Japan and the Developing Countries

Japan and the Developing Countries

A Comparative Analysis

Edited by Kazushi Ohkawa and Gustav Ranis
with Larry Meissner

*Published on behalf of the
International Development Center of Japan
and the Economic Growth Center
of Yale University*

Basil Blackwell

© International Development Center of Japan and
Economic Growth Center of Yale University 1985

First published 1985

Basil Blackwell Ltd
108 Cowley Road, Oxford OX4 1JF, UK

Basil Blackwell Inc.
432 Park Avenue South, Suite 1505,
New York, NY 10016, USA

British Library Cataloguing in Publication Data

Japan and the developing countries.
  1. Developing countries – Economic conditions
  2. Japan – Economic conditions – To 1868
  3. Japan – Economic conditions – 1868–1918
  I. Ōkawa, Kazushi   II. Ranis, Gustav
  330.9172′4   HC59.7
  ISBN 0-631-13792-0

Library of Congress Cataloging in Publication Data

Japan and the developing countries.
  "Published on behalf of the International Development Center of Japan
and the Economic Growth Center of Yale University."
  Includes index.
  1. Japan – Economic conditions – 1945–   – Addresses, essays, lectures.
2. Developing countries – Economic conditions – Addresses, essays, lectures.
I. Ōkawa, Kazushi, 1908–   . II. Ranis, Gustav.
III. Kokusai Kaihatsu Sentā.   IV. Yale University.
Economic Growth Center.

HC462.9.J3185   1985   330.952   84-12475
ISBN 0-631-13792-0

Typeset by Unicus Graphics Ltd, Horsham
Printed in Great Britain by T.J. Press Ltd, Padstow

Contents

Information contained in the tables and figures is indexed
Bibliographies follow each chapter

Preface

The essays in this book are the result of a major research effort, begun in the mid-1970s, focused on "Japan's Historical Development Experience and the Contemporary Developing Countries: Issues for Comparative Analysis," which has come to be called the Comparative Analysis or CA project. The original focus was on providing a clearer understanding of the basic Japanese historical pattern of development, guided by what we (as organizers) considered the unresolved major critical issues in the growth performance of less developed countries since World War II. The ultimate purpose was to determine, through a better understanding of the Japanese case, exactly which elements are peculiar to Japan, which are relevant only to less developed countries that are culturally related to Japan, and which are more generally transferable.

To this end, we initially examined various aspects of the historical experience of Japan and then contrasted it with cases of less developed countries, wherever possible, by marshalling a developed country–less developed country team effort. Not surprisingly, we did not always completely succeed, and we had to settle for something less than a fully comparative study. Thus, while this volume represents the capstone of the CA project, some essays may be better defined as offering a series of specific insights into the development process by authors who are keenly aware of development theory, Japan's historical experience, and the problems of contemporary less developed countries.

The project was launched with grants to the International Development Center of Japan (IDCJ) from the Japanese government's Economic Planning Agency and from the US Ford Foundation. In addition, we have received significant financial support from the Toyota Foundation, the Japan World Exposition Commemorative Fund, the Japan Foundation, and the Economic Growth Center at Yale University. A grant to aid English-language publication has been provided by ten Japanese donors through the CA Project Fund and the Economic Growth Center has provided the base of operations for shepherding the manuscript into print.

Saburo Kawai, president of IDCJ, has provided continual support and encouragement, and many IDCJ staff members, especially Yutaka Shimizu, Hirohisa Kohama, Tamiko Sakatani, and Hideko Hosono, have been of invaluable help in bringing the project to fruition and the various papers to publication. We also wish to thank Hugh Patrick, Director of the Economic Growth Center during the last part of the project, for his continuing support, as well as the Economic Planning Agency of Japan for permitting the use of results emanating from a related IDCJ-commissioned policy-oriented activity.

The Comparative Analysis Project was directed by the co-editors, with additional guidance provided by an Advisory Committee chaired by Nobel Laureate Simon Kuznets and including Shinichi Ichimura (Director, The Center for Southeast Asian Studies, Kyoto University), Shigeru Ishikawa (Professor, Institute of Economic Research, Hitotsubashi University), Shirley Wan-yong Kuo (Deputy Governor, Bank of China, Taipei, Taiwan), Mahar Mangahas (Vice-President, Research, Development Academy of the Philippines), H. M. A. Onitiri (Director, Nigerian Institute of Social and Economic Research), K. N. Raj (Professor, Center for Development Studies, Kerala, India), Miyohei Shinohara (Professor, Economics Department, Seikei University), and Miguel Urrutia Montoya (Vice-Rector, UN University, Tokyo).

Kazushi Ohkawa and Gustav Ranis

1 Introduction

KAZUSHI OHKAWA and GUSTAV RANIS

"Japan Inc." and "Japan as Number One" are clichés. There has been a plethora of books on what the United States can learn from Japan, and on why it has succeeded. Japan was a "latecomer" to development, and has in fact looked to the United States as a model of what its economy may evolve into, just as (with trepidation) many Americans currently look to Great Britain as indicative of the the direction in which the United States is heading. However, whether or not the interest in the 1980s in Japan's "success" in fact provides guidance for the United States, economists and policy-makers have long recognized Japan's historical experience as a source of possible insights for what here are called LDCs – less developed countries.

There has been a substantial volume of research in the postwar era on the causes of successful growth in the developing world as well as on the causes of failure, which is more frequently encountered. In connection with this, considerable attention has been paid to Japan's historical experience – with some observers characterizing the Japanese model as the "perfect guide" for contemporary LDCs and others rejecting it as completely irrelevant.

We have set ourselves the rather ambitious task in this book of presenting some potential lessons for contemporary developing countries that have been culled from the Japanese historical experience. This is a major purpose of the multi-faceted papers presented in this volume, a selection from studies carried out in the late 1970s and early 1980s as part of a project supported by the Ford Foundation and Japan's Economic Planning Agency on "Japan's Historical Development Experience and the Contemporary Developing Countries: Issues for Comparative Analysis." What, if anything, Japan can "teach" the LDCs is not just of academic interest, it is also of importance to policy-makers, North and South.

There is the substantive issue of what is, in fact, "relevant" (transferable) and what is "special" or ephemeral in Japan's attainment of modern economic growth. History surely does not repeat itself, at least not at the macro level, because the circumstances are never exactly the same. Still, just as the rules of grammar allow a variety of unique writing styles, understandable because of the

1

rules, we believe there exist patterns, still not fully discerned, common to the transition to modern economic growth, irrespective of time and place.

It is our conviction that, in the pursuit of a better understanding of what development is all about, the comparative historical laboratory has been seriously underutilized, especially relative to multi-country cross-sectional efforts, on the one hand, and strictly contemporary or forward-looking country-intensive efforts, on the other. The entire CA (Comparative Analysis) project has been based on the premise that analysis of past development experience, particularly of a generally "successful" case such as Japan, has something to teach us – not so much in terms of the precise transferability of a total societal experience, as something about the transferability and, at times, nontransferability of a number of special sectoral or functional dimensions considered important to an explanation of the Japanese experience.

The point of departure has been the research on the historical pattern of Japanese development, in particular the work undertaken at Hitotsubashi University under the LTES (Long-term Economic Statistics of Japan) project and the related micro and sectoral studies culminating (in English) in the volume *Patterns of Japanese Economic Development*, edited by Kazushi Ohkawa and Miyohei Shinohara (1979).

In examining the Japanese historical case, the participants in this follow-on research effort have been keenly aware throughout of the fact that economic development, or successful transition growth, is clearly a complicated mosaic, with each dimension part of a general equilibrium framework which cannot really be treated in isolation. The simultaneous-equation framework to approaching that problem, however, is a strait jacket with its own shortcomings, and we have departed from it to examine various pieces of the mosaic separately, at a sectoral or micro level – hopefully always keeping in mind the connectedness to the overall macro story of development.

The project has not been in a position to compare the Japanese historical experience in every dimension, or even all those considered crucial, or with representatives of every other typology of contemporary developing countries, where typologies are defined by different clusters of characteristics such as initial conditions, resource endowment, size, etc. Financial, human, and managerial resource constraints were clearly operative, and we had to be guided as much by the availability of individual researchers and funding opportunities as by any substantive master-plan for an ideal pattern of comparative studies. Thus the project necessarily fell short in the capacity to undertake comparative analysis both across major typologies (particularly the Latin American and African cases, which are more "distant" from the Japanese model), and across countries within "neighboring" typologies, for example, the South Asian and Southeast Asian cases.

In the selection of research topics and the ensuing results presented in this volume, the general areas focused on include an examination of the relevance of initial conditions and an overview of the historical experience (part I), the particular importance of technology choice and change in agriculture (part II) and in industry (part III), the flow of resources between the agricultural and nonagricultural sectors, and the role of institutions and policies in finance (part IV), and the relation between trade and development (part V).

We have set ourselves the rather ambitious task in this opening essay of not only introducing these papers, but also distilling the main lessons for contemporary developing countries that can be learned from the Japanese historical experience. It is easier and more productive to analyze the ingredients of success than the causes of failure – this is what has attracted researchers to the Japanese case in the first place – and so special attention has also been given to the postwar experiences of South Korea and Taiwan, members of the same typology, in juxtaposition to historical Japan.

In our attitude towards the policy conclusions to be extracted, we have tried to be consistently Kuznetsian – that is, we have taken the view that any such conclusions must be firmly grounded on a prior understanding of how the economy, or, as the case may be, a particular sector or market, is functioning or malfunctioning in relation to the basic economic forces at work. Once such an understanding has been reached, or at least the effort has been made to approach it, existing government policy can be viewed as either accommodating or obstructing such underlying economic forces. Judgments can then be made about the appropriateness of policies and, thus, about the need for policy change in any given developing-country context.

We recognize, in other words, that the relevance of the Japanese experience to contemporary LDCs lies in what conclusions can be derived for policy. At the same time, we are humble enough to know that for each developing country the applicability of our conclusions must be assessed by local analysts and policymakers, possessed of the necessarily fuller understanding of the complexities inherent in any particular situation. Inevitably, all that studies of the type undertaken here can realistically hope to accomplish is to sensitize policy-makers to certain historical relationships and precedents that might be useful in some way to their country's transition to modern economic growth.

Initial Conditions

Not much can be accomplished by policy with respect to the initial endowment – the people, the land, the colonial heritage. But the time just prior to the attempt at transition growth is never quite "initial" with respect to the quality of the human resources and related organizational dimensions. Something can be done about these – and something markedly different, in fact, seems to have happened in different 19th-century Asian societies which appeared quite similar in terms of their level of economic well-being, their man–land ratios, and their overall economic structure. Significant differences in subsequent economic performance over time have been laid at the doorstep of differences in "social capability," some apparently inherited and cultural, but some more economic in origin.

To shed light on the possible causes of divergent development, Yasuba and Dhiravegin compare initial conditions, and institutional and socioeconomic policy changes in the late 19th century in Japan and Siam (now Thailand). In the mid-19th century, both countries were quite similar in a straightforward resource-endowment sense, yet in the period before World War II, economic development and industrialization were the main trends in Japan, whereas de-industrialization and specialization in primary commodities were the major tendencies in Thailand. The authors demonstrate several ways in which Thailand was simply not as well "prepared" as Japan was, and the contrasts help explain the subsequent differences in development.

Japan does indeed seem to have been well prepared for transition growth, and this went beyond such factors as wider basic education and literacy to higher levels of achievement motivation. More broadly based chances for gaining social status as well as private advancement undoubtedly contributed to a "progressive" attitude among the Japanese middle class. Related to this is the fact that change in Japan was carried out largely by a class with few vested interests. Whether educational attainment, entry, and mobility conditions are to be classified as essentially "cultural," and thus presumably beyond the reach of policy, or as part of economic development is, of course, debatable and will undoubtedly continue to be debated.

Two other dimensions of the initial conditions, unambiguously economic, which can be, and indeed were, affected by government policy, are the extent of government investment as well as the official attitude toward technology transfer during the first phase of transition growth. From the beginning, the Meiji government in Japan assisted the private sector by stressing infrastructure investments as well as the subsidized transfer and dissemination of knowledge from the West. Japan sent teams abroad to select what seemed most appropriate, and employed foreign advisers for only a limited time. The Japanese government invested directly, for example, in textiles as well as in some heavy industries. But this was always largely on a "model factory" basis, with government assistance increasingly of the subsidy type, and most public enterprises, except those of military or strategic value, were closed down or sold to private investors within a decade or two. The initial, and continuing, hand of government has been heavier in most contemporary LDCs.

The abundance of cheap labor revealed in the lower level of real wages in Japan should not be viewed as an advantage in and of itself. Other countries, including Thailand, India, and China, had equally elastic supplies of unskilled labor during the 19th century, yet failed to develop, instead witnessing a decline in domestic industry. Rather, such an abundant supply of relatively educated, but industrially unskilled labor can apparently be converted into a real advantage only in the context of a favorable "total" environment, including an industrial entrepreneurial class and the right policy package to mobilize it effectively in a balanced growth context.

Following Simon Kuznets's vision of modern economic growth and assessing "development" as an effort at transition from a prior epoch of agrarianism to one of modern growth, Fei, Ohkawa, and Ranis provide a framework for understanding that transition via a number of identifiable phases. Their overview develops the notion that it is analytically useful to divide the contemporary less developed world into typologies (families) depending on such factors as initial conditions, resource endowments, and size. This typological-cum-phases approach is applied to the experiences of Japan, Taiwan, and South Korea.

These three nations are members of the same family of developing countries, having begun with a large labor surplus, limited natural resources, extensive human resources, and a fairly equally distributed land area. The authors found substantial similarities as well as some differences with respect to the identification of meaningful phases of transition growth, changing behavior of the system across such phases, and the overall performance with respect to growth, employment, and distribution in these three countries.

The essay recognizes differences in the international environment in which 19th-century Japan and the contemporary East Asian NICs (newly industrializing countries) were attempting their respective transitions to modern growth, as well as differences in the element of time culminating in contemporary efforts to "telescope" earlier experience. Still, grouping countries by common characteristics is seen not only to shed light on shared elements, but also to help spotlight differences from the group "norm" that make each country unique. Such an approach can help policy-makers assess the relevance of other countries' experiences. Thus, while the relative transferability or nontransferability of the Japanese experience in a particular dimension is recognized as being profoundly affected by the typological as well as temporal "distance" between a specific developing country and the Japanese case, the framework and analysis of phasing is found useful as a reference point for policy-makers in this as well as other families of developing countries.

Agricultural Development

Various strands of research under the CA project tend to confirm the importance of the agricultural sector in determining the success of the transition growth effort. In the early phases, agriculture does, or can, provide savings (a topic discussed in later chapters), along with foreign exchange, raw materials, and labor, as well as a market for the products of the new industrial sector. Three studies at the micro level provide insights into the major potential contributions of technology to the sector and into the kinds of economic and policy environments which favor such contributions.

An important implication of these chapters is that creating the technical and economic conditions for the adoption of land-saving technology change is even more important to LDCs in the 1980s than in 19th-century Japan, given the greater population pressure on land today. Although the means may exist to forestall the world of Ricardo, they are not always being implemented quickly enough.

Irrigation, improved locally-adapted crop varieties, fertilization, and other means of more intensively using land have a much higher return than expanding onto ever more marginal land, and have the potential to improve employment opportunities and the distribution of income. Nevertheless, for a number of reasons, improved varieties are still used on only about a third of the rice land and two-thirds of the wheat land in South and Southeast Asia. In addition, the existence of a more unequal distribution of land and more unequal access to such necessary inputs as credit, fertilizer, and water, frequently in conjunction with price signals that are artificially distorted in favor of widespread, early (and unconnected) mechanization, have prevented the appearance of equally favorable results on the employment and income-distribution fronts in many contemporary LDCs, compared to the historical Japanese experience.

This is clear from Kikuchi and Hayami's analysis of how Japan, Taiwan, Korea, and the Philippines have responded to population pressure on arable land. For these four monsoon Asian countries, improvements in irrigation systems have been the key to the development and diffusion of a land-saving technology, characterized by seed improvements and increased use of fertilizers, which has allowed agricultural productivity to increase markedly.

In Taiwan, in the 1960s, land-saving changes in technology (based on modern high-yielding varieties of rice, plus greater use of fertilizer and irrigation) led not only to faster growth, but also to an improvement in equity. Still, the impact of the so-called Green Revolution on income distribution has been somewhat controversial. To clarify this issue, Hayami and Kikuchi analyzed the new rice technology and its income-distribution effects in the light of the Japanese experience. Under the CA project, they undertook an intensive field survey of two neighboring Indonesian villages, one characterized by technological stagnation and the other by significant technological progress, and then compared them in order to isolate the precise effects of technology change.

One of the more interesting cases of technology change in Japanese agriculture before World War I is that of summer-fall cocoon-rearing which, by shifting the seasonal pattern from the spring, permitted much greater productive use of seasonally idle labor during the slack summer months. This labor-using type of change in process, moreover, favored the smaller-scale units and was undoubtedly helpful with respect to the distribution of income. A dramatic increase in cocoon production for export was made possible between 1890 and 1915, without causing a decline in rice production for domestic consumption.

A somewhat similar phenomenon occurred in Taiwan in the 1960s, with farmers – especially smaller units – beginning to grow mushrooms and asparagus (which, like silk in Japan, are exports) to complement rice. The experience indicates the importance, particularly in the case of densely populated, family-farm agriculture, of inducing the search for cropping patterns that make food and secondary, higher-valued, cash crops complementary. Such an environment in the cases of both Japan and Taiwan was closely related both to the organizational structure of agriculture (farmers' associations diffusing information on new technology and markets), plus the maintenance of a relatively price-response private-market setting.

Nghiep and Lynam show that much of the Asian development experience has only limited relevance to the situation in Latin America. The agricultural economies of Japan and most other Asian nations are characterized by a homogeneous farm-side distribution and by relatively small-scale farmers. Thus, land-saving and labor-using technologies are appropriate for most farming units. In contrast, in Latin American countries there is typically a wide range of farm sizes, which argues for a dual agricultural-development strategy, with quite different agricultural technologies for large-scale and small-scale farms.

As an example of products and processes appropriate for small-scale farms, the authors draw on their field work in Colombia to look at a new cassava technology, still in the experimental stage, combined with maize and sesame production. The technology change consists of an improved cassava variety and a fertilization method that releases fallow land, while in the sericulture case it consists of a new method of storing silkworm eggs. If the new method proves feasible, land use can be expanded in the Colombian case, in contrast to the more intensive use of given land in the Japanese case. But in both, there is a reduction in competition with existing food crops and support for the viability of small-scale producers.

Technology Choice in Industry

The CA project also focused on issues of technology choice and change at the micro level in the industrial sector, with particular attention given to the cotton textile industry. One major implication for policy from this work is the support it lends to the emerging conventional wisdom that a remarkably wide range of process choices (production methods) is available for both intermediate and final goods.

Additional flexibility comes from the hitherto relatively neglected dimension of product attributes (which, loosely, consists of product quality and capability). "Cheaper" products make sense in some markets. The whole arena of enhancing entrepreneurial capacities to make seemingly minor adjustments in both the process and product dimensions of technology change is probably still undervalued in policy importance, especially with respect to medium and small-scale (including rural) industry. All the evidence points to the importance of the capacity for adaptive local technology change, as opposed to the usually more heavily emphasized choice of imported technology.

Four essays deal with cotton spinning and textiles. Each approaches the topic from a different angle, covering the choice of technologies, the quality of the labor force, and the quality of the product produced, as well as a comparison between the Japanese and Indian experiences.

The Ranis and Saxonhouse chapter provides an introduction to technology choice in industry, offering an explanation of why the concept of "appropriate" technology is often so slow in emerging as an element of the LDC decision-making process. Drawing on their analysis of the Japanese and Indian cotton spinning industries, the authors proceed beyond the simple factor price distortion and protectionist stories in explaining comparative technological performance in the two countries, emphasizing instead the different types of environments decision-makers face.

The cotton spinning industry was the first industry of the Industrial Revolution whose technology followed its goods out of proximity to the North Atlantic to Eastern Europe and Russia, to Mexico and Brazil, to India and to Japan. By 1900, even though an enormous volume of international trade in cotton goods continued, and even though the British industry remained dominant, major textile industries existed at numerous locations on three continents.

At the beginning of the 1880s, the relatively well established Indian and the relatively recently established Japanese cotton textile industries had substantially similar initial conditions. The subsequent difference in development is quite startling. Both operated in labor-surplus economies, and both obtained initial technology and early technical advice from Britain, mostly from the same firm. During the 1880s, major changes occurred in cotton spinning technology. Japan transformed that technology in ways appropriate to its economy much better than India. In the last decade of the 19th century, the Japanese cotton textile industry rapidly changed from an importer of Indian yarn to a strong competitor in the Chinese market, and went on to dominate Asian markets in cotton textiles in the pre-Pacific War period.

As output expanded in Japan, the industry initially became relatively more labor-intensive, a highly desirable outcome in a labor-surplus economy. Such success is quite rare in contemporary LDC industrialization experience. In seeking to identify the reasons why this occurred, the Ranis and Saxonhouse chapter focuses on constraints on the exercise of technology choice. They argue that the choices made by the individual Japanese entrepreneur, in contrast to his Indian counterpart, illuminate the importance of differences in institutional and organizational environment. In India, a management system insulated by institutional constraints from fully harnessing entrepreneurial incentives represents a situation much closer to that of contemporary LDCs.

Product quality also plays an important role in determining the appropriateness of a technology. Saxonhouse and Ranis explore the relationship between technology choice and input–output quality in LDCs by analyzing the historical experience of the Japanese cotton textile industry. A product is likely to fulfill a variety of needs: just as a production process may be inappropriate, so may attributes of the product.

Turning from the quality of the product to the quality of the workers making it, Saxonhouse and Kiyokawa compare the labor forces of the Indian and Japanese cotton spinning industries, focusing on the relationship between the operation of the labor market and labor quality. The starting point of the analysis is a remarkable 1897 survey of the Japanese spinning labor force. The data are so rich that a clear picture can be given of what kinds of incentives were offered to the workers, and how they responded.

The international spread of ring-spinning technology is analyzed by Saxon-house. Using entirely new sources of information, he re-evaluates the British and Indian experiences in adopting ring technology and sets them within an interpretive framework which includes as part of its historical sample Japan, the United States, Canada, France, Austria, Russia, Switzerland, Italy, and Brazil.

Technology transfer can help LDCs attain higher rates of economic growth. Often, this is simply the importation of capital-intensive methods without modification, called nonadapted borrowed technology. Such technology tends to lower labor's relative share of national income, and to restrict employment opportunity in the modern sector. Adaptive borrowing involves modification to reflect domestic factor prices. Besides avoiding unfavorable effects on labor's relative share and employment opportunities, this process promotes learning-by-doing, and thereby increases technological capability.

Ono analyzes technology borrowing in the early Japanese iron and steel industry, and then looks at the extent of the similarity between the experiences of Japan, Brazil, and India. His analysis offers insights into why Japan ceased adaptive behavior and why LDCs tend to select capital-intensive (generally, nonadapted) production methods, pointing out that it is, in fact, not always irrational.

Intersectoral Resource Flows and Finance

The ability of agriculture to play its potentially crucial developmental role hinges in part on how successfully agricultural resources are mobilized. This requires, in the first instance, the generation of resources available for mobilization – that is, increasing agricultural productivity during the early growth phases. Such increases allow a net outflow of agricultural savings, both via private and public channels, which serve as an important source of funding for nonagricultural production and infrastructural investments. Moreover, if there is balanced progress in both sectors, labor is released more or less in relation to the creation of employment opportunities in nonagriculture. Finally, agricultural wage goods, augmented if necessary by imports, can be supplied without encountering the deleterious effects of a marked deterioration in the industrial sector's terms of trade.

Japan benefited from a labor-using type of change in agricultural technology in the 19th and early 20th centuries, first in the form of the diffusion of traditional best practice and then in the improvement of best practice via the introduction of modern "Green Revolution" type inputs. The sectoral terms of trade did not change markedly between 1880 and 1915. Once the increase in agricultural productivity did finally run out of steam, around 1918, imports of food from colonial Taiwan and Korea were utilized to keep the domestic terms of trade from rising too strongly against industry.

Taiwan's effort after World War II to follow the Japanese historical example was substantially aided by the much larger technological possibilities available to help generate a rapid pace of agricultural-productivity growth. Although undoubtedly aided by the choice of a relatively brief and mild set of import-substitution policies during the 1950s, the ability to telescope the exhaustion of the agricultural labor surplus into twenty years (1952–72), compared to fifty years in Japan (1870–1920), must be laid in large part at the door of much greater technological opportunities, international and domestic, often termed the "Green Revolution." The terms of trade did not turn markedly against agriculture in the import-substituting 1950s or against agriculture in the export-substituting 1960s in Taiwan.

Korea's performance is somewhat more ambiguous. More investment was required in agriculture, given the less favorable soil and climatic conditions, as well as lower levels of irrigation construction during the Japanese colonial period. Korea paid less attention, at least at first, to creating a policy and institutional environment that would not discriminate against domestic agriculture. The role of the "easy" availability of food aid in reducing agricultural incentives, thereby leading to a larger than necessary, earlier than necessary, dependence on food imports, as well as depriving the economy of a potential source of development funding, is a controversial issue. Policy changes in the early 1980s seem to indicate an effort to redress such missed opportunities.

By contrast, the Indian agricultural performance after World War II was unambiguously less favorable than in any of the East Asian cases, and thus the sector made no similar savings contribution to the rest of the economy during the corresponding growth period. Although this is, in part, due to differences in initial conditions, such as the need for more irrigation and other infrastructural investments within Indian agriculture, it is also in considerable part attributable to a much lower rate of technology change which, in turn, was heavily influenced by a much more pronounced and much more prolonged import-substitution policy regime, carrying its well-known tendency to discriminate against the agricultural sector.

Two essays in this volume look at aspects of the terms of trade between agriculture and nonagriculture. To find the role of the terms of trade in economic development, Hondai analyzes its effect on the transfer of labor between agriculture and nonagriculture, and the factors affecting changes in the terms of trade, from the perspective of economic development in Japan and Taiwan. His concern is with the allocation of resources between the two sectors, and his chapter offers insight into the major determinants of long-run movements of the terms of trade.

Mody, Mundle, and Raj analyze and compare the experience of Japan following the Meiji Restoration with that of India after Independence with regard to one major facet of agriculture's contribution to industrial development: resource flows from agriculture. To this end they have pulled together different estimates and sources of piecemeal data to present a more carefully cross-checked and comprehensive treatment of the problem than has been available hitherto.

The Japanese land tax served as the major instrument of transferring savings in the 19th century and was increasingly replaced by the intermediation of private voluntary savings. The same sequence may be noted for Taiwan. In India, in the absence of a large agricultural surplus to be siphoned off, the net flow of public revenues has been into agriculture, not only for infrastructure (primarily support for research), but also for current inputs (fertilizers and pesticides). By contrast, Japan placed much greater reliance, in the same early phase, on traditional inputs, plus the diffusion of best indigenous technology and improvements in it through a learning-by-doing process.

While the possibilities for fully harnessing the agricultural sector to a balanced growth path naturally differ with differing initial endowments, it remains true that too many developing countries still find it convenient to try to avoid the difficult domestic agricultural mobilization task, especially in basic foods, choosing instead to rely excessively, and at times much too soon, on imports. Outside Singapore and Hong Kong, agriculture is a substantial sector in East Asia, as it is elsewhere in the developing world, and it is difficult to march into modern growth dragging it along, particularly when the sector can play an important supportive role.

As far as the financing of development is concerned, we have already noted the substantial contribution of Japanese agricultural saving to the total investment fund. In the years before World War I, there was a gradual shift in how investment funds flowed – from government reliance on the land tax to finance infrastructural investment and provide subsidies to the private sector, to the channeling of private agricultural saving, later supplemented by industrial profits, through a growing financial intermediation network. Especially given the absence of any substantial inflow of foreign capital, at least during the 19th century, the way the Japanese organized their financial institutions and policies should be of considerable relevance to contemporary developing countries.

Various research efforts in this general area indicate Japan's experience in financial markets is especially worthy of analysis for comparative purposes, with respect to both institution-building and the policies in place. In fact, Japan was quite careful from the very beginning to continuously modify the financial intermediation network in order both to attract specialized savers and to serve specialized investment needs on a flexible basis. In addition, early heavy government-credit support for the commercial banking system was quickly reduced and arm's-length relationships established. Thirdly, and undoubtedly most important, Japan, at least until World War II, consistently followed a policy of flexible, market-determined interest rates, permitting, at the same time, a positive inducement to savers, an efficient allocation for borrowers, and an effective defense against inflationary pressures. All this stands in considerable contrast to the situation in most contemporary developing countries.

Our studies clearly imply that part and parcel of any strategy of enhanced participation of medium and small-scale industrial entrepreneurs, as well as farmers, must be a policy allowing relatively realistic official interest rates, rates that narrow the customarily wide gap between the official and curb markets and allow for more efficiency-oriented criteria for official lending. Removal of interest-rate ceilings is often viewed as both hurting the "little man" and causing a decline in investment. In fact, the little man is better off having access to credit at a reasonable price than having no access at a subsidized price. In addition, the rate of return on investment in most LDCs is sufficiently high that the prevalence of substantially positive real rates of interest is not likely to dampen investment. This has certainly been demonstrated not only in Japan, but also in the course of credit-market reforms in Korea and Taiwan during the 1960s.

Both the Teranishi and the Patrick and Moreno chapters deal with comparative aspects of the Japanese and Philippine banking systems. In the Philippines, there has been specialization of financial institutions and, surprisingly, substantial channeling of agricultural savings. However, the system still depends heavily on government credit, bail-outs, and other types of intervention.

Modern finance has penetrated rural areas of the Philippines, and Teranishi's study of rural banks shows they have been crucial in this process. His essay looks at the development and role of rural banks, and then compares rural banks and Philippine government-credit policy to the Japanese experience in the late 19th and early 20th centuries, a similar period in Japan's banking development. Teranishi notes a major contrast between what happened in the Philippines and in Japan is the elimination of extensive government credits to the banking system in Japan.

Patrick and Moreno look at the other end of the banking spectrum, analyzing private commercial banks. The authors examine such factors as lending policies and management quality as they affect bank growth. The interactions among the banks, private corporations with related or common owners, and the government are also taken up.

The contrast between Japan and the Philippines is undoubtedly most marked with respect to the general interest-rate policy followed. At least until June 1981, the Philippines represented a clear case of what has been called "financial repression," with interest-rate ceilings in force at both the deposit and lending levels, and with a substantial gap permitted between them to ensure banking profitability. Such a low official interest-rate policy constitutes an integral part of the usual import-substitution policy package. Its consequences in the Philippines and elsewhere include the existence of pronounced dualism in financial markets, discrimination with respect to official credit against small, new, and rural borrowers, as well as a general disincentive to savers, and a weakened defense against inflationary pressures.

In Japan, the Philippines, and some other developing countries, we encounter a small group of relatively wealthy individuals and powerful companies establishing close links between their industrial and financial-market activities, in both of which they may exercise considerable market power. The net economic impact of this set of non-arm's-length relationships is unclear. It is also puzzling how this type of interlocking family-dominated business configuration can have been functional in both the competitive markets of prewar Japan and the repressed financial markets of the Philippines. To some extent, this "powerful-group" phenomenon is, of course, an inevitable concomitant of narrowly based, primary import-substitution growth. The question remains, however, whether this pattern is likely to persist and what effect it has on growth and equity in subsequent phases of development.

Foreign capital has played a much larger role during the early phases of transition in virtually all of the contemporary developing countries than in 19th-century Japan. It certainly helped with the telescoping of fifty years of transition growth in Japan into twenty years in Taiwan. The reliance on foreign capital in Korea, given the relatively lower contribution from domestic agricultural savings, was, of course, even larger. If one abstracts from the very helpful indemnity paid by China after the 1893–94 war, foreign capital was virtually absent in 19th-century Japan. Korea and Taiwan, on the other hand, saw foreign aid, pre-dominant during import substitution, gradually phased out and replaced by private foreign capital during their subsequent export-oriented growth phase.

In the case of most other contemporary developing countries, concessional flows have continued, indicating there has as yet been no successful graduation from the need for bilateral or multilateral aid. It should, moreover, be noted that, although the CA project as such did not carefully analyze the issue, foreign aid has been helpful, for example in Taiwan, not so much in terms of amount (investment augmentation) as in its qualitative contribution, by buffering the painful effects of the policy changes of the late 1950s and early 1960s.

Foreign Trade and Development

In both historical Japan and contemporary LDCs, foreign trade has clearly played a very important role, although just how important is partly a function of the relative size of each country. Perhaps luckily, Japan did not at first have the tariff autonomy required to construct import-substitution, hot-house conditions for its industries. By comparison, in most contemporary LDCs, the level of effective protection, built up through a combination of tariffs and quotas, overvalued exchange rates, etc., is quite formidable. Only a few countries have thus far found it politically possible to overcome the vested interests of large-scale industrialists, organized workers, and civil servants to achieve across-the-board movement toward a more open economy.

Instead, the industrialization and trade patterns of many contemporary LDCs present clear cases of continued import-substitution growth under a variety of protectionist devices, followed by some effort at promoting exports. The evidence suggests that if such policies continue to be followed, efficient, internationally competitive firms are unlikely to evolve, mainly because the infant industries will not have the same need to "grow up."

Where there is a suitable combination of economies of scale and small domestic markets, opportunities may exist for regional integration and import substitution on a regional basis. The experience of such efforts in both Asia and Latin America would lead one to hypothesize, however, that it is better, at least for relatively small economies, to rely on multilaterally negotiated reductions in protection.

The essay by Yamazawa and Tambunlertchai provides an overview of the overall trade and development pattern in Japan, comparing it to the Thai case, and relating both to the product-cycle model. The Thai textile industry's development from import substitution to export substitution is taken as a case in point. Why export performance differs among Thai firms, as well as the export orientation of Thai entrepreneurs, are analyzed in this context. This part of their discussion brings us full circle, back to cultural aspects and the divergent paths of Thailand and Japan. It is interesting to note that the mid-20th-century responses in Thailand bode better for achievement of modern economic growth than did the 19th-century responses analyzed by Yasuba and Dhiravegin.

Motivated by the need to increase foreign-exchange earnings, many contemporary developing countries are eager to develop new exports as well as explore new markets for their traditional exports. Being aware of the difficulties involved, they have been interested in Japanese GTCs (general trading companies) because of their successful performance in the context of Japan's foreign-trade expansion, and wondered about its usefulness in non-Japanese cultural contexts. Some developing countries, including Korea, Thailand, and Brazil, implemented GTC promotion policies in the 1970s with the expectation this would in itself help to expand their exports rapidly. Not surprisingly, the experience has been somewhat mixed, because the results are heavily dependent on the underlying macro-policy setting. Although these institutions have been set up only recently, it is possible to assess their early development and, because Japan's GTCs have been the model, to compare development experiences. This task is undertaken in the essay by Yamazawa and Kohama.

Most developing nations view a domestic automobile industry as a symbol of success. Consequently, many have sought to establish domestic car production early on, with the development of a domestic machinery industry as one intended by-product. In his essay, Odaka seeks to assess what the results have been. Drawing on field studies made in the latter half of the 1970s, he reviews the performance of an important segment of the industry, parts suppliers, with special emphasis on the growth of smaller firms in the machinery industry. The overall question is in the title of the paper: Is the division of labor limited by the extent of the market? The answer is "Yes, but ... " Six Asian nations are studied, five that began to promote the industry in the 1970s (Indonesia, Malaysia, Thailand, the Philippines, and Korea), and Japan, where the industry started in the 1930s, but did not become significant until the 1950s. Japan's experience in the 1950s is compared with that of the five other countries in the 1970s.

Some Final Reflections

Returning to our basic premise that there are many instructive similarities between transition growth efforts in Japan and contemporary developing countries, a comment on the issue of differences between the 19th- and 20th-century international environment and the related issue of technology is in order. Some contemporary observers consider Japan's historical experience largely irrelevant, especially given the rising protectionist sentiments in developed countries that face any would-be export-substituting NIC (newly industrializing country). Although it is difficult to measure the comparative extent of effective protection across centuries, it can certainly be said that the most successful contemporary cases we have looked at – Korea and Taiwan – were successful in spite of increased import quotas in developed countries; this is mainly as a consequence of the flexibility and resilience their entrepreneurs acquired along the course of the transition path chosen.

Secondly, it is true that Japanese growth was favored by such unique initial conditions as a prior period of seclusion, which affected consumption patterns, and an ability to keep population pressure at much lower levels (near 1 percent) than the 2–3 percent in most LDCs today. No doubt this made it possible for substantially lower growth rates in agricultural and nonagricultural productivity to be sufficient for "success." But again, we must note that, partly as a consequence of efforts in family planning, but largely as a consequence of socioeconomic change itself, fertility levels can be, and have been, brought down.

Moreover, there are important entries on the other side of the ledger which tend to support the contention that, if anything, the international environment after World War II has been, and remains, substantially better for transition growth than that which Japan encountered. Most important here is the much larger opportunity for "appropriately" borrowing technology from the more advanced nations, emphasized so strongly by Simon Kuznets as a crucial ingredient in the move towards modern growth. This is especially relevant in agriculture, where Japan had no "Green Revolution" technology offered to it, and had to rely instead on improving its best traditional practices and diffusing them. The point also increasingly applies to the choice of industries and industrial technology. Foreign capital, first largely public and concessional, then primarily private and commercial, is more available now than it was to Japan. Moreover, the developed world's growth from World War II until at least the 1973 oil shock was unprecedented, offering ready markets.

Combined with the greater contemporary potential for the movement of goods, factors, and technology is the broader diffusion of impatience. Japanese leaders experienced a "felt need" to develop in order to protect their country from becoming a colony. But they moved cautiously, nonetheless, shifting from a land-intensive to a labor-intensive growth pattern, before moving on to more sophisticated capital and technology-intensive output and export mixes. Contemporary LDCs, on the other hand, by and large want to develop quickly in order to satisfy promises made to "close the gap" between themselves and the already-developed nations, in the context of wider understanding in their own countries of how large that gap is. In this effort, they are more likely to seek ways to accelerate and telescope the process.

In any case, it took "successful" Japan about fifty years, whatever advantages it may have had, to do what Taiwan and Korea achieved in approximately twenty years. It is difficult to avoid concluding that today's international economic environment, while it certainly can stand considerable improvement, is not the principal stumbling block keeping developing countries from achieving successful transition growth.

Reference

Ohkawa, Kazushi, and Miyohei Shinohara, with Larry Meissner (1979), *Patterns of Japanese Economic Development, a Quantitative Appraisal* (PJED), New Haven, CT: Yale University Press.

PART I   Initial Conditions

2 Initial Conditions, Institutional Changes, Policy, and their Consequences: Siam and Japan, 1850-1914

YASUKICHI YASUBA and LIKHIT DHIRAVEGIN

Siam (Thailand) and Japan shared striking similarities when they entered the modern period. In the preceding period, both had closed themselves to most western contact, and then were more or less forced open to trade, Siam in 1855 and Japan in 1859; yet both remained independent. Both started to modernize (westernize) in contemporary reigns. In Siam, this took place under Chulalongkorn (1868-1910), in Japan, during Meiji (1868-1912). For most of the period, both had to trade under procedures prescribed by the western powers. In the late 19th century, trade expanded rapidly and the terms of trade improved considerably. Initial trade patterns were similar; both exported mostly primary commodities in exchange for manufactured goods.

Yet development was widely divergent. Siam gradually gave up most of its early industries and became more and more specialized in the production of a few primary commodities, particularly rice. Commercialization proceeded, but neither economic development nor industrialization occurred to any significant degree. In Japan, domestic producers soon offered substitutes for imports and eventually some of these industries became exporters.

Economic development and industrialization were the main trends in Japan, whereas de-industrialization and specialization in primary commodities were the major tendencies in Siam. What caused these divergent courses? This chapter compares initial conditions, institutional changes in the late 19th century, and socioeconomic policies after the institutional changes, in an effort to shed light on this question.

The authors are grateful to Professors Simon Kuznets and Gustav Ranis for helpful comments, and to Professor Chatthip Nartsupha for his generous assistance in providing source material.

Initial Conditions

The center-periphery thesis does not apply, as both countries worked under basically the same external conditions, and started with similar trade patterns.[1] The commercial treaties of the 1850s prevented the use of tariffs and quotas to protect industries. Siam had a lower maximum, 3 percent, compared to 5 percent for Japan, and Japan precluded foreign investment by prohibiting ownership of land and free movement of foreigners, something Siam did not. Not much foreign direct investment, however, was made in Siam in the 19th century.

One version of the center-periphery thesis asserts the center exploited the periphery by exercising monopolistic or monopsonistic powers (Prebisch 1959). This cry was raised by the Japanese in the 19th century, but the thesis is dubious in view of relative price movements at the time. The price differential on raw silk between Yokohama and London was 113 percent in 1861, which probably did indicate monopsonistic forces. However, the margin shrank rapidly, even while foreigners dominated trade, reaching 43 percent by 1867, a figure comparable to the 34 percent differential between Suwa, the supply center, and Yokohama (Miyamoto et al. 1965: 554). The terms of trade improved by about 120 percent between the 1860s and 1920 for both Japan and Siam (Miyamoto et al. 1965: 553; Yamazawa 1975: 539; Feeny 1979: 115). These findings contradict several versions of the center-periphery thesis.

Comparison of income is hazardous, but what evidence there is suggests initial per-capita income in Japan was not much higher than that of Siam. It has been estimated at $239 for Japan in 1876 (1965 prices) (Ohkawa 1976: 6). Per-capita gross national product (GNP) for Siam in 1950 is estimated at $216 (1970 dollars) (data from World Bank 1981: 194, adjusted for price differentials from Kravis et al. 1978: 233). No estimate is available for Siam in the late 19th century, but from descriptive evidence there is little reason to believe real per-capita GNP increased much between the 1850s and 1950.[2]

Daily wages were much lower in Japan than in Siam. In the 1880s, the average wage of male day laborers in Japan was less than one-third that in Bangkok. Even Japanese carpenters received only two-thirds of the unskilled wage in Bangkok (Naikaku Tokeikyoku 1890: 175–76; Feeny 1979: 116 – local currency is converted to sterling for comparison). Given the notorious hesitation of Siamese peasants to work for others, their income may have been much lower than the Bangkok wage. What we can say is that wages of the

---

[1] The center-periphery thesis contends that some regions (nations, classes) are central to the system (economically dominant), whereas others are peripheral, and the condition of being peripheral is caused by the relationship between the center and periphery. See Wallerstein (1979) for a more complete discussion of the concept.

[2] Technology in agriculture is said to have been the same, and the yield of rice, at least in the 20th century, declined as population moved to less fertile land (Ingram 1971: 216).

Chinese in Bangkok were quite high, and it was difficult to employ Siamese even at these wages (Ingram 1971: 212-13).

Japan had some initial advantages, both absolute and relative to Siam. Siam had 5 or 6 million people, compared to 35 million in Japan in the late 19th century. The abundant supply of cheap labor may be a factor explaining the resilience of domestic industries and the thrust to industrialize Japan. Thailand had sufficient arable land not to be subject to much population pressure. This should not be overemphasized, however, as China and India had an elastic supply of cheap labor, yet experienced a collapse of domestic industries and did not develop new factory-type industries as fast as Japan. Japan's large population was a potentially lucrative domestic market, with its own tastes. One consequence of this is the fact that traditional Japanese manufacturing suffered little displacement by imports.

A major socioeconomic factor is an apparently progressive outlook of middle-class Japanese and a fatalistic one in Siam. Samurai scholars were eager to engage in western studies in the first half of the 19th century: some experimented with western science and technology; engineers and farmers overcame traditional fatalistic attitudes toward nature, and introduced new methods (see Ichii 1980: chs 15-18). Such an attitude was largely lacking in Siam (Chittiwatanapong 1976: 18). While such socioeconomic differences are intangible, and thus difficult to measure, we can identify several others.

Monetary instruments, including paper money and promissory notes, were widely used in Tokugawa Japan, whereas in Siam silver lumps, cowrie shells and later, Mexican dollars, circulated until the mid-19th century only around Bangkok. The first bank in Siam was not established until 1888, and then it was a foreign one. In Japan, the tradition of money exchanges made the transition to commercial banks easier.

In premodern industry, inventions and technological transfers were limited to scattered cases such as Egawa Tarozaemon's iron furnace, Tanaka Giemon's machines, and Hiraga Gennai's electrical devices. But the speed and breadth of the adoption and adaptation of technology during Meiji indicates the ability was widely dispersed among Tokugawa artisans.

Japan's paddy land was nearly all irrigated by the mid-19th century, which facilitated the spread of new varieties and, later, of commercial fertilizer. Even during Tokugawa, treatises on agriculture were written and peasants improved techniques. Many progressive peasants became landlords or ventured into commerce, local industry, or moneylending. By contrast, the general male population in Siam was subject to the corvee system, which limited the opportunity to develop rural elites that could bring about technological development and economic change in the rural community (Dhiravegin 1981b).

At the back of these premodern developments in Japan lay the diffusion of mass culture and practical education. Mass culture appeared in the early 19th century, when low-brow novels by Ryutei Tanehiko, satirical stories by Juppensha Ikku, and above all, how-to books by Ohkura Nagatsune and others attracted interest. Best-sellers, including books on agriculture, sold over 10,000 copies (Konta 1977: 53 et passim). Because wood-block-printed books were expensive, book-lenders prospered in large cities – there were over 500 in Edo and about 300 in Osaka at the beginning of the 19th century (Kinugasa 1963: 115). People went to school to learn to read and write, and this increase in education in turn furthered the spread of mass culture.

The tradition of having many schools of thought facilitated the adaptation of western materials to the Japanese context. While *gogaku* (which primarily trained future bureaucrats and scholars) taught mostly Chinese classics and calligraphy in the 18th century, such practical subjects as medicine, arithmetic, astronomy, and western studies became popular in the early 19th century (Ishikawa 1953: 256). The number of *terakoya* (temple schools), which gave commoners practical education, increased from some 600 in 1751–88 to over 3,000 in 1789–1829, and doubled by 1867 (Passin 1965: 14). Dore puts the school-attendance ratio in the early 1860s at more than 40 percent for males (1965: 254).

No such developments took place in premodern Siam, and most people were illiterate. The Siamese counterpart of Japanese mass culture was Buddhism, which was taken very seriously. The *wat* (temple) schools gave religious training to small children, and virtually all males spent some time in temples as monks. In short, premodern Japanese culture was conducive to modern economic growth, whereas premodern Siamese culture was not.

Another possible cause of divergence was the family system. The bilateral family system in Siam lacked a sense of lineage and was unfavorable for the accumulation of capital.[3] The Chinese population in Siam maintained a unilineal system and did accumulate wealth. However, most intended to stay only a short time and then return to China with their savings. This meant that the Chinese tended to invest in commerce and moneylending, rather than industry. The importance of the Chinese in the economy may have had deleterious effects on Siam's development (see Ingram 1971: 204–5; Skinner 1975: 113 and 224).

Japan's unilineal *iye* system, almost corporate in nature, was presumably very conducive to capital accumulation, even in industry. Typically, the *iye* consisted of a main family maintained by the ideology of continuity and primogeniture. Although inheritance by the eldest son was the norm, adoption was not unknown, particularly in commercial families where the original heir did not look promising. (See Nakano 1964; Yui 1973; Hori 1965).

The emerging Japanese leadership, lower-level samurai mainly from four outlying domains, did not represent substantial vested interests, and hence tended to favor drastic institutional changes. They also had an advantage in

---

[3] Bilateral families do not distinguish between male and female children, or birth order, in distributing inheritances. This does not, however, mean all children share equally. It is commonly asserted this leads to splitting up of property among many heirs, and thus works against accumulation of capital, and also diffuses a sense of lineage. Bilateral families are general throughout Southeast Asia.

evaluating the foreign threat, as they occupied strategic positions in both the political and military fields. (This is believed to have been important in the Sino-Japanese comparison; see Eto 1968: 242; Sakata 1970: 2.) The Siamese leadership also had a political-military background, and used it skillfully in diplomacy. Reform leadership, however, came from above, from the king, a few of his half-brothers, and other members of the traditional ruling class. The king had to modernize in the face of a colonial threat, and he could not go too fast or too far, as that might undermine his power.

These differences in initial conditions go a long way toward explaining the difference in what happened in the two countries in later years. What follows shows how these differences affected institutional changes and policy.

Institutional Changes

The late 19th century saw the end of feudalism in Japan and the end of serfdom and slavery in Siam. A centralized political system replaced a decentralized one, and legal reforms were introduced. However, modernization occurred earlier and went further in Japan. Institutional changes in Siam took place 20 to 30 years later than in Japan. External and internal forces induced the Meiji Restoration in 1868. No comparable internal pressure was at work in Siam, and the Bowring Treaty, willingly accepted by King Mongkut, reduced foreign pressure. King Chulalongkorn was the major force in the Chakkri Reformation. He and his followers, known as the Young Siam, encountered formidable conservative elements, the Old Siam and the Conservative Siam cliques, ready to obstruct reform.

Initial attempts, including abolition of slavery, judicial and financial reforms, and formation of a Council of State and Privy Council, ran into immediate difficulties. This was reflected in the Front Palace Crisis (1874-75) and the Fanny Affair Crisis (1879) (Wyatt 1969: 50-59). The domestic power struggle led to intervention by western powers, threatening independence. It also warned the king against further reforms. As a result, Chulalongkorn had to make do with a less controversial policy, road construction and canal digging. Only after the death of the ex-Regent in 1883, and of the Prince of the Front Palace in 1885, was the king in full control, and able to introduce more far-reaching reforms (Wyatt 1969: 84-89; Adams 1977).

Institutional changes were more far-reaching in Japan. Much of the pressure for change came from below or, at any rate, from the new leadership. The old rulers were deprived of most of their privileges and simply became part of a new nobility. The Emperor Meiji became a constitutional monarch; authority was exercised primarily by previously lower-ranking samurai. To be sure, the members of the new elite could rule only because they were allied with rising businessmen and powerful landlords, but it is clear that much of the initiative for institutional changes and policy came from them.

Because Tokugawa Japan was a loosely-united entity consisting of some 280 *han*, an integrated nation-state had to be formed. This meant a series of semi-revolutionary changes, including replacement of feudal dues with a land tax, pensioning off the old aristocracy (*daimyo* and samurai), creation of a national army and navy, and establishing a political system based on a constitution. The pensioning-off amounted to confiscation of the old stipend at progressive rates. Though this was less hard on the lower-level samurai, those not employed by the new government faced a difficult situation. In vain, some rebelled against the central government. The government offered them land in northern Japan, and extended loans and subsidies for starting businesses (Kikkawa 1935).

Such reforms were pushed only halfway or not at all in Siam. The centralization of localized authority was implemented. Fiscal and legal reforms were undertaken. Slavery was ultimately abolished (in 1905) and the corvee system was replaced by a head tax. Military organization along western lines was developed. (See Vongkomolshet 1958: 145–79.) Although the king was successful in turning Siam into a centralized state, there was no political participation by the masses. Chulalongkorn ruled as he saw fit. Petition by a number of members of the ruling elite in 1885 for adoption of a constitution, creation of an appointed cabinet, and use of a merit system in the bureaucracy was turned down by the king as untimely. The leaders thought in terms of modernizing only as much as necessary to survive in power and maintain the status quo. Changes were allowed as necessary, but were kept as limited as possible (Dhiravegin 1981b). A constitution was not adopted until the coup of 1932. Reform of economic institutions also came later. In fact, even today political scientists and institutional economists speak of the patrimonialism of Siamese society (Dhiravegin 1970; Jacobs 1971; Yano 1980).[4]

Policy

The Japanese government was very heavily involved in developmental policy, whereas relative inaction characterized the Siamese government. Both invested in infrastructure, but Japan went much further. The Meiji government financed railroads, bridges, harbors, water-supply systems, electric utilities, and the postal and telegraph systems. In 1885–89, government investment in fixed capital was over 15 percent of total expenditure, 1.7 percent of GNP. These are less than the comparable figures after World War II, but in an era of small government, they were substantial. By the 1910–14 period, the shares were 27.7 percent and 4.5

[4] Patrimonialism is a system of power and property relations preceding capitalism, in which the goods and services available to the society are allocated by noneconomic means. In particular, a priest or bureaucratic class is able to pre-empt resources for itself. The term originated with Weber; for a contemporary discussion of the concept, see Jacobs (1971: ch. 2).

per cent respectively. (Data from Ohkawa and Shinohara 1979: 251-53, 348-52, and 370-71.)

We do not have comparable statistics for Siam for the early years, but government expenditure seems to have been concentrated on defense, internal security, and the court, leaving little for economic development (Nartsupha and Prasartset 1979: 22). From 1892, we have rough statistics on revenues and expenditures. According to Ingram's estimates, the average ratio of capital expenditure to "ordinary" revenue was 10 percent for 1892-1900 and 9 percent for 1901-10 (1971: 328).

Siam emphasized investment in roads, railways, canals, and postal stations as a means of strengthening political centralization. Special emphasis was placed on railroads, which were considered particularly important for such a purpose. But even here backwardness was evident. In 1900, when Japan had 6,200 km of railroad, Siam had only 264 km. Siam did little to develop its most important infrastructure, canals. Foreign advisers, particularly van der Heide, repeatedly recommended construction of a large system in central Siam. The idea was rejected on the grounds there were insufficient funds.

During the 19th century, Siam kept a very conservative monetary and fiscal policy, restricting borrowing abroad and raising revenue from new taxes (Ingram 1971: 194-99). In contrast, Japan did not hesitate to borrow abroad, in order to pension off the former ruling class and build its first railway. Particularly in the 20 years between the Sino-Japanese War and World War I, foreign capital played a significant role. Gross liabilities to foreigners, mostly bonds, formed 41 percent of GNP in 1913. More important, Japan imposed a series of new taxes and increased old ones, so revenue as a proportion of GNP increased, rising from 10 percent in 1885 to 13 percent in 1914, despite the rapid increase in GNP.

We feel the most important difference between the two countries was the keenness of interest in importing foreign knowledge, whether technical, cultural, or institutional. Such interest was avid in Japan, but weak in Siam.

In the last years of the Tokugawa and in the early Meiji period, government factories were established in a number of industries, including silk-reeling, silk and cotton spinning, woolen weaving, various types of mining, iron and other metals, munitions, shipbuilding, tools, machinery, boilers, cement, bricks, and glass. They were established and operated, usually at a loss, largely with a view of transferring western technology. When they were sold to private interests during the 1880s, cries of corruption were raised, as many factories were priced far below the original investment. The factories played significant roles in transferring technology (Kobayashi 1965: 304-44). No factories were established by the Siamese government in this period. The one significant private factory was Siam Cement, founded in 1913. Only after revision of the trade treaties in 1926 were many private and government factories established.

Both governments, and the Japanese model factories, employed foreign advisers, but there was a fundamental difference in attitudes. Whereas Japan employed foreigners as teachers, who were to transfer technology and other knowledge, Siam kept them as more or less permanent advisers. As late as 1909, the Siamese government employed 319 foreigners. The number of foreigners employed by the Japanese government declined from a peak of 527 in 1875, to 155 in 1886, to 79 in 1895. At the height of the era of *oyatoi gaijin* (employed foreigners) in the mid-1870s, nearly 40 percent of them were at the Ministry of Industry, and their wages accounted for over one-third of the ministry's budget (see Umetani 1968: 52-71). Most foreign advisers in Siam were in the public sector, whereas in Japan they were employed in the private sector – over 90 percent of them in 1879-81 (Ogata 1961: 119).

The Japanese government also used study missions to import technology and knowledge. The most important was the Iwakura Mission, which visited the United States and Europe for nearly two years in 1871-73. Many of the 51 high-ranking officials of the new government who comprised the mission played important roles in modernization. Early in his reign, Siam's King Chulalongkorn wanted to make a trip to Europe, but his request was rejected by the Regent, who was the real power in the 1870s. In 1871, the king did visit the Dutch East Indies, India, Burma, and the Straits Settlements (Singapore) and though the trips made a strong impression on the king, they could not serve as substitutes for a trip to the West.

Japan had nearly 6,000 students abroad by 1881. They represented a fairly wide segment of the society, including former lower-ranking samurai (Ogata 1961: 68; Umetani 1968: 201). Until the late 1890s, Siam sent abroad only members of the royal family. The early groups of middle-class students later provided the leaders of the constitutional coup in 1932 (Akagi 1977; Ammarinrat 1979).

Education is the major means of disseminating new knowledge, particularly technical knowledge. Japan introduced compulsory education in the 1880s, which proved vastly successful, partly because of the foundation laid during the Tokugawa period. School enrollment for the required six years was almost 100 percent in 1915. Emphasis then shifted to expanding secondary, and then college and university education. Table 2.1 shows enrollment trends.

In contrast, Siamese children went to school simply in the hope of one day entering government service. As a result, enrollment fluctuated with the king's political fortunes, increasing when Chulalongkorn's power was on the rise, and falling when his power declined. There was also a fear that enrollment meant recruitment for military service. Thus only those of Chinese origin enrolled in great number. Compulsory education was not introduced until 1921.

The difference in emphasis was most distinct in higher education. In Japan, science and engineering have been emphasized from the start. When the first national university was established in Tokyo in 1877, the faculties were humanities, law, natural sciences, and medicine, and there was a separate college of engineering (which became part of the Imperial University in 1886). Until 1887, the proportion of the two schools' graduates in natural sciences, medicine, engineering, and agriculture exceeded 80 percent (Nakayama 1967: 375-80).

Table 2.1: Percentage of children in school in Japan, 1873-1915

	School level		
Year	Primary[a]	Secondary[b]	Tertiary[c]
1873	28.1	nd	nd
1880	41.1	nd	nd
1895	61.2	4.3	0.3
1905	95.6	8.8	0.9
1915	98.5	8.1	1.0

[a] Grades 1-6
[b] Grades 7-11

[c] College and university
nd No data

Source: Mombusho 1962: 39, 50, 180

The forerunner of Chulalongkorn University, Siam's oldest university, was the Royal Pages School, established in 1902. The aim was to provide a general education, with emphasis on training in government administration. It was not until 1913 that an engineering school was established at Hor Wang.

The Japanese government sponsored and participated in many domestic and international trade and industrial fairs. It collected economic data and made them available to the public; it promoted, set standards, and inspected exports; it established technological institutes and agricultural extension services, including teaching tours. In a later period, Siam showed interest in improving agricultural productivity. The government began sponsoring fairs in 1907, and established an experimental rice farm in 1916, a Bureau of Agricultural Science in 1923. These appear to have "achieved little immediate success," although they laid a foundation for more active and scientific efforts after World War II (Feeny 1979: 126).

Thus, although the involvement of the government was unusually heavy, Japanese economic development and industrialization were promoted largely through the construction of infrastructure and the transfer and dissemination of knowledge from the West. The government did subsidize the establishment of first-generation factories, and helped former samurai go into business. But, in general, the government did little to underwrite private-sector industrialization on an ongoing basis. After the 1880s, subsidies were limited. They went to agriculture, railroads (until they were nationalized in 1906), and, mostly, to shipping and (after 1896) shipbuilding, which were considered quasi-military (LTES vol. 7; Inoue 1973; Blumenthal 1976). As for tariffs, the only thing the government could do before revision of the treaties was to abolish import duties on raw cotton and export duties on cotton textiles. After 1899, it could and did raise import duties, but they remained moderate until World War I.

Military expenditure increased rapidly in the period before the Sino-Japanese War, and then remained high. The heavy burden may have retarded growth, by wasting resources which could have been used for capital formation or other development purposes. On the other hand, the weaponry increasingly was procured domestically, from both government and private factories. Because military factories served as training and research and development centers, the emphasis on domestic procurement of weaponry may have had a significant bearing on development (Yamamura 1977).

Technology Transfer

Technology can be imported in three ways. The first approach is to adapt, taking only ideas and parts of machines appropriate to domestic factor proportions. The second method is to take the most advanced western technology in labor-intensive industries, with or without modification for local conditions. The third is to use the advanced technology, irrespective of its capital intensity, in an effort to produce the most advanced products (for a discussion of this in connection with the steel industry, see chapter 11).

Silk-reeling is the most important example of the first type of imported technology for Japan. French and Italian machinery was introduced in government factories in Tomioka and Maebashi. Some factories using similar technology were built by private interests, but the tendency was to adopt a modified technology. Moreover, a still more traditional technology, which adopted only gears and the method of multiple-yarn reeling, proved to be a strong competitor until wages became too high in the 20th century. Most of these factories and workshops were located in the countryside. A lack of foreign direct investment, freedom from regulation during the Tokugawa period, and the existence of local innovators and mechanics presumably explain the occurrence of such development.

Agriculture and forestry still had by far the largest employment at the end of the period, employing about one-third of the labor force in 1910. The sector grew at 1.5 percent per annum between 1880 and 1910 (Ohkawa and Shinohara 1979: 78 and 372). Much of the growth can be attributed to technical progress, primarily the spread of higher-yielding rice varieties, more extensive use of commercial fertilizer, and improvements in non-rice production (Yamada and Hayami 1979: 89–93; and also chapter 4 below).

The second type of technology transfer is exemplified by cotton spinning, which was an urban industry. The most advanced large-scale factories were transplanted by a private consortium organized by Shibusawa Eiichi. Several capital-saving modifications were made, including operating two shifts (Ranis 1957: 594–607; and chapter 10 below). In most of the capital-intensive industries, modifications were more difficult, and they did not expand rapidly until later in the development process.

The third transfer method was adopted by military-related industries, particularly those owned by the government. Here the government factories played an overwhelmingly important role. In 1903, government factories employed 63 percent of the factory workers and 78 percent of the horsepower used in the machinery and equipment industries. After the cruiser *Kongo* was delivered by a British shipbuilder in 1912, all naval vessels were built in domestic yards.

Consequences

In the course of industrialization, rapid structural changes take place. Particularly striking was what occurred in Japan's trade structure. Just as with contemporary less developed countries (LDCs), Japan's initial exports were mostly primary or quasi-primary commodities, such as raw silk, tea, and marine products, in exchange for manufactured goods. But domestic manufacturers soon started substituting for imports, particularly in light industries, and eventually some of these became export industries. By 1914, Japan's major exports included such former imports as cotton yarn and cloth, in addition to traditional items such as raw silk and copper. And primary commodities, such as cotton, sugar, soybeans, and petroleum, had already become major imports. Table 2.2 shows the change in composition of Japanese trade between 1880 and 1910.

Siam's trade structure changed significantly in the 19th century, but the changes were mainly among types of primary products (see table 2.3). Rice as a percentage of total exports rose from a very small figure in the 1850s to 41 percent in 1867, and to about 70 percent after 1890. The four major exports – rubber, tin, and teak, in addition to rice – constituted some 90 percent of exports in the 1890s. More than 80 percent of the labor force was engaged in agriculture and forestry.

In Siam, technical progress was scattered and limited (Nartsupha and Prasartset 1979: 16). In rice production, even though total output and exports increased greatly, average yield probably declined as cultivation moved onto marginal land. This was certainly the case in the first half of the 20th century, for which we do have data (Ingram 1971: 214–16). The development of manufacturing was confined to areas such as rice milling, wood sawing, and machine repairing. Even though we do not have figures, there is little ground to believe per-capita output increased substantially during the period. Male real wages in Bangkok, while fluctuating widely, were stagnant or declined as a trend between 1865 and 1925 (Feeny 1979: 116).

In Japan, between 1885 and 1914, real per-capita output increased more than 50 percent (LTES vol. 1: 237). Real wages in manufacturing industries also rose substantially, by 45 percent in the period 1880–1914 (LTES vol. 8: 134 and 246). There is little doubt the engine of economic development was running in Japan. Japanese economic development and industrialization undoubtedly were

Table 2.2:   Percentage distribution of Japanese trade by major commodities, 1880 and 1910

Exports			
1880		*1910*	
Percentage exported	*Commodity*	*Percentage exported*	*Commodity*
31.0	raw silk	26.7	raw silk
27.0	tea	9.2	cotton yarn
4.7	waste silk	6.6	silk cloth
2.5	tangles[a]	5.7	cotton cloth
2.3	sardines	4.2	copper

Imports			
1880		*1910*	
Percentage imported	*Commodity*	*Percentage imported*	*Commodity*
21.1	cotton yarn	33.4	raw cotton
15.8	wool cloth	10.1	sugar
15.1	cotton cloth	3.0	petroleum[b]
3.8	petroleum[b]	3.0	soybeans
2.9	wrought iron[c]	2.8	wood

[a] Tangles are a kind of seaweed
[b] Petroleum and petroleum products
[c] T- and angle-bars, and other wrought-iron material used in construction

Sources: Computed from various primary sources; underlying data also available in LTES vol. 14

greatly facilitated by institutional changes and policy. The Meiji Restoration and related changes drastically redistributed income and opportunity, laying the foundation on which the private sector grew. Development was enhanced by such measures as model factories, subsidies of early private factories, and provision of extension and exposition services in an effort to close the gap in knowledge, as well as a strong emphasis on infrastructure and education.

The private sector in Japan responded vigorously to the initiatives taken by the government, and ultimately (rather soon in most cases), activities in fields other than military-related industries shifted to the private sector. Despite the basically oligarchic character of the government, the economy in the latter half of the Meiji period appears to have behaved more or less as neoclassical economists like to see.

Table 2.3: Percentage of Siam's total exports accounted for by three major commodities, 1867–1916

Year	Rice	Tin	Teak	Total
1867	41.1	15.6	nd	56.7
1890	69.7	11.1	5.5	86.4
1906	69.1	11.0	11.2	91.3
1915–16	70.1	15.9	3.9	89.9

The values are only for exports from Bangkok, which is believed to have handled 80 percent of total exports. However, rubber, the fourth major commodity in Siamese trade, was always shipped from other ports during this period. In 1925–39, rubber was 2.3 percent of total exports

nd No data

Source: Ingram 1971: 94

In contrast, a base for economic development appears to have been lacking in Siam. The abundant supply of land may have retarded industrialization, but the problem does not seem to have been industrialization as such; rather, the lack of technical progress in both industry and agriculture. The government did not actively create a base for development. The infrastructure was far from adequate and serious efforts to learn from abroad or to propagate knowledge domestically were lacking. Moreover, patrimonial institutions reduced initiative.

Lack of interest in technical progress was decisive in Siam's failure to develop in the 19th century. Institutional changes did not remove inhibiting forces as thoroughly, or as soon, as in Japan, and the policy of relative inaction, motivated by the ruling elite's desire to continue to hold power, did not help either. Given such a contrast in initial conditions, institutional changes, and policy, the divergence in economic development between Siam and Japan is probably what we should expect. Siam followed the path most colonies pursued, and found itself at the lower end of the vertical international division of labor by the end of the 19th century.

References

Adams, David (1977), "Monarchy and Political Change: Thailand under Chulalongkorn (1868–1885)," Ph.D. dissertation, University of Chicago.
Akagi, Osamu (1977), "The Impact of Western Educated Thai Students on the Thai Monarchy," paper presented at the Seventh Conference of the International Association of Historians of Asia, Bangkok.
Ammarinrat, La-oongtong (1979), "Karn song nukrian pai suksatoh tangprates tangtae Poh Soh 2411–2475," M.A. thesis, Faculty of Arts, Chulalongkorn University, Bangkok.

Blumenthal, Tuvia (1976), "The Japanese Shipbuilding Industry," in Hugh Patrick with Larry Meissner, eds, *Japanese Industrialization and its Social Consequences*, Berkeley, CA: University of California Press.

Chittiwatanapong, Prasert (1976), "The Modernization Base in Japan and Thailand: Education and Science," in *The Emergence of Modern States: Thailand and Japan*, Thailand-Japan Studies Program.

Dhiravegin, Likhit (1970), "Contrasting Modernization in Chulalongkorn's Siam (1868-1910) and Meiji's Japan (1867-1912)," *Journal of Social Sciences*, 7(1) (January).

Dhiravegin, Likhit (1981), "The Role of Political Leadership in the Modernization of Chulalongkorn's Siam (1868-1910) and Meiji's Japan (1867-1912)," presented at a seminar on the Centennial Celebration of Ataturk, in August 1981, sponsored by the Turkish government and the History Association of Thailand.

Dore, Ronald P. (1965), *Education in Tokugawa Japan*, Berkeley, CA: University of California Press.

Eto, Shinkichi (1968), "Kinsei Chugoku seijishi kenkyu," *Todai shakaikagaku kenky sosho 26*, Tokyo: Daigaku Shuppankai.

Feeny, David (1979), "Competing Hypotheses of Underdevelopment: A Thai Case Study," *Journal of Economic History*, 39(1) (March).

Horie Yasuzo (1965), "Nihon no keizai to 'iye'," *Keizai Kenkyu*, 16(2) (April).

Ichii, Saburo (1980), *Kinsei kakushin shiso no keifu*, Nihon Hoso Shuppan Kyokai.

Ingram, James (1971), *Economic Change in Thailand 1850-1970*, Stanford, CA: Stanford University Press.

Inoue, Yoichiro (1973), "Meiji koki no kaiji seisaku," in Yoshio Ando, ed., *Nihon keizai seisakushiron*, Tokyo: Daigaku Shuppankai.

Ishikawa, Ken (1953), *Gakko no hattatsu*, Iwasaki Shoten.

Jacobs, Norman (1971), *Modernization without Development: Thailand as an Asian Case Study*, New York: Praeger.

Kikkawa, Shuzo (1935), *Shizoku jusan no kenkyu*, Tokyo: Yuhikaku.

Kinugasa, Yasuki (1963), "Minshu bunka no hakyu," in *Koza Nihon bunkashi*, vol. 6, Sanichishobo for Nihonshi Kenkyukai.

Kobayashi, Masaaki (1965), "Kindai sangyo no keisei to kangyo haraisage," in Mitsuhaya Kajinishi, ed., *Nihon keizaishi taikei 5*, Tokyo: Daigaku Shuppankai.

Konta, Yozo (1977), *Edo no honyasan — kinsei bunkashi no sokumen*, Nihon Hoso Shuppan Kyokai.

Kravis, Irving B., Alan W. Heston, and Robert Summers (1978), "Real GDP Per Capita for More Than One Hundred Countries," *Economic Journal*, 88(350) (June).

LTES (*Estimates of Long-Term Economic Statistics of Japan*), series edited by Kazushi Ohkawa, Miyohei Shinohara, and Mataji Umemura, Tokyo: Toyo Keizai Shimposha.

  vol. 1, *National Income* (1974), Kazushi Ohkawa, Nobukiyo Takamatsu, and Yuzo Yamamoto.

  vol. 7, *Government Expenditure* (1966), Koichi Emi and Yuichi Shionoya.

vol. 8, *Prices* (1967), Kazushi Ohkawa, Osama Noda, Nobukiyo Takamatsu, Saburo Yamada, Minoru Kumasaki, Yuichi Shionoya, and Ryoshin Minami.

vol. 14, *Foreign Trade* (1979), Ippei Yamazawa and Yuzo Yamamoto.

Miyamoto, Mataji, Yotaro Sakudo, and Yasukichi Yasuba (1965), "Economic Development in Preindustrial Japan, 1859-1895," *Journal of Economic History*, 25(4) (December).

Mombusho (Government of Japan, Ministry of Education) (1962), *Nihon no seicho to kyoiku*, Teikoku Chiho Gyosei Gakkai.

Naikaku Tokeikyoku (Government of Japan, Cabinet Statistics Bureau), *Nihon teikoku tokei nenkan*, published annually from 1881, Tokyo; the 1980 (10th) issue was used.

Nakano, Takashi (1964), *Shoka dozokudan no kenkyu*, Miraisha.

Nakayama, Shigeru (1967), "Kokuei kagaku," in Isao Sugimoto, ed., *Kagaku-shi*, Tokyo: Yamakawa Shuppansha.

Nartsupha, Chatthip, and Suthy Prasartset (1979), *The Political Economy of Siam 1851-1910*, Social Science Association of Thailand.

Ogata, Hiroyasu (1961), *Seiyo kyoiku inyu no hoto*, Kodansha.

Ohkawa, Kazushi (1976), "Initial Conditions – Rough Notes," prepared for the Research Planning Conference on ... Comparative Analysis, April 2-4, Tokyo, International Development Center of Japan.

Ohkawa, Kazushi, and Miyohei Shinohara, with Larry Meissner (1979), *Patterns of Japanese Economic Development*, New Haven, CT: Yale University Press.

Passin, Herbert (1965), *Society and Education in Japan*, New York: Columbia University Press.

Prebisch, Raúl (1959), "Commercial Policy in the Underdeveloped Countries," *American Economic Review*, 49 (suppl.): 251-73 (May).

Ranis, Gustav (1957), "Factor Proportions in Japanese Economic Development," *American Economic Review*, 47: 594-607 (September).

Sakata, Yoshio (1970), "Nihon kindaika no shuppatsu to tenkai," *Jimbun Gakuho*, Jimbun Kagaku Kenkyusho, Kyoto University.

Siffin, William J. (1966), *The Thai Bureaucracy: Institutional Change and Development*, Honolulu: East-West Center Press.

Skinner, G. William (1975), *Chinese Society in Thailand, an Analytical History*, Ithaca, NY: Cornell University Press.

Smith, Thomas (1970), *The Agrarian Origins of Modern Japan*, Stanford, CA: Stanford University Press.

Umetani, Noboru (1968), *Oyatoi gaikokujin*, vol. 1, Kashima Shuppankai.

Vongkomolshet, Detchard (1958), "The Administrative, Judicial and Financial Reforms of King Chulalongkorn," M.A. thesis, Cornell University.

Wallerstein, Immanuel (1979), *The Capitalist World Economy*, Cambridge: Cambridge University Press.

World Bank (1981 edn), *World Tables*, Washington, DC: World Bank.

Wyatt, David (1969), *The Politics of Reform in Thailand*, New Haven, CT: Yale University Press.

Yamada, Saburo, and Yujiro Hayami (1979), "Agriculture," in Kazushi Ohkawa and Miyohei Shinohara, with Larry Meissner, eds, *Patterns of Japanese Economic Development*, New Haven, CT: Yale University Press.

Yamamura, Kozo (1977), "Success Illgotten? The Role of Meiji Militarism in Japan's Technological Progress," *Journal of Economic History*, 37(1) (March).

Yamazawa, Ippei (1975), "Yushutsunyu Kakaku Shisu," in Kazushi Ohkawa and Ryoshin Minami, eds, *Kindai Nihon no keizai hatten*, Tokyo: Toyo Keizai Shimposha.

Yano, Toru (1980), *Tonan Asia sekai no ronri*, Chuo Koronsha.

Yui, Tsunehiko (1973), "Nihon no kindaika to Tokugawa shonin," in Jiro Kamishima, Ed., *Nihon kindaika no takushitsu*, Tokyo: Azia Keizai Kenkyusho.

3 Economic Development in Historical Perspective: Japan, Korea, and Taiwan

JOHN C. H. FEI, KAZUSHI OHKAWA, and
GUSTAV RANIS

The economic development of Japan between 1870 and 1970, and of Taiwan and Korea over the period 1950–75 are examples of attempted transition into the epoch of modern growth in the style of Kuznets (1966). This paper looks at the period of transition growth in these three countries, in terms of both country typology and the identification of phases.

From a long-run perspective, the dominant feature of the epoch of modern growth is the routinized contribution of science and technology. This characteristic is shared by virtually all types of mature economies, even though countries may undergo different sequences or phases, due to differences in initial conditions and in their behavior over time. We believe that the detailed examination of the transition from the long epoch of agrarianism to one of modern growth benefits from the identification of phases.

Analysis of comparative growth suggests that sets of countries can be grouped around basic family affinities, a certain uniqueness not necessarily shared by other types of developing countries. However, even within a family of less developed countries (LDCs), there may exist important, and instructive, differences. Recognition of such differences as well as similarities in behavior among developing economies permits the generation of a more flexible evolutionary view of development, based on the notion that each phase in the transition is

The authors wish to acknowledge the helpful comments of Professors Simon Kuznets and Ryoshin Minami, as well as other participants in the Comparative Analysis Project. We also received substantial help from Shirley Kuo and Ms Liu with respect to Taiwan, from Moo-ki Bai, Young-ie Chung, and Toru Yanagihara with respect to Korea, and from Nobukiyo Takamatsu and Shokichi Motai with respect to Japan.

This paper represents a further development of Ohkawa and Ranis (1978).

characterized by a distinct structural form (morphology) and a distinct mode of operation (physiology). Such phases may be identified through a combination of inductive evidence and deductive reasoning.

This evolutionary view complements the more traditional analysis of shifts in the sectoral composition of output and labor allocation among the agricultural, industrial, and services sectors. As has been pointed out by Colin Clark and, more rigorously, by Kuznets, we usually encounter in the course of development a relatively shrinking agricultural sector, an expanding industrial sector, and a fairly stable (if markedly changing in composition) services sector. Such structural changes reflect changes in final demand as well as in capacity, or – in an open economy – in changing comparative advantage, as per-capita income rises. The phasing developed in this essay focuses on the same question, the underlying issue being how increases in productivity are allocated among sectors as income rises.

The approach represents something of a halfway house between the unacceptable proposition that there is a general fixed evolutionary model followed by all developing countries, and the equally unacceptable proposition that every country is *sui generis*, its transition growth defying generalization and transferability. Our typological framework aims to bring into clearer focus the elements of affinity, while at the same time noting instructive differences.

Family affinity and differences among Japan, Korea, and Taiwan represent significant aspects of the success of transition growth and are more easily observable empirically during the early phases. Our statistic analysis of later growth concentrates more on Japan; the work on Korea and Taiwan is necessarily still only propositional in this respect.

The next section presents an overview of the phases that Japan, Korea, and Taiwan have passed through. This elementary picture raises all the essential aspects of transition growth dealt with in this chapter, including the labor force and its allocation, which is a key element in understanding the development process. The early metamorphosis of the three economies is then discussed in the section entitled "The early transition phases," giving operational content to our phasing and typology. This section includes important differences in how each of the three traversed their early phases, and discusses the rapidity of development in each, including the related notion of "telescoping" of the growth process in Korea and Taiwan. In the next section, the later phase of development is taken up.

We then look in greater detail at the labor force. Topics covered include wage rates, capital/labor ratios, labor reallocation and income distribution, including linking of the time paths of the wage rate and wage shares with the labor-allocation process, and the surplus of labor-dualism question. Finally, we consider the relevance of our methodological approach to a better understanding of contemporary development efforts in the typologies found in Africa, Latin America, and other parts of Asia.

Transition Growth and Typology

Our study of comparative growth in Japan, Taiwan, and Korea presumes a commonality among them, a basic family affinity distinguishing them as a group from other types of developing countries, such as Latin America, African, or even other, larger, Asian countries. The underlying affinity among Japan, Taiwan, and Korea is, in part, based on cultural and geographic proximity. All are in East Asia, have high population densities, are poor in natural resources, and initially possessed a surplus labor force endowed with an unusually favorable level of literacy and general education. All initiated their transition after major disturbances: the collapse of the Tokugawa shogunate in Japan, the Korean War and, for Taiwan, retrocession to China followed by a separation from the mainland.

The structural forms and modes of operation demarcating growth phases may be described by the pattern of resource flows. The patterns and phases identified for our three systems are shown in table 3.1, which, with figure 3.1, contains the expository core of our analysis.

The development of Korea and Taiwan through phases P1 and P2 after World War II is roughly comparable with the same phases in Japan between about 1880 and 1920. By implication, what happened during P3 in Japan is somewhat indicative of what is likely to happen in Taiwan and Korea. We refer to P1 and P2 as the early transition period, and to P3 as the late transition period.

Table 3.1: Modes of operation in development phases

Symbol	Japan	Taiwan	Korea
P0	*Before 1870* isolation heritage	*Before 1950* traditional export expansion	*Before 1953* traditional export expansion
P1	*1870–1900* traditional export expansion, coupled with mild primary import substitution	*1950–62* primary import substitution	*1953–64* primary import substitution
P2	*1900–20* primary export substitution	*1962–70* primary export substitution	*1964–72* primary export substitution
P3	*After 1920* secondary import and export substitution	*After 1970* secondary import and export substitution	*After 1972* secondary import and export substitution

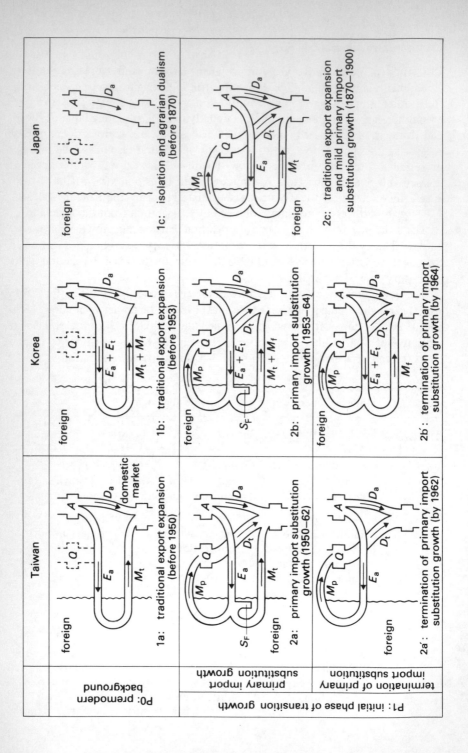

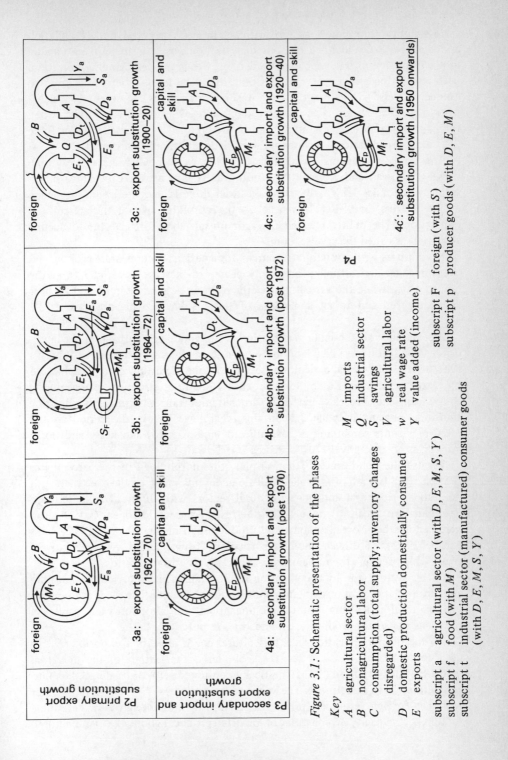

Figure 3.1: Schematic presentation of the phases

Key

A   agricultural sector
B   nonagricultural labor
C   consumption (total supply; inventory changes disregarded)
D   domestic production domestically consumed
E   exports

M   imports
Q   industrial sector
S   savings
V   agricultural labor
w   real wage rate
Y   value added (income)

subscript a   agricultural sector (with D, E, M, S, Y)
subscript f   food (with M)
subscript t   industrial sector (manufactured) consumer goods
             (with D, E, M, S, Y)

subscript F   foreign (with S)
subscript p   producer goods (with D, E, M)

P2 primary export substitution growth

3a: export substitution growth (1962–70)

3b: export substitution growth (1964–72)

3c: export substitution growth (1900–20)

P3 secondary import and export substitution growth

4a: secondary import and export substitution growth (post 1970)

4b: secondary import and export substitution growth (post 1972)

4c: secondary import and export substitution growth (1920–40)

P4

4c′:   secondary import and export substitution growth (1950 onwards)

It is natural to begin our analysis with an emphasis on population. (Population and labor force are identical, for our analytical purposes.) A major phenomenon of the transition into the epoch of modern growth is the demographic transition, with population growth rates rising from "historical levels," before declining to "modern levels." The strength of the upsurge determines the extent to which a labor-surplus condition is accentuated or prolonged. (Surplus labor exists when roughly the same level of output can be maintained by a smaller labor force with some organizational reforms and very little additional investment.)

The levels of Japan's population explosion were much more modest than those of Taiwan and Korea after World War II, but all three began as labor-surplus economies. The early transition in all three is characterized by a decline in the relative, as well as – eventually – the absolute, size of the agricultural population. The point at which the agricultural labor force begins to decline absolutely is called the reversal point.

In countries with few natural resources, food deficits become more pronounced over time, as agricultural productivity ceases to increase as rapidly as at the outset. Thus, while the agricultural sector plays an active role in P1 and P2, it is ultimately reduced to an appendage of the system, and plays a passive role during P3.

Associated with the labor reallocation is the gradual exhaustion of the labor-surplus condition; unskilled labor becomes a scarce factor by the end of P2. This shift of labor from the agricultural sector to nonagriculture, much emphasized by Kuznets, represents a key long-run characteristic of structural change during the transitional process, and is of crucial importance to understanding the transition phasing in table 3.1. In this regard, we believe the period around 1920 represents something of a significant landmark for Japanese transitional growth, as do the early 1970s for Korea and Taiwan.

Besides the condition of labor surplus, the morphology of the early phases (P1 and P2) is that of an open dualistic economy – that is, the coexistence of domestic agricultural and nonagricultural sectors with different rules of wage determination (dualism) trading with the rest of the world (openness). Dualism here denotes both organizational and product dualism (see Ohkawa 1972; Ranis and Fei 1982). All three economies, particularly Taiwan and Korea, are relatively small, which renders their openness an especially important feature.

In this system, the total population is allocated as either agricultural or non-agricultural labor. Labor combines with land as the major factors of production, yielding total agricultural output; the nonagricultural labor force and capital in the industrial sector produce total industrial output.

On the output-allocation side, agricultural goods are either exported (E_a) or used for domestic consumption (D_a). Similarly, the output of the industrial sector is either exported (E_t), domestically consumed (D_t), or used as inputs into agriculture, or as investment. The value of total exports ($E = E_a + E_t$), together with net foreign resources (private-capital inflow and foreign aid), determine total import capacity M, consisting of imported producer goods M_p, manufactured consumer goods M_t, and food M_f. The total domestic supply (consumption) of consumer goods is thus $C_a = D_a + M_f$ for food and $C_t = D_t + M_t$ for industrial consumer goods. In this way, the direction of the output flows in each sector give operational content to the concept of open dualism. (Note we are not concerned here with the service sector or inventory changes.)

Under our simplifying assumption, wage rates are the same in agriculture and nonagriculture, total wage payments in industry are wB, and in agriculture, wV, where w is the real wage rate, B is the nonagricultural labor force, and V is the agricultural labor force. With Y indicating value added, the industrial real wage share is wB/Y_t and wV/Y_a is the real wage share in agriculture. These functional income-distribution considerations are a part of the transition story, which we develop later, as the wage rate and the wage share reflect both the labor-surplus condition and the technological aspects of production in the two sectors.

In the industrial sector, total income (value added) Y_t is used either for consumption C_t or savings S_t. Similarly, value added in agriculture, Y_a, can be divided into consumption C_a and savings S_a. The per-capita consumption of agricultural goods and of nonagricultural goods defines the welfare implications of growth. Total savings $S = S_a + S_t$, which, together with S_F (the capital inflow from abroad), add up to total investment, of course affect the rapidity of growth. We assume part of agricultural savings is used to finance industrial-sector investment.

While this is an oversimplification of reality, it is nonetheless consistent with reality. Thus, staying within the confines of this system, we can glean a number of useful insights into the development process.

The Early Transition Phases (P1 and P2)

As Japan, Korea, and Taiwan embarked on their transitions to modern growth, their economic structures were gradually transformed into a full open dualistic system. We first take up the transitional growth of Taiwan and Korea, and relate it to the phasing of table 3.1, explore the family affinities, and note some of the differences between the two countries. The experiences of these two latecomers is then compared with the early transition period of Japan, primarily in terms of instructive differences. The telescoping (shortening) of the early transition by Taiwan and Korea, compared to Japan, is then discussed.

Two conditions prevail during this early period: the agricultural sectors plays a dominant role, and labor-surplus conditions prevail. That these two conditions occurred in all three systems is the main element of the family affinity that constitutes the basis for our analysis. The focal point in this section is the structure of resource flows or the market orientation of the two main producing sectors and their interaction with the rest of the world. To illustrate the discussion that follows, the flows and orientation of each country during each phase are shown in figure 3.1.

Transition Growth in Taiwan and Korea

Korea and Taiwan exhibit the set of initial economic and geographic conditions commonly defined as a labor surplus, natural resources poor, open, dualistic economy. This is demonstrated by the striking resemblance in the evolution of their economic structures through P0, P1, and P2 (see figure 3.1).

During P0, the pre-transition phase, under what we call traditional export expansion or triangular colonialism, the agricultural sector (A) produces the domestic food supply plus goods for export (E_a), which help finance imported manufactured nondurable consumer goods (M_t), such as textiles. Both Taiwan and Korea experienced the same triangular pattern under colonialism during P0, with the difference that Korea also exported some nonagricultural goods early on.

Taiwan and Korea initiated modern growth during P1, via a primary import-substitution (PIS) pattern, which focuses on manufactured nondurable consumer

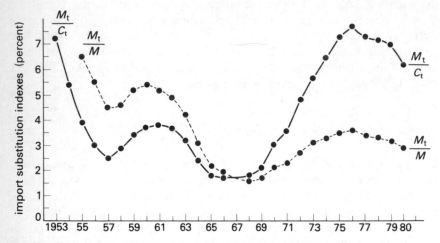

Figure 3.2: Import substitution indexes: Taiwan, 1953–80

Five-year moving averages with 3-year averages for the end years

M_t are products with codes 1, 6, 8, and 9 in the SITC (standard industrial trade classification)

M_t/C_t manufactured consumer goods imports as a percentage of total consumption of manufactured consumer goods (i.e. excludes food and services)

M_t/M manufactured consumer goods imports as a percentage of total imports

Sources: See figure 3.3

goods. Phase P1 is initiated when earnings from traditional exports (augmented by foreign-capital inflows) are reallocated to industrial-sector activities, aimed at replacing previously-imported manufactured consumer goods. Korea commenced its PIS phase P1 around 1953, Taiwan around 1950.

During PIS, part of primary product earnings (E_a) is diverted from importation of consumer goods (M_t) to importing producer goods (M_p). An emerging industrial sector (Q) uses the producer goods to make domestically the goods previously imported (M_t). In this way, domestic production (D_t) substitutes in domestic markets for imports (see figure 3.1, row 2).

The fall in M_t/D_t signifies that domestic demand for manufactured nondurable consumer goods is increasingly satisfied by the domestic output of the import-substituting industries (D_t), while the decline in M_t/M_p signifies that foreign exchange is increasingly being allocated away from the importation of manu-

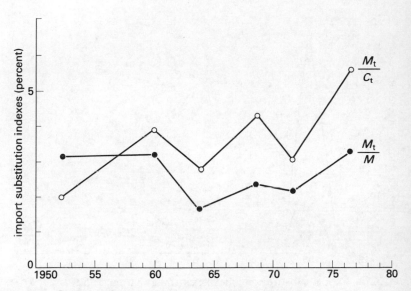

Figure 3.3: Import substitution indexes: Korea, 1952–78

Single-year data

Sources

Taiwanese data are from various government statistic sources, including the annual *Statistical Abstract of the Republic of China*, the monthly *Statistics of Exports and Imports* (published by the Ministry of Finance), and the *Commodity Trade Statistics of the Republic of China, 1954–74*
Korean data are from various government statistical sources, primarily the Bank of Korea's *Economic Statistics Yearbook*

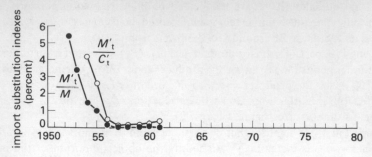

Figure 3.4:   Import substitution indexes, clothing: Taiwan, 1952–61
Single-year data

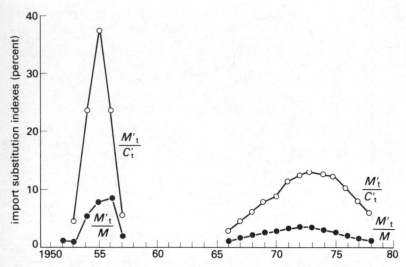

Figure 3.5:   Import substitution indexes, clothing: Korea, 1952–78
1952–57, single-year data; 1966–78, 5-year moving averages

M'_t/C'_t expenditure for imported clothing as a percentage of total
             expenditure for clothing
M'_t/M clothing imports as a percentage of total imports

Sources: see figure 3.2

M'_t is from a United Nations series on imports of cotton piece goods in its *Yearbook of
International Trade Statistics*

factured consumer goods and towards the importation of producer goods. Import substitution in the domestic-market sense is thus shown by a decline in M_t/D_t over time, and substitution in the foreign-exchange-allocation sense by M_t/M_p, also declining over time. The process is illustrated for Taiwan in figure 3.2 and for Korea in figure 3.3. This is even clearer for the performance of one type of consumer good, textiles, than for all consumer products, where the output mix changes (figures 3.4 and 3.5).

Such primary import substitution represents a natural metamorphosis out of colonial triangularism in three senses. First, the system's import capacity is still based on traditional primary-product exports, which represent the country's basic comparative advantage. Second, these exports pay for the producer-good imports that represent the major instrument for carrying modern science and technology into the system. And, finally, the domestic market for modern nondurable consumer goods was already there, developed by the importers, making life easier for the relatively inexperienced local entrepreneurs.

Most LDCs initiate transition growth with such a primary import-substitution phase. Because growth is fueled mainly by traditional agricultural or raw-material exports and the domestic market for consumer goods is limited, the duration of this phase depends on the potential for maintaining or expanding these two markets. For countries with relatively abundant natural resources (for example, some Latin American countries), the process can be prolonged rather easily. However, for countries with a relatively poor natural-resource endowment, the process is necessarily short. It must end when all manufactured nondurable imports have been substituted for by domestic output, or when all foreign-exchange earnings have been allocated to imports of producer goods. Any further industrialization then has to slow to the pace of population plus per-capita income growth. This is shown in figure 3.1, row 3.

When P1 came to its inevitable end, both Korea and Taiwan moved to exporting labor-intensive manufactured products (E_t). This new type of export gradually assumes the role of the traditional primary-product exports (E_a); therefore the phase is called primary export substitution. It began around 1964 in Korea and 1961 in Taiwan.

The system's comparative advantage base in foreign trade has now shifted from land to unskilled labor. The logical necessity of the transition from P1 to P2 is based on both negative and positive factors. Negatively, there are the limitations of natural resources and domestic markets, already noted above. Positively, entrepreneurs and the labor force have gained experience and skills needed to create efficiency-oriented industries capable of penetrating world markets for labor-intensive manufactured goods.

The inevitability of the emergence of P2 after P1 is part of a natural evolutionary thesis applicable to a developing country with an abundance of labor, but a dearth of natural resources. Policy changes accommodating the new system include more realistic interest and foreign-exchange rates, the establishment of export processing zones, and the reduction, first, of quantitative restrictions, then of tariffs.

Phase P2 also signifies that, for the first time, the system has a dependable outlet for its abundant labor supply: embodied in labor-intensive, nondurable consumer goods, it is exported. For this reason, both industrial-sector labor absorption and GDP growth rates are likely to be much higher during P2 than during P1. It is through such a process that the labor-surplus condition is ultimately exhausted, bringing a marked upturn in unskilled real wages.

P2 also marks a considerable shift in the nature of the basic socioeconomic problems of the society. First, the pervasive sense of massive labor abundance and unemployment of P1 is replaced by one of labor utilization and, ultimately, labor scarcity, coupled with concern that the increase in real wages will threaten the competitive position in world markets. Second, the perennial sense of foreign-exchange shortage during P1, with import capacity dependent on traditional export earnings plus foreign aid, is replaced by growing foreign-exchange resources fueled by growth of the new industrial exports, plus foreign investors anxious to participate in P2 growth.

During P1, the infant entrepreneurial class benefited from an array of government policies that provided windfall profits – earnings not related to productive efficiency. Other sources of saving – in particular, agricultural savings – were tapped and transferred to this new industrial class. During P2, in contrast, entrepreneurs are ready to take advantage of an environment favoring more realistic prices and greater market orientation, and thus conducive to the requirements of a more efficiency-oriented growth phase.

The family affinity between Taiwan and Korea is based largely on the emergence of such an externally-oriented industrialization phase at the end of primary import substitution. Other characteristics corroborating this affinity can be summarized in five points.

First, the degree of external orientation can be expected to fall or remain low during P1, in contrast to the colonial-trade regime, as trade (imports or exports) as a percentage of national income probably declines. In contrast, during P2 the trade ratio increases in a sustained fashion ($E/$GDP in figures 3.6 and 3.7). The trade-ratio decline during P1 is due partly to limits on the expansion of exports of natural resources and partly to the autarkic tendencies inherent in import substitution. The increase during P2 is due to the much greater external orientation of this phase, as the economy becomes more competitively market-oriented and labor-intensive industrial exports account for an increasing portion of national income.

Second, the composition of exports undergoes a dramatic change. During P1, traditional agricultural exports dominate total exports. During P2, nontraditional manufactured goods take over, indicating the power of the primary export-substitution process (E_t/E in figures 3.6 and 3.7).

Third, real unskilled wages begin to rise near the end of P2. There is a relative stability of unskilled real wages in both sectors as long as the unlimited supply of

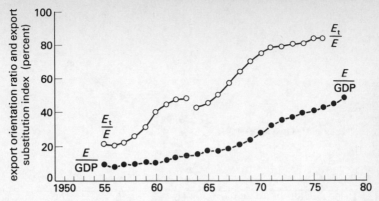

Figure 3.6: Export orientation ratio and export substitution index:
Taiwan, 1955–78

E_t/E plots single-year data; E/GDP is a 5-year moving average

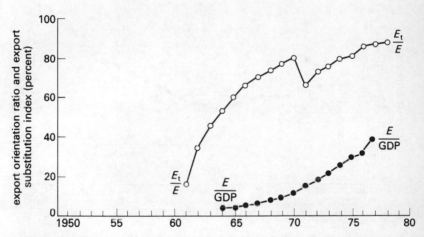

Figure 3.7: Export orientation ratio and export substitution index:
Korea, 1961–78

Before 1966, single-year figures; after 1966, 5-year moving averages

E_t/E manufactured goods as a percentage of total exports
E/GDP exports as a percentage of GDP

Sources: see figure 3.2

labor lasts. During P2, surplus labor is gradually exhausted, bringing the economy
to the commercialization point. That is, when the labor surplus is exhausted,
labor becomes a scarce commodity that is compensated in a competitive neoclassical fashion (wage equal the marginal product of labor) (figures 3.8 and 3.9).

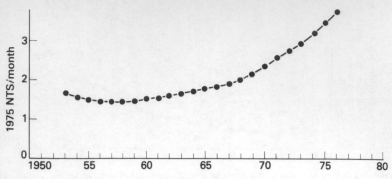

Figure 3.8:   Unskilled real wage rates: Taiwan, 1953–76

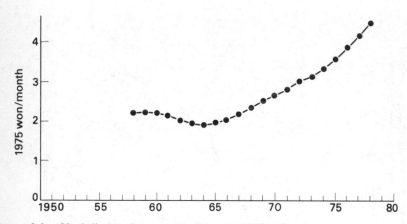

Figure 3.9:   Unskilled real wage rates: Korea, 1958–78

The real unskilled wage rate is defined here as the monthly average earnings for textile workers deflated by the GNP deflator, an average being taken of male and female wages.

The data are plotted as 5-year moving averages, except the end-year figures are 3-year averages

Sources

Taiwanese data are from the *Statistical Abstract of the Republic of China*. For wages, the 1978 edn (pp. 280–81); for the GNP deflator, the 1980 edn (pp. 170–73) converted to make 1975 equal to 1

Korean data are from the Bank of Korea's *Economic Statistics Yearbook*. Wages are from the 1980 edn (pp. 258–59) and equivalent tables in earlier editions; the GNP deflator has been calculated by the authors from current- and constant-priced GNP series in the *Yearbook*

Fourth, the rapidity of labor reallocation accelerates during P2. In this phase, the now more export-oriented industrial sector absorbs labor at a much faster pace than was possible by import-substituting nonagricultural activities during P1. While a moderate decline in the relative size of the agricultural workforce occurred during P1, in P2 the process is more rapid, and there is possibly even an absolute decline in the agricultural labor force. This decline, the reversal phenomenon, if it occurs, is a major transition point. We return to it later. The combination of plentiful labor with a now more mature entrepreneurial class capable of penetrating international markets makes the increase in the labor-reallocation rate an integral part of the transition process.

Finally, the speed of the growth process accelerates. During P1, the rate of income growth per-capita tends to be respectable overall, perhaps higher initially, but then falling slightly as the primary import-substitution process runs out of steam. During P2, the growth rate of real GNP per-capita accelerates substantially and is maintained at a much higher level, as the system has developed the capacity to make more effective use of its labor force.

An additional crucial feature is the comparative performance of the agricultural sector during the early transition period. Agricultural labor productivity grew steadily in both economies. This occurred in Korea, despite less favorable production conditions, including climate and soil salinity, as well as the fact that under Japanese colonial rule the Korean agricultural sector received relatively less attention, including less infrastructural investment (irrigation) and less institutional investment (farmers' associations, etc.). Post-colonial agricultural policy diverged somewhat, at least until the mid-1970s, when Korean agricultural productivity spurted.

Statistically, the performance of the two agricultural sectors can be compared not only by examination of the levels and rates of increase of agricultural productivity, but also by examining the composition of traded items (both imports and exports). Korea, with agricultural labor productivity initially lower and at first rising more slowly, exported a higher percentage of nonagricultural goods and imported a higher percentage of food from the beginning. A related major difference is the early appearance of net food imports in Korea, a phenomenon that persisted throughout the early transition. Early on, Korea had to spend foreign exchange for food imports, whereas in Taiwan food exports continued to contribute to foreign-exchange earnings. Another consequence of this contrast is Korea's lower level of agricultural savings and the much larger volume of foreign debt. Korea had to rely much more on foreign savings (S_F in figure 3.1), first in the form of foreign aid, later of private capital, a difference not without consequences in the post-1973 era.

Early Transition Growth in Japan

The transition-growth experience of Japan demonstrates a striking similarity to both Taiwan and Korea during the early period. This is shown morphologically by the evolution of the economic structure in figure 3.1. Figures 3.10–3.13 present for Japan the series given for Korea and Taiwan in figures 3.2–3.9.

The relatively mild import substitution of P1 (1870–1900) was characterized in Japan by an expansion, from a previous "no trade" position, of traditional

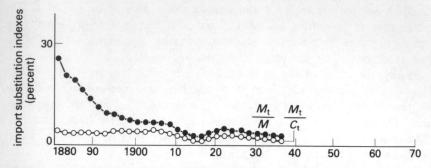

Figure 3.10:   Import substitution indexes: Japan, 1880–1935

Five-year moving averages, except the end years are 3-year averages
For notation, see the notes to figure 3.2

Sources: Data are from LTES, vol. 14: M_t: p. 201 (col. 1); M: p. 201 (col. 5) and pp. 180–81; C_t is M_t plus domestic manufacturing consumption use, taken from PJED: 315–18

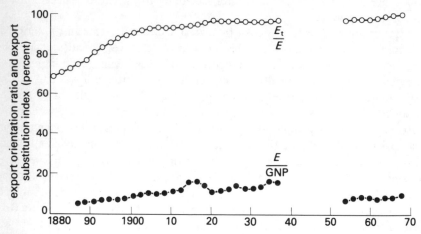

Figure 3.11:   Export orientation ratio and export substitution index: Japan, 1880–1970

Five-year moving averages, except the end years are 3-year averages
For notation, see the notes to figure 3.7

Sources: Data on E_t are from PJED: 315–18; E is $E_t + E_a$, data on E_a are from LTES, vol. 14: 177–79; GNP is GNE from PJED: 256–60

exports (silk cocoons, tea, and other agricultural goods) financing the importation of producer goods and manufactured consumer goods. During the export substitution of P2, changes in the economic structure of Japan again are similar, although not so obvious in outline. The changes are characterized by the rapid relative expansion of nondurable consumer-goods exports (silk, cotton textiles,

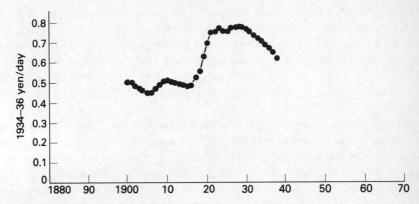

Figure 3.12:   Unskilled real wage rates: Japan, 1897–1937

Five-year moving averages, except end years are 3-year averages
See notes to figure 3.8

Sources: Data are daily textile wages from LTES, vol. 8: 247 (col. 7) deflated by the GNP deflator given in PJED: 387–88

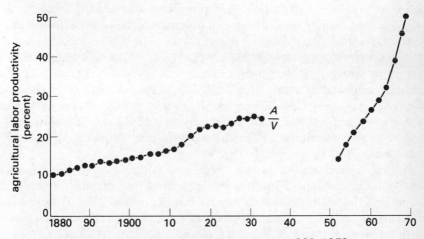

Figure 3.13:   Agricultural labor productivity: Japan, 1880–1970

Five-year moving averages, except end years are 3-year averages

Sources: Data are authors' estimates based on series in LTES, vol. 9 and PJED

and rubber products), and an increase, but much less spectacular, in the system's overall trade orientation.

From the viewpoint of the labor-reallocation process over time, in the sequential order followed (P1, P2) as well as in the ability to graduate from classical dualism, the fundamental underlying similarity among the three countries is confirmed. Yet differences in initial conditions, in the international environment, as well as in behavior over time, are also instructive.

Turning first to the differences in initial conditions, Japan did not have a colonial heritage, but instead emerged from centuries of self-imposed seclusion. This can be depicted by the absence of the triangularism found in Taiwan and Korea during P0. Figure 3.10 shows Japan had a slightly increasing trade ratio E/GNP during P1 as, starting from a negligible base, trade expanded; this is in sharp contrast with the tendency towards greater autarky found in Taiwan and Korea.

Secondly, although the three systems had in common the absence of a modern nondurable consumer-goods industry at the beginning, consumption habits in Korea and Taiwan provided a visible market for these goods. Japan had not acquired a taste for such items. Although Meiji Japan quickly began to import consumer goods, initially they were destined mainly for luxury or upper-class consumption. Thus, before import substitution in Japan could take place, the requisite markets had to be created, and because most of the population retained traditional tastes for some time, this was a gradual process. The task facing the new industrial class in Japan therefore may be said to have been more difficult and taken longer – 30 years, compared with 10 to 15 years in Taiwan and Korea.

Japan's inability, under the unequal treaties imposed by western powers, to engage in full-fledged domestic-market protection was another factor in the relatively mild primary import-substitution pattern of the 19th century. Japan's main trade-related task during this period seems to have been the enhancement of its import capacity through the (delayed) expansion of agriculture-based exports, in order to purchase the producer goods needed for the expansion of a modern manufacturing sector. This is why 1870–1900 is often called a period of traditional export expansion. These special circumstances resulted in a relatively mild primary import-substitution pattern, as well as the later commingling of primary export substitution P2 with early secondary import substitution P3 after the turn of the century.

Postwar Taiwan and Korea have been more intensely technology-impacted than 19th century Japan. This is especially true of the potential for change in the agricultural sector. Although Japan's early (pre-World War I) agricultural productivity performance was quite remarkable for its time, it was based largely on the improvement and diffusion of traditional practices (Hayami and Yamada 1968). In contrast, postwar agricultural technical change has involved biologically-based innovations and the deployment of modern inputs. During P1 and P2 in both Taiwan and Japan, the increase in agricultural productivity implies that the agricultural sector played a more active role than in Korea. This is so, even though the infusion of modern inputs into agriculture came much earlier in transition growth in Taiwan and Korea than in Japan.

In all three systems, technological change was land-saving during P1 and P2, but become more labor-saving near the end of P2 and during P3. As long as the agricultural population per unit of land increased, new technology had to be labor-using, a bias rendered more feasible by the use of modern inputs such as double cropping, and the biological-chemical innovations of the early transition experience. Toward the end of P2, as agricultural population per unit of land decreased, agricultural technological change became increasingly labor-saving, with the mechanization type of innovation taking over. The reversal point, followed by the end of the labor-surplus condition, brought about this pattern of innovation in the agricultural sector.

During their first transition phase (P1), all three systems experienced a pattern of international trade not in keeping with the longer-term comparative advantage expected from their underlying resource endowment. In order to acquire modern producer goods, all three, in fact, initially exported traditional primary products in which they had a longer-term comparative disadvantage. As import substitution progressed and the entrepreneurial maturation process bore fruit, labor-intensive nondurable consumer-goods industries could absorb the surplus labor by producing for world markets. This led not only to the gradual solution of the labor-surplus or underemployment problem in all three systems, but also to a pronounced shift in the center of gravity of the economy and in its comparative advantage position from agriculture to nonagriculture.

Telescoping and Transition Growth

If exhausting the labor surplus, or reaching the commercialization point, is taken as a major objective for our typological set of developing countries – one attempting transition in the mid-19th century, the other two in the mid-20th – consideration of the time required to achieve this is essential to our analysis. The 50 years of transition-growth experience in Japan (P1 and P2) clearly were telescoped by Taiwan and Korea. First of all, it took Japan 30 years (1870–1900) to pass through P1, more than twice as long as Taiwan (1950–62) or Korea (1953–64). This relates in part to the fact that Japan began the transition process with a per-capita income level substantially below those of postwar Korea and Taiwan. The latter two countries were thus in a better initial position and undoubtedly even more impatient to "get there" than Meiji Japan. Second, global GNP growth has been much faster during the second half of the 20th century than it did in the late 19th century.

The phenomenon is also partly accounted for by the fact that consumer demand for factory-produced goods pre-existed in the contemporary cases, whereas it first had to be created in Japan. Finally, the expansion of agricultural productivity in 19th-century Japan was based on traditional technological change, which had much less impact than that based on the use of modern inputs such as new seed and fertilizer combinations. Together, these factors more than overcome Japan's initially lower population density and much lower population growth rate throughout P1 and P2.

During P2 (1900–20), Japan experienced a slower pace of export expansion and labor reallocation than Taiwan (1962–70) or Korea (1964–72), that is, once again the transition process was substantially telescoped. This compression was possible in the contemporary LDCs because the faster growth of agricultural productivity and of industrial technological opportunities more than overcame the disadvantage of faster population growth, which increases the size of the labor surplus that needs to be reallocated in the first place. But it was undoubtedly helped most by the unprecedented expansion of world income and the even more rapid expansion of world trade during the 1960s.

The inflow of foreign resources also played a much larger role in both phases of early transition growth in Korea and Taiwan than in Japan. It is only in the era following World War II that long-term capital movements have taken on the special form of foreign aid, later supplemented and supplanted by both direct and portfolio private capital. Given its more productive agricultural sector and the larger role accorded its domestic agricultural savings, Taiwan required much less foreign capital than Korea throughout the period under observation. Japan financed virtually all its industrial growth from domestic sources, agricultural savings, and reinvested nonagricultural profits. The substantial volume of foreign capital, first aid, and then private investment, available in the second half of the 20th century contributed substantially to the telescoping phenomenon.

Development in the Later Transition Phases (P3 and P4)

Although it has been relatively easy to characterize and define the early phases of growth (P1 and P2) for all three systems, it is both theoretically and empirically harder to accomplish this for later phases. And for contemporary LDCs that have only recently emerged from the P2 labor-surplus condition it is particularly difficult.

Looking first at Japan, where we have the advantage of a longer time perspective, we may divide the later transition into the interwar period P3 (1920–40) and the postwar period P4 (1950 onward). When Japan lost its dualistic structure after 1920, a new era and a new mode of operation of the economy began, which was centered on nonagriculture, and composed of manufacturing and services subsectors. Manufacturing during P3 can be further divided into a large-scale component and a medium and small-scale component, while services divide into trade-related (commerce and transportation), professional (doctors, teachers, engineers, accountants, etc.), and government employees (civil servants and soldiers). The nonagricultural sector that the transitional-growth phenomenon centered on was thus highly differentiated and heterogeneous (Ohkawa and Rosovsky 1965: ch. 2).

The primary factor inputs of the manufacturing sector are capital, used by all sizes of industry, as well as skilled labor, mainly for large-scale industry, and unskilled labor for all scales of manufacturing. Together with the skilled and unskilled workers in the services sector, the human-resources input is also highly heterogeneous and differentiated in quality.

We observe two types of markets. There is a domestic market for consumer goods (manufactured items and services), as demanded by the households that receive national income. A domestic market for producer goods also exists; this is still largely supplied by imports, as demanded by the industrial sector.

The market orientation of the manufacturing sector is thus partly towards the domestic market for nondurable and durable consumer goods, and partly towards the exports of the previous primary export-substitution phase (P2). In addition, the manufacturing sector also produces investment goods, financed by domestic savings. The new phenomenon in P3 is that the manufacturing sector now begins to engage earnestly in construction of producer goods and consumer durables for the domestic market. To the extent similar goods previously imported are now replaced by domestic production, this process is called secondary import substitution, secondary being used to differentiate it from the primary (consumer nondurable goods) import substitution of P1. There is an increased need for capital and skilled labor in secondary import substitution.

Secondary Import and Export Substitution

The extent of secondary import substitution can be assessed best in the domestic-market sense. If we let $g = M_p/D_p$ be the ratio of imported producer goods (M_p) to domestically made producer goods (D_p), the decline of g through time presents a rough indication of secondary import substitution. We could also separate out imported intermediate goods and look at the trend for these and for capital goods separately (see figure 3.10 for Japan).

Early in P3, most intermediate and capital goods are still imported, which indicates that the economy does not yet have the capacity to produce these goods efficiently. While, during P2, secondary import substitution begins to occur, as the higher skills required for the domestic manufacture of such goods are acquired, this becomes a widespread phenomenon only during P3. Some of this early (P2) secondary import substitution is different from that of the post-commercialization era (P3) in at least two ways. First, it cannot offset the basic external orientation of the economy, traced to the continuing overwhelming expansion of labor-intensive nondurable consumer goods. Second, consistent with the overall labor surplus, substitution is likely to be in nonelectrical machinery, which is relatively labor-intensive and not very demanding of labor skills or capital. In short, early secondary import substitution is likely to shift only gradually from the economy's comparative advantage in the form of unskilled labor.

From a long-term perspective, microscopically, the substitution problem is associated with the emergence of ever-newer industries with growing strength to compete. The observable consequence on a product-by-product basis is manifested by the growth of new producer-goods and durable consumer-goods industries, which first compete successfully with foreign producers in the domestic market, and subsequently compete successfully with them in foreign markets.

During P3, secondary import substitution can be verified by the waves of new industries moving into domestic production and then into exporting, aptly described as a flying-geese pattern by Kojima (1958). According to this microscopic view, import substitution, industry by industry, is but a prelude to export expansion, with the extent of any lag between the two very much a function of the strength of the economies of scale and the size of the country. The more pronounced such economies of scale (e.g. in passenger cars) are, relative to the size of the domestic market, the more likely it is that the industry, to be efficient, will have to export relatively soon.

In this respect, because of the relatively smaller size of their domestic markets, P3 in Taiwan and Korea has been, and can be expected to continue to be, somewhat different from that in Japan. The narrower the domestic market, the shorter the wings of the flying geese must be. Thus, in many contemporary LDCs industrial growth during P3 has to be more export-oriented from the beginning.

There is another – macro – dimension attached to secondary import substitution. The trade ratio (exports share of GNP) declines during P1. This internally-oriented growth has been replaced by an external orientation during P2, with the trade ratio moving upward dramatically. During secondary import substitution, in P3, there is at first a renewed tendency towards self-sufficiency, as protection is raised against imported producer goods and resources are diverted to their production at home. For the industrial sector as a whole, this decline in the trade ratio is likely to be more pronounced when, at the end of P2, the country has achieved an unusually high export ratio, allowing a larger domestic market for secondary import substitution. On the other hand, the smaller the country, the sooner secondary export substitution will have to follow, which prevents the ratio from falling too much. For Taiwan and Korea, which reached very high trade ratios at the end of P2, we expect the ratio to decline in the years ahead, certainly as compared to prewar Japan, which merely showed a slowdown in the increasing trend exhibited during P2.

As secondary import and secondary export substitution progresses, we can expect the country to add more and more value domestically to its raw-material imports. This means a higher contribution from capital and domestic skilled labor and a falling contribution from natural resources and unskilled labor in both domestic output and, gradually, in exports.

One way of looking at what ultimately distinguishes P4 from P3 is that the dynamic flying-geese pattern of P3 is characterized by the importation and adaptation of foreign technology in the context of increasingly capital and skilled-labor-intensive output mixes, whereas P4 is associated with the capacity for routinized indigenous technological change. In other words, P3 represents a period of learning to compete with the rest of the world in an ever-more sophisticated range of goods, whereas P4 adds learning to invent domestically and routinely, one of the key characteristics of modern economic growth, as emphasized by Kuznets.

During primary import substitution (P1), governments protect the domestic nondurable consumer-goods market from import competition. Thus, domestic consumers pay an artificially high price due to the relative inefficiency of the import-substituting industries. During P2, import protection is gradually reduced, while exports are often assisted. During the secondary import- and export-substitution phases (P3 and P4), there is renewed pressure for temporary protection; but industries such as petrochemicals and plastics cannot be protected without hurting downstream industries such as textiles. Thus, duties imposed on imported producer goods or raw materials harm the competitive position of textiles in world markets, as foreign consumers are not inclined to pay for the inefficiency of domestic producers. Consequently there is a tendency during P3 and P4 toward the gradual consolidation and then lowering of tariffs.

Labor Reallocation, Wages, and the Distribution of Income

The modern epoch is one of science and technology, manifested in higher skill levels in the labor force. Before 1920 (during P1 and P2), the Japanese economy was endowed with an ample supply of unskilled labor, the very abundance of which characterized early growth. Then, around 1920, Japan reached a major landmark in the transition-growth process. This had two aspects. First, the country lost its dualistic characteristic, as the agricultural sector became an appendage. Second, the labor surplus gave way to a labor force with a scarcity value typical of a mature economy.

The unskilled wage rate during P1 and P2 reflects the labor-surplus condition prevailing in both the agricultural and nonagricultural sectors and, for this reason, is relatively stable. After the turning point, real-wage increases occur neoclassically, that is, in relation to innovation and the rate of capital accumulation relative to population growth. With the exhaustion of surplus labor, wages are determined by labor's scarcity value and tend to increase more rapidly.

Wage Rates

During P3, as human capital accumulates, an initially relatively homogeneous labor force is differentiated into many skill varieties. Termination of the surplus-labor condition means that the conversion of unskilled to skilled labor through investment in human resources becomes the basic issue. Skilled labor takes time to develop, as it involves experience as well as formal training and education.

It is thus by no means an accident that in the late 1970s Taiwan and Korea became preoccupied with the notion that a new growth phase was being reached and that a much more serious effort would have to be directed at developing a skilled labor force. One key aspect of this technological revolution is the increasing dichotomy between skilled labor (L_k) and unskilled labor (L_u) in manufacturing. A time profile of L_k, L_u, and their ratio $z = L_k/(L_u + L_k)$ shows the triplet (L_k, L_u, and z) consistently increasing through time, indicating that skilled workers are an increasing percentage of the total manufacturing labor force.

Let w_k and w_u be the wage rates for the two types of labor, with $r = w_k/w_u$ ($r > 1$). The wage ratio r passes through three periods, one of increasing relative skill shortage, one of increasing relative skill abundance, and one of a near-constant relative supply of skills. Figure 3.14 shows this as something of an inverse U-shaped pattern for the first two periods, most pronounced in Taiwan's case.

The first period, when r increases, is related to changing endowment and income trends; these are likely to lead, first, to a demand for skilled labor not matched by supply, because of lagging investment in human resources. The opposite is true during the next period, when increasing skill abundance accounts for a falling r. Finally, we can expect to drift toward a constant magnitude, reflecting a sustainable education and experience premium for skilled labor. Thus, the final skill premium is likely to be lower than the initial one, because investment in human resources ultimately does catch up with demand.

Capital-Labor Ratios

As long as the labor-surplus condition prevails, the absorption of labor by the industrial sector tends towards a constant capital-labor ratio. If, encouraged by relatively stable wage rates, technological innovation tends to be labor-using (or at least not very labor-saving), we may even expect to see a capital-shallowing phenomenon, that is, a decrease in the capital-labor ratio, as a result of faster labor absorption.

Looking at the real wage for cotton textile workers and the capital-labor ratio in the cotton textile industry of Japan, we do, in fact, encounter capital shallowing before 1905, modest capital deepending thereafter, and substantial capital deepening after the 1920 commercialization point. Reliable capital-labor ratios cannot be computed for Taiwan and Korea, but wages initially fell (figures 3.8, 3.9, and 3.12). If we plot the capital-labor ratios for the entire Japanese industrial sector, thereby reflecting changes in the industrial-output mix as well as in technology, we note a mild deepening trend before, and a severe deepening trend after the end of the labor-surplus condition was reached. In combination with a possibly faster growth of the capital stock, this capital-deepening is observable in most industrially mature economies.

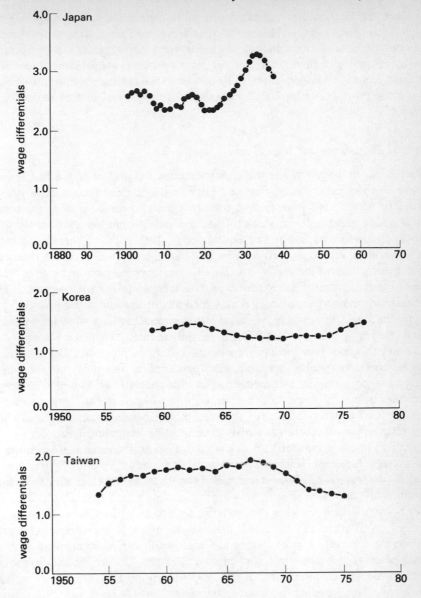

Figure 3.14: Wage differentials, skilled versus unskilled: Japan (1897–1937), Korea (1957–78), and Taiwan (1954–75)

Five-year moving averages, except end years are 3-year averages
Ratio of the average monthly earnings (for Japan, daily earnings) of machinery workers to those of textile workers (both sexes)

Sources: Japanese data are from LTES, vol. 8: 247–48; for Korea, the Bank of Korea's *Economic Statistics Yearbook* (1980 edn: 258–61) and equivalent tables in other years; for Taiwan, the *Statistical Abstract of the Republic of China* (1978 edn: 280–81)

Once the labor-surplus condition terminates, the industrial real wage begins to increase more rapidly. The agricultural sector no longer is the source of an unlimited supply of labor. Induced by the increase in the real wage and expectations of further such increases, technology change shifts in a labor-saving direction. Japan's real-wage behavior after 1920 is thus explained mainly in terms of the rate of growth of the capital stock and the strength and bias of technology change.

Income Distribution and Wage Share

What does the wage share in the nonagricultural sector (that is, the functional distribution of income) imply about equity or the size distribution of income? Property income and wage income represent the two components of the total value added generated in a sector. These are paid to families that supply the labor services or own the land or capital goods. Total family income is the sum of wage income plus property income. It is empirically well accepted that the pattern of property income is distributed more unequally across families than that of wage income. This is why a relative increase in the labor share can be assumed, *ceteris paribus*, to make family income distribution more equal.

In the dualistic economy, we must differentiate between what happens to rural (mainly agricultural) and to urban (mainly industrial) families. Not only do we need to know how income from work and from property (both land and capital) are distributed across rural and urban families over time, but also what shifts are occurring as a consequence of the gradual reallocation of family activities from agricultural to nonagricultural pursuits. (See Fei, Ranis, and Kuo (1979) for a fuller discussion of the relationship between the functional and size distributions of income, as well as the impact of sectoral reallocation.)

Labor's share in industrial activity is equivalent to the ratio of the real wage to average industrial labor productivity. When, during the early transition period, the wage is relatively stable, labor's share increases whenever its average productivity decreases. This follows from the simple fact that labor's share is $wB/Y = w/p$, where p is labor productivity, defined as Y (the value of its output) divided by B (the size of the industrial labor force). If industrial capital per worker is constant, a given percentage increase in capital would lead to the same percentage increase in labor employed, leaving the productivity of labor unchanged. On the other hand, if the labor-absorption process leads to capital shallowing, labor productivity tends to decrease.

Technological change biased in a labor-using direction (that is, a change contributing to a faster rate of labor absorption) leads to a more equitable pattern of family income distribution because it tends to increase labor's share. In contrast, after the turning point, the behavior of labor's share reflects two types of forces that operate in opposite directions. On the one hand, the capital-deepening process tends to increase labor's share (see Fei and Ranis 1964: ch. 3). On the other hand, a labor-saving technology bias tends to depress labor's share.

In the mature economy, some observers have noted an empirical tendency for labor's share to remain relatively stable over the long run. However, in the short run, as the economy moves from P2 to P3, labor's share is likely to increase because of continued rapid capital accumulation, coupled with a likely slow-down in population growth, plus the fact that innovations are unlikely to be very labor-saving immediately. Thus, labor's share will probably increase for a time after the commercialization point, bringing about a more equitable pattern in family income distribution.

The data for Taiwan permit a relatively full analysis of the level and changes in income distribution over time. As a consequence of the initial stability and later increase in the functional share of labor, and of the reallocation of family income from a less-equally-distributed agricultural to a more-equally-distributed (but still largely rural) nonagricultural income, we observe a more equal pattern of family income distribution even before the commercialization point (around 1968).

The Gini coefficient was about 0.4 in 1960, dropped to just over 0.3 between 1964 and 1968, and then to under 0.3 in the early 1970s. Although Korean data are not as reliable as those of Taiwan, the level of the Gini coefficient was 0.37 in 1964, 0.35 in 1970, and 0.41 in 1975 (Choo 1977). This relatively stable and favorable level during P2 is what we expect from the level and trend in labor's functional share.

It is more difficult to determine the pattern of the size distribution of income for Japan prior to World War II. Even the behavior of labor's relative share is by no means clearly established (see Otsuki and Takamatsu 1982; Minami and Ono 1978). The Minami–Ono data suggest that the wage share fell during P2 primarily because output-mix changes overcame labor-using technology change, which was induced by the low level and stability of the real wage. After 1920, the labor share continued to rise because of capital deepening in the industrial sector, despite the continued moderate tendency for innovations to be labor-saving. Finally, labor's share declined a bit because the capital-using nature of innovations induced by the expectation of continued increases in the real wage apparently overwhelmed the capital-deepening effect.

The present state of empirical and conceptual understanding of the prewar situation does not permit more than propositional statements to be made. The impressive once-and-for-all upward shift of the wage share in Japan after World War II, which is not in dispute, is clearly related to such postwar reforms as a strong boost for unions and an increase in minimum wages. Labor's relative share is currently apparently fairly constant, as has been observed in other industrially mature economies.

Surplus Labor and Dualism

A final word on surplus labor in the context of the different kinds of dualism within the nonagricultural sector is warranted. During P1 and P2, as the economy retained its agricultural-industrial dualism, surplus labor in agriculture may be viewed as something of a reserve army, with the movement of labor out of agriculture into industry shrinking that pool, while population growth is augmenting it. The existence of surplus labor, while by no means guaranteeing a constant unskilled real wage, thus contributed to holding down its rate of increase until the end of P2.

After 1920, the disappearance of agricultural-industrial dualism in Japan was accompanied by the emergence of an intra-industrial dualism, as another reserve army made its appearance. This reserve is unskilled labor in services and in medium and small-scale industries. The shift of labor out of this pool during P3 and P4 plays something of the same role as the earlier shift from agriculture. In industry and services, as previously in agriculture, roughly the same level of output can be produced by a smaller labor force given some organizational reforms and a little additional investment. The appearance of trading firms, supermarkets, mail-order houses, department stores, etc., to replace small retail-trade establishments are examples of the kind of organizational reform which releases labor with very little additional capital, especially when inventory changes are taken into account.

Related to this is the controversy in the literature concerning the dating of the commercialization point in Japanese development. Minami, for example, found unskilled industrial real wages rising after 1920 but falling again in the 1930s, exhibiting a sustained rise only in the 1960s (Minami 1973). Our interpretation is that the decline in the 1930s was caused by the impact of the Great Depression, which had a similar effect in other mature economies. Moreover, the pool of surplus labor of the second type, which undoubtedly existed in Japan during P3 and even P4, was swollen by the wartime destruction of capital and the postwar return of soldiers to the labor force. We believe the first turning point (in 1920) has the distinguishing characteristic that, before then, the real wage was determined independently of the rapidity of labor absorption by nonagriculture. We do not believe that Minami's 1960s turning point has this characteristic. To argue that the labor-surplus condition really terminated in 1965 may be viewed as a complementary, rather than competitive, explanation of the Japanese historical case.

Conclusions

In this chapter we have examined the common and the disparate elements of the transition-growth experience of three typologically related economies. The effort has been based on the notion that economic history represents a still much underutilized laboratory for analyzing contemporary development issues. The basic ideas we have built on include the identification of transition phases during which the *modus operandi* of the system substantially changes; the notion of sectoring the economy by heterogeneous organizational behavior; and the retention of the analytical view of an economy's performance as an integral whole.

We hope our approach sheds some light on other labor-surplus economies currently engaged in the transition-growth effort, and that the general methodology, suitably adjusted, may also prove useful for the analysis of similar phenomena in typologically different situations. We do not believe there is one inevitable and natural sequence for any particular type of developing country which must somehow be replicated – just as we do not believe in the predictive content of average cross-sectional patterns of LDC behavior (e.g. the "patterns" approach of Chenery and his associates – see, for example, Chenery and Syrquin 1975). Both approaches represent, at best, only the "beginning of wisdom."

Thus, if we observe labor-surplus countries, say in Latin America, attempting to skip the labor-intensive export-substitution phase (P2) and move directly from P1 into P3, we would examine the causes, in terms of differences in colonial antecedents, initial endowments, or a set of less rather than more accommodating public policies. If Brazil appears to behave as something of a deviant Latin American type and Korea as something of a deviant East Asian type, their similarities across basic typologies may substantially enhance our understanding. In short, although we do not believe in the existence of an ideal or standard growth path, it is our conviction that the analysis of differences and similarities within families as well as between them constitutes an amalgam of theory and history potentially helpful in the ever-elusive pursuit of a more general understanding of transition growth.

References

Chenery, Hollis, and Moises Syrquin (1975), *Patterns of Development, 1950–1970*, Oxford: Oxford University Press, for the World Bank.

Choo, Hak Chung (1977), "Probable Size Distribution of Income in Korea," paper prepared for the *Income Distribution by Sector and Over Time in East and Southeast Asian Countries* project, Tokyo: JERC (Nihon Keizai Kenkyu Center).

Clark, Colin (1967), *Population Growth and Land Use*, New York: St Martin's Press.

Fei, John C. H., and Gustav Ranis (1964), *Development of the Labor Surplus Economy*, Homewood, IL: Richard D. Irwin.

Fei, John C. H., Gustav Ranis, and Shirley W. Y. Kuo (1979), *Growth with Equity: The Taiwan Case*, Oxford University Press.

Hayami, Yujiro, and Saburo Yamada (1968), "Technological Progress in Agriculture," in Lawrence Klein and Kazushi Ohkawa, eds, *Economic Growth: The Japanese Experience Since the Meiji Era*, Homewood, IL: Richard D. Irwin.

Kojima, Kiyoshi (1958), *Nihon boeki to keizai hatten*, Tokyo: Kunimoto Shoba.

Kuznets, Simon (1966), *Modern Economic Growth: Rate, Structure and Spread*, New Haven, CT: Yale University Press.

LTES (*Estimates of the Long-Term Economic Statistics of Japan*), series edited by Kazushi Ohkawa, Miyohei Shinohara, and Mataji Umemura, Tokyo: Toyo Keizai Shimposha.

   vol. 8, *Prices* (1967), Kazushi Ohkawa, Osama Noda, Nobukiyo Takamatsu, Saburo Yamada, Minoru Kumazaki, Yuichi Shionoya, and Ryoshin Minami.

   vol. 9, *Agriculture and Forestry* (1966), Mataji Umemura, Saburo Yamada, Yujiro Hayami, Nobukiyo Takamatsu, and Minoru Kumizaki.

   vol. 14, *Foreign Trade* (1979), Ippei Yamazawa, and Yuzo Yamamoto.

Minami, Ryoshin (1973), *The Turning Point in Economic Development*, Tokyo: Kinokuniya.

Minami, Ryoshin, and Akira Ono (1978), "Relative Income Share of Labor: Long-run Trend and Fluctuations in Prewar Japan and their Implications," in *Papers and Proceedings of the Conference on Japan's Historical Development Experience and the Contemporary Developing Countries*, Tokyo: International Development Center of Japan.

Ohkawa, Kazushi (1972), *Differential Structure and Agriculture: Essays on Dualistic Growth*, Tokyo: Kinokuniya.

Ohkawa, Kazyshi, and Ryoshin Minami, eds (1975), *Kindai Nihon no keizai seicho*, Tokyo: Toyo Keizai Shimposha.

Ohkawa, Kazushi and Gustav Ranis (1978), "On Phasing: A Preliminary View," in *Papers and Proceedings of the Conference on Japan's Historical Development Experience and the Contemporary Developing Countries*, Tokyo: International Development Center of Japan.

Ohkawa, Kazushi, and Henry Rosovsky (1965), "A Century of Japanese Economic Growth," in William L. Lockwood, ed., *The State and Economic Enterprise in Japan*, Princeton, NJ: Princeton University Press.

Otsuki, Toshiyuki, and Nobukiyo Takamatsu (1982), "On the Measurement and Trend of Income Inequality in Prewar Japan," *Papers and Proceedings of the Conference on Japan's Historical Development Experience and the Contemporary Developing Countries, phase II*, Tokyo: International Development Center of Japan.

PJED (*Patterns of Japanese Economic Development*), Kazushi Ohkawa and Miyohei Shinohara, with Larry Meissner, eds (1979), New Haven, CT: Yale University Press.

Ranis, Gustav, and John C. H. Fei (1982), "Lewis and the Classicists," in M. Gersovitz et al., eds, *The Theory and Experience of Economic Development: Essays in Honor of Sir W. Arthur Lewis*, Hemel Hempstead: George Allen and Unwin.

PART II Agricultural Development

4 Agricultural Growth against a Land-Resource Constraint: Japan, Taiwan, Korea, and the Philippines

MASAO KIKUCHI and YUJIRO HAYAMI

The topic of this chapter is the process that mobilized public efforts to improve land infrastructure in response to population pressure on limited land resources in four monsoon Asian countries. For Japan, Taiwan, Korea, and the Philippines, improvements in irrigation systems represent a key to the development and diffusion of land-saving technology, which is characterized by seed improvements and increased use of fertilizers. Greater control of water not only facilitated the more efficient response of improved rice varieties to fertilizer, but also encouraged fertilizing by reducing the risk of crop failure.

According to Ricardo and other classical economists, population pressure on land eventually results in agricultural and economic stagnation, bringing high food prices, real wages rates barely sufficient for subsistence, and a high share of rent in total income. The classical view has been challenged by several researchers. Schultz shows the share of land in the value of agricultural output did not rise, but actually declined in the process of economic development (1953: 124-45). Clark and Haswell (1964) and Boserup (1965) suggest that population pressure may induce changes in both agricultural technology and agrarian structure so as to increase the intensity of land utilization. Further, Hayami and Ruttan (1971) have provided a historical perspective showing countries like Japan, unfavorably endowed with land resources, could achieve rates of growth in agricultural output as high as countries favorably endowed, such as the United States, by developing technology appropriate to their resources. North and Thomas (1973) have likewise developed a European perspective, showing population pressure on land was the basic factor inducing institutional and technological changes.

The history of Japan since the Meiji Restoration (1868) represents a prototype for the removal of a land-resource constraint, initially conditioned by high population density, through the development of land-saving technology (Okhawa and Rosovsky 1960; Johnston 1966; Hayami et al. 1975). The experience of

An earlier version of this paper was published in the *Journal of Economic History* (1978 December), 38: 839-64.

Taiwan and Korea during the interwar period provides relevant comparisons to developing countries in Asia today, as their agricultural growth, based on the transfer of Japanese technology, paralleled rapid population growth. Finally, the Philippines of the 1950s and 1960s represents more recent experience in the tropical world.

First, we compare the broad historical patterns of agricultural growth in the four countries for periods that include the initial spurts in agricultural productivity, and pose the hypothesis that population pressure, while causing deterioration in the land-labor ratio, induced increases in land productivity. Then we outline the mechanism of land productivity increase – an improved infrastructure (primarily irrigation) and the development of highly fertilizer-responsive rice varieties (seed-fertilizer technology). We next demonstrate how such increases in land productivity, called internal land augmentation, have the same effect on output as an expansion of cultivated land area, called external augmentation. Cost curves are derived for internal and external land augmentation, and seed-fertilizer technology is shown to have had the effect of counteracting the rising cost of irrigation as construction moved from easier to more difficult sites. The momentum of internal augmentation has been maintained through the complementarity of better technology and land-infrastructure improvements.

Patterns in Agricultural Growth

The periods chosen as meaningful for comparison are 1880–1938 for Japan, 1913–37 for Taiwan, 1920–39 for Korea, and 1950–69 for the Philippines. These periods encompass the initial spurts in agricultural productivity. For Japan, Taiwan, and Korea, the early years roughly correspond to the completion of cadastral surveys which laid a foundation for modern agricultural development.

Initial Conditions

Table 4.1 gives estimates of agricultural output per male worker and per hectare of agricultural land. Labor productivity in Japan, Taiwan, and Korea at their initial stages of agricultural development was roughly similar to that in the Philippines in recent decades. Large differences do appear, however, in the initial land productivity, which was substantially lower in the Philippines. Population pressure on land in Taiwan was probably much lower in the 19th century, with a land–man ratio on a level comparable with the Philippines in the 1950s and 1960s (see Lee 1971).

Land area in the Philippines in the 1950s and 1960s was about 2 hectares per male worker; it was less than 1 hectare in Japan in the 1880s and in Taiwan in the 1910s, and barely above 1 hectare in Korea in the 1920s. In Japan and Taiwan, these unfavorable ratios were offset by higher levels of land productivity, resulting in comparable levels of labor productivity.

Table 4.1: Labor and land productivities, and land–man ratios: Japan, Taiwan, Korea, and the Philippines (selected years)[a]

Country	Year	Agricultural output per male worker (Y/L) (wheat units)[b]	Agricultural output per hectare of cultivated land area (Y/A) (wheat units)[b]	Cultivated land area per male worker (A/L) (hectares)
Japan	1880	2.5	2.9	0.86
	1900	3.4	3.6	0.93
Taiwan	1913	2.8	3.6	0.78
Korea	1920	3.0	2.9	1.03
Philippines	1950	3.3	1.8	1.83
Japan	1938	7.4	5.5	1.34
Taiwan	1937	5.7	6.8	0.84
Korea	1939	3.8	3.9	0.96
Philippines	1969	4.1	2.1	1.95

[a] 5-year averages centering on the years shown
[b] One wheat unit is equivalent to one ton of wheat. All agricultural commodities are converted into wheat equivalents by relative prices

Sources: Inter-country cross-section estimates of land and labor productivities in agriculture for 1960 by Hayami and Ruttan (1971: 70) are extrapolated by land and labor-productivity indexes for respective countries. The indexes are from: Ban 1979; Crisostomo and Barker 1979; Lee and Chen 1979; Yamada and Hayami 1979

The differences in land productivity can be explained primarily by differences in land infrastructure. Japan inherited from its premodern period a well-developed irrigation system. Already in 1880, practically all the paddy area, about 60 percent of cultivated land, was irrigated. The proportion of irrigated to total paddy area was almost 60 percent in Taiwan in the 1910s, and less than 50 percent in Korea as late as the mid-1920s. In the Philippines, although strictly comparable data are not available, irrigation appears to have been much less developed in the 1950s than in Taiwan in the 1910s or Korea in the 1920s.

Growth Paths

On the eve of World War II, labor productivity in agriculture in Japan and Taiwan was substantially higher than in Korea, and even higher than in the Philippines in the late 1960s. A common feature of agricultural growth in Japan, Taiwan,

Table 4.2: Agricultural output growth rates and relative contributions: Japan, Taiwan, Korea and the Philippines

| | Total output $G(Y)$ (1) | Labor $G(L)$ (2) | Land $G(A)$ (3) | Labor productivity $G(Y/L)$ (4) | Land productivity $G(Y/A)$ (5) | Contribution of land-productivity growth | |
						to total output growth $(6) = (5)/(1)$	to labour-productivity growth $(7) = (5)/(4)$
Japan[a]							
1880–1900	1.65	0.09	0.47	1.56	1.18	71	76
1900–1920	1.99	−0.63	0.73	2.62	1.26	63	48
1920–1938	1.03	−0.23	0.13	1.26	0.90	87	71
Taiwan[a]							
1913–1920	2.24	−0.48	1.05	2.72	1.19	53	44
1920–1930	4.29	0.95	0.83	3.34	3.41	79	102
1930–1937	3.84	1.48	0.72	2.36	3.12	81	132
Korea[a]							
1920–1930	0.46	0.60	0.07	−0.14	0.39	85	279
1930–1939	2.92	0.33	0.13	2.59	2.79	96	108
Philippines[a]							
1950–1960	4.08	2.81	3.38	1.27	0.70	17	55
1960–1969	3.45	1.84	1.63	1.61	1.82	53	113

[a] Annual compound growth rates between 5-year average centering on the year shown

Sources: Ban 1979; Crisostomo and Barker 1979; Lee and Chen 1979; Yamada and Hayami 1979

and Korea was that the increase in land productivity acted as a major contributor to the growth of both total output and labor productivity. When defined in terms of the axes of land and labor productivities, however, the growth paths diverged over time (table 4.2 and figure 4.1).

Japan's growth was accompanied by a gradual movement in the land–man ratio, and labor productivity increased more than land productivity. Taiwan's growth was achieved despite a slightly deteriorating land–man ratio. Initially, the potential for expanding the cultivated area in Taiwan was relatively large, but it was soon exhausted. From the 1910s to the 1920s the land–labor ratio changed from a positive to a negative contributor to labor-productivity growth. As for Korea, growth in labor productivity was slower than in Taiwan, because the land–labor ratio continued to decline throughout the interwar period.

With all three countries having little land for expansion, the contrasting growth paths resulted primarily from differences in population growth and labor absorption outside agriculture. In Japan, the population growth rate rose from about 1 percent annually in the late 1880s to around 1.5 percent in the 1930s.

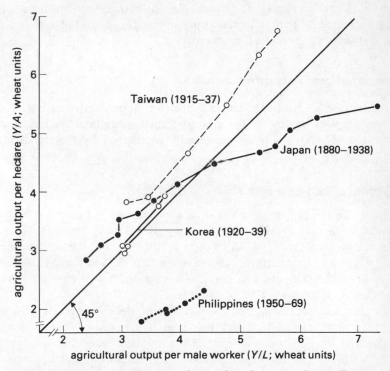

Figure 4.1: Historical growth paths of agricultural output: Japan, Taiwan, Korea, and the Philippines

Five-year averages

In Taiwan, it rose from about 1 percent in the 1910s to 2.5 percent in the 1930s; and in Korea, from about 1 percent in the 1920s to 2 percent in the 1930s. Industrialization in Japan was sufficient to provide nonfarm employment, so the agricultural labor force did not increase. In Taiwan and Korea, on the other hand, industrial development lagged, partly due to Japanese colonial rule, and the pressure of population on the land continued to increase.

The growth pattern of Philippine agriculture in the 1950s and 1960s was similar to that of Taiwan during the interwar period. During the 1950s, rapid growth in agricultural output was brought about primarily by opening new land. By the end of the decade, the supply of unused land was exhausted by the extremely high rate of population growth (exceeding 3 percent per year). The land–labor ratio then began to deteriorate. However, high rates of growth in output and labor productivity were maintained in the 1960s by increasing the yield per hectare.

The observed trends in agricultural productivity in the four countries suggest the following hypothesis: population pressure, while causing a deterioration in the land–labor ratio, induced the increase in land productivity. In Japan, the land-productivity increase was accompanied by an improvement in the land-labor ratio. In this case, it seems probable that even before the beginning of modern economic growth, population pressure had accumulated to the point of igniting efforts to increase land productivity.

Mechanism of Land Productivity Increases

The underlying mechanism inducing increased land productivity is taken up in this section. Rice was by far the most important agricultural product, and the trends in land productivity were primarily determined by the trends in rice yield.

The Process of Increasing Rice Yield

Trends in rice yield in the four countries are compared in figure 4.2. From the beginning of modern development, the rice yield was much higher in Japan than in Taiwan or Korea, reflecting differences in irrigation. But the gap was reduced as yields began to rise sharply in Taiwan in the 1920s and in Korea in the 1930s. The spurt in the Philippines in the 1960s is similar, but its absolute level was lower because of the lower level of irrigation.

The processes accounting for the increases in yield are compared in figure 4.3. They illustrate the technical and institutional changes prompted by the imbalance or disequilibrium inherent in the process of economic development. The 1890-1920 spurt in Japan paralleled the spread of improved seed and fertilizer technology. At this time there was no appreciable improvement in infrastructure. However, the proportion of improved land began to rise during the 1910s, as improved rice varieties became dominant.

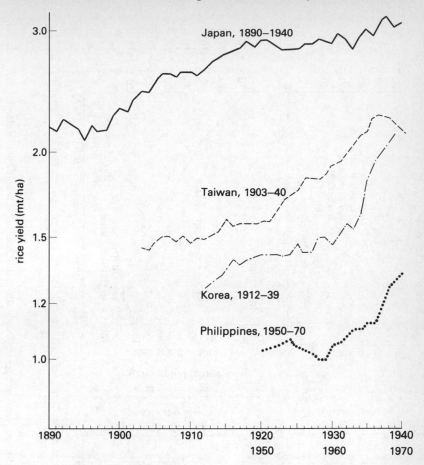

Figure 4.2:   Rice yield per hectare planted: Japan, Taiwan, Korea, and the Philippines

Five-year moving averages; semi-log scale; million tons per hectare in brown rice equivalents

Source: Korean Government-General 1939 and the sources listed in table 4.1

The lag of infrastructure investment behind seed-fertilizer technology can be attributed to feudal heritage. By the beginning of the modern era, the irrigation and drainage systems in areas such as Kinki (the region centered on Kyoto and Osaka) and Northern Kyushu had been developed sufficiently to introduce fertilizer-responsive high-yielding rices. Those varieties were selected mostly by veteran farmers (*rono*), and were further tested and improved by government experimental stations. As the diffusion of the technology approached the limit

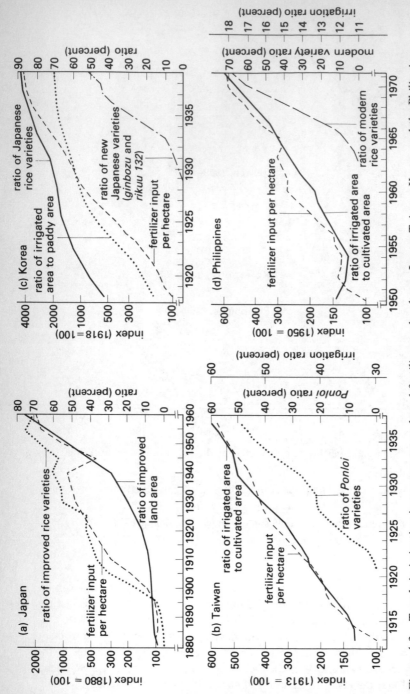

Figure 4.3: Trends in irrigation improvement and seed-fertilizer technology: Japan, Taiwan, Korea, and the Philippines

Five-year moving averages

Fertilizer is expressed in equivalents of N + P₂O₅ + K₂O

Improved land means land covered by the land-improvement projects, irrigation, drainage, and land consolidation

Source: Hayami et al. 1975: 175; Hayami et al. 1976; Kikuchi 1976

of the area with adequate water-control facilities, infrastructure became the major constraint.

When this happened, anxiety over the food supply induced public investment and institutional innovation. As early as 1899, public concern about national security, arising from Japan's position as a net importer of rice after the Sino-Japanese War (1894–95), resulted in the enactment of the Arable Land Replotment Law (revised in 1905 and 1909). The law required compulsory participation by farmers and landlords in a land-improvement project if two-thirds of the landlords, together owning two-thirds of the land involved, agreed. This was an institutional innovation similar to the Enclosure Acts in England.

The rice riots caused by high prices during World War I led to another innovation, the Rules of Subsidization of Irrigation and Drainage Projects. These authorized the central government to give a 50 percent subsidy to large irrigation and drainage projects undertaken by prefectural governments. (For further details about infrastructure development, see Nogyo Hattatsushi Chosakai (1954: 117–320); Hayami et al. (1975: 270–92).)

The sequences in Taiwan and the Philippines stand in sharp contrast to those of Japan. In Taiwan, the development of land infrastructure preceded by almost a decade the introduction of Ponlai rice, which had been adapted to Taiwan's environment from Japanese varieties. The irrigation investment in the late 1910s was part of a major infrastructure program funded by the colonial government. The improvements enabled planting of Japanese varieties of rice in the 1920s, which was in accord with Japan's policy of fostering Taiwan as its granary. In effect, the infrastructural development created the conditions for increasing land productivity in compensation for the decline in the land–labor ratio. (See Kawano 1941; Hayami and Ruttan 1971: 205–7.)

As for Korea, the lead-lag relation between irrigation and seed-fertilizer technology is not so clear. An increase in the percentage of paddy fields irrigated paralleled an increase in the area planted with Japanese varieties. During the 1920s, despite rapid increases in both of these, yield did not rise very rapidly. This apparent contradiction can be explained by the direct transfer of rice varieties from Japan to Korea. When Japanese colonial policy attempted to increase the export of rice from Korea to Japan, because of similar climatic conditions, Japanese varieties initially were introduced without much adaptive research, in contrast to what had been done in Taiwan. Moreover, because of Korea's precarious water supply and in the absence of adequate irrigation facilities, the first varieties introduced were not highly fertilizer-responsive.

The Rice Production Development Program for Korea, launched in 1920 in response to the rice riots in Japan, allocated most of its funds to the construction of irrigation systems. As the infrastructure was improved, the less-responsive rices were replaced by those with higher fertilizer responsiveness, such as *ginbozu* and *rikuu 132*, either imported from Japan or developed in experimental stations in Korea. As a result, the rice yield in Korea rose sharply in the 1930s. (See Kobayakawa 1959; Hayami and Ruttan 1971: 207–10.)

The sequences of irrigation and technology development in the Philippines were similar to those in Taiwan. The dramatic development and diffusion of semi-dwarf varieties since the late 1960s, heralded as the Green Revolution, were preceded by more than a decade by a spurt of investment in irrigation.

The experiences of Taiwan, Korea, and the Philippines demonstrate the role of irrigation as a precondition for the introduction of seed-fertilizer technology. Large public investment in land infrastructure was required to create the conditions for sustained increases in land productivity.

Land-Supply Constraint and Land-Infrastructure Development

Improvement in land infrastructure, especially irrigation, is a precondition for successful adoption of the seed-fertilizer technology that makes sustained increases in land productivity possible. If the constraint of land resources in the face of mounting population pressure was the factor inducing an increase in land productivity, we should find a close association between the limited supply of land and the development of land infrastructure. Such an association is, in fact, clear for Japan and the Philippines (figure 4.4).

Although Japan was densely populated at the beginning of modern economic growth, there remained some room for expansion of the cultivated area, mainly in Hokkaido and Tohoku (northern Japan). But by the 1910s, even this had been exhausted. In dramatic fashion, acceleration in land-infrastructure improvement coincided with the halt in the expansion of cultivated area and the land-labor ratio. This implies acceleration in infrastructure improvement following the Arable Land Replotment Law embodied the response of both the private and public sectors to the increasing scarcity of land.

In the Philippines, good-quality cultivated land expanded more rapidly than the agricultural labor force on Mindanao, Visayas, and Luzon until the late 1950s. But since then, the growth rate of the cultivated area has decelerated, and the land–labor ratio has declined. In contrast, irrigation development has accelerated. The process and the underlying mechanism appear the same as in Japan.

Hypothesis

The increase in land productivity from improving infrastructure and developing seed-fertilizer technology has the same effect on output as expansion of cultivated area. The former may be called internal augmentation, the latter, external augmentation. Building on our earlier work (see Hayami et al. 1976), the shifts in the momentum of output growth from external to internal augmentation, as observed in the histories of Japan, Taiwan, Korea, and the Philippines, may be conceptualized as follows.

As population pressure pushes the cultivation frontier onto inferior land, the marginal cost of increasing production through expansion of the cultivated area

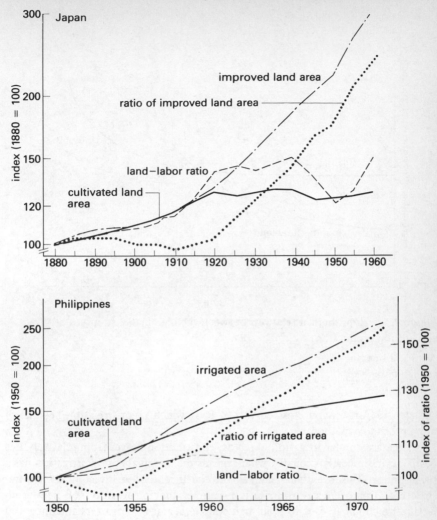

Figure 4.4: Trends in irrigation improvement, cultivated land area, and land-labor ratio in Japan and the Philippines

Sources: Hayami et al. 1975; 175; Hayami et al. 1976; Kikuchi 1976

rises relative to the marginal cost of intensification. Eventually, internal augmentation becomes less costly. This is illustrated in figure 4.5.

The marginal cost of increasing output by opening new land is represented by curve A, and by constructing irrigation facilities, by curve I. With abundant land, curve A is horizontal and below curve I, indicating a relative advantage for external over internal augmentation. As the cultivation frontier moves to inferior

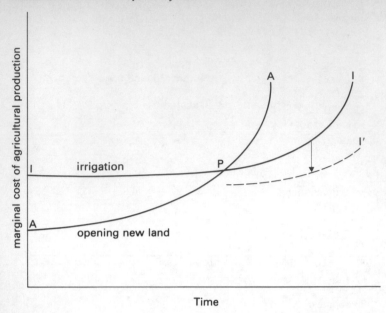

Figure 4.5: Hypothetical relations between the marginal cost curves of agricultural production

A = land opening
I = irrigation

land, curve A rises, and cross curve I at P, at which point irrigation becomes a more profitable method.

As the area under irrigation expands, construction moves from relatively less costly to more costly projects, which means the marginal cost of irrigation has a rising trend. This eventually chokes off the incentive to invest in land infrastructure. Improvement in irrigation permits the introduction of new seed-fertilizer technology. Due to their high complementarity, fertilizers and improved seeds have the effect of reducing the cost of irrigation required to produce a unit of additional income, as illustrated by the shift of the irrigation cost curve downward, from I to I′. This downward shift increases the incentive to invest in infrastructure rather than to expand cultivated area. These relationships emerge in the transition of momentum from expanding cultivated area to increasing land productivity.

It may appear anomalous to assume the marginal cost of production using irrigation constructing diverges downwards from the marginal cost of opening land, because the optimum resource allocation is supposed to establish an equality in the marginal rates of returns among investment alternatives. This may be explained by the time-lag involved in adjusting to the economic opportunity represented by the crossover point. Typically, private individuals settle new areas, either as legal homesteaders or as illegal squatters; they open the new land using their own labor and capital. In contrast, irrigation systems, especially the gravity type usual in monsoon Asia, are characterized by indivisibility and externality, requiring group action by farmers or public investment by the government. Group action requires leadership and discipline. These cannot be developed immediately as the need arises; rather, their development may require several generations. Thus, the marginal cost of building irrigation systems tends to diverge downwards because of underinvestment in irrigation, which is in turn due to slow development in rural organization.

It is possible for the government to fill this gap, but it can hardly be expected that government investment in irrigation can quickly re-establish equality in the marginal rates of returns of the two alternatives. Moreover, a government response of investing in infrastructure depends on its ability to perceive the social need, as well as on its revenue. The dynastic cycle, in China in particular, can be cast in these terms. There was major new construction and rehabilitation of existing irrigation systems during the early decades of a new dynasty. But, as the bureaucracy lost its vitality, the systems were allowed to deteriorate, and agricultural production declined. Ultimately, there were peasant riots which, often together with foreign invasion, resulted in the fall of the dynasty.

In terms of our hypothesis, the modern agricultural histories of Japan, Taiwan, Korea, and the Philippines may be interpreted as follows. Before modern economic growth began, Japan was already located to the right of point P. Meiji Japan was thus ready to move immediately from curve I to curve I' by developing the seed-fertilizer technology. Gradual population growth in the Tokugawa period caused the economy to pass point P, but because the shift was very gradual, there had been sufficient time for village communities to develop an organization capacity to mobilize communal labor to build and maintain local irrigation facilities. Feudal lords had also taken the responsibility of controlling rivers and major irrigation systems. The decentralized power structure of the feudal system might have contributed to this response to local needs.

It appears that Korea was also located to the right of P before modern agricultural growth began. However, partly due to the incapacity of the Yi dynasty at the end of the 19th century, and partly due to the highly centralized, despotic structure of the government, irrigation systems were not extensive. Therefore, initial large-scale investment in irrigation was required before the shift from curve I to I' could commence.

Taiwan, in contrast, seems to have reached P in the late 1910s. The increase in the Japanese colonial government's investment in irrigation during this period played a large role. But an even more basic factor appears to have been the increase in the relative advantage of irrigation over land opening. Government investment provided the condition for shifting from I to I' in the 1920s and 1930s.

The Philippines seems to have reached P only in the late 1950s. The nationalistic desire to achieve self-sufficiency in food, together with foreign-exchange considerations, helped focus public attention on the need to invest in irrigation, which had become a relatively less costly means to increase rice output. The way for the shift from I to I' in the mid-1960s was thus prepared.

Estimating the Cost Curves

As a test of our hypothesis, we have estimated curves A, I, and I', in terms of the marginal cost of land opening and irrigation development to produce an additional unit of income from agricultural production. The marginal cost–benefit ratios (C/B) are calculated as:

$$C/B = i\left[\frac{(1+i)^{m+n}}{(1+i)^{n}-1}\right](K+H)/B$$

where

B = annual benefit flow due to the investment per hectare;
H = annual operation and maintenance costs per hectare;
i = interest rate (assumed to be 10 percent per annum);
K = capital cost per hectare;
m = middle year of the construction period;
n = usable life, in years.

Simplifying assumptions are that all capital costs occur in the middle year of the construction period, and both benefits and operation-maintenance costs begin in the year following completion of construction and are constant over the project's usable life.

The cost (C) consists of the annual service flow of initial capital investment and the annual cost of operation and maintenance per hectare of new area brought into either cultivation or irrigation. The corresponding benefit flow (B) is measured by the increase in gross value added per hectare, and is estimated by subtracting the cost of seeds, fertilizers, and chemicals from the value of additional output produced. Both costs and benefits are measured at constant prices – 1934–36 for Japan, Taiwan, and Korea, and 1970 for the Philippines. For Japan, drainage and land consolidation are included under irrigation. We tested four levels of seed-fertilizer technology for each country in order to analyze the complementarity between irrigation and seed-fertilizer technology. The selection of fertilizer-application levels was based on both actual farm survey data and optimum levels derived from fertilizer response functions. Additional details on the calculations are given in a note at the end of this chapter and in Kikuchi (1976). The results are summarized in table 4.3.

As expected, the real cost of irrigation development to produce an additional unit of income shows a rising trend for each level of technology in every country.

Table 4.3: Costs of irrigation construction and land opening to produce an additional unit of agricultural income

	Irrigation				Land opening	
	Traditional varieties		Improved varieties			
Japan[a]	N = 40 kg	N = 80 kg	N = 80 kg	N = 120 kg		
1902	0.89 (11)	0.64 (15)				
1905	0.80 (13)	0.57 (17)				
1910	1.11 (9)	0.80 (12)				
1915	1.25 (8)	0.90 (11)				
1920	1.32 (7)	0.96 (10)	0.70 (14)	0.64 (15)	1.00 (10)	
1925	1.26 (7)	0.92 (11)	0.66 (15)	0.61 (16)	0.78 (12)	
1930	1.49 (6)	1.07 (9)	0.78 (13)	0.67 (14)	1.06 (10)	
1932	1.32 (7)	0.95 (10)	0.69 (14)	0.64 (15)	1.17 (9)	
Taiwan[a]	N = 0 kg	N = 50 kg	N = 50 kg	N = 100 kg	Case A	Case B
1907	0.40 (26)	0.33 (31)				
1910	0.60 (17)	0.49 (21)			0.96 (10)	1.15 (9)
1915	0.76 (13)	0.62 (15)				
1920	0.65 (16)	0.53 (19)				
1925	0.87 (11)	0.71 (14)	0.47 (20)	0.42 (22)		
1930	1.15 (9)	0.94 (11)	0.61 (15)	0.55 (17)		
1932	1.27 (8)	1.04 (10)	0.68 (14)	0.61 (16)		
Korea[a]	N = 0 kg	N = 50 kg	N = 50 kg	N = 100 kg	Case A	Case B
1911	0.53 (28)	0.42 (36)				
1915	0.61 (19)	0.49 (26)				
1920	0.52 (24)	0.42 (30)			0.61 (17)	
1925	1.02 (10)	0.82 (13)	0.42 (27)	0.39 (29)	0.70 (15)	0.48 (22)

Table 4.3 continued

	Irrigation				Land opening	
	Traditional varieties		*Improved varieties*			
					Case A	Case B
1930	1.04 (10)	0.84 (13)	0.43 (26)	0.39 (28)	1.20 (8)	0.82 (13)
1932	1.11 (9)	0.89 (11)	0.46 (24)	0.42 (26)	1.26 (8)	0.86 (12)
Philippines[b]	N = 0 kg	N = 15 kg	N = 20 kg	N = 60 kg		
1951	0.44 (26)	0.42 (27)				
1955	0.48 (24)	0.45 (25)				
1960	0.61 (18)	0.58 (19)				
1965	0.59 (19)	0.56 (20)				
1970	0.69 (15)	0.72 (15)	0.35 (32)	0.31 (36)		
1972	0.76 (14)	0.72 (15)	0.38 (28)	0.34 (32)	1.19 (9)	0.80 (12)

[a] 1934-36 constant prices
[b] 1970 constant prices

Fertilizer levels are indicated by N (nitrogen) in kilograms
Values inside parentheses are the internal rates of return calculated as rates that satisfy

$$\frac{K}{B - H} = \frac{(1 + r)^n - 1}{r(1 + r)^{m+n}}$$

Sources: Ban 1979; Crisostomo and Barker 1979; Lee and Chen 1979; Yamada and Hayami 1979

There was a tendency for costs to increase faster than benefits when irrigation investment accelerated. Looking across the columns shows the rising trends in marginal cost–benefit ratios for irrigation were totally compensated by successive downward shifts of curve I to I'. These results support our hypothesis that the development of seed-fertilizer technology had the effect of counteracting the rising cost of irrigation as construction moved from easier to more difficult sites.

Only incomplete data are available for investments in land opening. For Japan, aggregate time-series data are available after 1918. The estimates in table 4.3 show the marginal costs were about the same as for irrigation used with traditional rices. But because improved varieties had already been introduced widely by the 1920s, the profitability of irrigation would clearly have been higher than land opening.

The data for Japan are not sufficient to infer the relation between the cost curves of land opening and irrigation hypothesized in figure 4.5. The Korean data are more informative in this respect. Cases A and B in table 4.3 correspond to a traditional technology level (zero nitrogen and traditional rices), and improved technology (100 kg of nitrogen and improved varieties), respectively, for rice planted in newly opened paddy fields. For the traditional technology, the real cost of both land opening (case A) and irrigation rose sharply from the beginning of the 1920s (figure 4.6). The irrigation cost curve rose more sharply until the mid-1920s, reflecting a short-run increase in cost due to the sudden increase in government irrigation investment under the Korean Rice Production Development Program. The longer-run trend, however, seems steeper for the land-opening curve than for the irrigation curve.

A more interesting observation for Korea is the relation between the land opening (case B) and the irrigation curves for the improved technology. While development of seed-fertilizer technology was successful in counteracting the increase in the cost of irrigation, it did not stop the rise in the land-opening cost curve. This divergence clearly demonstrates the role of complementarity between irrigation and technology in shifting the momentum of agricultural growth from external to internal augmentation.

Unfortunately, no aggregate time-series data on land-opening investment are available for Taiwan or the Philippines. In the case of Taiwan, the estimated costs of land opening are for the government land-settlement project of 1909–17. Cases A and B assume different crops planted on the new land – two crops of upland rice, and one of sugar cane, respectively. The results show much higher cost–benefit ratios for land opening than for irrigation investment, which suggests a rationale for the colonial government's heavy investment in irrigation after about 1915. In an earlier stage of development in Taiwan, several land-settlement projects were undertaken by the colonial government and the sugar companies, but almost all of these failed. (See Taiwan Government-General 1919; Yanaihara 1929.) One of the few projects that was successful in settling Japanese immigrants was the one analyzed here, and even it was terminated in 1917, leaving incom-

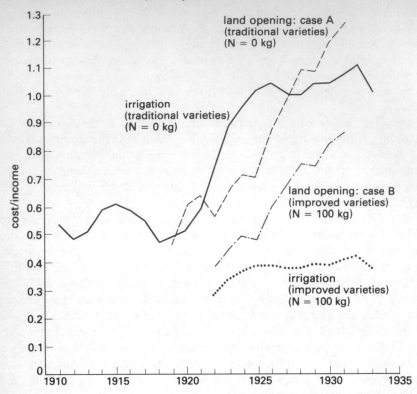

Figure 4.6: Trends in the cost–benefit ratios for building irrigation systems and opening new land for Korea (1934–36 constant prices)

plete a large part of the original plan. Such unsuccessful attempts correspond well to the low rates of return to land opening estimated in this study.

In the Philippine case, the estimates of the costs of land opening are from 1973 projects by the Bureau of Land Resettlement. Cases A and B assume one crop of upland rice, and two of corn, respectively. The results show irrigation improvement was more profitable or less costly, especially with fertilizer-responsive varieties.

The four countries have in common rising irrigation cost curves, yet there were differences in the levels of marginal cost–benefit ratios for irrigation (figure 4.7). The curves for Japan for different technologies are located well above those of Taiwan and Korea throughout the period under study.

Japan entered the modern period with a relatively well-developed irrigation network, which means the easier locations already had systems. On the other hand, the initial irrigation infrastructure in Taiwan and Korea was inadequate for the succcessful introduction of seed-fertilizer technology. The possibility of

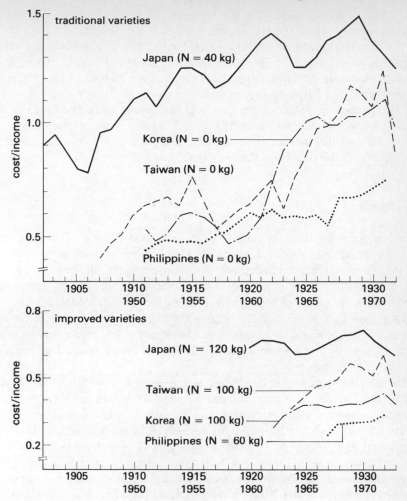

Figure 4.7:   Trends in the cost–benefit ratio for irrigation improvement in Japan, Taiwan, Korea, and the Philippines

achieving increased output at a relatively low cost by exploiting irrigation potential was a basic factor inducing public investment in irrigation systems in Taiwan and Korea under the Rice Production Development Programs.

The gap in the irrigation cost–benefit ratios between Japan and its colonies began to narrow during the 1920s, as a result of rapid development of the less costly sites. Had there been no agricultural depression in Japan in the 1930s, and thus no interruption in the irrigation-development programs in the colonies, the ratios of Taiwan and Korea would have continued to approach the Japanese level. Such a process seems to imply movement towards an equilibrium in rice production costs within the Japanese Empire.

The marginal cost–benefit ratio of irrigation for the Philippines in the 1950s was at the same level as for Taiwan and Korea in the initial stage of their agricultural development. This may imply the Philippines was endowed with an equally large potential for irrigation development. The fact the irrigation cost curve did not rise in the Philippines in the 1960s as fast as in Taiwan and Korea in the 1920s may mean the potential in the Philippines has not been exploited quite as fast as in the other two countries. In any case, it is clear profitable irrigation development is still possible in the Philippines.

Conclusions

Broad comparisons of the agricultural histories of modern Japan, Taiwan, Korea, and the Philippines suggest a major shift in the momentum of agricultural growth, from external to internal augmentation, emerged; this resulted from the rise of population pressure to a point where the latter became less costly than the former. The results of cost–benefit analysis show clearly that, for the period when growth in land productivity became the major contributor to the growth in output, the profitability of investment in irrigation was higher than in land-opening projects, assuming improved fertilizer-responsive rice and high levels of fertilizer application.

Perhaps the most important finding is the process by which irrigation and technology emerged. In Japan, the feudal heritage of relatively extensive irrigation systems provided a base for development of seed-fertilizer technology. As the technology diffused, land infrastructure became a bottleneck. This induced public investment and institutional innovation for the further development of land infrastructure. In both Taiwan and Korea, the infrastructure was not adequate when the initial transfer of the seed-fertilizer technology from Japan was attempted during the late 1910s and early 1920s. Thus, large-scale investment in irrigation was made by the colonial governments. Irrigation and technology proceeded almost concurrently, reinforcing each other.

In the 1960s, land productivity in the Philippines, hitherto stagnant, rose, demonstrably as a compensation for the decline in the expansion of cultivated area. This change indicates the Philippines began to follow a route of agricultural growth similar to that of Japan, Taiwan, and Korea. The spurt in government irrigation investment in the late 1950s prepared for the dramatic diffusion of semi-dwarf varieties of rice, beginning in the mid-1960s. The rising cost as more marginal areas are irrigated has been countered by further improvements in rice technology. Without such developments, the Philippines would be trapped in Ricardian stagnation. Prewar Japan, Taiwan, and Korea similarly avoided that fate.

Population growth continues to press hard on limited land resources. Avoiding the Ricardian trap is by internal augmentation, that is, through investment in land quality and developing land-saving technology. The *sine qua non* for sustained agricultural growth is intensified investment by the public sector in irrigation and research.

Technical Note on the Estimation of Costs and Benefits for Investment in Irrigation and Land Opening

Assumed operation and maintenance costs:

for irrigation:

Japan: 3 percent of initial capital costs
Taiwan: 18 yen per hectare
Korea: 13 yen per hectare
Philippines: 60 pesos per hectare

for land opening:

Japan, Taiwan, Philippines: zero
Korea: 13 yen per hectare (the same as for irrigation, because all the land-opening projects included in our analysis had irrigation facilities)

Assumed usable life:

irrigation: 50 years in all countries
land opening: infinite, except 50 years for Korea

Deflators:

Japan: the price index of land-infrastructure construction from the National Research Institute of Agricultural Economics (1967)
Korea and Taiwan: the GNE implicit deflator for investments in construction compiled by Mizoguchi (1975)
Philippines: the GNP implicit deflator for investments in construction from the National Economic Development Authority (1973)

Projects Included and Data Sources

Japan: projects approved under the Arable Land Replotment Law (Norinsho, 1941)

Taiwan: irrigation projects undertaken by Governor-General's Office (Bank of Taiwan 1950); land-settlement projects in Hualien (Taiwan Government-General 1919)

Korea: projects under the Korean Rice Production Development Program (Korean Government-General)

Philippines: projects under the National Irrigation Administration (NIA, 1974) and the Bureau of Land Resettlement (who made unpublished data available to us).

Opportunity Cost of Labor

Increases in labor costs for crop production due to irrigation and land opening have not been subtracted, as increments in labor are assumed available at zero opportunity cost. In fact, there is little change in labor input for the wet-season crop because of irrigation. Labor use in the dry season in Taiwan and the Philippines increases as irrigation enables planting in the dry season. It seems reasonable, however, to assume that during the dry season farm labor remains primarily idle when there is no irrigation, and thus has a very low opportunity cost. It also seems reasonable to assume that workers who are resettled by the government land-opening projects are those who had difficulty finding productive employment in their prior locations.

References

Ban, S. H. (1979), "Growth Rates of Korean Agriculture, 1918–1968," in Yujiro Hayami, Vernon W. Ruttan, and Herman M. Southworth, eds, *Agricultural Growth in Japan, Taiwan, Korea and the Philippines*, Honolulu: University Press of Hawaii.

Bank of Taiwan (1950), *Taiwan shui li wenn tyi*, Taipei: Bank of Taiwan.

Boserup, Ester (1965), *The Conditions of Agricultural Growth: The Economics of Agrarian Change Under Population Pressure*, Chicago: Aldine.

Clark, Colin (1940), *The Conditions of Economic Progress*, 1st edn, London: Macmillan.

Clark, Colin, and M. Haswell (1964), *The Economics of Subsistence Agriculture*, London: Macmillan.

Crisostomo, C., and R. Barker (1979), "Growth Rates of Philippines Agriculture, 1948–1971," in Yujiro Hayami, Vernon W. Ruttan, and Herman M. Southworth, eds, *Agricultural Growth in Japan, Taiwan, Korea and the Philippines*, Honolulu: University Press of Hawaii.

Crisostomo, C. M., R. H. Meyers, T. B. Paris, B. Duff, and R. Barker (1971), "The New Rice Technology and Labor Absorption in Philippine Agriculture," *Malayan Economic Review*, 16: 117–58.

Hayami, Yujiro, and Vernon W. Ruttan (1971), *Agricultural Development: An International Perspective*, Baltimore, MD, and London: Johns Hopkins Press.

Hayami, Yujiro, in association with Masakatsu Akino, Masahiko Shintani, and Saburo Yamada (1975), *A Century of Agricultural Growth in Japan: Its Relevance to Asian Development*, Tokyo: University of Tokyo Press.

Hayami, Yujiro, C. C. David, P. Flores, and M. Kikuchi (1976), "Agricultural Growth Against a Land Resource Constraint," *Australian Journal of Agricultural Economics*, 29: 144–59.

Hooley, R., and V. W. Ruttan (1969), "The Philippines," in Richard L. Shand, ed., *Agricultural Development in Asia*, Canberra: Australian National University Press.

Johnston, Bruce F. (1966), "Agriculture and Economic Development: The Relevance of Japanese Experience," *Food Research Institute Studies*, 6: 251–312.

Kawano, S. (1941), *Taiwan beikoku keizai ron*, Tokyo: Yuhikaku.

Kikuchi, M. (1976), "Irrigation and Rice Technology in Agricultural Development: A Comparative History of Taiwan, Korea and the Philippines," Ph.D. dissertation, Hokkaido University.

Kobayakawa, K. (ed.) (1959), *Chosen nogyo hattatsushi*, Tokyo.

Korean Government-General (1939), *Nogyo tokeihyo*, Seoul: Korean Government-General.

Korean Government-General (1940), *Chosen tochikairyo jigyo yoran*, Seoul: Korean Government-General.

Lee, Teng-hui (1971), *Intersectoral Capital Flows in the Economic Development of Taiwan, 1895–1960*, Ithaca, NY: Cornell University Press.

Lee, Teng-hui, and Y. E. Chen (1979), "Growth Rates of Taiwan's Agriculture, 1911–1972," in Yujiro Hayami, Vernon W. Ruttan, and Herman M. Southworth, eds, *Agricultural Growth in Japan, Taiwan, Korea and the Philippines*, Honolulu: University Press of Hawaii.

Mizoguchi, T. (1975), *Taiwan Chosen no keizai seicho*, Tokyo: Iwanami.

National Economic Development Authority (1973), *National Income Accounts*, Quezon City: NEDA.

National Irrigation Administration (Philippines) (1974), *Revised Listing of National Irrigation Systems Operated and Maintained by the National Irrigation Administration, as of June 30, 1974*, Quezon City: National Irrigation Administration.

National Research Institute of Agricultural Economics (1967), *Tochi kairyo toshi no suekei*, Tokyo: National Research Institute of Agricultural Economics.

Nogyo Hattatsuchi Chosakai (1954), *Nihon nogyo hattatsushi*, vol. 4, Tokyo.

Norinsho (Government of Japan, Ministry of Agriculture and Forestry) (1941), *Dai 16-ji kochi kakucho kairyo jigyo yoran*, Tokyo.

North, D. C., and R. P. Thomas (1973), *The Rise of Western World: A New Economic History*, Cambridge.

Ohkawa, Kazushi, and Henry Rosovsky (1960), "The Role of Agriculture in Modern Japanese Economic Development," *Economic Development and Cultural Change*, 9: 43–47.

Schultz, Theodore W. (1953), *The Economic Organization of Agriculture*, New York: McGraw-Hill.

Taiwan Government-General (1919), *Kanei iminjigyo hokokusho*, Taipei: Taiwan Government-General.

Yamada, Saburo, and Yujiro Hayami (1979), "Growth Rates of Japanese Agriculture, 1880–1970," In Yujiro Hayami, Vernon W. Ruttan, and Herman M. Southworth, eds, *Agricultural Growth in Japan, Taiwan, Korea and the Philippines*, Honolulu: University Press of Hawaii.

Yanaihara, T. (1929), *Teikokushugi ka no Taiwan*, Tokyo: Iwanami.

5 Agricultural Technology and Income Distribution: Two Indonesian Villages viewed from the Japanese Experience

YUJIRO HAYAMI and MASAO KIKUCHI

The development and diffusion of modern rice and wheat varieties, often heralded as the Green Revolution, has had a profound impact on the economies of the developing countries in Asia. In assessing the "revolution," a major concern has been the effects on income distribution. Specifically, it has been charged that poorer peasants have become poorer, relatively if not absolutely. To shed some light on this issue, we undertook an intensive field survey of two villages in Java. This chapter analyzes the new rice technology and its effects on income distribution in the case-study villages in the light of the Japanese experience. Our conclusion is that land-saving technology can and has improved income equality. Although the Ricardian force of population pressure was countered by technological progress in one of the studied villages, in the other village stagnant technology has meant growing poverty and inequality of incomes.

We approach the problem from the side of functional distribution of income. The size distribution of income among individuals or households is determined by the functional distribution among production factors, and by the size distribution of production-factor endowments. The functional distribution is directly determined by technology and, hence, is the link in the analysis of the relationship between technology and the size distribution of income. This theoretical consideration, and the availability of data, mean that our study is based mainly on time-series and cross-sectional comparisons of factor shares.

In the first part of the chapter we have sought to identify the nature of technological change in Japanese agriculture through analysis of long-term trends in factor inputs, factor prices, and factor shares before World War II. The second

The field surveys in Indonesia discussed in this paper were supported jointly by the Agricultural Development Council, the Agro-Economic Survey of Indonesia, the International Development Center of Japan, and the International Rice Research Institute. More detailed discussions of the field work can be found in Kikuchi et al. (1980a and 1980b). Major findings are integrated with other village studies in Hayami and Kikuchi (1981).

part provides background on the Green Revolution and income-distribution issues with which we are concerned. Two villages in West Java – one characterized by technological stagnation and the other by significant technological progress – are then compared and the effects of technological change are examined. Implications of the case studies are discussed in the final part, in the light of the historical experience of Japanese agriculture.

Agricultural Technology and Factor Shares in Japan

As a basis of comparison with the Indonesian case-studies, this section seeks to identify the nature of technological change in Japanese agriculture and its effect on income distribution by reviewing the historical process of agricultural growth in Japan since the early Meiji period (the 1870s and 1880s). Observations are confined to the period before World War II, because the postwar Japanese experience, characterized by a sharp decline in the size of the agricultural labor force, is not relevant to most developing countries in Asia. The section draws on our earlier work (see Hayami et al. 1975: ch. 2).

Quantitative aspects of agricultural growth in Japan for the prewar period are relatively well established, though the data are not immune from substantial observational errors and index-number problems. Long-term trends in output, inputs, and productivity are shown in figure 5.1. Between 1880 and 1935, total agricultural output (the aggregate of all products minus intermediate products of agricultural origin) increased at an average annual compound rate of 1.6 percent. Inputs of the two primary factors, land and labor, changed slowly; the labor force (male-worker equivalents) declined slightly (0.2 percent annually); land area (paddy-field equivalents) showed a very modest increase of 0.4 percent annually. Capital also grew more slowly than output, 1.0 percent a year. At 3.2 percent annually, only current inputs showed an increase substantially higher than the output growth rate.

Overall, total input (the aggregate of all conventional inputs using factor share weights) increased at a rate of 0.4 percent a year, and total productivity (the ratio of total output to total input) increased at 1.2 percent. This implies only one-quarter of total output growth in agriculture was accounted for by increases in land, labor, capital, and current input; the rest was from technological progress, broadly defined here as a shift in the production function conventionally specified.

The nature of technological change can be inferred from a comparison of movements in factor inputs (figure 5.1) with the corresponding movements in factor prices relative to the price of farm products (figure 5.2). On the whole, the rates of change in respective factor inputs are inversely correlated with those in the factor prices. While the relatively stationary levels of labor and land were accompanied by rising trends in their prices, the rapid increase in current inputs was accompanied by a rapid decline in their prices.

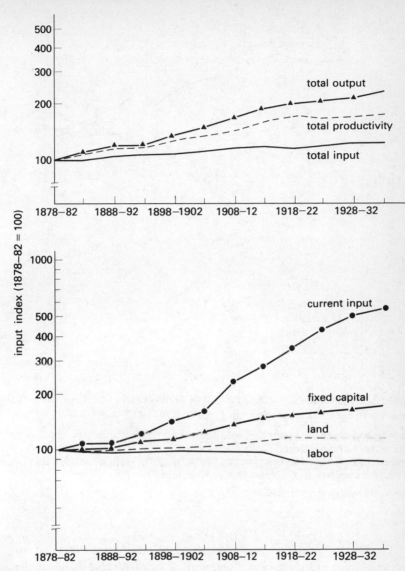

Figure 5.1: Trends in output, inputs, and productivity in Japanese agriculture, 1878–1932

This figure graphs an index of 5-year averages of output, inputs, and productivity on a semi-log scale, with 1878–82 = 100

Source: Hayami et al. 1975: 230 and 234; underlying data are also available in Yamada and Hayami 1979

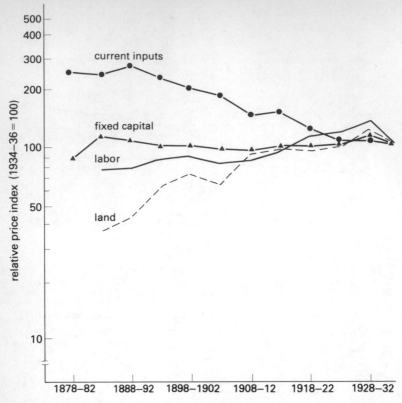

Figure 5.2: Indexes of prices of factors of agricultural production relative to the price of agricultural products in Japan, 1878–1932

This figure graphs on a semi-log scale an index of 5-year averages of prices of four factors of agricultural production relative to an index of agricultural product prices, with 1934–36 = 100. For more information on the data collection and compilation, see Yamada and Hayami (1979)

Source: Hayami et al. 1975: 232–33

The rapid rise in the price of farmland seems to reflect the fact that land was the most limiting factor in agricultural production. The rapid decline in the price of current inputs relative to land appears to be the major force that induced substitution of the current inputs, especially fertilizers, for land, thereby increasing the input of plant nutrients per unit of farmland area.

Considering the significant gain in total productivity, it is unlikely that factor substitutions in response to changes in relative prices represented movements along a fixed isoquant of a neoclassical production function, but instead were movements along an innovation possibility curve or an envelope of isoquants of potential production functions. It seems reasonable to hypothesize that the process involved technological change biased toward land saving and fertilizer using in Hicks's sense. (*Ceteris paribus*, the technology is such that increases in fertilizer input per unit of land at a constant fertilizer–land price ratio raises the output share of fertilizer at the expense of the share of land.)

As a test, we derived factor shares in the total cost of agricultural production. Because the factor inputs and their prices moved in opposite directions, the shares remained fairly stable. However, if we broadly compare the initial with the terminal decade, the basic trends are clear, as shown in table 5.1. The share of current input increased at the expense of land, while the capital and labor shares remained stable. These results are consistent with the hypothesis of a land-saving bias in technological progress in agriculture. Further evidence is provided from estimation of production functions (see Hayami et al. 1975: ch. 4). Underlying this process were the development and diffusion of fertilizer-responsive and high-yielding rices, improvements in land infrastructure such as irrigation and drainage, and expansion of less land-dependent enterprises such as sericulture.

Japan's success in developing land-saving technologies had critical implications in both growth and equity. If the land-saving technologies had not developed, the rapid increase in demand for food in the process of economic development would have resulted in sharp increases in both land rent and food prices. The increase in food prices would have implied increases in urban workers' cost of living and wage rates and, hence, reduction in the returns to industrial capital. Much of the increased agricultural income due to high food prices would have been captured by landowners in the form of increased land rent. Food could have been imported, but that implies a drain of foreign exchange needed for imports of capital goods and technical know how.

Table 5.1:   Percentage change in factor shares in agricultural production cost in Japan, 1888–97 and 1928–37

	1888–97 *(1)*	*1928–37* *(2)*	*(2)−(1)*
Current input	8.2	12.5	4.3
Capital	10.2	10.8	0.6
Land	30.8	25.5	−5.3
Labor	50.8	51.2	0.4
Total	100.0	100.0	0

Source: Yamada and Hayami 1979: table J-5

Thus, if land-saving technologies had not been exploited adequately, the industrialization and overall economic growth of Japan in its early phase would have been seriously constrained by the limitation of land endowment, in accordance with the Ricardian scenario. At the same time, income disparity in the rural sector between landlords and tenants (and small owner-farmers whose subsistence required outside wage employment) would have been much greater.

The Green Revolution Controversy

The need for land-saving technologies is more compelling for developing countries today than for Japan during its early development, since the former face much greater population pressure. Unlike Japan, the absolute size of their agricultural labor force has been rising rapidly, as population growth exceeds the labor-absorbing capacity of nonagriculture. The result has been declining land–labor ratios, often accompanied by decreases in real wage rates (Asian Development Bank 1977: 49–58).

Such economies closely fit the dismal view of Ricardo. As population growth presses on land resources under constant technology, cultivation frontiers expand to ever-more marginal land, and greater amounts of labor are applied per unit of cultivated area; the marginal return to labor input declines, and the cost of food production rises. This leads to higher food prices; real wage rates measured in food grain decline, and land rent increases. In the end, laborers' income is the minimum sufficient to maintain a stationary population, and all the economic surplus is captured by landlords as land rent.

In the real world, technology has not remained constant. In fact, remarkable progress has been made, including the expansion and improvement of irrigation systems in South and Southeast Asia since the 1950s, and the diffusion of modern semi-dwarf varieties of rice and wheat since the 1960s – the process heralded popularly (and misleadingly) as the Green Revolution. The modern varieties (MV), characterized by short, stiff stalks with pointed leaves that receive solar energy more efficiently and which withstand higher applications of fertilizers, have proven higher-yielding and more profitable under conditions of adequate water control and crop care.

The initial enthusiasm for MV during the Green Revolution bandwagon period has been superseded by criticisms such as "the failure of miracle rice," reflecting occasional crop failures due to insects, other pests, drought, and flood. However, MV have continued to diffuse rapidly, with MV planted on nearly 70 percent of the wheat area and 30 percent of the rice area in South and Southeast Asia (Dalrymple 1978). This seems sufficient evidence that MV represents an economically more efficient and profitable technology.

The MV propagated during the 1960s and early 1970s were those developed by international agricultural research centers such as IRRI (International Rice Research Institute in the Philippines) and CIMMYT (International Center for

Corn and Wheat Improvement in Mexico). These original MV have been steadily replaced by crosses of international center varieties and local ones developed by national experimental stations. As a result, the newer MV are more adapted to local conditions.

Facilitated by MV and improved irrigation, the application of fertilizers increased. The quantity of fertilizers applied per hectare, measured by the sum of nitrogen, phosphate, and potash, tripled in South and Southeast Asia from the late 1960s to the late 1970s. The development of irrigation infrastructure and seed-fertilizer technology appears to represent technological change similar to that in Japan. If so, it should significantly augment land, and thereby counteract decreasing returns to labor applied to the physically limited land area. However, the efforts of land augmentation seem to have been insufficient to overcome the extremely strong population pressure. The marginal productivity of agricultural labor has not risen; indeed, it has diminished in many areas, as reflected by declining or stagnant trends in real wage rates. However, if the technological change had not occurred, the situation would be much worse.

Despite the crucial contribution of the new rice and wheat technology to both efficiency and equity, it has often been attacked on the grounds it promotes inequitable income distribution. The arguments run as follows. The new technology tends to be monopolized by large commercial farmers who have better access to new information and credit. MV require higher applications of modern inputs such as fertilizers and pesticides; adoption of MV is difficult for small farmers with little capability to purchase these inputs. A large profit from MV adoption by a few large farmers induces them to enlarge by consolidating the farms of small non-adopters through purchase or tenant eviction. The ultimate result is polarization of rural communities into large commercial farmers and a landless proletariat.[1]

It is an empirical question whether the new technology has a land-saving bias and, thereby, counteracts the adverse effect of population pressure on the functional distribution of income. It is also an empirical question how strong such positive effects have been relative to the negative effects enumerated by the Green Revolution critics.

We approach the problem by comparing two Javanese villages, one of which is characterized by technological stagnation and the other by significant technological progress. By comparing the two, we seek to single out the effect of technological change. Java serves as a social observatory uniquely suited for the problem concerned, because rural poverty is especially serious, there is an extremely high population density, and it has long been feared that population pressure, together with modernizing forces such as the new technology, are

[1] Such arguments are mentioned by Wharton (1969), Johnston and Cownie (1969), Falcon (1970), Warriner (1973), and Palmer (1976). More radical views are expressed by Frankel (1971), Cleaver (1972), and Griffin (1974).

destroying traditional village institutions and are resulting in greater misery for the poor.[2]

Study of Two Indonesian Villages

The two villages chosen for the comparative analysis are among those covered by the Rice Intensification Survey (*Intensifikasi Padi Sawah*) conducted by the Agro-Economic Survey of Indonesia for 1968–72. Those data provide the benchmark from which changes can be ascertained. The villages are in the Kabupaten of Subang in West Java, immediately north of Bandung and about 120 km east of Jakarta. One is located in the foothills of the southern part of Subang – we call it South Village; it is surrounded by rice terraces. What we call North Village is located about 30 km to the north, on a completely flat coastal plain along the Java Sea. We conducted a complete enumeration survey in each village for both economic and institutional data. The survey periods were January 1979 for South Village and November–December 1979 for North Village.[3]

Agrarian Structure and Population Pressure

The agrarian structures are quite different in the two villages. As shown in table 5.2, South Village was a typical peasant community, with three-quarters of the households classed as small farm operators and only one-quarter as landless laborers. Only about two-fifths of North Village households were farm operators; the rest were landless laborers. The incidence of tenancy was significantly higher in North Village than in South Village; almost all tenants were sharecroppers, sharing output and costs fifty-fifty.

As is common in rural Java, both villages have very unfavorable land–man ratios. In South Village, as many as 419 people drew subsistence primarily from about 25 hectares of wet ricefield (*sawah*). The population density was higher for South Village, but the rate of population growth seems to have been much faster in North Village. Data on the number of children per mother suggest the natural rate of population growth in South Village had decelerated from about 3 percent annually to 1 percent over the last 40 years, and there is no sign of a significant inflow of migrants. In North Village, not only does the natural increase seem to be higher, but a large number of migrants flowed into the

[2] This third point was developed originally by Boeke (1953), and followed by others with different viewpoints and approaches; for a typical expression, see Collier et al. (1974).
[3] The community called a village in this study is a *kampung*. *Kampung* might more appropriately be translated as a hamlet, as it is nothing more than a cluster of houses. As such, *kampungs* are the indigenous community form. The official administrative unit in rural areas of Java is a *desa*, which includes several *kampungs*. A *kabupaten*, often translated as regency, is like a Japanese prefecture.

Table 5.2:   Land area, population, and number of households in the surveyed villages

	South Village (1978)	North Village (1979)
Total rice land (ha)	24.7	65.6
Total population (no.)	419	774
Total number of households	110 (100)[a]	191 (100)[a]
Farm operators	83 (75)	75 (39)
Landless laborers	27 (25)	116 (61)
Rice land per capita (ha)	0.06	0.08
Rice land per household (ha)	0.22	0.34
Rice land per farmer household (ha)	0.30	0.87

[a] The numbers in parentheses are percentages of total households
In addition to the rice fields, South Village had 3 hectares of land used for home gardens and fish ponds, and North Village had 8 hectares

Source: Authors' field surveys in 1978–79

village. According to old villagers, the number of households in North Village had been about 40 in 1940; it had increased to 191 at the time of our survey. Assuming no change in average family size, population growth for the past four decades has been as high as 4 percent annually.

Such differences in agrarian structure and demographic pattern can be explained by the histories of settlement. South Village is old; no one there knows when settlement began. In contrast, North Village was settled after 1920, because it was more difficult to build an irrigation system in a flat coastal plain than in the foothills. Initial settlers in North Village opened new land and practiced extensive farming under a rain-fed condition. Because the yield of rain-fed rice was very low, an operational holding of about 2 hectares was required for a family's subsistence. Thus, by Javanese standards, relatively large holdings were established. Yields rose significantly after a local irrigation system was built in the 1950s for the wet-season crop.

Intensification of rice farming due to irrigation increased labor demand and migrants flowed into North Village as landless laborers or sharecroppers. The process was repeated after the irrigation system had been extended. The class differentiations between relatively large farmers and a large number of landless workers, and between landowners and tenants, were thus developed through waves of migration.

Extension of the irrigation system was part of the Jatiluhur system, the largest in Java. Major laterals had been built by 1968, but it was not until 1972 that secondary and tertiary laterals were completed and the whole village

Table 5.3: Changes in multiple cropping, adoption of modern varieties, and rice yield in the surveyed villages

	South Village			North Village		
	1968–71[a]	1978[b]	Percentage change[d]	1968–71[a]	1978–79[c]	Percentage change[d]
Multiple-cropping ratio[e]	1.9	1.9	0	1.5	2.0	33
Ratio of MV adopters (%)	11	14	3	7	100	93
Rice yield (kg/ha):						
per ha of crop area	2.6	2.9	12	2.4	3.4	42
per ha of rice field area	4.9	5.5	12	3.6	6.7	86

[a] Averages of dry and wet seasons

[b] 1978 dry season

[c] Average of 1978–79 dry season

[d] Percentage increase from 1968–71 to 1978 or 1979, except for the "ratio of MV adopters," which is simply the 1978 or 1979 figure minus the 1968–71 figure

[e] Total crop area divided by total rice field area

Sources: For 1968–71, Rice Intensification Survey and, for 1978–79, authors' field surveys in those years

area became amenable to double cropping of rice. The introduction of double cropping was facilitated by the diffusion of MV that have early maturing and nonphotosensitive characteristics. The MV commonly used in 1979 were IR26, IR36, IR38, and Asahan, developed by the Central Agricultural Experiment Station at Sukamandi, near North Village. There was no difference in the MV adoption rate among farm-size classes and among tenure classes. The average rice output per hectare of wet paddy land per year increased by more than 80 percent during the 1970s (table 5.3).

In contrast to the dynamic changes in North Village, South Village was largely stagnant. The local irrigation system had been well developed as far back as people could remember. There had been no significant improvements in the system, nor any expansion in cultivated area since before World War II. The growing population increased fragmentation of landholdings through inheritance. The number of near-landless peasants increased, even though the ratio of completely landless laborers was not as large as in North Village (table 5.2).

As with North Village, MV were introduced in the late 1960s under the Bimas Program – a nationwide program of rice-production intensification, based on a package of modern inputs, credit, and extension services. However, because the MV were highly susceptible to insects (brown planthoppers) and pests (tungro virus disease), many farmers who tried them reverted to traditional varieties. At the time of our survey in 1979, only 14 percent of farmers still used MV, although as many as 83 percent had tried MV at least once. As a result, the rate of increase in the average rice yield per hectare of crop area in this village was much slower than in North Village (see table 5.3).

In South Village, it appears the population level which can be sustained on limited land under a constant technology had been reached several decades ago. Population data suggest that villagers suppressed the birth of children long before 1975, when the government program for birth control was introduced. Many women reportedly had abortions by indigenous methods, which were often harmful to their health. In short, the economy of South Village approximates the world of classical economists like Malthus and Ricardo, in which population pressure on a fixed land resource under constant technology results in a stationary state of no population growth with the minimum subsistence level of living.

Labor Employment and Wages

The different patterns of technological progress (defined here broadly as the shift of the production function due to both irrigation improvement and MV diffusion) between North and South Villages were reflected in sharp differences in the changes in rice-production inputs and input prices for the past decade (see tables 5.4 and 5.5).

In South Village, where technology was stagnant, the input of fertilizers per hectare of crop area increased at a rate below the rate of decline in the real price of fertilizers. On the other hand, in North Village, where fertilizer-responsive MV

Table 5.4:   Changes in inputs and input prices for rice production, South Village

	1968-71[a]	1978[b]	Percentage change from 1968-71 to 1978
Inputs			
Fertilizer (kg/ha)	191	229	20
Labor (hr/ha):			
land preparation	420	494	18
total (preharvest)	736	928	26
Carabao and cattle for land preparation (days/ha)	16.4	9.2	−44
Real input prices (in paddy)[c]			
Fertilizer (kg/ha)	1.5	1.1	−27
Labor wage (kg/day)[d]	9.5	8.5	−11
Carabao rental (kg/day)	6.2	9.5	53

[a] Average for wet and dry seasons
[b] Dry season
[c] Nominal price divided by paddy price
[d] Wage for land preparation, assuming a working day of 8 hours; includes lunch

Source: As table 5.3

were widely adopted, the per hectare input of fertilizers increased six times faster than the rate of decline in the price of fertilizers.

Dramatic contrasts can also be observed in the changes in the inputs of labor and animal power in relation to their price changes. In South Village, an increase in labor input was associated with a decline in the real wage rate. At the same time, the real rental rate of draft animals (carabao and cattle) increased. The decline in labor wage rates relative to animal rental costs resulted in a sharp decline in the use of animal power – a process involving substitution of hand hoeing for animal plowing and harrowing. It is clear that population pressure on the land under a stagnant technology resulted in a decline in the value of human labor relative to the values of both capital and food. In contrast, in North Village the data clearly show the increase in labor demand due to technological progress outpaced the increase in labor supply due to population growth, which meant rising wages despite the effort to substitute capital (animal power) for human labor.

Differences in the wage rates between villages within 30 km of each other appear anomalous. But, from our observations, the labor market is segmented between the coastal and hilly areas. Most of the migrants to North Village, both

Table 5.5: Changes in inputs and input prices for rice production, North Village

	1968-71[a]	1978/79[b]	Percentage change from 1968-71 to 1978/79
Inputs			
Fertilizer (kg/ha)[c]	75	209	179
Labor (hr/ha):			
land preparation	219	233	6 (42)[g]
total (preharvest)	638	701	10 (46)[g]
Carabao and cattle for			
land preparation (days/ha)[d]	9.6	13.2	38 (83)[g]
Real input prices (in paddy)[e]			
Fertilizer (kg/ha)	1.5	1.0	−33
Labor wage (kg/day)[f]	7.9	11.5	46
Carabao rental (kg/day)[d]	8.8	14.1	60

[a] Average for wet and dry seasons
[b] Averages for 1978/79 wet season and 1979 dry season
[c] Urea and TPS
[d] Data for wet season only
[e] Nominal price divided by paddy price
[f] Wage for land preparation, assuming a working day of 8 hours; includes lunch
[g] Number outside parentheses are the rates of increase in labor input per hectare of cropped area; numbers in parentheses are the rates of increase per hectare of paddy-field area

Source: As table 5.3

permanent and seasonal, came from the east along the coast. Not many people in South Village went to work on the coast. This might be due to ethnic differences: most of the people in South Village are Sudanese, whereas many people in North Village are Javanese. Anthropological investigation is needed to clarify this point.

Changes in Factor Shares

How were these differences in technological change reflected in income distribution? Data are not available to identify changes over time in the size distribution of income, but we have made inferences based on changes in the factor shares of income of rice production.

Changes in the average factor shares of rice output per hectare of crop area in South Village from 1968–71 to 1978 were estimated (table 5.6); factor payments are expressed in paddy terms by multiplying factor inputs by factor-product

Table 5.6: Changes in factor payments and factor shares in rice production, South Village

	Factor payment (kg/ha)			Factor share (%)		
		1978[b]			1978[b]	
	1968-71[a]			1968-71		
	Owner	Owner[c]	Tenant[d]	Owner	Owner	Tenant
Rice output	2,600	2,942	3,080	100.0	100.0	100.0
Factor payment[e]						
Current input[f]	380	328	356	14.6	11.1	11.7
Capital[g]	101	90	41	3.9	3.9	1.3
Labor	1,257	1,301	1,341	48.4	44.2	43.5
(family)	(427)[h]	(438)	(476)	(16.4)	(14.9)	(15.4)
(hired)	(830)[h]	(863)	(865)	(31.9)	(29.3)	(28.1)
Land	0	0	1,262	0	0	41.0
Operator's surplus	862	1,223	80	33.1	41.6	2.6

[a] Averages for wet and dry seasons
[b] 1978 dry season
[c] Averages of 74 owner farmers cultivating 20.4 hectares
[d] Averages of 9 tenant operators cultivating 1.8 hectares
[e] Factor payments converted to paddy equivalents by the ratios of factor to output prices
[f] Seeds, fertilizers, chemicals, and irrigation fee
[g] Animal rental for land preparation
[h] Assumes the same composition of family and hired labor as 1978

Source: As table 5.3

price ratios. During the period under consideration, the average yield per hectare increased by a little more than 10 percent. Both the payment to hired labor and the imputed cost of family labor increased very slightly, less than 5 percent. Operator's surplus (the residual) recorded a major increase for owner farmers. For tenant farmers, the operator's surplus was almost zero and the land rent paid to landlords equaled the owner farmer's surplus. Such results clearly show the operator's surplus of owner farmers consisted mainly of the return to their land. Thus, the major gain in owner farmer's surplus implies an increase in the economic rent of land. Altogether, the relative share of labor declined and the relative share of land increased.

What do such estimates imply about the income distribution between farmers and landless laborers? Table 5.7 shows how the income (value added) from rice production per hectare was distributed between farmers and hired laborers. Farmer's income consists of operator's surplus and the returns of family labor and capital. Laborer's income consists of wage earnings from hired farm work.

Table 5.7: Changes in shares of income from rice production, South Village

	Income in paddy (kg/ha)		Income share (%)	
	1968-71	*1978*	*1968-71*	*1978*
Value added[a]	2,220	2,614	100.0	100.0
Farmer:				
family labor	427	438	19.2	16.8
capital	101	90	4.6	3.4
operator's surplus	862	1,223	38.6	46.8
total	1,390	1,751	62.6	67.0
Hired laborer	830	863	37.4	33.0

[a] Output value minus current input cost

Farmer's total income in paddy terms increased by 25 percent between 1968-71 and 1978, whereas laborer's income increased by only 4 percent. Employment of hired labor increased because of more intensive cropping and substitution of human labor for animal power. But the increase was offset, to a large extent, by the decline in the wage rate. On the other hand, farmer's income increased significantly, primarily due to the increase in the return to land captured in the form of operator's surplus. As a result, farmer's income share increased and laborer's share declined. The data clearly suggest the income distribution became more skewed.

It is probable that the size distribution of income between farmers and laborers became more skewed than the data in table 5.7 show. From 1968-71 to 1978, the number of landless and near-landless households increased faster than the number of farmers. Therefore, the share of income per landless household should have declined by a greater extent than the share of income per hectare. It is highly likely that the income per household or per capita from rice production for landless and near-landless households declined in absolute terms, even though the rice income per hectare increased slightly.

We now move to the case of North Village, characterized by dynamic technological progress. Changes in the average factor shares of rice output per hectare in North Village from 1968-71 to 1978 are given in table 5.8. During this period, the average yield per hectare for wet and dry seasons increased by 40 percent. Nonetheless, the relative share of labor stayed almost constant. At the same time, the shares of both current inputs and capital increased. As a result, the share of operator's surplus declined for owner farmers.

In the case of tenant farmers, operator's surplus was almost zero and land rent paid to landlords was equivalent to owner farmer's surplus, implying the operator's surplus of owner farmers consisted mainly of the return to their land.

Table 5.8:   Changes in factor payments and factor shares in rice production, North Village

	Factor payment (kg/ha)			Factor share (%)		
	1968–71[a]	*1978/79*[b]		*1968–71*[a]	*1978/79*[b]	
	Owner	*Owner*	*Tenant*[c]	*Owner*	*Owner*	*Tenant*[c]
Rice output	2,342	3,237	3,272	100.0	100.0	100.0
Factor payment[d]						
Current input[e]	152	296	280	6.5	9.1	8.5
Capital[f]	47	151	154	2.0	4.7	4.7
Labor	947	1,343	1,295	40.4	41.5	39.6
(family)	(117)	(273)	(357)	(5.0)	(8.5)	(10.9)
(hired)	(830)	(1,070)	(938)	(35.4)	(33.0)	(28.7)
Land	0	0	1,495	0	0	45.7
Operator's surplus	1,196	1,447	48	51.1	44.7	1.5

[a] Average for wet and dry seasons
[b] Averages of 1978/79 wet season and 1979 dry season
[c] Data for share tenants
[d] Factor payments converted to paddy equivalents by the ratios of factor to product prices
[e] Seeds, fertilizers, chemicals, and irrigation fee
[f] Animal and tractor rental for land preparation

Source: As table 5.3

Thus, the results in table 5.8 are consistent with the hypothesis that technological progress in this village was biased in a land-saving and capital-using direction and was more or less neutral with respect to the use of labor – a factor-saving bias similar to that of Japan implied in table 5.1.

The data in table 5.8 are rearranged in table 5.9 to show how the income (value added) from rice production per hectare was distributed between farmers and hired laborers. Both groups recorded significant gains in their absolute incomes, while their relative shares remained largely unchanged. Such results contrast with the case of South Village, where the income of laborers did not show a significant increase and their relative-income share declined (see table 5.7).

Conclusions

The comparative analysis of the two West Javanese villages sheds some light on the net effect of technological change on income distribution. In South Village,

Table 5.9: Changes in shares of income from rice production, North Village

	Income in paddy (kg/ha)		Income share (%)	
	1968–71	*1978/79*	*1968–71*	*1978/79*
Value added[a]	2,191	2,903	100.0	100.0
Farmer:				
family labor	117	252	5.3	8.7
capital	47	154	2.1	5.2
operator's surplus	1,197	1,427	54.6	49.2
total	1,361	1,833	62.1	63.1
Hired laborer	830	1,070	37.9	36.9

[a] Output value minus current input costs

population pressure reached its limit long ago, and population growth decelerated, but the labor force continued to increase; technology was stagnant because modern varieties of rice that were effective in the environmental conditions of this specific location were not available; fertilizer application increased not because of new technology, but because of subsidized fertilizer prices. Gains in rice yields were not significant. The increase in the labor force against limited land resources under stagnant technology resulted in a decrease in the economic return to labor; the real wage rate for land preparation declined, inducing the substitution of hand hoeing for animal plowing; and labor's income share declined relative to land's share. The dismal process of growing poverty and inequality in South Village approximates the classical model of Ricardo.

In North Village, the Ricardian force of population pressure was countered by technological progress. Improvement of the irrigation system, together with diffusion of MV, not only increased the average yield per hectare of rice, but also contributed to a dramatic expansion in the area under double cropping; labor demand increased and the real wage rate rose significantly, despite the inflow of migrant laborers and farmers' efforts to substitute animal power for human labor; the relative-income share of labor rose relative to that of land, and the income of hired laborers increased absolutely, if not relatively.

These observations suggest the hypothesis that the technological change based on irrigation, modern varieties of rice and wheat, and fertilizers that has been progressing in South and Southeast Asia, including North Village, is of the same nature as the change in Japan before World War II. Land is the most limiting factor of agricultural production in this region. Essentially, the new technology saves the use of land (prevents its factor share from rising), and to the extent the technological change is land-saving, income inequality between the land-owning and the landless classes does not increase.

In a sense, South Village may be considered a counterfactual simulation of the prewar Japanese economy in the absence of land-saving technological progress in agriculture. If land-saving technologies had not been developed in Japan, agricultural production would have been constrained by the limitation of land. Reduction of the domestic food supply would have adversely affected industrial development, either through increased food prices that necessitated an increase in the nominal wages of industrial workers or through the drain of foreign exchange from large-scale importation of foodstuffs. An inevitable consequence would have been a lower rate of labor absorption in nonagriculture. As in South Village, a decline in the return to labor relative to land would also have been inevitable.

Recognizing the hazard of generalizing from micro case-studies, the results of the village studies presented here, viewed from the historical experience of Japan, suggest a key to high rates of economic growth and more equal distribution of income in densely populated land-scarce economies in South and Southeast Asia is the generation of land-saving technological progress at a rate that can overcome population pressure. Because that population pressure is so much greater than it was in Japan, the necessary technological progress must be much faster than that experienced in Japan.

References

Asian Development Bank (1977), *Rural Asia: Challenge and Opportunity*, New York: Praeger.

Boeke, Julius S. (1953), *Economics and Economic Policy of Dual Societies as Exemplified by Indonesia*, Institute of Pacific Relations.

Cleaver, Harry M. (1972), "The Contradictions of the Green Revolution," *American Economic Review*, 72: 177–88 (May).

Collier, William L., et al. (1974), "Agricultural Technology and Institutional Change in Java," *Food Research Institute Studies*, 13(2): 169–94.

Dalrymple, Dana P. (1978), *Development and Spread of High-yielding Varieties of Wheat and Rice*, Foreign Agricultural Economic Report no. 96, US Department of Agriculture.

Falcon, Walter P. (1970), "The Green Revolution: Generations of Problems," *American Journal of Agricultural Economics*, 52: 698–710 (December).

Frankel, Francine R. (1971), *India's Green Revolution: Economic Gains and Political Costs*, Princeton, NJ: Princeton University Press.

Griffin, Keith (1974), *The Political Economy of Agrarian Change: An Essay on the Green Revolution*, Cambridge, MA: Harvard University Press.

Hayami, Yujiro, and Masao Kikuchi (1981), *Asian Village Economy at the Cross Roads*, Tokyo: University of Tokyo Press, and Baltimore, MD: Johns Hopkins University Press.

Hayami, Yujiro, in association with Masakatsu Akino, Masahiko Shintani, and Saburo Yamada (1975), *A Century of Agricultural Growth in Japan*, St

Paul, MN: University of Minnesota Press, and Tokyo: University of Tokyo Press.

Johnston, Bruce F., and John Cownie (1969), "The Seed–Fertilizer Revolution and Labor Force Absorption," *American Economic Review*, 59: 569–82 (September).

Kikuchi, Masao, Anwar Hafid, Chaerul Saleh, Sri Hartoyo, and Yujiro Hayami (1980a), "Class Differentiation, Labor Employment, and Income Distribution in a West Java Village," *Developing Economies*, 18: 45–64 (March).

Kikuchi, Masao, Abrar Yusuf, Anwar Hafid, and Yujiro Hayami (1980b), *Technological Progress and Income Distribution in a Rice Village in West Java*, IRRI Research Paper Series no. 55, Los Baños, Philippines: International Rice Research Institute.

Malthus, Thomas R. (1976 edn), *An Essay on the Principle of Population*, edited by Philipp Appelman, New York: Norton.

Palmer, Ingrid (1976), *The New Rice in Asia: Conclusions from Four Country Studies*, Geneva: United Nations Research Institute for Social Development.

Ricardo, David (1951 edn), *On the Principle of Political Economy and Taxation*, 3rd edn, edited by Piero Sraffa, Cambridge: Cambridge University Press.

Warriner, Doreen (1973), "Results of Land Reform in Asian and Latin American Countries," *Food Research Institute Studies*, 12(2): 115–38.

Wharton, Clifton R. J. (1969), "The Green Revolution: Cornucopia or Pandora's Box," *Foreign Affairs*, 47(3): 464–76 (April).

Yamada, Saburo and Yujiro Hayami (1979), "Agricultural Growth in Japan, 1880–1970," in Yujiro Hayami, Vernon W. Ruttan, and Herman M. Southworth, eds, *Agricultural Growth in Japan, Taiwan, Korea and the Philippines*, Honolulu: University Press of Hawaii.

6 The Impact of Improved Cassava Technology on Small Farming in Colombia

LE THANH NGHIEP and JOHN K. LYNAM

Agricultural growth in Latin America takes place within a farm-size structure that is highly skewed. Heterogeneity in production units, defined by a large variance in internal factor proportions – especially land and labor – results in substantial heterogeneity in production technologies, crop specialization, and factor productivities across farm-size units. The skewed distribution of land in relation to labor has resulted in the sector-wide underemployment of both of these factors (Berry 1975).

Within a highly skewed land distribution, rapid mechanization of large-scale farms can produce a very rapid treadmill effect, especially for underutilized mobile resources. Thus, very rapid migration from rural to urban areas characterizes Latin American economies, requiring substantial investments in social infrastructure, and in many cases swamping urban employment-generating capacity. With the political weight given to low food prices in urban areas, policies for developing a dynamic large-farm sector will probably continue. However, the downward rigidity of urban wage rates, continuing capital-intensive industrialization, and the large portion of the workforce still in agriculture argue for some moderation in the high potential rate of rural–urban migration, and thus for a labor-intensive small-farm development strategy as a necessary complement.

The feasibility of such a dual agricultural development strategy rests on minimizing competition between large and small farmers, which means crop specialization by farm size. This specialization will be determined by factor intensity in the production process, with small farmers having an obvious comparative advantage in the production of labor-intensive crops. A development strategy for small farms focuses on crops that also have the potential for productivity increases through improvement in technology.

Cassava is a traditional small-farm crop in Latin America, partly because of its moderate to high labor requirements and the difficulty in mechanizing harvesting, and partly due to high marketing risks. Another factor is its adaptability to

110

relatively poor agroclimatic conditions. Small farmers in Latin America are, in general, located in marginal land areas and concentrate on lower-value commodities adapted to such areas. Cassava is produced in the more marginal of these marginal zones, areas with relatively low rainfall or particularly severe soil constraints. Increasing productivity and expanding the area planted to cassava could increase the returns to both labor and land resources that are currently underutilized, given the important caveat that demand is sufficiently expansive and price elasticity is sufficiently elastic.[1]

Given cassava's high perishability after harvest and its low value to bulk ratio, the markets for its traditional use (human consumption in fresh form) are geographically relatively unintegrated and easily saturated. However, cassava has several potential alternative uses and, given price competitiveness with substitutes, could enter starch, animal feed, or, more recently, fuel alcohol, and feedstock markets. These are sufficiently elastic markets to guarantee significant demand for increased production, but the price levels necessary to be competitive are lower than the prices for current uses, and appear to be less than costs at current productivity levels. Access to these markets will necessarily require cost-reducing production technology. Thus, development of cassava would not only be directed at small-scale farmers and at marginal agroclimatic zones, but it would also be associated with the development of industrial markets.

Technical change in cassava will involve two principal components. First, traditional cassava-farming systems maintain soil fertility through a fallow system. Fallowing obviously creates a strong land constraint in a small-farming system. Substitution of fertilizer for fallow could release this constraint. Secondly, current yield-levels tend to be low in comparison to experimental yields – 6–8 tons per hectare, as compared to consistent experimental yields of 50–60 tons (CIAT 1979) – and much of this yield-gap is ascribed to differences in the genetic yield-potential of the varieties.

This essay presents an attempt to specify the impact that new cassava varieties would have on cropping patterns, farm incomes, factor shares, and the supply of

---

[1] Cassava, also known as manioc, tapioca, yucca, or mandicoca, is the principal, starchy root crop grown in the tropics. Originating from South and Central America, the crop was distributed to Africa and Asia shortly after the discovery of the New World, and is now a major food source for an estimated 300 million people. All cassava roots contain toxic prussic acid, but in varying amounts. Those varieties with low amounts, so-called sweet cultivars, are usually consumed by just peeling and boiling. The bitter varieties must be processed into such forms as roasted flour before being eaten, for example, *farinha de mandioca* in Brazil or *gari* in West Africa, fermented pastes such as *fufu* in West Africa, or griddle cakes such as *casabe* in the Caribbean. Processing the roots is also important because the roots deteriorate rapidly after harvest.

More recently, cassava has been increasingly utilized in non-food uses. Cassava starch, cassava pellets for animal feeds, and fuel alcohol derived from cassava have been the most important alternative markets. The crop's high carbohydrate-yields under a broad range of rainfall and soil conditions, and its multiple uses, give cassava substantial unexploited potential in the agricultural economies of tropical countries.

food and farm products for industrial use, with a special focus on the farm-size dimension of these. A simple linear-programming model is used, in which a representative farmer is assumed to maximize agricultural income through allocating family labor and land among different crops. The effects of improved cassava technology are derived by comparing the linear-programming solutions with and without the new technology. In the case of the traditional technology, technical coefficients of cassava varieties and alternative crops, and market constraints are based on farm-survey data in Media Luna, Colombia, a region where cassava dominates. Yield, labor input, and fertilizer input per hectare for the improved technology are synthesized from diverse interim results of the cassava program at CIAT (Centro Internacional de Agricultura Tropical), in Cali, Colombia. Findings for this cassava case from Colombia are compared to those for Japanese sericulture obtained in a study by Nghiep and Hayami (1979).

Cultivation Patterns

The Media Luna area produces three market crops: cassava, maize, and sesame. Cassava can be divided into early cassava monoculture, late cassave monoculture, and cassava–maize association. Sesame is a monoculture crop, and maize is principally cultivated in association with cassava. On average, in terms of culti-vated area, the proportion of cassava–maize association, monoculture cassava, and sesame is 4:1:1. The rainy season is May through November, with peaks in May–June and September–November. The crop year can be divided thus: May–June, July–November, and December–April. Late monoculture cassava is planted in July–November and must remain a year before it can be harvested. Early cassava, monoculture or in association with maize, is planted in May–June and the harvest can begin in December. Maize in the cassava–maize association is cultivated and harvested within the July–November period. Sesame is a three-month crop planted in August–September and harvested by November. The prices, production costs, and labor input per hectare of these crop activities are presented in tables 6.1 and 6.2.

Cassava has no well-defined harvest period; farmers dig it up when they have access to a market. Cassava can be left in the ground almost a year after maturity. Yields of cassava left unharvested remain constant through June and then, due to the effect of rain, increase. The marketing aspect is complicated by the existence of two markets: an urban market for direct human consumption of fresh cassava, and an industrial market for the starch content. There is a discount for the starch market, and cassava sold fresh is subject to quantity and high-quality constraints. The share of cassava going to the fresh market is 37 percent in December–April, 23 percent in May–June, and 12 percent in July–November. Maize and sesame are not subject to such market constraints.

As in other regions of Colombia, the present cassava cropping in Media Luna requires fallowing to maintain soil fertility. In Media Luna, cassava typically is

Table 6.1: Labor requirements for different crops at Media Luna, Colombia (days/ha)

Period	Activity	Cassava–maize association	Cassava monoculture		Sesame
			Early planting	Late planting	
May–June	Planting	8.0	5.5	–	–
	First weeding	14.4	13.0	–	–
	Second weeding	14.5	14.5	–	–
July–November	Planting	–	–	5.5	3.0
	Weeding	11.4	12.3	13.0	14.0
	Weeding	2.2	2.2	14.5	–
	Maize–sesame harvest	4.0	–	–	12.0
	Cassava harvest (following year)	–	–	16.0	–
December–April	Cassava harvest	16.0	16.0	–	–
	Total	70.5	63.5	49	29

Source: Our sample survey at Media Luna

Table 6.2: Prices of activities: existing cassava technology

| | Cassava–maize association | | | | | | |
| | December–April | | May–June | | July–November | | Sesame |
	Fresh market	Industrial market	Fresh market	Industrial market	Fresh market	Industrial market	
Price of maize ($/kg)	5.0	5.0	5.0	5.0	5.0	5.0	—
Yield of maize (kg/ha)	610	610	610	610	610	610	—
Production value of maize (kg/ha)	3,050	3,050	3,050	3,050	3,050	3,050	—
Price of cassava or sesame ($/kg)	2.7	1.7	2.7	1.7	3.5	1.7	14.0
Yield of cassava or sesame (kg/ha)	7,600	7,600	7,600	7,600	9,200	9,200	550
Production value of cassava or sesame ($/ha)	20,520	12,920	20,520	12,920	32,200	15,640	7,700
Total production value ($/ha)	23,570	15,970	23,570	15,970	35,250	18,690	7,700
Capital cost ($/ha)	1,500	1,500	1,500	1,500	1,500	1,500	1,500
Purchased current inputs ($/ha)	87	87	87	87	87	87	268
(seed)	(87)	(87)	(87)	(87)	(87)	(87)	(268)
(fertilizers)	(0)	(0)	(0)	(0)	(0)	(0)	(0)
Total production cost ($/ha)	1,587	1,587	1,587	1,587	1,587	1,587	1,587
Value added ($/ha)	21,983	14,383	21,983	14,383	33,663	17,103	5,932

Source: Our sample survey at Media Luna

sown for three or four consecutive years, with a fallow of two and a half to three years. Fallow is necessary when using existing varieties and no fertilizers – surveys show the number of years in fallow gives an almost exact ordering of yields (CIAT 1980). Fertility-maintenance ability is dependent on the amount of available land, with small farmers having a short fallow period and thus lower yields. Fertilizer-responsive, high-yielding cassava would be profitable to growers; and the profits are expected to be higher to small-scale farmers.

The cropping of cassava is relatively labor-using. As shown in table 6.1, the number of labor days required for one hectare of cassava is 70.5 per year, 2.5 times that of sesame. Allowing for the fallow period (4 years cassava, 3 years fallow), the effective labor requirement is 40.3 days per hectare, 1.4 times that of sesame. This difference in labor-absorbing capacity between the two crops provides an indication why cassava is dominant on small-scale farms with high labor–land ratios. Farm sizes in the area vary from 2 to 10 hectares, with a mode of 5. Usually women do not work in the fields and older children only occasionally do so. Thus, 1.5–2 workers are available per family. Land preparation is carried out by hired tractor. The cost of land preparation, plus the cost of maize seed and sesame seed, are more than 90 percent of farmers' expenditure for purchased inputs.

Improved Cassava Technology

The CIAT cassava program began in 1972. Given the limited prior research and the fact seven years was needed to develop a hybrid, there is not yet a technology assuring high, stable yields over a large area. For our discussion here, we therefore assume a variety with synthesized properties, based on the data from various physiological, varietal, agronomic, and economic research work done at the Center. CIAT has tested an early hybrid line in Media Luna. In the first year of the trials, the hybrid doubled the yield of the traditional local variety, Secundina, over a wide range of management conditions (CIAT 1981). Although in the second year much of the yield advantage was lost due to susceptibility to root-rot diseases, the physiological yield-gain due to breeding was demonstrated even by this very early hybrid line.

The role of fallowing in cassava cropping systems is multi-faceted. Besides recycling leached nutrients from lower layers of soil, fallowing also plays an important role in conserving organic matter, in controlling erosion, and apparently in maintaining effective mycorrhiza populations.[2] The ability of fertilizer to substitute completely for fallow depends very much on soil type and slope. While on phosphorus-deficient oxisols and ultisols, fertilizer is not a complete

[2] Mycorrhiza are fungi which are indigenous in the soil and which form a symbiotic association with plant roots. After root infection, hyphae are produced which enter the soil and which are particularly effective at translocating phosphorus. Because cassava has a particularly inefficient root system, an effective mycorrhiza association is essential for adequate nutrient uptake.

substitute for fallow, on the flat, sandy soils of Media Luna a single year of trials showed fertilizer on unfallowed land could raise yields to those obtained under fallow conditions (CIAT 1982). Moreover, where fertilizer-responsive varieties are used, there are apparently larger yield gains in the substitution process.

The new cassava variety is thus assumed to have yields of twice the traditional variety, Secundina, at the farm level. Yields are maintained by fertilizer application, thereby releasing fallow land; fertilizer cost is assumed to be half of the increased production value. As with Secundina, the new variety is cultivated in association with maize and with similar labor and capital requirements. Cassava roots of this new variety are of lower quality, and thus are more for industrial use; sales in the fresh markets are half of those of the traditional variety. Yields, labor requirements, capital cost, prices, and values added assumed for the hypothesized cassava variety are given in table 6.3.

The Linear-Programming Model

The problems of how the technology just described affects farm incomes, in which directions change in cropping pattern and factor shares can be expected, and how the mix between direct human consumption and industrial use shifts are illustrated by a linear-programming (LP) model of a representative farm. The owner is assumed to have family labor and land, and to maximize income through allocating these factors to the production of cassava, maize, and sesame under market constraints. The two cassava technologies are assumed to differ from each other in yield, fallow period, and fertilizer requirement. These are incorporated in the model with varying prices and land coefficients. For simplification, monoculture cassava – only 15 percent of the total cassava area in the region – is omitted.

The model covers three cropping years. The existence of two markets and three harvest periods means six cassava-maize activities each year. Consequently, the model has 21 activities, one objective function, nine labor constraints, nine land constraints, and nine market constraints. The model is given in table 6.4.

The presence of a (fallow) in the land coefficients of the cassava–maize association is the key element of the model. A positive value implies using fallow to maintain soil fertility. For the improved cassava technology, a zero value is assigned to a to incorporate the assumption that fertilizers substitute for fallow.

Market constraints are presented by nine exact equations instead of the usual inequalities. The reasons for this treatment are as follows. The farmer wants to sell as much of the cassava as possible to the fresh market when the price is high, but the proportion of suitably high-quality roots in total production and access to the fresh market are limited. Thus, there is an upper bound to the quantity sold on the fresh market in each period of the year. On the other hand, we want to know if the hypothesized technology can shift the supply of farm products

Table 6.3: Price of activities: hypothesized cassava technology

| | Cassava-maize association | | | | | | |
| | December–April | | May–June | | July–November | | Sesame |
	Fresh market	Industrial market	Fresh market	Industrial market	Fresh market	Industrial market	
Price of maize ($/kg)	5.0	5.0	5.0	5.0	5.0	5.0	—
Yield of maize (kg/ha)	610	610	610	610	610	610	—
Production value of maize (kg/ha)	3,050	3,050	3,050	3,050	3,050	3,050	—
Price of cassava or sesame ($/kg)	2.7	1.7	2.7	1.7	3.5	1.7	14.0
Yield of cassava or sesame (kg/ha)	15,200	15,200	15,200	15,200	18,400	18,400	550
Production value of cassava or sesame ($/ha)	41,040	25,840	41,040	25,840	64,400	31,280	7,700
Total production value ($/ha)	44,090	28,890	44,090	28,890	67,450	34,330	7,700
Capital cost ($/ha)	1,500	1,500	1,500	1,500	1,500	1,500	1,500
Purchased current inputs ($/ha)	6,547	6,547	6,547	6,547	6,547	6,547	268
(seed)	(87)	(87)	(87)	(87)	(87)	(87)	(268)
(fertilizers)	(6,460)	(6,460)	(6,460)	(6,460)	(6,460)	(6,460)	(0)
Total production cost ($/ha)	8,047	8,047	8,047	8,047	8,047	8,047	1,768
Value added ($/ha)	36,043	20,843	36,043	20,843	59,403	26,283	5,932

Table 6.4:   The linear-programming model

Objective function

$$(1) \quad Z = \sum_{i=1}^{3} \left(\sum_{j=1}^{3} \sum_{k=1}^{2} x_{ijk} PC_{jk} + y_i PS \right)$$

Labor constraints

$$(2) \quad \sum_{j=1}^{3} \sum_{k=1}^{2} x_{ijk} b_1 + \sum_{k=1}^{2} x_{i-11k} b_3 \leqslant L_1 \qquad\qquad (i = 1, 2, 3)$$

$$(3) \quad \sum_{j=1}^{3} \sum_{k=1}^{2} x_{ijk} b_2 + \sum_{k=1}^{2} x_{i-12k} b_3 + y_i b_4 \leqslant L_2 \qquad\qquad (i = 1, 2, 3)$$

$$(4) \quad \sum_{k=1}^{2} x_{i3k} b_3 \leqslant L_3 \qquad\qquad (i = 1, 2, 3)$$

Land constraints

$$(5) \quad \sum_{j=1}^{3} \sum_{k=1}^{2} x_{ijk} (1 + a) + \sum_{j=2}^{2} \sum_{k=1}^{2} x_{i-1jk} (1 + a) \leqslant A \qquad\qquad (i = 1, 2, 3)$$

$$(6) \quad \sum_{j=1}^{3} \sum_{k=1}^{2} x_{ijk} (1 + a) + y_i \leqslant A \qquad\qquad (i = 1, 2, 3)$$

$$(7) \quad \sum_{j=1}^{2} \sum_{k=1}^{2} x_{ijk} (1 + a) \leqslant A \qquad\qquad (i = 1, 2, 3)$$

Market constraints

$$(8) \quad d_j x_{ij1} - c_j \sum_{j=1}^{3} \sum_{k=1}^{2} d_j x_{ijk} = 0 \qquad\qquad (i = 1, 2, 3; j = 1, 2, 3)$$

Definitions

Market 1	fresh cassava
Market 2	industrial cassava
Period 1	May–June (2 months)
Period 2	July–November (5 months)
Period 3	December–April (5 months)
x_{ijk}	area (ha) of cassava–maize association with cassava being cultivated in year i, harvested in period j, and sold in market k
y_i	area (ha) of sesame cultivated, harvested and sold in year i
PC_{jk}	value added per hectare ($/ha) obtained from the cassava–maize association, with cassava being harvested in period j and sold in market k

Table 6.4   continued

PS	value added per hectare ($/ha) of sesame
L_j	labor-days available in period j
A	total land area
a	fallow input per hectare of cassava's cultivated area (ha/ha)
b_1	per hectare labor input of the cassava–maize association in period 1 (days/ha)
b_2	per hectare labor input of the cassava–maize association in period 2 (days/ha)
b_3	per hectare labor input of the cassava–maize association for cassava harvest
b_4	per hectare labor input (days/ha) of sesame in period 2
c_j	share of cassava sold to fresh market in period j in total cassava production of the year
d_j	yield (tonne/ha) of cassava harvested in period j

for industrial use upward without causing a decline in food supply. Thus, it is necessary to set a lower limit to the quantity available for direct human consumption.

In the case of the existing technology, c_j represents the actual fresh-market shares of cassava in Media Luna. For the hypothesized technology, halves of these shares are used. Improved cassava varieties are considered less tasty, which is reflected in this model by the smaller percentage of fresh cassava. Because higher yields are assumed, smaller fresh-market shares are also necessary to keep the supply of fresh cassava at a level that can be absorbed. Technical coefficients of the LP model are given in appendix tables 6.A1 and 6.A2.

Implications of Improved Cassava Technology

The income-maximizing solutions of the LP model for the traditional and improved technologies, assuming 40 labor-days a month and 5 hectares of land, are shown in tables 6.5–6.7. Changes in cropping pattern and farm incomes at different levels of labor endowment are given in table 6.8. The optimal planted areas of cassava–maize and sesame differ slightly in each year in the three-year cropping period, but all solution sets show a clear tendency towards stable cropping patterns. Data presented in the tables are for the third year.

Impact on Cropping Pattern

The LP solutions assuming 40 days of labor a month show adoption of the improved technology almost maintains the cultivated area of the cassava–maize association at the previous level; most released fallow land is allocated to the production of sesame. Specifically, the cultivated area in cassava–maize association increases slightly, from 1.96 hectares in the traditional case to 2.05 for the improved cassava, while the area of sesame almost doubles, from 1.57 to 2.95 hectares.

Table 6.5: LP solution: traditional cassava technology[a]

	Area (ha)	Value added ($) Per ha	Value added ($) Total	Production (kg) Per ha	Production (kg) Total	Marginal value product Land ($/ha/year)	Marginal value product Labor ($/day/year)
Cassava	1.95979		43,151.8		16,005	0	1,078.8
Fresh market	1.47442		34,850.5		11,540	0	871.3
December–April	0.77919	21,983	17,128.9	7,600	5,922	0	428.2
May–June	0.48547	21,983	10,694.1	7,600	3,697	0	267.4
July–November	0.20876	33,663	7,027.5	9,200	1,921	0	175.7
Industrial market	0.48537		8,301.3		4,465	0	207.5
December–April	0	14,383	0	7,600	0	0	0
May–June	0	14,383	0	7,600	0	0	0
July–November	0.48537	17,103	8,301.3	9,200	4,465	0	207.5
Maize	(1.95979)			610	1,195	0	
Sesame	1.57037	5,932	9,315.4	550	864	5,932	−508.6
Fallow	1.46984						
Total	5		52,467.2			5,932	570.2

Values added of maize are included in those of cassava

[a] Assuming a total of 40 labor-days per month and 5 hectares of land

Table 6.6: LP solution: improved cassava technology[a]

	Area (ha)	Value added ($)		Production (kg)		Marginal value product	
		Per ha	Total	Per ha	Total	Land ($/ha/year)	Labor ($/day/year)
Cassava	2.05145		64,601		35,501	0	1,615.0
Fresh market	0.81760		32,172		12,798	0	804.3
December–April	0.43208	36,043	15,573	15,200	6,568	0	389.3
May–June	0.26976	36,043	9,723	15,200	4,100	0	243.1
July–November	0.11576	59,403	6,876	18,400	2,130	0	171.9
Industrial market	1.23385		32,429		22,703	0	810.7
December–April	0	20,843	0	15,200	0	0	0
May–June	0	20,843	0	15,200	0	0	0
July–November	1.23385	26,283	32,429	18,400	22,703	0	810.7
Maize	(2.05145)			610	1,251	0	
Sesame	2.94855	5,932	17,491	550	1,622	5,932	−304.2
Fallow	0					0	
Total	5		82,092			5,932	1,310.8

Values added of maize are included in those of cassava

[a] Assuming a total of 40 labor-days per month and 5 hectares of land

Table 6.7: Impacts of cassava technology on factor shares[a]

	Traditional technology			Improved technology		
	Marginal value product ($)	Imputed factor cost ($)	Factor share (%)	Marginal value product ($)	Imputed factor cost ($)	Factor share (%)
Labor	570.2	22,808	39.1	1,310.8	52,432	50.5
Land	5,932	29,660	50.8	5,932.0	29,660	28.6
Current inputs[b]	—	591	1.0	—	14,220	13.7
Capital[c]	—	5,295	9.1	—	7,500	7.2

[a] Assuming a total of 40 labor-days per month and 5 hectares of land
[b] Including sesame seed, maize seed, and fertilizer
[c] Tractor rents for land preparation

Table 6.8: Labor endowment and income changes[a]

Labor	Income ($)		Income change	
(days/month)	Traditional technology	Improved technology	Dollars	Percentage
10	19,132.6	23,431.2	4,298.6	22.5
20	38,265.2	46,862.4	8,597.2	22.5
30	39,350.4	61,569.0	2,218.6	56.5
40	52,467.2	82,092.0	29,624.8	56.5
50	65,584.0	102,615.0	37,031.0	56.5
60	69,884.7	123,138.0	53,253.3	76.2
70	69,884.7	143,661.0	73,776.3	105.6

[a] Assuming 5 hectares of land

Interesting changes in the cropping pattern are also observed, when the LP solutions for different levels of labor endowment are compared. With the traditional cassava technology, increases in labor up to 22 labor-days a month result in a land surplus, and both cassava–maize and sesame increase in area. Then the two begin to compete for land, and cassava–maize increases at the expense of sesame area. At about 52 labor-days a month, labor becomes redundant. Thus, in the traditional cropping system, the larger the labor–land ratio, the more farmers cultivate cassava, even though cassava requires a substantial portion of land for fallow.

Because the cassava cropping system no longer requires a fallow period, the land constraint is less restrictive for the improved technology. Unused land disappears and the area of sesame reaches its peak at a larger amount of labor. After the labor endowment exceeds 28 days a month, the area of sesame declines, but at a slower pace than before. Labor becomes redundant at 92 days a month.

Impact on Labor Productivity

The improved cassava technology is labor-using. This can be demonstrated through comparisons of the marginal productivities of labor and the labor-absorption ability of the two alternative technologies. The LP solutions at 40 labor-days a month indicate the marginal productivity of labor increases by 30 percent if the improved variety is adopted, and the marginal productivity of land remains virtually unchanged (tables 6.5 and 6.6). The utilization of family labor increases from 38 to 52 percent of available time. Consequently, the marginal productivity curve of labor shifts upward and the maximum labor requirement for 5 hectares reaches 92 days a month.

Impact on Factor Shares

Table 6.7 shows the factor shares of the two alternative technologies. The imputed factor costs of labor and land are the products of the marginal productivities available from the LP solutions and the levels of labor and land inputs. Current input costs indicate expenditures for sesame seed, maize seed, and – in the improved cassava case – fertilizers for cassava. Capital costs are rents paid for tractors used in land preparation. As expected, the shares of current inputs and labor increase, while that of land decreases. The improved cassava technology results in raising the functional share of labor. Expected benefits from this type of technology are thus larger for small farming, where labor is relatively abundant. Table 6.8 shows the larger the amount of available labor, the higher the projected increase in agricultural incomes in both pesos and labor share.

Impact on Cassava Supply

Supplying sufficient food and producing raw materials for industrial use are the major roles of agriculture, if a country is to achieve sustained high rates of economic growth. It is thus critical that the improved cassava technology is consistent with these roles. In the Colombian economy, fresh cassava and maize are used mainly for human consumption, industrial cassava is for processing into animal feed and starch, and sesame is for vegetable oil and oilcake. Comparisons of the LP solutions indicate that both the food supply and the production of farm products for industrial use can be improved. For foodstuffs, the supply of fresh cassava and maize increase slightly, from 11.5 tons and 1.2 tons to 12.8 and 1.25, respectively. At the same time, the quantity of industrial cassava increases fivefold from 4.5 to 22.7 tons, and that of sesame almost doubles. Thus, cassava technologies of the type assumed increase both foodstuffs and industrial raw materials, thereby making food supply and raw-material supply less competitive with each other for resources.

Comparison to Japanese Sericulture and Conclusions

Nghiep and Hayami's study (1979) of the summer–fall raising technology for sericulture in Japan provides findings comparable to those for cassava. Traditionally in Japan, spring was the period of cocoon culture, and this coincided with the peak labor requirement for rice. Summer–fall raising enabled cocoon culture in months of slack labor, between rice planting and harvesting. Two major contributions of the technology to the Japanese economy were identified. First, it increased the labor-absorption capacity of a given land area and, therefore, sericulture was carried out in the framework of small-scale family farming. Second, the dramatic increase in silk production, which was the major source of Japan's foreign-currency earnings in the prewar period, did not impinge on rice production.

The cassava case dealt with in this chapter is technically different from Japanese sericulture, but has similar implications. In the cassava case, an improved variety and fertilization are expected to release fallow land; in the sericulture case, technical progress occurred in the method of storing silkworm eggs, which enabled production in the slack labor period in the summer and fall. Two sorts of changes were observed in Japan: more intensive land use (double cropping), and a more even distribution of family labor throughout the year. In the case of the hypothesized cassava technology, the main effects also were more effective use of available land, followed by an increase in labor demand in what was a labor-surplus area.

The agricultural economies of Japan and other Asian countries are characterized by a homogeneous farm-size distribution and by relatively small-scale farms. Thus, land-saving and labor-using technologies, like summer–fall sericulture, are appropriate for most farming units. In Latin American countries, the wide range of farm sizes argues for a dual agricultural-development strategy, with quite separate agricultural technologies for large-scale and small-scale farms.

There is thus a role for Asian development experience within a Latin American environment, but in a limited context. The improved cassava technology would have an impact on small-scale agriculture in Colombia and other tropical Latin American countries, similar to that of summer–fall sericulture in Japan. The cassava technology weakens the land constraint and brings about increases in labor productivity and farm incomes. By such means not only are the high rates of out-migration from the agricultural sector potentially reduced, but there is also an increase in food supplies (fresh cassava and maize) and industrial raw materials (low-quality cassava and sesame). Although the demand for land-augmenting and labor-using technology arises in Asia from the constraints on available land and in Latin America from the very skewed distribution of land resources, the very real impact of such technologies on agricultural development warrants further research on identifying small-farm technologies.

References

Berry, R. Albert (1975), "Special Problems of Policy Making in Technologically Heterogeneous Agriculture: Colombia," in Lloyd G. Reynolds, ed., *Agriculture in Development Theory*, New Haven, CT: Yale University Press.

CIAT (Centro Internacional de Agricultura Tropical) (1979–82), *Cassava Program Annual Report*, Cali, Colombia: CIAT.

Nghiep, Le Tranh, and Yujiro Hayami (1979), "Mobilizing Slack Resources for Economic Development: the summer–fall rearing technology of sericulture in Japan," *Explorations in Economic History*, 16: 163–81.

Table 6.A1: LP coefficients: existing cassava technology

Row					Variables					
	1	2	3	4	5	6	7	8	9	10
0	21,983	14,383	21,983	14,383	33,663	17,103	21,983	14,383	21,983	14,383
1	36.9	36.9	36.9	36.9	36.9	36.9	0	0	0	0
2	17.6	17.6	17.6	17.6	17.6	17.6	0	0	0	0
3	16.0	16.0	0	0	0	0	0	0	0	0
4	0	0	16.0	16.0	0	0	36.9	36.9	36.9	36.9
5	0	0	0	0	16.0	16.0	17.6	17.6	17.6	17.6
6	0	0	0	0	0	0	16.0	16.0	16.0	16.0
7	0	0	0	0	0	0	0	0	16.0	16.0
8	0	0	0	0	0	0	0	0	0	0
9	0	0	0	0	0	0	0	0	0	0
10	1.75	1.75	1.75	1.75	1.75	1.75	0	0	0	0
11	1.75	1.75	1.75	1.75	1.75	1.75	0	0	0	0
12	0	0	1.75	1.75	1.75	1.75	0	0	0	0
13	0	0	0	0	1.75	1.75	0	0	0	0
14	0	0	0	0	0	0	1.75	1.75	1.75	1.75
15	0	0	0	0	0	0	0	0	1.75	1.75
16	0	0	0	0	0	0	0	0	0	0
17	0	0	0	0	0	0	0	0	0	0
18	0	0	0	0	0	0	0	0	0	0
19	4.788	-2.812	-2.812	-2.812	-3.404	-3.404	4.788	-2.812	-2.812	-2.812
20	-1.7556	-1.7556	-5.8444	-1.7556	-2.1552	-2.1552	0	0	0	0
21	-0.912	-0.912	-0.912	-0.912	8.096	-1.104	0	0	0	0
22	0	0	0	0	0	0	4.788	-2.812	-2.812	-2.812

	11	12	13	14	15	16	17	18	19	20	21
23	0	0	0	0	0	0	−1.7556	−1.7556	5.8444	−1.7556	−1.7556
24	0	0	0	0	0	0	−0.912	−0.912	−0.912	0	0
25	0	0	0	0	0	0	0	0	0	0	0
26	0	0	0	0	0	0	0	0	0	0	0
27	0	0	0	0	0	0	0	0	0	0	0

| | | | | | *Variables* | | | | | | |
Row	11	12	13	14	15	16	17	18	19	20	21
0	33,663	17,103	21,983	14,383	21,983	14,383	33,663	17,103	5,932	5,932	5,932
1	0	0	0	0	0	0	0	0	0	0	0
2	0	0	0	0	0	0	0	0	29.0	0	0
3	0	0	0	0	0	0	0	0	0	0	0
4	36.9	36.9	0	0	0	0	0	0	0	0	0
5	17.6	17.6	0	0	0	0	0	0	0	29.0	0
6	0	0	0	0	0	0	0	0	0	0	0
7	0	0	36.9	36.9	36.9	36.9	36.9	36.9	0	0	0
8	16.0	16.0	17.6	17.6	17.6	17.6	17.6	17.6	0	0	29.0
9	0	0	16.0	16.0	0	0	0	0	0	0	0
10	0	0	0	0	0	0	0	0	0	0	0
11	0	0	0	0	0	0	0	0	1.0	0	0
12	0	0	0	0	0	0	0	0	0	0	0
13	1.75	1.75	1.75	1.75	1.75	1.75	1.75	1.75	0	0	0
14	1.75	1.75	1.75	1.75	1.75	1.75	1.75	1.75	0	1.0	0
15	1.75	1.75	0	0	0	0	0	0	0	0	0
16	1.75	1.75	1.75	1.75	1.75	1.75	1.75	1.75	0	0	0
17	0	0	1.75	1.75	1.75	1.75	1.75	1.75	0	0	0
18	0	0	0	0	1.75	1.75	1.75	1.75	0	0	0

Table 6.A1   continued

	Variables										
Row	11	12	13	14	15	16	17	18	19	20	21
19	0	0	0	0	0	0	0	0	0	0	0
20	0	0	0	0	0	0	0	0	0	0	0
21	0	0	0	0	0	0	0	0	0	0	0
22	−3.404	−3.404	0	0	0	0	0	0	0	0	0
23	−2.1552	−2.1552	0	0	0	0	0	0	0	0	0
24	8.096	−1.104	0	0	0	0	0	0	0	0	0
25	0	0	4.788	−2.812	−2.812	−2.812	−3.404	−3.404	0	0	0
26	0	0	−1.7556	−1.7556	5.8444	−1.7556	−2.1552	−2.1552	0	0	0
27	0	0	−0.912	−0.912	−0.912	−0.912	8.096	−1.104	0	0	0

Var. 1: x_{131} Var. 7: x_{231} Var. 12: x_{222} Var. 17: x_{321}
Var. 2: x_{132} Var. 8: x_{232} Var. 13: x_{331} Var. 18: x_{322}
Var. 3: x_{111} Var. 9: x_{211} Var. 14: x_{332} Var. 19: y_1
Var. 4: x_{112} Var. 10: x_{212} Var. 15: x_{311} Var. 20: y_2
Var. 5: x_{121} Var. 11: x_{221} Var. 16: x_{312} Var. 21: y_3
Var. 6: x_{122}

Row 0:   Objective function
Rows 1–9: Labor constraints

Rows 10–18: Land constraints
Rows 19–27: Market constraints

Table 6.A2: **LP** coefficients: hypothesized cassava technology

Row	Variables									
	1	*2*	*3*	*4*	*5*	*6*	*7*	*8*	*9*	*10*
0	36,043	20,843	36,043	20,843	59,403	26,283	36,043	20,843	36,043	20,843
1	36.9	36.9	36.9	36.9	36.9	36.9	0	0	0	0
2	17.6	17.6	17.6	17.6	17.6	17.6	0	0	0	0
3	16.0	16.0	0	0	0	0	0	0	0	0
4	0	0	16.0	16.0	0	0	36.9	36.9	36.9	36.9
5	0	0	0	0	16.0	16.0	17.6	17.6	17.6	17.6
6	0	0	0	0	0	0	16.0	16.0	0	0
7	0	0	0	0	0	0	0	0	16.0	16.0
8	0	0	0	0	0	0	0	0	0	0
9	0	0	0	0	0	0	0	0	0	0
10	1.0	1.0	1.0	1.0	1.0	1.0	0	0	0	0
11	1.0	1.0	1.0	1.0	1.0	1.0	0	0	0	0
12	0	0	1.0	1.0	1.0	1.0	0	0	0	0
13	0	0	0	0	1.0	1.0	1.0	1.0	1.0	1.0
14	0	0	0	0	0	0	1.0	1.0	1.0	1.0
15	0	0	0	0	0	0	0	0	1.0	1.0
16	0	0	0	0	0	0	0	0	0	0
17	0	0	0	0	0	0	0	0	0	0
18	0	0	0	0	0	0	0	0	0	0
19	12.388	-2.812	-2.812	-2.812	-3.404	-3.404	0	0	0	0
20	-1.7556	-1.7556	13.444	-1.7556	-2.1552	-2.1552	0	0	0	0
21	-0.912	-0.912	-0.912	-0.912	17.296	-1.104	0	0	0	0
22	0	0	0	0	0	0	12.388	-2.812	-2.812	-2.812

Table 6.A2   continued

| | Variables | | | | | | | | | |
Row	1	2	3	4	5	6	7	8	9	10
23	0	0	0	0	0	0	-1.7556	-1.7556	13.444	-1.7556
24	0	0	0	0	0	0	-0.912	-0.912	-0.912	-0.912
25	0	0	0	0	0	0	0	0	0	0
26	0	0	0	0	0	0	0	0	0	0
27	0	0	0	0	0	0	0	0	0	0

| | Variables | | | | | | | | | | |
Row	11	12	13	14	15	16	17	18	19	20	21
0	59,403	26,283	36,043	20,743	36,043	20,843	59,403	26,283	5,932	5,932	5,932
1	0	0	0	0	0	0	0	0	0	0	0
2	0	0	0	0	0	0	0	0	29.0	0	0
3	0	0	0	0	0	0	0	0	0	0	0
4	36.9	36.9	0	0	0	0	0	0	0	0	0
5	17.6	17.6	0	0	0	0	0	0	0	29.0	0
6	0	0	0	0	0	0	0	0	0	0	0
7	0	0	36.9	36.9	36.9	36.9	36.9	36.9	0	0	0
8	16.0	16.0	17.6	17.6	17.6	17.6	17.6	17.6	0	0	29.0
9	0	0	16.0	16.0	0	0	0	0	0	0	0
10	0	0	0	0	0	0	0	0	0	0	0
11	0	0	0	0	0	0	0	0	1.0	0	0
12	0	0	0	0	0	0	0	0	0	0	0
13	1.0	1.0	0	0	0	0	0	0	0	0	0

Row											
14	1.0	1.0	0	0	0	0	0	0	0	0	0
15	1.0	1.0	0	0	0	0	0	0	0	1.0	0
16	1.0	1.0	1.0	1.0	1.0	0	0	0	0	0	1.0
17	0	0	1.0	1.0	1.0	0	0	0	0	0	0
18	0	0	1.0	1.0	1.0	0	0	0	0	0	0
19	0	0	0	0	0	0	0	0	0	0	0
20	0	0	0	0	0	0	0	0	0	0	0
21	0	0	0	0	0	0	0	0	0	0	0
22	-3.404	-3.404	0	0	0	-2.812	-2.812	-2.812	-3.404	-3.404	0
23	-2.1552	-2.1552	0	0	0	-1.7556	-1.7556	-1.7556	-2.1552	-2.1552	0
24	17.296	-1.104	0	0	0	-0.912	17.296	-0.912	-3.404	-1.104	0
25	0	0	12.388	-2.812	-2.812	-3.404	-3.404				
26	0	0	-1.7556	13.444	-1.7556	-2.1552	-2.1552				
27	0	0	-0.912	-0.912	-0.912	17.296	-1.104				

Var. 1: x_{131} Var. 7: x_{231} Var. 12: x_{222} Var. 17: x_{321}
Var. 2: x_{132} Var. 8: x_{232} Var. 13: x_{331} Var. 18: x_{322}
Var. 3: x_{111} Var. 9: x_{211} Var. 14: x_{332} Var. 19: y_1
Var. 4: x_{112} Var. 10: x_{212} Var. 15: x_{311} Var. 20: y_2
Var. 5: x_{121} Var. 11: x_{221} Var. 16: x_{312} Var. 21: y_3
Var. 6: x_{122}

Row 0:   Objective function
Rows 1–9:   Labor constraints
Rows 10–18:   Land constraints
Rows 19–27:   Market constraints

PART III Technology Choice in Industry

7 Determinants of Technology Choice: the Indian and Japanese Cotton Industries

GUSTAV RANIS and GARY SAXONHOUSE

The importance of improving the quality of technologies in less developed countries (LDCs), with direct consequences for productivity and growth, and indirect effects that aid achievement of a more equitable or more employment-intensive growth path, has for some time been recognized by analysts and policy-makers both within the developing countries and outside. Indeed, few subjects have received more attention in the recent literature on development. While concern with the role of science and technology has been mounting, progress in providing answers has lagged behind considerably. This should not be surprising, in view of the deficiencies of our understanding of the subject, even in the context of the developed countries. For this reason, any effort to improve even marginally our understanding of how more or less "appropriate" technology is chosen and developed is clearly bound to have a high payoff. This is especially true in the context of societies critically short of conventional inputs, a scarcity lying at the heart of their state of underdevelopment.[1]

The potential for a large payoff is illustrated by the dramatic performance of a small set of contemporary developing countries. Despite poor endowments of natural resources, since the 1950s systems such as Taiwan and Korea have not only managed to grow rapidly, they have at the same time experienced considerable equity in income distribution. This stands in sharp contrast to many other developing countries. Fast-growing Latin American nations such as Mexico

This research has been partly supported under a National Science Foundation grant. An earlier version of this paper was presented to the 1980 annual meeting of the American Association for the Advance of Science, and is included as "International and Domestic Determinants of LDC Technology Choice" in Lucas and Freedman (1983). Excerpted by permission. Research by Saxonhouse (see chapter 10) supersedes some of the data in the earlier versions.

[1] An "appropriate technology" is one that is efficient in terms of domestic factor costs. In part, because labor is the least mobile, and in contemporary LDCs the most abundant, factor, the term is often used popularly to imply a labor-using, as opposed to a highly machine-oriented, technology. Our use is not so restricted.

and Colombia, in spite of more favorable endowments of natural resources at the end of World War II, have failed to do as well, either in terms of growth – though this has been respectable – or in achieving distributional, employment, and poverty-alleviating goals.

The inability of these Latin American countries to ease the painful tradeoffs between output, employment, and distributional objectives seems to be associated with considerably less technological flexibility, or less ability to innovate adaptively in labor-using directions, compared to the Asian examples. There are marked differences not only in the intersectoral composition of growth at the aggregate level, with more initial attention being paid to agriculture in the Asian countries, but also in the greater scope for labor-intensive technologies afforded by an export-oriented industrial output mix. As a consequence, in contrast to most Latin American countries, we see in the Asian cases a much more rapid absorption of underemployed and unemployed, accompanied by relatively equitable levels of income distribution. Industrial capital–labor ratios seem to be substantially lower in the Asian countries, and the direction of technology change appears much less labor-saving, and thus more "appropriate," than in the majority of contemporary developing countries.

The stakes are high, and thus there is a case for trying to understand the role of appropriate technology as an ingredient in differential performance since the end of World War II. It is a pity so much of the analysis of technology choice and change has been directed towards the impact of technology on selected aggregate variables, such as employment and income distribution, and so little on the proximate causes of differential technology performance that are likely to be uncovered by disaggregation. But, as long as too many planners, along with virtually all engineers, believed in the absolute tyranny of fixed-factor proportions and fixed-attribute bundles, there was little sense in discussing the search for technological alternatives and the inducement mechanism for selecting the appropriate technology at the level of the individual firm.

Despite the general neglect, we do know a good deal more in this area now than we did in the 1950s. We now recognize that there is, in principle, a fairly wide range of alternative technology choices, except in a few continuous process industries. We also now acknowledge the importance of including in our analysis the quantitatively-important product attribute or quality change, not just process change, which is easier for economists to handle. These represent important advances in our understanding.

As a consequence, research has broadened to address the question of what causes more or less appropriate technology choices to be made and what induces a more or less appropriate direction of technology change over time. Put another way, because a choice can be made from a wide variety of techniques, and because this spectrum presumably can be further broadened through technological change, why is the range of techniques actually used in developed and developing countries so narrow, much narrower than expected on the basis of conventional theory, given the international differences in factor endowments?

Although we recognize cultural and human-resource differentials across countries, our basic premise is that the environment surrounding economic agents is of crucial significance to the answer. Though a supply of information about alternative technologies and appropriate goods remains essential, an equally key ingredient is the active demand for such information by entrepreneurs concerned with the effect on the profitability of their choices. This aspect is often neglected in discussions of science and technology. The care exercised in technology choice and the level of investment and research activity directed towards technological change depend, to a significant extent, on the type of incentives faced by decision-makers within each firm. Our research emphasis can be summarized simply by stating we have selected a number of variables affecting these incentives, and are exploring their effects on technological choice and change in the context of development.

The first variable is industrial structure. At one extreme of the industrial-structure continuum is agriculture. With the exception of some cash-crop plantations, farming units are generally small and competitive. Individual units have very weak incentives to invest in research and inventive activity. The legal mechanism of the patent is particularly ineffective for biologically-based technology, because of the ease of replicability and the difficulty of policing infringement. This makes generation, adaptation, and diffusion of agricultural technology a public good, and it is widely recognized as such.

In the industrial sector, small firms that approximate a competitive industry may also have relatively weak incentives to invest in inventive activity. The presence of many rival firms makes it difficult to amass such market power, even with new technology, or to retain innovation profits; moreover, relatively small size may make it difficult to obtain the resources necessary for the pursuit of technology change, and render the impact of potential cost savings less than would be enjoyed by a larger firm. Some of these reasons suggest that firms near the opposite end of the continuum, in fairly concentrated industries, have comparatively strong incentives to conduct research. However, these inducements are somewhat offset by the lack of competitive pressure on oligopolistic firms to perform at full potential. Even an industry "workably competitive" in structure can be made to feel more or less pressure to innovate, depending on the degree of competition from sources outside the industry, particularly imports.

Protective measures taken by national governments are the second variable we wish to concentrate on. We expect, *ceteris paribus*, firms in industries more shielded from foreign competition by tariffs, import quotas, and the like to feel less pressure to innovate and consequently to engage in less inventive activity than otherwise. Similarly, firms in industries heavily subsidized through credit, foreign-exchange rationing, price controls, or other measures are likely to adopt a less appropriate technology, other things being equal, than firms in unprotected industries.

We have designed our research to capture the effects of these two variables through a series of comparisons. We are investigating technology change and choice in agriculture, in a competitive industry (cotton spinning and textiles), and in a less competitive industry (agricultural machinery). Differences between the technological performance in these three cases should yield insights into the effects of market structure, and the extent and nature of government intervention as part of the environment of the individual firm's decision-making.

This chapter presents early findings from one aspect of this continuing activity, an examination of the historical experience of the 19th and 20th century Japanese and Indian cotton textile industries. In the first part, we focus on the differences in the observed performance with respect to technology. In the second part, we consider why this occurred, and focus on the differences in the economic and institutional environment of the two countries.

Differential Performance

The relatively well established Indian and relatively recently established Japanese cotton textile industries had substantially similar initial conditions at the beginning of the 1880s. The Indian industry in its modern form is usually dated from the founding of three successful mills in 1854. By 1882, 65 mills were in operation, housing over 14,000 looms and 1.6 million spindles, almost all mules (Pearse 1930: 22). Short-staple Indian cotton, augmented by about 3 percent imported cotton, was spun into relatively coarse yarn. Working in factories modeled after those in Lancashire, mill operatives, mostly male, worked a single dawn-to-dusk shift, which meant from 10 hours in winter to 14 hours in summer. In Japan, relatively few mills had been erected after the first in 1867. As in India, machine spinning was done on mules, mostly by male workers in single shifts. About 60 percent of the yarn consumed was domestically produced by traditional hand-spinning methods, and most of the remainder was imported from India, mainly in counts of 20s or higher.[2]

In the decade of the 1880s, major changes in cotton spinning technology put an end to this similarity. The major innovations and less spectacular adaptations of this decade can be conveniently divided into two distinct phases. In the first, between 1882 and 1884, the spinning mule remained at the center of the technology and other changes were made around it. In the second phase, 1887–89, the core process changed, with ring spinning replacing mule spinning and alterations being made in adjusting to rings.[3]

[2] Yarn is measured by weight, and yarn size by a measure relating weight to length. The metric unit is the tex, the weight in grams of 1,000 m of yarn. The English system uses count, which indicates the length of a pound of the yarn. For cotton, one count is 840 yards (one hank). Most final-output yarn has several plys twisted together; hence 20/3 (read 20-count 3-ply) is a yarn 5,600 yards long per pound (20 times 840 divided by 3). Single-ply yarn is abbreviated as an "s" after the count number, so 16s is a 16-count single-ply. A coarse yarn is up to 20s; medium is 21s to 40s; fine, 41s to 80s; and over 80s are superfines.

[3] For a brief description of how these work, see chapter 10 below.

The new techniques were adopted quickly and widely in Japan, but spread slowly in India. As output expanded in Japan, the industry became relatively more labor-intensive, even as average labor productivity increased, a highly desirable outcome in a labor-surplus economy like that of Japan during this period. Such success is quite rare in contemporary LDC industrialization experience, and thus warrants particular attention.

Early Change in Japan

The data in table 7.1 show the general effects of the changes in Japan. Their labor-using character is demonstrated by the substantial decline in the capital-labor ratio between 1886–90 and 1891–95. This capital shallowing was combined with an equally dramatic decline in the capital–output ratio. Innovational intensity was large enough to provide an increase in average labor productivity, despite the strong labor-using bias of the changes adopted (Fei and Ranis 1965).

The first significant change in Japan was the adoption of two shifts of eleven hours each, in place of one shift; this was made possible by the increased use of electric lighting and the availability of sufficient supervisory personnel. Labor continued to be mostly male. This change reduced by almost half the capital-labor ratio in the core spinning processes. Such a sudden and significant intensification of capital use also reflected more reliable motive power, due to a change from water power to steam.

Beginning in the same period, the emphasis in production shifted to coarser yarns, from 16s to a range of 12s–16s. This change was important in itself, as higher-count Indian imports and domestic hand-spun yarn were replaced by lower-count machine-spun yarn with qualities more suited to Japanese weather. It also linked well with advances being made in weaving, through the adoption of Batten- and Jacquard-derived improvements on the traditional handloom. These improvements included the addition of a roller, so that the physically difficult task of moving the shuttle back and forth by hand as the weft is carried through the warp was considerably eased, and thus made more accessible to female labor. A second, even more important improvement pertaining to the Japanese version of the Batten loom was the substitution of wood for the metal used on the French models. This cut capital costs by half and accommodated a lower-count yarn. The less-rigid, lighter wooden looms vibrated more, which meant the cloth produced was less strong, but it still provided the warmth required.

The spinning of coarser yarn was of even greater significance in preparing the way for the industry's central technological improvement of the 1880s. Ring spinning, the major alternative to mule spinning, is especially well suited to lower counts. In the space of two years, 1887–89, virtually the whole Japanese industry shifted to rings. The importation of mules, apart from a limited number assigned to fine-count production, ceased completely within one year. Aided by fires which conveniently destroyed a substantial portion of the existing mule stock, a virtually instantaneous switch from mules to rings occurred.

Table 7.1: The Japanese spinning industry: overview

Year (average annual)	(1) Capital (average working spindles per day)	(2) Labor (operatives, male and female)	(3) Output (yarn in kan per day)	(4) Capital–labour ratio (1) ÷ (2)	(5) Capital–output ratio (1) ÷ (3)	(6) Labour productivity 1,000 × (3) ÷ (2)
1886–90	148,516	5,992	7,887	24.8	18.8	1.32
1891–95	406,419	29,178	42,902	13.9	9.5	1.47
1896–1900	1,013,987	57,857	105,176	17.5	9.6	1.82
1901–05	1,296,471	67,840	120,256	19.1	10.8	1.77
1906–10	1,614,581	80,852	149,419	20.0	10.8	1.85
1911–15	2,331,236	109,228	242,847	21.3	9.6	2.22
1916–19	3,354,972	147,251	303,409	22.8	11.1	2.06

The sharp drop in the average annual capital–labor ratio for the industry as a whole between 1886–90 and 1891–95 looks suspicious, but can be confirmed directly from individual mill records. The capital–labor ratio for Osaka Spinning dropped from 22.0 in August 1889 to 11.6 in June 1893; for Naniwa, from 33.9 to 9.8; Kanegafuchi, from 22.0 to 14.2; and for Mie, from 18.2 to 14.6

Source: Nippon teikoku tokei nenkan: nos 10–40

This rather dramatic shift in technology in the core spinning process was followed by improvements in ancillary processes. The ring machinery had a clear advantage over mules in requiring less skill per worker. Moreover, by adding workers to tie broken yarn, rings could be run at higher speeds. For these and other reasons, rings are more labor-intensive than mules for any given yarn count up to at least the 40s. Increasingly, young women were hired at low wages to provide the needed unskilled labor. At the same time, the shift to cotton mixing, a labor-intensive operation, made it possible to marry the use of the ring to a lower average staple length. The short-staple cotton, grown and generally imported by Japan, was not readily spun on rings; it could be spun on mules. Cotton mixing had been employed elsewhere, and the Japanese were able to avoid a substantial increase in average staple length in switching from mule to ring because of their own substantial innovations in cotton mixing. Thus, mixing is an important element in the ring's success in Japan.

The overall decline in the capital–labor ratio in Japanese cotton spinning during the second phase of technology change was thus mainly related to three linked factors: the basic shift from mule to ring spinning, the policy of running the machines at higher speeds, and the increased utilization of cotton mixing. These changes augmented the earlier labor-using innovation of the double shift, and continued the emphasis on producing low-count yarn.

Early Change in India

Indian technological performance in the 1880s, as well as later, was dramatically different. Given the initial endowment – at least as much labor surplus and equal access to technology – similar types of labor-using changes could be expected. Table 7.2 presents an aggregate picture of the changes that did in fact occur.

Because Indian statistics for the period do not distinguish between spinning and weaving workers in the same mill, it was necessary to estimate the capital-labor ratio for selected years using the average spindle-per-worker ratio in mills with no weaving workers. Despite this shortcoming, it is safe to say that Indian capital–labor ratios were consistently higher than those of Japan, and there was probably no drop in the capital–labor ratio comparable to the Japanese experience, at least in the period for which estimates could be made. Thus, although the Indian industry did not become more capital-intensive over time, as is customary in contemporary LDC experience, neither did it increase its labor intensity. Instead, it experienced capital widening, with little apparent movement either in the capital–output ratio or in average labor productivity.

At a time when a new technology was being suggested to both Japanese and Indian mills by British machinery suppliers, examination at a more disaggregate level leaves the same impression of a relative technological inertness in India. The most striking example is the slow adoption of ring spinning. The number of rings did increase steadily, and Indians viewed their adoption as the most significant technical development of the 1880s. Nonetheless, according to the records of the six main British textile machinery suppliers, well over two million

Table 7.2: The Indian spinning industry: overview

	(1) Annual average number of working spindles	(2) Annual average number of millhands employed daily	(3) Annual average yarn output (millions of pounds)	(4) Capital-labor ratio (spindles per worker)	(5) Capital-output ratio	(6) Average labor productivity[a]
1895/96–1899/1900	4,210,360	152,406	468.9	32.8	8,975.5	3.9
1900/01–1904/05	4,932,343	183,074	571.7	34.7	9,275.7	4.0
1905/06–1909/10	5,616,835	221,211	651.6	31.1	8,619.9	3.4
1910/11–1914/15	6,257,852	250,739	651.6	30.0	9,603.3	3.0
1915/16–1919/20	6,546,723	287,543	669.8[b]	35.1	9,774.3	3.5

[a] The labor averages used were computed by dividing the average number of spindles in column 1 by the estimated spindle per worker ratio in column 4
[b] Output for 1919–20 was not available, and so is not included in the average

Sources: Columns 1 and 2: *Report of the Indian Tariff Board* 1928: 232–33. Column 3: *Statistics of British India* 1921, vol. 1: 59. Column 4 has been computed using the total spindles and total workers in mills with no looms, reported in the *Financial and Commercial Statistics of British India* (for 1895–96, the 1897 edn: 416–19; for 1903–04, the 1904 edn: 349–50), *Statistics of British India* (for 1908–09, the 1911 edn, vol. 1: 36–37; for 1918–19, the 1921 edn: 56–58), and for 1913–14, the *Statistical Abstract of British India* 1915 edn, vol. 1: 55–57. These figures agree in magnitude with an independent estimate made by an anonymous mill manager and cited in the "Report of the Textile Factories Labour Committee" (Parliamentary Papers 1907, Cd 3617, p. 71). He reports 28 workers per thousand spindles, which is 35.7 spindles per worker

Table 7.3: Imported raw cotton used in Indian spinning

	(1) *Average annual cotton imports to British India (cwt)*	(2) *Average annual Indian cotton consumption (cwt)*	(3) *Imports as percentage of consumption*
1880/81–1884/85	51,004	1,652,854	3.1
1885/86–1889/90	73,636	2,837,505	2.6
1890/91–1894/95	89,087	4,256,052	2.1
1895/96–1899/1900	89,377	5,124,087	1.7
1900/01–1904/05	116,422	5,936,090	2.0
1905/06–1909/10	130,937	7,027,437	1.9
1910/11–1914/15	243,637	7,208,410	3.4
1915/16–1919/20	53,876	7,334,676	0.7

Sources: Column 1: *Financial and Commercial Statisitcs* 1897 edn: 518 and 1904 edn: 408; *Statistics of British India* 1913 edn, vol. 1: 14 and 1922 edn, vol. 1: 138. Column 2: Pearse 1930: 22

new mules were imported into India between 1883, the date of the first Indian experimentation with rings, and 1900. In sharp contrast with the sudden halt of Japanese mule imports, large numbers of mules continued to be imported into India. (See chapter 10 below.)

The Indian cotton spinning industry also failed to realize the full labor-using effects of other technological changes, in contrast to Japan. Male workers continued to predominate throughout the period, with women accounting for no more than 25 percent, and children forming a small and decreasing proportion of the total (Morris 1965: 66). Some mills lengthened the working day to fifteen hours in the early part of the century (Morris 1965: 104), but as late as 1930 the single shift was considered normal (*Report* 1932: 113). Cotton mixing was certainly practised, but its purpose was viewed differently. There is evidence mills tried to work with as short a staple as possible, and probably increased their labor use through this practice, but they did not use mixing to reduce their reliance on mule technology. Medium and long-staple cotton had to be imported; the import data in table 7.3 suggest how little mixing was done.[4]

[4] The Victorian Jubilee Technical Institute, established in 1882, included instruction in cotton mixing, and Mehta (1954) includes a photograph of a lecture on mixing given in 1896.

An 1899 petition by employees in the spinning and weaving mills in Bombay cited cotton quality as a reason why Indian mill hands were less productive than the English. "The breakage in the thread . . . is so continuous here on account of the bad quality of the cotton, that mill-owners are compelled to employ more men." (Parliamentary Papers 1890–91, vol. 59: 107).

Consequences in the Market

Evidence the Japanese were forging ahead of the Indians technologically is clearly visible in the relative performance of the two industries when competing for markets. In the infancy of the Japanese industry, India had exported yarn to Japan. Indian exports to Japan fell from a peak in 1910/11 of 2.8 million yards of cloth, and nearly 3 million pounds of yarn, to less than 1 percent of these levels in 1930 (*Annual* 1913–14, vol. 2: 370 and 1929–30, vol. 2: 320). Table 7.4 shows the increasing penetration of Japanese cloth and yarn into India.

The same period saw Japanese yarn entering the Chinese market, which had been supplied mainly by Indian products, and winning the dominant position by 1915. Trade was only part of the Japanese involvement in China. Japanese-owned mills in China, which were organized and operated like mills in Japan, expanded capacity more than eightfold between 1915 and 1928, when they accounted for over one-third of total spindlage (Moser: 66). The number of Japanese-owned looms increased 15 times over the same period, and accounted for nearly half of total Chinese weaving capacity in 1928 (Moser: 87). This expansion makes the Japanese rout of the Indian industry even more thorough than the trade figures indicate. Whether in foreign markets or within the Indian

Table 7.4:   Indian–Japanese foreign trade competition

	(1) Japanese yarn exports to India[a] *(millions of lbs)*	*(2)* Japanese cloth exports to India[a] *(millions of yards)*	*(3)* Japanese yarn exports to China and Hong Kong *(millions of lbs)*	*(4)* Indian yarn exports to China and Hong Kong *(millions of lbs)*
1895	–	–	15.3	163.3
1900	–	0.0	88.2	208.4
1905	0.0	0.2	97.9	240.6
1910	0.3	0.2	102.4	171.3
1915	1.4	34.0	179.3	152.4
1920	13.7	133.9	111.1	80.6
1925	26.0	169.2	–	–
1930	8.3	380.6	–	–

[a] Data for Japan are listed for the calendar year in which a fiscal year ends

Sources: Columns 1 and 2 are computed from the *Annual Statement of Seaborne Trade of British India* (various issues from the 36th to the 64th); and the *Report of the Indian Tariff Board* 1932: 25 and 28. Columns 3 and 4 are computed from the *Report* 1927: 96

domestic market, the rapid diffusion discussed earlier gave Japan a decided advantage wherever Indian and Japanese cotton textiles competed.

Analysis of Causes

The difference in the technological development of the Japanese and Indian textile industries is indeed quite startling. Both operated in labor-surplus economies, and both obtained initial technology and early technical advice from Britain, mostly from the same firm. Yet one transformed that technology in ways appropriate to its economy much better than the other did. Our objective here is to identify as many plausible reasons as possible why this occurred; it is necessarily difficult, if not impossible, to present any single satisfactory causal explanation. The search focuses on constraints on the exercise of technology choice, that is, on differences in the competitiveness of the macroeconomic environment and in the pattern of final demand. In what follows, we have attributed at least qualitative weights to various plausible causal explanations.

Distortions in Factor Prices

One may suspect that the so-called distortion of relative factor prices, inducing entrepreneurs to use too much scarce capital and too little surplus labor, was more at play in India than in Japan. However, in the absence of data on relative factor availabilities or shadow prices in the two countries, it is difficult to make a clear-cut judgment on the initial extent of relative distortion. Inspection of the available evidence reveals some difference in the trend of relative factor prices over time. The relative movements of wages and the price of capital are summarized in table 7.5 for Japan, and table 7.6 for India.

For Japan, the cost ratios presented suggest that capital was initially very high and only began to fall sharply relative to labor after 1900. This pattern is consistent with the aggregate endowment picture over time (Ohkawa and Rosovsky 1968; Ranis 1959). Indian data present a rather different picture. The ratios of a rough index of the cost of capital to the wages of cotton textile workers increase sharply until about 1900, and remain more or less constant thereafter. In both countries, investment in cotton mills came from private sources, not through any institutional channel that was regulated, and entrepreneurs were not offered artificially-low interest rates as the opportunity cost of their capital.

Other evidence does allow us to venture the hypothesis that capital was initially underpriced and labor overpriced in both India and Japan. The nominal wage in India was constant or rose only slowly over the latter half of the 19th century (Buchanan 1934; Sarkar: 216–21). The interest rates at which the Indian government borrowed internally were in an overall downward trend throughout the course of the 19th century (such rates were printed periodically in the Parliamentary Papers). The opposite trend occurred in Japan, where

Table 7.5: Indexes of the costs of capital and wages in Japan, in nominal and real terms (1928–32 ≡ 100)

	(1) Capital goods price index	(2) Loan-rate index	(3) User cost of capital index (1)×(2)/100	(4) GNP price deflator	(5) Real user cost of capital (3)×100/(4)	(6) Money wages index for cotton spinners	(7) Real wage index for cotton spinners (6)×100/(4)	(8) Ratio of user cost of capital to wages
1887	32.6	–	–	17.6	–	–	–	–
1888–1892	35.0	144.2	50.5	20.2	250.0	9.6	25.9	5.26
1893–1897	42.1	137.5	57.9	25.7	225.3	11.2	26.9	5.17
1898–1902	53.1	146.5	77.8	35.8	217.3	18.0	33.9	4.32
1903–1907	57.2	127.9	73.2	43.8	167.1	21.5	33.9	3.40
1908–1912	59.3	113.9	67.5	50.5	133.7	27.0	39.4	2.50
1913–1917	75.4	–	–	62.1	–	32.0	39.4	–
1918–1922	148.0	115.0	170.2	127.6	133.4	92.4	61.4	1.84
1923–1927	132.7	116.3	154.3	126.2	102.3	112.9	80.9	1.37
1928–1932	100.0	100.0	100.0	100.0	100.0	100.0	100.0	1.00
1933–1937	106.1	86.1	91.4	100.9	90.6	73.0	68.0	1.25

Sources: Ranis 1957; Asahi Shimbun 1930; Goto 1970

Table 7.6: Indexes of the costs of capital and wages in India, 1890–1912 (1908–12 ≡ 100)

	(1) Capital goods price index[a]	*(2)* Loan-rate index[b]	*(3)* User cost of capital *(1)×(2)/100*	*(4)* Money wage index for cotton textiles	*(5)* Ratio of user cost of capital to wages
1890–92	75	71	53	75	0.7
1893–97	79	98	77	77	1.0
1898–1902	90	108	92	82	1.1
1903–07	95	99	94	90	1.0
1908–12	100	100	100	100	1.0

[a] This index is the average of the price indexes for metals and building materials
[b] This index is the average of the mean annual interest rates on demand loans on government paper issued by the Presidency Banks of Bengal, Bombay, and Madras. A list of interest rates on outstanding loans chargeable to the Indian government was printed periodically in the Parliamentary papers

Source: Computed from data in Datta 1914. Column 1, from vol. 1: 29; column 2 from vol. 4: 448; and columns 3 and 4, from vol. 3: 2–3

slower population growth and higher marginal-savings rates tended to give weak support to the conclusion that India experienced somewhat more repressed financial markets or credit rationing than Japan.

Although it is difficult to judge differences in the initial extent of factor-price distortions, the fact capital was becoming relatively more expensive over time in India and dramatically less expensive in Japan indicates substantially less rigid factor prices than are usually encountered in contemporary import-substituting LDCs. In any case, the relevance of differential factor-price distortions in explaining the slower diffusion of capital-saving production methods in India is limited. Indeed, if anything, the divergent trends in relative factor-price movements, everything else being equal, should have led to relatively more rapid Indian adoption and relatively slower Japanese adoption of the ring-spinning machine and other capital-saving practices.

Tariff policy is another common source of distortions. Table 7.7 presents tariff rates for both cotton yarn and cloth for selected years. For Japan, the unequal treaties imposed in the 1850s prevented more than a 5 percent *ad valorem* tariff on imports until the first decade of the 20th century. The freedom of the Japanese government to apply this duty selectively, however, did allow substantial effective protection for Japanese cotton textile manufacturers, which was denied their Indian counterparts. In the early 1890s, Boren (the All Japan Cotton Spinners' Association) was able to persuade the government to

Table 7.7:   Tariff rates on cotton yarn and cotton cloth

	Yarn		Cloth	
	Japan	India	Japan	India
1893	4.28	0.0	5.26	0.0
1898	2.94	0.0	4.12	3.5
1903	5.79	0.0	7.12	3.5
1908	4.08	0.0	5.98	3.5
1913	8.33	0.0	10.97	3.5
1918	3.37	5.0	3.59	7.5
1924	1.19	5.0	3.18	11.0
1928	3.77	5.0	14.23	11.0
1933	3.02		0.81	75.0

Figures in each column are percentages

Sources: Japan: Yamazawa 1975; India: Vakil and Munshi: 41–43

remove the 5 percent duty on raw cotton. This allowed substitution of imported longer-staple raw cotton for the very short-staple Japanese raw cotton. In addition, because raw cotton was between 75 and 85 percent of the total cost of producing yarn, removal of the 5 percent duty on raw cotton, while retaining a 5 percent duty on yarn and cloth, greatly increased effective protection for Japanese products.

By direct contrast, in India the duty on imported cloth was designed explicitly as a revenue-generating measure. Domestic machine-produced cloth was taxed at exactly the same rate to rule out any semblance of protection. For administrative reasons, handloom weavers were not subject to the excise tax. This differential treatment of machine and handmade cloth delayed the growth of machine weaving in India, thereby creating disincentives for the adoption of ring spinning. Because rings, unlike mules, spin yarn onto heavy wooden bobbins, ring mills are at a particular disadvantage in attempting to send their yarn to far-flung handloom-weaving operations.

Product Differences

Bringing quality differences into the analysis allows a substantially better understanding of technology choice. Rings and mules have features which are advantageous or disadvantageous, depending on the characteristics of the yarn being spun. A major advantage of rings over mules lies in the spinning of comparatively low-count yarns with the application of relatively more labor. The disadvantage of using rings to produce low-count yarn lies in the extra stress the process places on the fiber.

Coarse yarn is suitable for weaving medium or heavy-weight fabrics, but cannot be worked into finer fabrics, which require a higher count. Before mechanization, traditional hand-crafted cotton textile products in Japan had been of the coarser type. Consumers were accustomed to such cloth and had developed their styles around it. Further, the latitude at which Japan lies makes a warm cloth climatically appropriate. It was therefore natural for Japanese spinners to emphasize the production of low-count yarn. This led to the adoption of the ring rather than the mule, because Japanese spinning mills, unlike mills elsewhere in the world, developed sophisticated, but very labor-intensive, techniques for mixing raw cotton. This mixing, by allowing the ring to use very cheap cotton, negated the primary advantage the mule retained over the ring in the spinning of low-count yarn.

The traditions of the Indian industry before mechanization were different. Indian spinners had long worked in fine counts, and the greatest demand both in foreign and domestic markets was for fine fabrics (Chaudhuri 1980). India's climate tends to make heavier fabrics less acceptable to consumers; moreover, more variety seems to have been demanded. When Indian textile mills began production, British imports supplied the finer yarn and cloth, leaving the lower-count yarn to the Indian mills. Over time, however, the Indians moved increasingly into higher counts. Mehta (1954: 9) reports the average count spun was 13 in 1907–08, and by the end of World War I it was in the high teens. In 1933–34, it was 20, and in 1938–39, 27.

The preference of Indian consumers for finer-count products, signaled through the market, was certainly one factor leading to the relatively greater use of mules and the delayed introduction of rings in India. Moreover, Indian producers wished to respond to this demand by producing high-quality cloth using locally grown cotton. In the absence of adopting then-unknown Japanese mixing practices, this led directly to the use of the mule (see chapter 10 below). We have here an example of the general rule that technology choice involves not only a choice of method, but also a choice of product characteristics, and that this quality dimension in technology choice can significantly affect the labor-intensity of the choice. The consistency of ring technology with cloth appropriate to Japan's climate as well as with indigenous Japanese consumer tastes, which apparently were not greatly affected by international demonstration patterns, allowed a more labor-intensive expansion path for the Japanese textile industry. In India, the climate and consumer tastes both worked against such an outcome.

The Organizational and Institutional Environments

There are differences in the organizational and institutional environments facing the two countries, and these provide more of an explanation than the old chestnut of relative factor-price distortions in its simple-minded version. We are referring here, in the first instance, to differences in the extent of workable competition, as reflected, for example, in relative freedom of entry, access to credit, and pressure in commodity markets. As Scherer (1970) puts it, "What is needed for rapid technological progress is a subtle blend of competition and monopoly, with more emphasis in general on the former than the latter, and with the role of monopolistic elements diminishing when rich technological opportunities exist." Such opportunities clearly existed in cotton spinning, as is evident from the correspondence between Platt and its Japanese and Indian customers. But the difference in response was related in large part to differences in organizational structure, affecting the relative pressures on management to innovate.

At the time India's modern cotton textile industry was being established, the country's capital markets were very imperfect. The main source of capital available for investment in early mills was the personal wealth of successful merchants and financiers (Lokanathan 1935: 135–36). Commonly, one individual would provide most of the initial capital which might be supplemented by a small group of family members and associates. This individual would then be designated as the manager of the mill, and would receive payment for this function in addition to a return on his investment. This pattern, called the managing-agency system, was prevalent throughout the industry. The managing agency constituted a separate firm, supplying management to the mill on a commission basis and often running other firms as well, including other textile mills.

One special feature of the Indian cotton textile industry was the relative absence of British participation in providing capital and senior management, even while providing much of the industry's technical expertise. Even though sales agents of British machinery manufacturers were early participants (Koh 1966), the industry can be characterized as having been owned and managed primarily by Indians. This is in contrast to the heavy British investment in other enterprises (see Lokanathan 1935: 136; Buchanan 1934: 206; Mehta 1954: 42).

The managing-agency system as practised bore several defects which undoubtedly reduced the average quality of entrepreneurial ability in the industry (Fukazawa 1965: 231–33). The managers were not industrialists, and they generally also had no managerial or technical training or experience. They tended to concentrate on financial affairs to the neglect of the technical aspects of the mill (see Koh 1966: 127). Managerial ability was spread over the mill, the agency firm itself, and other managed enterprises. Infusion of talent was limited by the agents' long, guaranteed tenure and the practice of handing down the agency from father to son.

But perhaps the most serious was the incentive structure, which often did not effectively induce the agent to act in the best interests of the mill. In many cases, particularly in the early period, commissions were based on physical output or sales, not on profits (*Report* 1927: 87). After 1885, however, commissions based on profits became more common, but depreciation was not treated as a charge against profits. In many cases, the managers also received, as purchasing agents, commissions on the machinery they bought for the mill. The bias towards import and capital-intensity created by these last two features is obvious. The failure to link commissions to profits, if not totally perverse in effect, undoubt-edly reduced the incentive to search intensively for innovations, especially as the managing agents often sold their capital holdings in the mill at a later date.

The central defect of the Indian managing-agency system thus was not so much that good management was prevented, but that it was not adequately encouraged. Certainly, there were some managers of exceptional ability. An outstanding, frequently cited example is J. N. Tata, a mill owner who was also a pioneer in India's steel industry. In 1883, a technical advisory mission Tata had sent to England shipped two ring-spinning frames to India (for details, see Mehta 1954: 43; Wacha 1915: 35; Sahlatvala and Khosia: 30). Their output of low-count yarn proved to far exceed the output of mules, and experimentation and adaptation continued under the direction of British technicians. Tata immediately began replacing mule spindles with rings, as did some other mills. However, the statistics on the Indian adoption of rings indicate replacement was restricted to a relatively small number of managers, in contrast to the almost instantaneous diffusion in Japan (also see chapter 10 below).

Given the substantial restraints on entry imposed by the capital requirements, differences in managerial and technical performance among firms could be maintained without serious threat to the position of a poorly-performing manager (Mehta 1954: 52 and 84). Even nine years after Tata successfully used rings, most Indian managers failed to appreciate their superiority. In an 1892 issue of the *Indian Textile Journal*, Japan was ridiculed for its use of rings and for its mixing of cottons. The same article further maintains that the short-staple length Indian cotton would continue to make the ring inappropriate, something the subsequent experience of both Indian and Japanese spinning mills proved totally incorrect. The appearance of such an article in a respected Indian journal nine years after Tata successfully used rings clearly indicates that substantial portions of the Indian industry maintained a self-satisfied posture long after the Japanese (who were large purchasers of Indian cotton) had shifted entirely to rings.

It is understandable that technically inexperienced Indian managers would rely heavily on British staff, and virtually all technical positions were filled by British workers until the 1880s, when Indians began to fill junior posts (Mehta 1954: 101). Though it would have been impossible to run the mills without them, this heavy emphasis on a foreign technical class probably also served to retard technological progress in the industry. First, the managers, from whom one expects the impetus for technological progress to come, found it difficult to control technicians (Mehta 1954: 106). Second, the foreign staff rarely knew the mill workers' languages, and few of the latter spoke English. This brought about another pervasive feature of Indian mill organization, the jobber, which impeded technological advance (Morris 1965: 129–38; Thakker).

Although the social origins of jobbers are not entirely clear, they seem to have been drawn from the same class as the workers, and so continued to function as an intermediary when Indian technicians from the middle class became more numerous. Whether through evolution or deliberate decision, jobbers acquired the middle-management tasks of work supervision, discipline, and labor recruitment. Once again, the incentives were badly suited to induce behavior profitable to the mill. Paid a placement fee by new workers, and with no hope of moving up within the organization on the basis of the productivity or performance of a stable, well-trained labor force, jobbers concentrated on increasing labor turnover, thus maximizing their revenue from side payments. (An alternative explanation of the high labor turnover is given by Mazumdar 1973.) The level of education and literacy of India's middle-management cadre also probably compared unfavorably with the Japanese situation, in which upward mobility and a task-oriented reward system encouraged the search for greater efficiency.

The Labor Force

How much weight should be given to the differential characteristics of the industrial labor force itself is an interesting and unanswered question. Frequent mention is made in the literature of poor Indian work habits, including absentee-ism and long, irregular breaks; the well-disciplined hard-working Japanese mill hand seemed to provide a sharp contrast. (See, for example, the comparison made between Indian and Japanese labor in Pearse 1930: 11.) Visiting Japanese missions also made much of the enervating influence of Indian weather con-ditions, while Indian writers stress the low levels of labor productivity associated with low levels of nutrition and health.

The smaller proportion of female labor in India, compared with Japan, has been related to the much greater reluctance of both Muslim and Hindu women to enter the labor force. The persistence of a single shift is often attributed to the unreliability and individualism of the Indian worker, in contrast to the more cooperative, community-oriented Japanese. Such differences in the inherent cultural background and quality of the unskilled labor might be enough to provide some bias in favor of greater capital intensity and the prolonged retention of the mule in India. But absenteeism was as high in Japan and, if anything, Indian operatives had more work experience (Saxonhouse 1976). Many of the differences in performance must thus reflect more on the incentives facing managers in the two countries than on the labor they directed.

Industrial Associations

Some of the deficiencies in the quality of the managerial and entrepreneurial environment in India might have been offset in part, if a good social mechanism had existed for pooling technological information and experience. Such an organization functioned extremely well in Japan (Saxonhouse 1976: 115–18). Spinners representing over 97 percent of the country's spindles were members of Boren (the All Japan Cotton Spinners' Association). The rapid diffusion of new technical information through Boren was clearly aided by Boren's simultaneous control over the allocation of imported raw cotton to its members.

In India, the organizations most closely corresponding to Boren were the various mill-owner groups, the largest of which was BMOA (the Bombay Mill Owners' Association). Several reasons suggest themselves as to why BMOA and similar groups did not serve the same technological function as Boren. Judging from their actions, their role was more political, including involvement in early controversies over tariffs, and this turned the focus away from technology. This may have been a case of energy being diverted away from profits derived from more appropriate technology choices and towards profits from changes in the provision of government favors, credit, etc. – that is, rent-seeking activities. Also, BMOA was patterned largely after British industrial organizations, which meant there was no precedent for extensive technology sharing.

Conclusions

The lessons of economic history permit us to proceed beyond the simple factor-price distortions story in explaining comparative technological performance. Given the common British-produced spinning technology, the choices made by the individual Japanese entrepreneur, in contrast to his Indian counterpart, illuminate the importance of differences in institutional and organizational environment. Adoption of the two successive waves of labor-using innovations came quickly in Japan and only slowly and reluctantly in India, primarily because of the relative strength of workable competitive pressures at home, enhanced by Boren's structure and diluted by India's managing-agency system.

Product quality plays an important role in determining the appropriateness of a technology. In the specific case of ring versus mule spinning, Japan had the good fortune to have a market consistent with the type of yarn that rings spun best, and this was not true of India.

In Japan, dependable technological information channels led to early and rapidly diffused switches in technology, including acquisition of shelf technology (technology embodied in stock machinery or standard procedures) and modifications and adaptations of how it was used. In India, a management system that was insulated by institutional constraints from fully harnessing entrepreneurial incentives represents a situation much closer to that of contemporary LDCs. The ability to create and maintain an environment placing a minimum of workable competitive pressure on the decision-maker is crucial to the appropriateness of technology choices and the direction of technology change.

References

Annual Statement of the Seaboard Trade of British India.

Asahi Shimbun (1930), *Nihon keizai tokei sokan*, Tokyo.

Biswas, M. R., in cooperation with Robert Evenson (1980), "UNCSTD in Retrospect," *Mazingira*, 4(2), 36–53.

Buchanan, D. H. (1934), *The Development of Capitalist Enterprise In India*, New York.

Chaudhuri, K. N. (1980), "The Structure of Indian Textile Industry in the Seventeenth and Eighteenth Centuries," *Indian Economic and Social History Review*, 17: 127–82.

Datta, K. L. (1914), *Report on the Enquiry into the Rise of Prices in India*, 5 vols, Calcutta.

Fei, John C. H., and Gustav Ranis (1965), "Innovation intensity and Factor Bias in the Theory of Growth," *International Economic Review*, 6: 182–98 (May).

Fukuzawa, H. (1965), "Cotton Mill Industry," in V. B. Singh, ed., *Economic History of India*, Bombay.

Goto, Shinichi (1970), *Nihon no kinyu tokei*, Tokyo: Toyo Keizai Shimposha.

Koh, Sung Jae (1966), *Stages of Industrial Development, a Comparative History of the Cotton Industry in Japan, India, and Korea*, Philadelphia: University of Pennsylvania Press.

Lokanathan Palamadai S. (1935), *Industrial Organization in India*, London: G. Allen and Unwin (reprinted in 1970 by Kraus Reprints).

Lucas, Barbara A., and Stephen Freedman (1983), *Technology Choice and Change in Developing Countries: Internal and External Constraints*, Dublin: Tycooly International Publishing.

Mazumdar, D. (1973), "Labour Supply in Early Industrialization: the Case of the Bombay Textile Industry," *Economic History Review*, second series 26(3): 477–96 (August).

Mehta, S. D. (1954), *The Cotton Mills of India*, Bombay: Textile Association.

Morris, Morris D. (1965), *The Emergence of an Industrial Labor Force in India*, Berkeley, CA: University of California Press.

Moser, C. K., *The Cotton Textile Industry of Far Eastern Countries*.

Ohkawa, Kazushi, and Henry Rosovsky (1968), "Postwar Growth in Historical Perspective: A Second Look," In Lawrence Klein and Kazushi Ohkawa, eds, *Economic Growth, The Japanese Experience since the Meiji Era*, Homewood, IL: Richard D. Irwin for the Economic Growth Center, Yale University.

Pearse, Arno S. (1930), *The Cotton Industry in India*, Manchester.

Ranis, Gustav (1957), "Factor Proportions in Japanese Economic Development," *American Economic Review*, 47: 594–607 (September).

Ranis, Gustav (1959), "The Financing of Japanese Economic Development," *Economic History Review*, second series (11): 440–54 (April).

Report of the Indian Tariff Board, annual; the 1927 and 1932 edns were used.

Sahlatvala, B. Sh., and K. Khosia, *James Tata*.

Sarkar, *The Economics of British India*.

Saxonhouse, Gary (1976), "Country Girls and Communication Among Competitors in the Japanese Cotton-Spinning Industry," in Hugh Patrick with Larry Meissner, eds, *Japanese Industrialization and its Social Consequences*, Berkeley, CA: University of California Press.

Scherer, F. M. (1970), *Industrial Market Structure and Economic Performance*, Chicago: Rand McNally.

Thakker, G., *Labour Problems of the Textile Industry: A Study of the Labour Problems of the Cotton Mill Industry in Bombay*.

Vakil, C. N., and M. C. Munshi, *Industrial Policy in India*.

Wacha, D. E. (1915), *The Life and Work of J. N. Tata*, Madras: Granach.

Yamazawa, Ippei (1975), "Industrial Growth and Trade Policy in Pre-war Japan," *The Developing Economies*, 13(1): 62 (March).

8 Technology Choice and the Quality Dimension in the Japanese Cotton Textile Industry

GARY SAXONHOUSE and GUSTAV RANIS

Economists traditionally have neglected the quality dimension in their analysis of technology choice. Since the assumption of homogeneity in the specified inputs and outputs is so basic to much of our analytical apparatus, they have, understandably, usually found it convenient to assume a certain standard quality of both the primary and intermediate inputs, as well as of the resulting output. When it comes to empirical application, they have either waved their hand or, if more conscientious, endeavored as far as possible to disaggregate the inputs, such as labor, by skill level and the output by selecting the most disaggregate level of industrial classification feasible.

Sometimes, when evidence on residual differences in quality is so overwhelming as not to be easily ignored, an attempt is made to homogenize the input or output index (for example, by using efficiency units in the case of labor, or yarn counts in the case of cotton spinning as the converter).

Such quality variation, either in output or in the use of primary or intermediate inputs, may, of course, occur unintentionally at any level of aggregation, as in the absence of quality control, or intentionally, as in the effort to procure raw materials from a different source or supply a different market. Of particular interest to us is that either explicitly or implicitly planned variations in input or output quality may be accompanied by substantial variations in the quantities of such assumed homogeneous primary factors as abundant unskilled labor, which can be efficiently absorbed by a given amount of physical capital.

A single product with many dimensions or characteristics is likely to fulfill a variety of needs and, in the same way that process technology developed in advanced countries is often inappropriate for the LDC factor endowment, many of the characteristics built into a particular product by advanced countries may be inappropriate for LDC income levels, real consumption preferences, and other

155

conditions.[1] The shedding of "excess" or inappropriate product characteristics by itself can represent a significant potential resource saving for LDCs.

If products may be usefully viewed in terms of their possibly "excess" or inappropriate quality characteristics, the same is of course true for inputs. Unlike product attributes, it has long been understood that input attributes are most important for interpreting manufacturing phenomena in LDCs in general, and in particular the disappointing contribution of the industrial sector to employment growth. As early as 1958, Hirschman (1958), for example, argued that capital may not be the only scarce factor of production in LDCs and that capital-labor choices have to be made with consideration for such scarce third factors as managerial talent. With a somewhat different slant on the same general problem, Gerschenkron (1952), writing even earlier, observed that the stable, reliable, disciplined labor force required by industrialization was not the kind found in abundance in most late developing countries and, therefore, capital-intensive industrialization strategies were not necessarily inappropriate.

For all the importance of these early insights, there has been curiously little work done within the LDCs to test these or equally cogent alternative hypotheses.[2] What little work that has been done on these topics has been inconclusive. A 1968 study using international data supported Hirschman's and Gerschenkron's findings that higher-quality labor is complementary with unskilled labor and a substitute for capital (Yahr 1968). This finding was supported by Solomon and Forsyth (1977), using data from the Ghanaian manufacturing sector. By contrast, a number of recent studies using exclusively American data found skilled and unskilled labor to be highly substitutable, and skilled labor and capital to be complementary (Berndt and Christensen 1974; Denny and Fuss 1977). These findings challenge the conventional, if still largely untested, wisdom on the subject for the LDCs.

In what follows, the relationship between technology choice and the various dimensions of input and output quality in LDCs is examined by analyzing the historical experience of the Japanese cotton textile industry. Using market-generated data, it is shown that there exist tradeoffs among a variety of quality dimensions of the commodity (cotton cloth), and these tradeoffs are closely related to the demand for inputs of varying scarcity and quality. The nature of the tradeoffs among these inputs of varying quality is also identified.

The Japanese textile industry created a range of cotton cloth products which were of lower quality than had been generally hitherto manufactured in India, Europe, and America, but which were well suited to East Asian markets and to the demands of the lower-income classes elsewhere. The Japanese were

---

[1] The analytical implications of this view of consumer demand were first taken up systematically in Lancaster (1966). An early explicit application of Lancaster's work to LDCs appears in Stewart (1972).
[2] This is true, despite a continuing stream of papers examining factor substitution under conventional assumptions of homogeneous outputs and homogeneous capital and labor. See, for example, Behrman (1972), Kintis (1977), Sines (1979), and Sapir (1980).

successful in profitably producing this cloth, in large measure because they creatively explored the complementarity and substitution possibilities between varying grades of raw cotton and between varying grades of labor. They became capable of producing cotton cloth of a particular quality, using lower-quality raw cotton and lower-quality labor than had previously been thought possible or desirable.

In the following section, the analytical framework for examining the choice of output quality and input mix is outlined. The next section discusses the data used in the estimation of this framework. A regression analysis is used to explain the pricing between 1906 and 1935 of various brands of Japanese cotton cloth in terms of their quality attributes. This analysis identifies the implicit market evaluation of these various attributes. These estimated implicit attribute prices are then used to help estimate the derived product attribute supply functions and derived input demand functions. With this estimated framework, it will be possible in the final section to explore in some detail the relationship between technology choice and the various dimensions of input and output quality in Japan's prewar cotton textile industry.

The Analytical Framework

Assume Japanese textile firms between 1906 and 1935 maximized a variable profit function of the following form:

$$\Pi(\mathbf{P}; -\mathbf{X}) = \sum_{i=1}^{I} \sum_{j=1}^{I} \sum_{j=1}^{I} a_{ij}(1/2P_i^2 + 1/2P_h^2)^{1/2} x_j + \sum_{i=1}^{I} \sum_{j=1}^{J} c_{ij} P_i X_j$$

$$+ \sum_{i=1}^{I} \sum_{j=1}^{J} \sum_{j=1}^{J} b_{jk} X_j^{1/2} X_k^{1/2} P_i \tag{1}$$

where:

$\mathbf{P} \equiv$ vector or prices of variable outputs and inputs
$\mathbf{X} \equiv$ vector of fixed inputs
$\Pi \equiv$ profit operator
$a_{ih} = a_{hi}$
$b_{jk} = b_{kj}$
$a_{ii} = 0$
$b_{jj} = 0$

The variable profit function Π gives the maximum profits that the firm can obtain, allowing a subset of inputs and outputs to be variable, while another subset of inputs is held fixed.[3] The form of the profit function in equation (1) is such that if Π is differentiated with respect to the prices of output and variable inputs, then for positive prices and positive values of the fixed inputs the solution to equation (2) may be obtained.

$$\frac{\partial \Pi}{\partial P_i}(\mathbf{P}; -\mathbf{X}) = U_i(\mathbf{P}; -\mathbf{X})$$

$$= \sum_{h=1}^{I} \sum_{h=1}^{J} a_{ih}(1/2P_i^2 + 1/2P_h^2)^{1/2}P_iX_j + \sum_{j=1}^{J} c_{ij}X_j$$

$$+ \sum_{j=1}^{J} \sum_{k=1}^{J} b_{jk}X_j^{1/2}X_k^{1/2} \quad \text{for } i = 1, 2, \ldots, n \tag{2}$$

where U_i is the operator for the profit-maximizing derived product-attribute supply function or the profit-maximizing derived input-demand function. (The general form of this result is known as Hotelling's lemma and is proved in Gorman (1968).)

There will be one derived product-attribute supply function or derived input-demand function for each of the variable quantities. When the parameters of equation (2) are estimated, it is possible to characterize fully the production

---

[3] The concept of a variable profit function was first suggested in Samuelson (1953). Gorman (1968) rigorously determined many of its properties. The profit function's use in econometric work is presented in Diewert (1973). Given that firms are making both a quantitative and qualitative choice with respect to output, the optimization problem here is slightly different from what is routinely encountered. Solution to the problem begins by forming a cost function with quantity, quality of output, and factor prices of inputs as arguments. This function may be derived by minimizing input costs, subject to production function constraints relating quantity and quality of output and inputs. The resulting cost function is used as data by the profit-maximizing firms in choosing the optimal quality and quantity of output.

In this context, note that firms are competitors and not monopolists, even though the marginal costs of attributes are not constant, because all establishments observe the same prices and cannot affect them by their individual production decisions: price is independent of quantity. The firm will make a decision on the optimal quality and quantity of production by adding attributes until the marginal revenue from additional attributes equals their marginal cost of production per unit sold and by increasing quantity of production up to the point where unit revenue equals marginal cost evaluated at the optimal bundle of attributes. The first-order conditions from this profit-maximization problem can be solved for amounts of the attributes in the cloth chosen by the firm to produce, and the quantity of this cloth actually produced in terms of the implicit attribute prices and the product price. Given that the quantity and quality of output has now been determined, by Shepherd's lemma the optimal inputs can be determined from the cost function previously derived. It is the process of choosing optimal values of quantity and quality of output and inputs characterized here which is embedded in the profit function in equation (1). For more on this optimization process, see Rosen (1974).

relationships. This is because by duality theory it is possible to show that there is a unique relationship between an underlying production function and Π (Diewert 1973). Note that the particular functional form chosen for Π provides a second-order approximation to an arbitrary, twice continuously differentiable, variable profit function which satisfies the necessary conditions for this unique relationship and for equation (2) to hold (Diewert 1973). It will be noted that, other than symmetry, no a priori conditions are imposed on equations (1) and (2). Product attributes and inputs are not treated as separable groups. This is because output mix is hypothesized to be closely related to raw-cotton mix and labor mix. This is a central concern of the analysis here.

The Data

Variable Quantities

The price vector $\mathbf{P}$ in equations (1) and (2) includes fifteen elements:

$P \equiv$ price of cloth
$P_1 \equiv$ price of cloth attribute – weight
$P_2 \equiv$ price of cloth attribute – warp yarn count
$P_3 \equiv$ price of cloth attribute – weft yarn count
$P_4 \equiv$ price of cloth attribute – ends per inch
$P_5 \equiv$ price of cloth attribute – picks per inch
$P_6 \equiv$ price of cloth attribute – plain weave (categorical variable)
$P_7 \equiv$ price of cloth attribute – twill weave (categorical variable)
$P_8 \equiv$ price of cloth attribute – width
$P_9 \equiv$ wages
$P_{10} \equiv$ price of Chinese cotton
$P_{11} \equiv$ price of East Indian cotton
$P_{12} \equiv$ price of American cotton
$P_{13} \equiv$ price of Egyptian cotton
$P_{14} \equiv$ price of other cotton

The eight cloth attributes being treated as variables do not exhaustively characterize each type of cloth, but, given the limited number of degrees of freedom, they do account for much of the variance between most brands.[4]

It should be noted that the threads running the length of a bolt of cloth are called warp threads and those lying cross-wise are called weft threads. A bolt of cloth is woven by pulling the weft threads through the prepared warp. The weft

[4] Discussion of different attributes of cotton cloth are given in Hunter (1924), Whiteside (1940), and Hoye (1942), among other places. See also the very useful dissertation on the American cotton textile industry by Doane (1969).

fills in the warp structure to create cloth. The thread itself is referred to as yarn. Each type of yarn is given a count number equal to the number of hanks of that yarn (1 hank = 840 yards) necessary to equal one pound. The higher the count, the finer the yarn. The number of warp threads per inch or ends and the number of weft threads per inch gives a measure of the denseness with which yarn is laid in the cloth.

The weave is another important product attribute. The theoretical variety of weaves is limited only by the permutations and combinations which can be worked out in the positions of such groups of warp and weft threads relative to each other on the loom. In practice, there are two major options – interweaving every thread at every opportunity, or skipping threads here and there. The first option is the plain weave. Under the second option, most non-plain Japanese cloth produced during the period of this study was either twill or satin. In the twill weaves, after passing under one crossing thread, the thread rides on top of two or more others, and when this step is arranged in a regular rotation, a diagonal ridge (twill) is produced. In the satin weave, also produced by floating one thread across several others, the formation of a rib is avoided. The weave attributes will be represented in the analysis here by two dummy variables which take on the value 1 if the weave is plain or twill, respectively. If the weave is satin or some other type, both categorical variables will take on the value 0.

The cloth-width attribute primarily defines whether the output will be used to make traditional or western-style clothing. Japanese *kimono* are made from bolts of cloth no more than twelve to fifteen inches wide. Western-style clothing and other western-style cloth products are cut from cloth which is double to triple these widths.

Given the other cloth attributes, an extra variable for weight may seem unnecessary. In fact, the Japanese textile industry was extremely successful in effecting wide variations in the weight (and therefore the quality) of cloth of given dimensions by the addition of starch to the warp yarns. Starch might account for as much as 6 percent of British or American cloth weight. Some Japanese brands of cloth contained as much as 23 percent starch (Clark 1914).

Variable input attributes in this analytical framework are exclusively different grades of raw cotton. Raw cotton is graded primarily, but not exclusively, by the length of its fiber, otherwise called its staple length. The longer the staple length, the less the fiber will break when it is being spun and woven. Because higher-count yarn requires more spinning, the probability of breakage is higher and therefore higher-count yarn generally requires longer-staple raw cotton. Similarly, warp yarns must be stronger than weft yarns, and in consequence also require longer-staple raw cotton. Among raw cottons used in substantial quantities by the Japanese in the period under consideration here, Chinese raw cotton had the shortest staple. Next came Indian raw cotton, followed by raw cotton from the American South. Finally, the longest staple used by the Japanese, as by the English, was from Egypt.

Fixed Quantities

The **X** vector in equations (1) and (2) containing the fixed inputs includes as elements:

$X_1 \equiv$ spindle hours
$X_2 \equiv$ loom hours
$X_3 \equiv$ length of shift
$X_4 \equiv$ experience of the work force
$X_5 \equiv$ education of the work force

It is assumed that decisions as to the levels of each of these five inputs are exogenous to the decisions with respect to level and mix of output and level of the labor input. For much of the period under investigation here, increases in capacity depended more or less intimately on imported capital goods. The lag between order and delivery was sufficiently and unexpectedly varied that a spinning-mill manager's control over the time-path of his mill's capacity could be quite limited. (For further discussion, see Saxonhouse (1975).)

In other words, once the capacity was in place, the mill manager had only limited discretion with respect to capacity utilization and length of shift. The Japanese cotton spinning industry was, during the period under study, and remains today, an interesting blend of competition and oligopoly. Thus, although entry into the industry was always unrestricted and decisions regarding output *per se* were left to the individual firms, the trade association or cartel executive body, throughout virtually the entire period under study, determined the limits of capacity utilization and the length and number of working shifts.

Available evidence also suggests that individual firms had little control over the quality of their labor force, or else made decisions with a different, longer horizon in mind. Throughout most of the pre-Pacific War period, the spinning industry relied on young female recruits from the most underdeveloped regions of Japan. As late as 1893, very few of these recruits had been exposed to any kind of formal education. Due to an explicit change in government policy, by 1910 98 percent of the recruits from the very same poor families had attended primary school. Notwithstanding their increased education, the time-path of departure of an entering cohort of recruits remained unchanged between the 1890s and the 1930s. The work experience of the average member of the spinning-industry labor force rose from 14 months in 1891 to over 44 months in 1930, largely because a small constant proportion of each entering cohort became members of the permanent work force. Whatever policies the mills may have had to establish a permanent work force, they were unimportant by comparison with the simple maturation of the industry. (These topics are treated in more detail in Saxonhouse (1976).)

Data Sources

The system of equations in (2) will be estimated using 903 firm observations over a 29-year period, between 1906 and 1935. This is a subset of the sample of 2,138 observations over 45 years which have been used in some of the previous work on the prewar Japanese spinning industry. This subset is defined by the availability of brand price and attribute data. The input data are taken from the records of Boren (the All Japan Cotton Spinners' Association), and the brand price is taken from the regular quotations made by the Osaka Cotton Merchants' Union. For the entire period between 1906 and 1935, the Osaka Cotton Merchants' Union quoted prices regularly on all the major brands and many of the minor brands of cotton yarn and cloth. Characterizations of these brands in terms of the seven attributes discussed above are also readily available.

The Implicit Prices of the Attributes of Japanese Cloth and Yarn

The prices of cloth and yarn attributes required for the estimation of equation (2) are not explicit market prices. Rather, following earlier work on hedonic price indexes, cloth prices are first regressed on cloth characteristics to obtain a hedonic price function:

$$P_c = \sum_i \sum_j d_{ij} u_i^{1/2} u_j^{1/2} \tag{3}$$

where u_i and u_j are cloth attributes, and P_c is the price of cloth.[5] By differentiating equation (3) after estimation, it is possible to obtain the implicit prices of the cloth characteristics:

$$P_i = \frac{\partial \hat{P}_c}{\partial u_i} = \frac{1}{2} \Sigma d_{ij} \left(\frac{u_j}{u_i}\right)^{1/2} \tag{4}$$

While one relationship is used to characterize the temporally pooled observations on firm brand prices, it is clear from the form of equation (4) that, in general, the implicit prices of attributes will vary from firm to firm and over time as the attribute composition of a product varies. This will occur even as these firms are at any one time operating in the same market and is at least theoretically possible, because of the nature of the demand for cloth and the technology associated with its production.[6]

---

[5] The approach taken here follows, among others, Rosen (1974) and Lucas (1975). In equation (3) it is assumed that $d_{ij} = d_{ji} = 0$.
[6] Had the functional form of the hedonic price function in equation (3) been linear, the implicit prices of attributes would be constant, even as the amount of a particular attribute embodied in a brand of cloth varied.

The worldwide market for cotton cloth in which the Japanese participated between 1906 and 1935 consisted of a number of separate, but highly inter-related markets. These markets for cloth were primarily differentiated according to taste and custom, climate, income levels, etc., a differentiation which occurred internally as well as internationally. In Japan, it was exemplified by the separate markets for traditional and modern cloth. Internationally, the light-weight, finely woven cloth which was climatically required in such Japanese export markets as India and Southeast Asia, was not abundantly used in Japan. And again, the heavily-sized, sparsely-woven cloth that Japan sold in the 1930s to the poorer regions and lower-income groups throughout the world would scarcely have been purchased by anyone with even moderate, not to mention substantial, means.

If the attributes of the cloths were all traded separately in explicit markets, the nonlinear form of equation (3) would not make sense. Competition should have made the price of an attribute everywhere the same. (Yarns of varying counts were traded in explicit markets.) Because clothing attributes which satisfied a variety of different ultimate demands came packaged as cloth and could not be trivially unraveled and recombined, because consumers in the world market differed in their tastes, needs and wealth, and because firms differed in their capabilities, or may have chosen to specialize in the satisfaction of particular markets by producing particular attribute packages, differences in the implicit prices of the same attribute could occur in competitive markets. (See the discussion in Rosen (1974) and Triplet (1976).)

Equation (3) is estimated using generalized, least-squares methods which allow for unmeasured time-specific and firm-specific effects using dummy variables. Some of the results of this estimation are presented in table 8.1. These results should be interpreted with some care. The hedonic price regression is not a substitute for the estimation of the decision-making framework laid out in equations (1) and (2). The hedonic price function may be thought of as a relationship that traces out the transactions generated by the intersection of the attribute buyer's implicit compensated demand functions with the attribute seller's implicit compensated supply functions. Because buyers and sellers differ among themselves in the ways outlined above, the hedonic price function is generated by many different demand functions intersecting with many different supply functions. The hedonic price function duplicates econometrically the market information known to buyers and sellers. If, however, we wish to understand the determinants of the implicit transaction prices for each of the attributes, rather than "simply" the implicit transaction price itself, demand and supply functions must be identified and estimated.

In table 8.2, some attempt is made to summarize the market information obtained from estimating equation (3). The average implicit price for each characteristic, the coefficient of variation of this price among firms, and the average amount of this characteristic packaged in a piece of cloth are presented for five-year intervals.

Table 8.1: The hedonic price regression coefficients

	d_{i1}	d_{i2}	d_{i3}	d_{i4}	d_{i5}	d_{i6}	d_{i7}	d_{i8}
$i=1$ weight	0	0.893×10^{-5} (0.3×10^{-5})	0.851×10^{-5} (0.3×10^{-5})	0.531×10^{-6} (0.2×10^{-6})	0.941×10^{-6} (0.5×10^{-6})	0.632×10^{-8} (0.6×10^{-1})	0.319×10^{-7} (0.4×10^{-2})	0.131×10^{-4} (0.6×10^{-5})
$i=2$ warp yarn number		0	0.132×10^{-2} (0.9×10^{-3})	0.623×10^{-3} (0.6×10^{-3})	0.916×10^{-3} (0.7×10^{-3})	0.511×10^{-4} (0.1×10^{-1})	0.238×10^{-5} (0.2×10^{-1})	0.273×10^{-2} (0.2×10^{-2})
$i=3$ weft yarn number			0	0.497×10^{-3} (0.4×10^{-3})	0.724×10^{-3} (0.2×10^{-3})	0.290×10^{-4} (0.2×10^{-4})	0.321×10^{-7} (0.3×10^{-7})	0.323×10^{-3} (0.3×10^{-3})
$i=4$ ends per inch				0	0.561×10^{-2} (0.2×10^{-3})	0.438×10^{-2} (0.1×10^{-2})	0.228×10^{-2} (0.1×10^{-2})	0.113 (0.3×10)
$i=5$ picks per inch					0	0.517×10^{-2} (0.3×10^{-2})	0.196×10^{-2} (0.1×10^{-2})	0.263 (0.4×10)
$i=6$ plain weave						0	0.000 (0.000)	0.592×10^{-2} (0.4×10^{-2})
$i=7$ twill weave							0	0.681×10^{-2} (0.3×10^{-2})
$i=8$ width								0

$R^2 = 0.779$. The numbers in parentheses are standard errors. The eight cloth attributes are indexed by i as above

While great care must be exercised in interpreting tables 8.1 and 8.2, a number of observations should be made, First, dissimilar trends are found in the average implicit prices of the cloth attributes. The attributes of yarn fineness, sizing, and width show increasing prices, whereas the cloth-density variables show decreasing trends. At the same time, these differing trends can be loosely related to changes in attribute weight or quantities. Positive price trends are associated with increases in attribute quantities. Declines in implicit price also seem to be associated with small declines in attribute quantities. Since the hedonic price equation is not a structural equation, no real interpretation of these associations may be given. Only when the profit function has been estimated can such an interpretive linking of prices and quantities be made.

If the average piece of Japanese-made cloth was getting wider and being more heavily sized, and came to use finer yarns which were less densely woven, it is also true that Japanese production was becoming more heterogeneous over time. This is certainly reflected in the coefficients of variation of the implicit individual firm prices of the attributes. For all the eight attributes, there are nontrivial variations in the implicit attribute prices among firms. For all eight attributes, this variation becomes more pronounced with World War I and continues to increase sharply 1935.

The Estimation of Derived Product Attribute Supply Functions and Derived Input Demand Functions

Implicit prices calculated using the coefficient estimates in table 8.1 are used in the estimation of the equation (2). Note that these implicit prices are not pre-determined variables. Although textile firms being modeled did not have market power, brand choice and implicit prices were determined simultaneously. It is also plausible to assume that elements of the stochastic terms in different derived product attribute supply and derived input demand will have nonzero covariance. These two factors together suggest that a variant of three-stage least squares should be used in estimating equation (2).[7]

Once these demand and supply functions have been estimated, it is possible to describe fully the technical relationships between the differing attributes of and inputs into the production of cloth in Japan. Table 8.3 presents partial elasticities of transformation between attributes, partial elasticities of substitution between inputs, and partial elasticities of transformation between attributes and inputs. These elasticities are defined in terms of the profit function in Diewert (1974).

[7] Given that the same being used here is a time-series of cross-sections, it is easy enough to imagine firm and time effects having nonzero covariances.

The instrumental variables actually used in estimating values for equation (2) include (a) money borrowed on promissory notes, (b) formally educated technicians per plant, (c) managerial experience, (d) price of coal, (e) cotton yarn inventory, (f) exports, (g) rate of dividends, (h) paid-in capital, and (i) horsepower.

Table 8.2: The implicit price of cloth characteristics

	1906	1911	1916	1921	1926	1931	1935
Weight (lb per square yard)[a]							
Real implicit price (index)	100.0	108.2	105.7	112.1	115.8	124.3	124.6
Coefficient of variation of price	0.043	0.041	0.038	0.069	0.052	0.097	0.103
Quantity (index)	100.0	100.7	100.4	108.9	106.4	109.5	108.7
Warp yarn number (hanks)							
Real implicit price (index)	100.0	109.5	107.3	110.1	115.4	120.2	133.4
Coefficient of variation of price	0.85	0.83	1.36	3.22	2.67	4.13	3.63
Quantity (index)	100.0	103.6	104.1	104.9	110.6	114.6	119.2
Weft yarn number (hanks)							
Real implicit price (index)	100.0	109.9	107.9	108.8	109.1	124.3	128.0
Coefficient of variation of price	0.81	0.79	1.28	2.93	2.58	4.01	3.43
Quantity (index)	100.0	103.1	103.4	104.2	108.5	111.2	115.9
Ends per inch							
Real implicit price (index,	100.0	106.9	105.5	89.4	92.7	89.8	83.4
Coefficient of variation of price	2.01	1.89	2.99	4.28	3.50	5.25	4.63
Quantity (index)	100.0	104.2	105.1	100.0	101.2	99.8	100.3

Picks per inch							
Real implicit price (index)	100.0	105.8	104.1	86.0	90.7	96.3	89.1
Coefficient of variation of price	0.962	0.884	1.31	1.73	1.55	1.94	1.83
Quantity (index)	100.0	103.4	103.9	98.4	99.1	99.0	99.6
Plain weave							
Real implicit price (index)	100.0	100.2	97.9	103.3	102.2	98.1	97.3
Coefficient of variation of price	0.18	0.22	0.25	0.33	0.36	0.29	0.32
Quantity (index)	100.0	97.2	92.5	97.4	89.6	98.5	97.0
Twill weave							
Real implicit price (index)	100.0	101.3	103.6	107.2	105.3	106.3	110.7
Coefficient of variation of price	0.13	0.14	0.17	0.38	0.32	0.35	0.39
Quantity (index)	100.0	104.6	108.3	110.4	107.5	109.3	109.4
Width (inches)							
Real implicit price (index)	100.0	107.8	105.0	109.2	115.8	138.3	147.7
Coefficient of variation of price	4.47	5.49	5.43	8.87	7.35	7.91	8.16
Quantity (index)	100.0	132.1	147.3	163.5	176.9	195.0	231.8

[a] As with most such prices in prewar Japan, changes in the price of cloth are dominated by fluctuations in the business cycle. In an effort to avoid imposing still greater complexity on the estimation of the hedonic price function, prices of cloth have been deflated by the price of raw cotton

Table 8.3: Partial elasticities of transformation and substitution

	Weight 1	Warp yarn number 2	Weft yarn number 3	Ends per inch 4	Picks per inch 5	Plain weave 6
1. Weight	−0.509 (2.78)	1.73 (9.30)	0.394 (2.54)	1.43 (0.526)	1.65 (0.589)	0.170 (32.3)
2. Warp yarn number		−14.3 (5.18)	−1.72 (0.510)	−5.50 (1.42)	−1.10 (3.72)	3.05 (3.28)
3. Weft yarn number			−9.26 (3.72)	−1.91 (0.901)	−5.41 (0.878)	4.78 (3.39)
4. Ends per inch				−1.64 (0.804)	−6.35 (2.26)	5.45 (5.05)
5. Picks per inch					−3.15 (0.518)	2.65 (4.97)
6. Plain weave						−18.0 (10.7)
7. Twill						
8. Width						
9. Labor						
10. Chinese cotton						
11. East Indian cotton						
12. American cotton						
13. Egyptian cotton						
14. Other cotton						

The numbers in parentheses are standard errors. The elasticities calculated in this table are for mean values of the variable quantities and fixed inputs only

The results in table 8.3 confirm that the technical relationships in Japanese cloth production were such that Japanese textile firms could make significant adjustments in the attributes of the cloth they produced in response to changing conditions in both product and factor markets. Of the 35 elasticities of transformation for attributes in table 8.3, 17 are statistically significantly different from zero. Tradeoffs clearly existed among cloth attributes. Variations were possible in response to changing demand conditions.

Substitution was also possible among the different kinds of raw-cotton input. Of the 15 partial substitution elasticities (including own elasticities) among the five different grades of raw cotton, nine are statistically significant from zero, and only one has a sign which is a priori implausible. Given that each of these

Twill 7	Width 8	Labor 9	Chinese cotton 10	East Indian cotton 11	American cotton 12	Egyptian cotton 13	Other cotton 14
0.708 (119.0)	0.928 (1.56)	−0.401 (0.454)	−0.777 (127×10)	−1.91 (28.0)	0.993×10^{-1} (193×10)	−0.602 (1.84)	0.389 (1.44)
1.96 (5.58)	−4.79 (21.2)	1.85 (0.459)	−6.84 (2.49)	−4.61 (1.29)	3.78 (5.86)	2.46 (2.46)	−1.93 (316×10)
0.639 (0.720)	−0.536 (3.52)	2.74 (1.31)	−7.60 (3.55)	−4.33 (0.487)	7.02 (4.31)	1.39 (1.72)	0.000 (0.100)
4.52 (3.65)	0.758×10^{-1} (120×10^3)	0.686 (0.388)	−2.25 (0.547)	−3.19 (1.19)	9.90 (6.11)	0.534 (460×10^6)	3.82 (543×10)
1.99 (1.45)	0.104 (278×10^2)	1.20 (0.449)	−4.00 (2.33)	−3.52 (1.64)	11.0 (6.96)	0.657 (165×10^3)	5.25 (1.75)
8.16 (1.23)	0.821 (0.472)	0.555 (286×10)	-0.348×10^{-2} (674)	-0.402×10^{-1} (108×10^3)	-0.153×10^{-4} (0.158×10^{-1})	0.146 (0.375)	−3.90 (3.79)
−13.4 (5.51)	−0.244 (0.156)	0.819 (11.0)	-0.655×10^{-4} (0.655×10^{-1})	-0.947×10^{-2} (170)	0.180×10^{-4} (5.55)	0.595×10^{-5} (0.999×10^{-5})	−2.58 (2.05)
	−1.13 (0.294)	1.04 (0.680)	0.318×10^{-1} (63.2)	0.898×10^{-2} (1.11)	0.651×10^{-4} (7.37)	-0.441×10^{-1} (4.84)	−0.144 (4.13)
		−1.82 (0.938)	−14.6 (9.07)	−9.09 (4.55)	1.56 (0.647)	3.88 (2.71)	0.915 (1.04)
			−15.2 (10.2)	0.397 (0.208)	16.23 (7.66)	7.82 (4.49)	8.51 (8.56)
				−13.5 (7.46)	0.868 (0.543)	5.34 (2.14)	0.960 (3.20)
					−10.9 (4.66)	1.25 (0.727)	4.98 (7.89)
						6.31 (6.19)	12.4 (116×10^2)
							0.555 (396×10)

partial elasticities is calculated on the assumption that all other attributes and inputs are being held constant, these results are a potent demonstration of the character of Japanese cotton mixing or blending techniques. The following quotation from a former president of the Toyo Spinning Company is instructive:

> When we say "cotton blending" we refer to the technical skill and ability to choose most cheaply and economically those varieties among the world's cotton embodied with the necessary and sufficient use values to spin yarns of a given quality. Normally speaking, however, since there is no single variety of raw cotton that will simultaneously meet their qualifica-

tions, men contrive to fulfill their conditions by blending and mixing various varieties of raw cotton ... cotton blending consists of skill in choosing and purchasing cheaper cotton as well as the mechanical skills needed to put this cotton to use in the mills.

In America where cotton of a uniform quality is plentiful and readily available, there is no economic need to resort to blending, so these skills have not developed there. England, however, is in a geographical position similar to Japan which should encourage consideration of adopting blending procedures. They have not, however, developed these either partly perhaps [*sic*] because trade unions have a voice in the usage of raw cotton. Cotton blending has therefore come to be known world-wide as a technique unique to the Japanese. (Quoted in Seki 1956)

Of special interest to this study are the elasticities of transformation in table 8.3 between variable input and output attributes. For example, as observations on actual practice confirm, the finer the yarn in the Japanese cloth, the greater the input of high-quality (American and Egyptian) raw cotton. Similarly, the more densely the yarn has been laid in the cloth, the greater the input of raw cotton.

In view of the continuing interest in the process of labor absorption in LDCs, special attention centers on the elasticities of transformation and substitution associated with the labor variable. Of the 15 elasticities presented in table 8.3, eight are statistically significant with plausible signs. These estimated elasticities clearly suggest that the more slack there was in the labor market, the more appropriate it was to produce coarser yarn. Specifically, as table 8.3 indicates, a 1 percent decline in the price of labor relative to the price of yarn was associated with a 1.8 percent decline in the count of warp yarn and a 2.7 percent decline in the count of weft yarn produced. In other words, the lower-quality cotton is significantly associated with larger labor absorption. This makes sense, as coarser yarn, by being twisted less, made relatively less use of the most capital-intensive processes of the textile mill, whereas more labor could be used to repair the larger number of broken ends in the spinning process.

The elasticities also show that the lower the real wages in the labor market, everything else being equal, the easier it was to use lower-quality raw cotton. Raw-cotton mixing and blending was a relatively labor-intensive process. With cheap labor available, short-stapled Chinese and East Indian cotton could be substituted for American and Egyptian cotton. Table 8.3 shows that a 1 percent decline in the price of labor relative to the price of Chinese raw cotton is associated with a 14.6 percent increase in the amount of Chinese raw cotton being used by each laborer. By contrast, a 1 percent decline in the price of labor relative to the price of American raw cotton is associated with a 1.6 percent decline in its use.

Finally, it is also clear from table 8.3 that the number of warp and weft threads in a square inch of cloth were adjusted to the character of the labor market. For a given count (or yarn number), weft yarn, because it was filling, could use lower-quality, shorter-staple raw cotton. To survive breakages in weaving, warp yarns required higher-quality raw cotton. For this reason, an increased use of weft yarn may be viewed as a relatively labor-using innovation. This is consistent with our findings, which show that the decline in the real wages of labor led to an increase in the number of picks per inch (weft) relative to the number of ends (warp).

An estimation of equation (2) also makes it possible to obtain estimates of the elasticity of transformation (in this context, sometimes called the elasticity of intensity) for each of the variable output attributes and inputs and the fixed inputs. On the basis of these results, the earlier observations on this subject by Hirschman and Gerschenkron and the contrasting more recent empirical work seem rather too simple. The two quality-dimensions of labor have rather different implications for labor absorption. The more experienced the labor force becomes, the more productive it becomes, but also the greater the demand for labor. Worker experience within the Japanese textile industry, in other words, was labor-absorbing. By contrast, while more exposure to formal primary education also meant a more productive textile worker, this way of improving labor quality diminished the demand for labor. Worker education in the Japanese textile industry was labor-displacing.

Why, then, should two different dimensions of labor quality have such different implications for labor demand? First, it should be understood that changes in the "environment" of the production process embodied in a particular input do not necessarily augment that input alone or at all (Tobin 1967). The improvement in the quality of labor, for whatever reason, need not be simply labor-augmenting.

In the case of the Japanese textile industry, the change in the two dimensions of labor quality actually relate to two different classes of workers. Experience of the average workers in this industry increased because a corps of permanent workers developed over time in the industry, not because the rate and time-pattern of departure of new recruits changed. From each entering cohort of workers, a few stayed on and gained supervisory positions on the mill floor. It is certainly plausible that such supervisors could have been complementary with unskilled labor. In this sense the findings here do support Gershenkron (1962), Hirschman (1958), and Yahr (1968).

Even though the pattern of separation of new workers from the textile industry remained unchanged during the first 35 years of the 20th century, the educational background of the new workers did improve. The fact additional workers were exposed to primary education did make a difference. Within the primary school, the future mill operative learned for the first time to respond to the discipline of a nonfamily adult. The demands for constant attention and regular attendance, the necessity of confronting new situations and mastering them – how similar this was to life in the mill compound! The better-educated recruit was a better textile worker. In this instance, an improvement in labor

Table 8.4: Elasticities of transformation between fixed inputs and variable quantities

$i =$	Spindle hours	Loom hours	Length of shift	Experience	Education
1. Weight	0.723 (0.681×10^{-1})	0.440 (0.509×10^{-1})	-0.849×10^{-3} (0.522×10^{-2})	2.77 (1.41)	1.59 (0.874)
2. Warp yarn number	0.238×10^{-3} (0.312×10^{-4})	0.745×10^{-4} (0.463×10^{-4})	-0.132×10^{-1} (0.121×10^{-1})	-0.243×10^{-1} (0.155×10^{-1})	0.682×10^{-1} (0.383×10^{-1})
3. Weft yarn number	0.241×10^{-3} (0.352×10^{-4})	0.529×10^{-4} (0.311×10^{-4})	-0.828×10^{-2} (0.121×10^{-1})	-0.992×10^{-2} (0.557×10^{-2})	0.319×10^{-1} (0.132×10^{-1})
4. Ends per inch	0.514×10^{-5} (1.52)	0.381×10^{-1} (0.492×10^{-1})	-0.562×10^{-2} (0.715×10^{-2})	0.197 (0.938×10^{-1})	0.736×10^{-2} (0.750×10^{-2})
5. Picks per inch	0.881 (544)	0.334×10^{-1} (0.831×10^{-2})	-0.264×10^{-2} (0.196×10^{-2})	0.212 (0.702×10^{-1})	0.681×10^{-2} (0.482×10^{-2})
6. Plain weave	0.621×10^{-4} (0.114)	-0.139×10^{-4} (0.128×10^{-4})	0.158×10^{-3} (0.235×10^{-3})	0.630 (0.406)	0.132 (0.132)
7. Twill weave	0.735×10^{-4} (0.166)	0.167×10^{-2} (0.225×10^{-2})	0.710×10^{-4} (0.249)	0.593×10^{-2} (0.544×10^{-2})	0.101×10^{-1} (0.871×10^{-2})

8. Width	0.320×10^{-3} (0.168 × 10^{-1})	0.726×10^{-1} (0.338 × 10^{-1})	0.001 (1.00)	-0.112×10^{-4} (0.179 × 10^{-2})	0.532×10^{-3} (0.106 × 10^{-2})
9. Labor	0.861 (0.165)	0.391 (0.200)	0.561 (0.140)	1.80 (0.561)	−0.657 (0.132)
10. Chinese cotton	0.505 (0.110)	−1.34 (0.871)	0.231 (0.234)	1.07 (0.252)	-0.219×10^{-1} (0.259)
11. East Indian cotton	0.892 (0.146)	0.361×10^{-2} (0.195 × 10^{-2})	0.149 (0.244)	0.125 (0.321)	0.571×10^{-1} (0.192)
12. American cotton	0.715 (0.160)	0.517 (0.157)	0.474 (1.89)	0.223 (0.327)	1.03 (0.526)
13. Egyptian cotton	1.01 (0.301)	1.21 (1.29)	0.840×10^{-2} (0.641 × 10^{-2})	-0.991×10^{-1} (0.703 × 10^{-1})	1.14 (0.770)
14. Other cotton	0.529 (0.542)	0.141×10^{-1} (0.358 × 10^{-1})	0.437×10^{-2} (0.200)	-0.182×10^{-1} (0.193 × 10^{-1})	-0.849×10^{-2} (0.136 × 10^{-1})

The numbers in parentheses are standard errors. The elasticities calculated in this table are for mean values of the variable quantities and fixed inputs only

quality might be thought of as labor-augmenting. If this is the case, an increase in the proportion of workers with primary-school education could lead to a decline in the demand for workers measured in natural units.

Some additional information on the influence of changing labor quality on the production process, as well as some corroboration of the above analysis, may be obtained by examining the sign and significance of the elasticities of transformation between experience and education and nonlabor inputs and output attributes which are presented in table 8.4. For example, the results in the experience column of table 8.4 provide support for the hypothesis that a more experienced work force will mean, *ceteris paribus*, more sizing of cloth, a lower weft-count number, more threads per given area of cloth, and greater use of Chinese and East Indian cotton. The results with respect to new cottons and yarn count are consistent with the finding that a more experienced labor force led to a more labor-intensive mode of production. In addition, the finding that a more experienced labor force led to a significant increase in sizing is consistent with the previous treatment of experience as something of a proxy for the supervision of the mill labor force. It is well known in the technical literature of the textile industry that heavy sizing requires considerable supervision (Copeland 1912).

In contrast with the results for increased work experience, the results in the education column of table 8.4 associate increased formal education with higher counts of both warp and weft yarns, and relatively greater use of American raw cotton. Again, this is consistent with earlier findings that an increasingly primary-school-educated labor force made possible a less labor-intensive mode of production.

Conclusion

Making use of an unusually rich data set, a number of results of potentially wide interest have been uncovered. The Japanese textile industry developed a new range of cotton cloths well-suited to East Asian markets and to the demands of lower-income classes elsewhere by aggressively taking advantage of the tradeoffs that clearly existed among a variety of the quality dimensions of cotton cloth. The Japanese were successful in profitably producing this unprecedently-shoddy product in large measure because they creatively explored the complementarity and substitution possibilities between varying grades of raw cotton and between varying grades of labor. Japanese manufacturers joined the production of newly-shoddy merchandise to the use of an overall lower quality of raw cotton and overall lower quality of labor force than was characteristic of their industrial predecessors in other countries. A good stripped of superfluous characteristics was developed to be mass-produced by a labor force in large measure without economic attributes other than those being exercised in their work in the textile industry.

The experience of the textile industry was not unique. Other Japanese industries later came to have similar experiences. It is a measure of how far Japan has come, when we remember that one or two generations ago Japan was associated in the public mind not with high-quality, but with poor-quality merchandise. In industry after industry, the poor durability of Japanese products was widely noted. Whatever quality dimensions were lacking, poor-quality Japanese machinery, light bulbs, matches, umbrellas, and the like were commercially successful. There were important markets for products with these characteristics, and they could be cheaply produced by Japan, a country rich in unskilled labor, but with a dearth of skilled labor.

References

Behrman, J. R. (1972), "Sectoral Elasticities of Substitution between Capital and Labor in a Developing Economy: Time Series Analysis in the Case of Postwar Chile," *Econometrica*, 40(2): 311–26 (March).

Berndat, E., and L. Christensen (1974), "Testing for the Existence of a Consistent Aggregate Index of Labor Inputs," *American Economic Review*, 64: 391–404 (June).

Clark, W. A. Graham (1914), *Cotton Goods in Japan*, Washington: US Government Printing Office.

Copeland, M. T. (1912), *The Cotton Manufacturing Industry of the United States*, Cambridge, MA: Harvard University Press.

Denny, M., and M. Fuss (1977), "The Use of Approximation Analysis to Test for Separability and the Existence of Consistent Aggregates," *American Economic Review*, 67: 404–18 (June).

Diewert, W. D. (1973), "Functional Forms for Profit and Transformation Functions," *Journal of Economic Theory*, 6: 284–376 (June).

Diewert, W. D. (1974), "Application of Quality Theory," in Michael D. Intriligator and David Kendrick, eds, *Frontiers of Quantitative Economics*, vol. II, Amsterdam: North Holland.

Doane, Donna (1969), "Regional Structure of the Cotton Textile Industry," Ph.D. dissertation, Purdue University.

Gerschenkron, Alexander (1962), *Economic Backwardness in Historical Perspective*, Cambridge, MA: Harvard University Press.

Gorman, W. (1968), "Measuring the Quantities of Fixed Factors," in J. Wolfe, ed., *Value, Capital and Growth*, Chicago: Aldine Publishing Company.

Hirschman, A. (1958), *The Strategy of Economic Development*, New Haven, CT: Yale University Press.

Hoye, J. (1942), *Staple Cotton Fabrics*, New York: McGraw-Hill.

Hunter, J. (1924), *Cloth and the Cloth Trade*, London: Pitman.

Kintis, A. A. (1977), "Capital–Labor Substitution in a Developing Country – The Case of Greece: Comments and Some New Results," *European Economic Review*, 9: 379–82 (August).

Lancaster, K. (1966), "A New Approach to Consumer Theory," *Journal of Political Economy*, 74: 132–56 (April).

Lucas, Robert E. B. (1975), "Hedonic Price Function," *Economic Inquiry*, 13(2): 157–78 (June).

Rosen, Sherwin (1974), "Hedonic Prices and Implicit Markets," *Journal of Political Economy*, 82(1): 34–55 (January/February).

Samuelson, Paul A. (1953), "Price of Factors and Goods in General Equilibrium," *Review of Economic Studies*, 21(1): 1–20 (June).

Sapir, A. (1980), "Economic Growth and Factor Substitution: What Happened to the Yugoslav Miracle?" *Economic Journal*, 90: 294–313 (June).

Saxonhouse, Gary (1975), "Capital Accumulation, Labor Saving, and Labor Absorption Once More, Once More," *Quarterly Journal of Economics*, 89: 322–30 (May).

Saxonhouse, Gary (1976), "Country Girls and Communication among Competitors in the Japanese Cotton Spinning Industry," in Hugh T. Patrick, with Larry Meissner eds, *Japanese Industrialization and Its Social Consequences*, Berkeley, CA: University of California Press.

Seki, N. (1956), *The Cotton Industry of Japan*, Tokyo: Japanese Society for the Promotion of Science.

Sines, R. H. (1979), "Sectoral Elasticities of Substitution between Labor and Capital in Venezuelan Manufacturing: A Cross-Sectional Micro Analysis," *World Development*, 7: 79–82 (January).

Solomon, R., and D. Forsyth (1977), "Substitution of Labour for Capital in the Foreign Sector: Some Further Evidence," *Economic Journal*, 87: 283–89 (June).

Stewart, F. (1972), "Choice of Technique in Developing Countries," *Journal of Development Studies*, 9: 99–121 (October).

Tobin, J. (1967), "Comment," in Murray Brown, ed., *The Theory and Empirical Analysis of Production*, New York: Columbia University Press, for the National Bureau of Economic Research.

Triplet, J. (1976), "Consumer Demand and Characteristics of Consumption Goods," in N. Terleckyi, ed., *Household Production and Consumption*, New York: Columbia University Press.

Whiteside, A. (1940), *Whiteside's Textile Information and Conversion Tables*, Bloomfield, NH: Morse Press.

Yahr, M. (1968), "Human Capital and Factor Substitution in the CES Production Function," in P. Kenen and R. Lawrence, eds, *The Open Economy*, New York: Columbia University Press.

9 Supply and Demand for Quality Workers in Cotton Spinning in Japan and India

GARY SAXONHOUSE and
YUKIHIKO KIYOKAWA

In the last decade of the 19th century, the Japanese cotton textile industry rapidly changed from being an importer of Indian yarn to a strong competitor in the Chinese market, and went on to dominate Asian markets in cotton textiles in the pre-Pacific War period. Why this occurred and why India could not compete with Japan is the topic of this chapter. Our explanation focuses on the relationship between the operation of the labor market and labor quality.

Labor productivity in the Japanese cotton spinning industry was lower than in the Indian industry in the late 1890s. But by the first decade of the 20th century the reverse was true, and in subsequent decades the gap widened. Achievement of high labor productivity by Japanese spinners was basically due to an improvement in the capacity of Japanese management to deal with the least expensive labor available in the Japanese economy (teenage girls), and to the gradual improvement in the quality of this labor. Indian managers were less effective.

The starting point of our analysis is a remarkable 1897 survey of Japanese cotton spinners. The data allow us to describe the industry's labor force in some detail. Indeed, the sample is so rich and varied in detail on worker and company characteristics that it is possible to specify a behavioral function sufficiently general to allow time conditions of the 1890s to be treated as a special case. This is done in the first section of this chapter. Provided a function estimated from the cross-section data of the 1890s can be temporarily extrapolated, the changes in the labor-market conditions between the 1890s and later periods can easily be treated as changes in the values of variables included in our functions. This perspective forms the comparison of the Japanese and Indian industries made in the second part of the chapter.

The authors express their thanks to Prof. K. N. Raj for his valuable comments at the CA Project Conference, and to Dr. Kazuo Koike for his kind provision of crucial data.

177

This view of labor-market developments in Japan should not be considered simply as a mathematical trick. There is considerable substantive evidence worker behaviour in the 1890s persisted in later periods; it was the proportions of various types of workers that changed (Saxonhouse (1976) introduced this theme). Thus, for example, the pattern of departure of new recruits from the industry is similar in 1925 and 1895. Because there were fewer new recruits in the 1920s than in the 1890s, the statistics of the aggregate turnover suggest radical changes in behaviour that simply did not occur. Thus we feel, at least in this case, a function estimated from cross-section data can be extrapolated through time, and the changes in labor-market conditions after the 1890s can be treated as changes in the values of variables included in our functions.

We still must ask, however, how there came to be a larger number of experienced mill hands in the 1920s. Was it simply history? The almost inevitable logistic development of the industry meant faster growth, followed by slower growth. A new, faster-growing industry cannot have experienced workers – unlike an older, slower growing one. Or, did the spinning mills devise strategies that successfully encourage the growth of an experienced labor force?

The markets for job characteristics in early industrialization, which result from the interaction of company desires and capabilities with worker preferences and opportunities, have not been studied systematically for any period of any country's economic history. Thus, our explicit treatment of job and worker characteristics in the estimation of worker preference functions also makes possible the construction of hedonic worker compensation indexes. Neither the construction of the various well-known Japanese wage series, nor their interpretation deal adequately with either the changing quality of jobs or the changing quality of workers (see, for example, Minami 1973; Minami and Ono 1979). Yet these changes are extremely helpful in resolving conflicting interpretations of the series during the 1920s and 1930s. The preference function estimated here provides the basis for a proper treatment of these changes and for the construction of a new, more appropriate compensation series.

Workers in the Japanese Cotton Spinning Industry

The Japanese cotton spinning industry starting its explosive development at the beginning of the 1880s. The number of spindles rose from 76,600 in 1887 to 385,321 in 1892, and to 970,567 in 1897 – almost a 13-fold increase. This great expansion necessitated a rapid rise in the number of mill hands: 2,330 in 1887, 25,232 in 1892, 44,992 in 1897 – a 19-fold expansion. Given the small number of experienced mill hands available during this decade, the spinning labor market

---

[1] Although the subject probed is sensitive, the reliability of the data seems excellent. For example, Kanebo (the Kanegafuchi Spinning Mills) internal documents are virtually identical with what is in the report. The formation of the committee (*shokko jijo chosa i-inkai*) is discussed in Boren (1897).

was understandably tumultuous. Well-publicized raids between mills spawned headlines in the Japanese newspapers. (See Fujibayashi 1943: Sampei 1936.)

In our analysis of the Japanese cotton spinning labor market of the 1890s, the spinning mill is viewed as offering a bundle of job characteristics containing wages, pace of work, hazards and health care, and the availability and quality of dormitory life. Workers are viewed as having preferences with respect to varying bundles of job characteristics. Such preferences are assumed to vary with the traits of these workers; thus, age, experience, education, and other presumptively valuable traits shape the preferences of workers.

In 1897, as discussions in Noshomusho (the Ministry of Agriculture and Commerce) caused heightened concern among cotton spinning firms that strict factory legislation might be enacted, Boren (the then-infant All Japan Cotton Spinners' Association) established a working group of the representatives of 14 firms for the purpose of collecting information on the working conditions in the industry. This committee was exceedingly successful in meeting its charge: 71,000 workers in 75 mills were examined.

An unusually quantitatively detailed report in identical format was obtained from each mill on: (1) the recruitment practices and payments; (2) workers classified by age, work experience, and literacy; (3) number and length of rest periods during a working day, length of shifts, and number of days between shift rotation; (4) wage-payment systems; (5) expenditure for health care, number of doctors and nurses in attendance, incidence of sickness, injury, and death attributable to particular diseases and other causes; (6) availability of dormitories, including their rules and restrictions, food costs, and supervisory and educational personnel costs; and (7) the rate of workers' absenteeism and the time pattern of permanent separation from the mill. Underlying these reports were specially prepared worker registers, also in identical format.[1]

The summary of this investigation paints an interesting picture of mill life in the late 1890s. A significant percentage of the labor force of the industry was recruited hundreds of miles from the spinning mills. Already, the familiar pattern of the Kansai (Osaka, Kobe, and Kyoto) mills recruiting teenage girls from southern Kyushu and Shikoku, and the Kanto (Tokyo area) mills recruiting from northern Honshu was established. (After 1924, the exact regional distribution of recruits to the spinning industry is available from Koseisho.) The distribution in 1924 and thereafter was quite similar to the pattern reported in 1897. On recruitment, the worker's family received a bonus, which on average was equivalent to twenty days' starting wages. The typical recruit was a teenage girl. For the spinning mill's female labor force as a whole, the average age was 19, and almost 30 percent were aged 14 or younger.

The girls typically faced a working day almost 12 hours long, with some three rest periods totaling an hour for each shift. Half the mill labor force worked a day shift, usually beginning at 6 a.m., and half worked an evening shift beginning at 6 p.m. Shifts generally rotated every seven days, and one day was allowed off each week.

A large majority of the female workers lived in company-run dormitories. These dormitories, to some extent inspired by glowing reports of the early 19th-century experience at Lowell, Massachusetts, offered their workers many services, but placed many restrictions on their activities after work hours. Permisssion to leave the mill compound was restricted. Regulations varied; some mills allowed one or two hours outside the compound each day, others allowed none. Infractions of discipline, a less than excellent attendance record, and an otherwise poor work record led to a suspension of the privilege. However, many of the regulations were closer to ideals than actuality.

Included among the benefits were subsidized food in company dormitories, and health and education facilities. The implicit food subsidy per month was equivalent to a week's wages for an inexperienced recruit. Also, 63 of the 65 mills reporting on their provision of health care had dispensaries staffed by at least one full-time nurse, while 37 offered general education instruction to their workers. Having dispensaries in the mills certainly made sense, as at one time or another during a year, 75 percent of the labor force became ill. And, although it is difficult to ascertain the quality of the health care, the survival rate from sickness and accident was excellent. The mills surveyed experienced no more than 4.9 deaths per 1,000 workers during 1897. Given the age distribution of workers in the mills surveyed, mill workers experienced a lower mortality rate than the average of the age cohorts from which they were drawn.[2]

It is difficult to determine the quality of education offered. Among the 37 mills providing instruction, there was an average of just four instructors for 1,000 female workers. Because 30 percent of the work force was aged 14 or under, individual exposure was probably quite limited. This is not surprising. Typical classes lasted for two hours and were scheduled at 7 p.m. for the day shift and 7 a.m. for the night shift. The attentiveness of workers, who had completed an 11-hour shift, with an hour's mealtime between the end of the shift and the beginning of the class, can only be surmised.

The high turnover of workers, which was characteristic of the cotton spinning labor force during the entire pre-Pacific War period, was certainly indicated in the 1897 survey. Over 40 percent of the newly recruited workers left the mills within six months of their employment. This departure rate is lower than the rate characteristic of the industry for much of the prewar period at the level of both the individual mill and the aggregate industry. The average work experience

---

[2] The results should be qualified. The mortality rate for mill workers has been compared to mortality rates using the life-tables constructed for the late 19th century by Morita (1944) and Yasukawa (1971). That the mortality rate in the factories was lower than outside does not mean country girls reduced their risk of death by entering mill work. Sickly girls simply did not enter the mills. Workers who became ill might leave the mill, subsequently dying at home from a mill-contracted disease or injury. For a later period, reports of this happening are legion. Also, note that the mortality rate reported for 1897 is lower than the rate for cotton spinning workers reported by Noshomusho in 1907 and 1910. The 1907 rate is 5.4 deaths per 1,000 workers; the 1910 rate, 12.6 deaths.

of the spinning industry labor force in 1897 was no more than 18 months. Temporary absences from the work place were also high; 8.3 percent of dormitory workers were absent at any given time during the survey month.

The conditions described in the Boren report have an air of familiarity. The dormitories and classes for female workers call to mind Lowell, Massachusetts. The high rates of worker turnover are reminiscent of the Southern Piedmont region of the United States. And the age of the workers and the accidents described resemble, at least anecdotally, the findings of British parliamentary commissions in the early 19th century. What sets the Japanese apart is who did the study, and the quality of the report. The cotton spinning industry itself undertook a comprehensive survey. For all the internationally familiar circumstances, only the Japanese undertook such a massive, almost universal, survey on so many pertinent dimensions so early in an industry's history.

Conceptual Framework

The traditional theoretical treatment of job choice, which goes back as far as Adam Smith, has stressed wage differentials as compensating for differences in job attributes. Similarly, the historical treatment of job choice in early industrialization has highlighted the importance of working conditions and living environment, in addition to wages, in the decision to accept and continue factory work. For all the theoretical insight and historical suggestion, there has been virtually no systematic econometric analysis of the market for job characteristics, whether done on contemporary or traditional data. In part, the lack of appropriate data has been responsible. In part, there has also been the presumption that the forces producing observed wage variation are so varied and so complex as to preclude isolating the impact of individual effects.

However, it is not clear why price determination in labor markets should be more complex than in any other market where tied sales occur. Indeed, the hedonic reconstruction of demand theory suggests tied sales and package deals of product characteristics are the rule and not the exception in virtually all market exchanges. (For other applications of the hedonic approach to labor markets, see Smith 1976.) With this in mind, and given the availability of a rich data set, it is appropriate to proceed with this almost unprecedented investigation of workers' preferences with respect to place of employment.

The market being investigated is hypothesized to consist of profit-maximizing cotton spinning mills seeking workers of varying quality by offering wages plus the opportunity to work in a mill compound with amenities and disamenities, and of workers of varying traits who, in the course of attempting to maximize utility, are seeking high wages, good working conditions, and opportunities for future improvement. Because workers differ in quality, not everybody is offered the same wage rate for a given job.

The workers' utility functions are assumed to include off-the-job consumption, which can be purchased using job wages, and job characteristics. Worker traits are viewed as determining tastes, particularly with respect to job characteristics, and thus are also arguments of the utility function. For example, a worker is dissatisfied if her job requires more or less ability than she possesses. Whether a worker takes a job depends on the wage offered, the characteristics of the job, and the worker's personal traits. In choosing a job, in order to maximize utility, a worker acts to equate the marginal rate of substitution among the wage rate, each job characteristic, and the ratio of the shadow prices at the relevant point of the efficiency frontier in wage rate-job characteristics space. These equalities may be solved to provide a set of supply functions for each worker.

On the other side of the market, it can be hypothesized that mills maximize profits subject to a production function which accounts for the output of both goods and job characteristics, and to a market price schedule relating wages and worker traits and job characteristics. A spinning mill manager sought to obtain a labor force with a set of traits working at a particular structure of jobs by balancing the marginal contribution to the mill revenue product of particular worker traits against the marginal cost of acquiring the traits, given the mill's non-job characteristics. Mills with different non-job characteristics acquire different mixes of labor, depending on the precise complementaries among mill characteristics and worker traits in both the cotton spinning production function and the market-generated wage-traits-characteristics function.

Part of the cost of acquiring a labor force with a particular set of traits is the resources used in producing particular job characteristics. On the margin, these costs can be equated with the resulting market wage payments saved by the presence of these characteristics. Whether a worker is hired depends on the wage rate, the characteristics of the job being offered, and the personal traits of the worker. With the aid of the first-order conditions from mill profit maximization, it is possible to obtain mill demand functions for particular workers. In this same context, job-characteristic supply functions for mills can also be obtained.

In the market for quality in workers and quality in jobs, complete equilibrium is defined by the matching of plans on behalf of employes and employers. Wedding jobs and applicants in wage-job characteristics space is represented by common tangents of the appropriate acceptance and offer functions. It is assumed decisions by firms on the quality mix of workers hired and the amenities and disamenities are separable from other decisions by firms. Similarly, it is assumed worker decisions regarding the mix among wages and other amenities are separable from other consumption decisions.

The Model

Ignoring random terms, the model to be estimated can be written:

$$W_i(Z) = F^i(W_c, W_f, Z_1, \ldots, Z_N, T_1, \ldots, T_K) \tag{1}$$

$i = 1, \ldots, N$ demand for job characteristics

$$W_i(Z) = G^i(W_c, Z_1, \ldots, Z_N, T_1, \ldots, T_K, M_1, \ldots, M_M) \tag{2}$$

$i = 1, \ldots, N$ supply of job characteristics

where:

$W_i(Z)$ is the price of the job characteristic z_i
W_c is money wages available for off-the-job consumption
W_f is money fees (recruitment bonuses) available for off-the-job consumption
T_j is the jth worker trait
M_k is the kth non-job firm characteristic

The Ws, Zs, and Ts in the system of demand and supply equations (1) and (2) are assumed to be endogenous. The Ms are assumed predetermined. Thus, if $M > K + N + 1$, the demand equations are identified.

While data on the Z_i, W_c, W_f, T_j, and M are potentially available, the absence of explicit markets for individual job characteristics as opposed to jobs with bundles of characteristics means the W_i are not normally available. But the W_i can be computed from the derivative of the wage-explaining regression. Let wages be explained by:

$$W = H(Z_1, \ldots, Z_n, T_1, \ldots, T_K) \tag{3}$$

with

$$\frac{\partial W(Z)}{\partial Z_i} = W_i(Z)$$

In the estimation which follows, it is assumed equation (3) is semilogarithmic:

$$\ln W_{cf} = \Sigma a_i Z_i + \Sigma b_j T_j + \Sigma c_k R_k + W_0$$

It should be emphasized that estimation of equation (3) alone, without following through with estimation of the system of supply and demand equations, will not give us the information being sought here. $W_i(Z)$ may be thought of as a function that traces out the transactions generated by the intersection of Z_i buyers' compensated demand functions and Z_i sellers' compensated supply functions. In the markets for job characteristics studied here, workers clearly differ according to their traits and qualities, and firms clearly differ according to their cost conditions, if for no other reason than factor prices differed regionally in Japan. Thus, $W_i(Z)$ is generated by many different demand functions intersecting with many different supply functions. $W_i(Z)$ will be determined by the distribution of buyers and sellers in the 1897 sample. The slope of $W_i(Z)$ in W_i, Z_i space is not the slope of a demand curve nor the slope of a supply curve. If we wish to understand the determinants of the transactions prices for each of the job characteristics, rather than just the implicit transaction price itself, demand and supply functions must be identified and estimated.[3]

Implications of the Estimation

The results of estimating the wage-explaining relationships are presented in table 9.1. By the standards of semilogarithmic regressions of wages on explanatory variables, the results are interesting. For a one-tailed test of significance with a 5 percent critical region, six explanatory variables and the constant term are significant with the expected sign. When the critical region is expanded to 10 percent, another six variables become significant, and only three are not.

Agricultural Opportunities and Bonuses

In examining each of the explanatory variables, first notice that, despite all the long-distance recruiting, opportunities in the area in which the mill was located have a significant relationship with mill wages. Evaluated at the mean point, the elasticity of female mill wages to female agricultural wages is 0.827.

The analysis here does not directly tell us the character of the impact of the recruitment bonus on the decision to enter the spinning mill. The sign of the coefficient on Z_1 suggests the bonus came out of future wage payments. A spinning mill recruit receiving the industry-wide average wage and the industry-wide average recruitment bonus lost three yen of future wages for each yen initially received. The parents, rather than the girl, typically received the bonus.

Shifts and Rest Periods

A longer daily shift was compensated with higher daily wages, and longer rest periods during a shift meant lower wages. The size of the coefficient suggests

---

[3] Even if labor were perfectly mobile, W_t differs from mill to mill, provided the functional form of equation (3) is nonlinear. This is an issue that can be resolved empirically, but that a nonlinear form for equation (3) may be hypothesized at all requires some discussion. First, it must be assumed workers cannot repackage jobs. In the present context, this is quite easy to assume. Part-time work was not feasible at all for mill girls. Also, all remunerative work was done within the set mill environment. If mill workers slept in the dormitories and if their access to the world outside was limited, they could hardly fail to use company dining halls or company health facilities. Second, it is also assumed firm technology for designing or producing jobs is not linear. This is a common, but not universally made, assumption for production functions. The analytical framework in this section has drawn on Antos and Rosen (1975), and Lucas (1977), whose work should be consulted for further discussion of these issues.

Table 9.1: The estimation of $\ln W_{cf} = W_0 + \Sigma a_i Z_i + \Sigma b_j T_j + \Sigma c_k R_k$

Symbol		Variable	Coefficient
W_0	$\equiv$	constant term	0.763×10 [a]
Z_1	$\equiv$	bonus paid to recruitee (sen)	-0.350×10^{-4} [c]
Z_2	$\equiv$	length of working shift (hours)	0.362×10^{-1} [c]
Z_3	$\equiv$	length of rest periods during shift (hours)	-0.438×10^{-1} [b]
Z_4	$\equiv$	incidence of sickness and injury at firm (percent)	-0.289×10^{-2}
Z_5	$\equiv$	mortality at firm (percent)	0.259×10^{b}
Z_6	$\equiv$	living in dormitory (dummy variable = 1 if in dorm)	-0.190^{b}
Z_7	$\equiv$	if dormitory occupant, number of free hours per day	-0.403×10^{-3} [c]
Z_8	$\equiv$	food subsidy for dormitory workers (sen)	-0.149×10^{-4} [c]
Z_9	$\equiv$	company primary and department school instructional personnel per worker	-0.133×10^{2} [b]
T_1	$\equiv$	risk of recruit leaving within six months (percent)	0.348×10^{-4}
T_2	$\equiv$	age of worker (years)	0.303×10^{-1} [c]
T_3	$\equiv$	relevant experience of worker (years)	0.166×10^{-1} [c]
T_4	$\equiv$	rate of absenteeism (percent)	-0.179×10^{-2} [b]
T_5	$\equiv$	literacy of worker (dummy variable = 1 if literate)	-0.385×10^{-1}
R_1	$\equiv$	agricultural wage in area in which plant is located (sen)	0.694×10^{-3} [a]

[a] $\equiv$ significant at 1 percent level $W_{cf} \equiv$ female wage rate
[b] $\equiv$ significant at 5 percent level $R^2 = 0.93$
[c] $\equiv$ significant at 10 percent level

that typically the marginal compensation for additional work by mill hands was less than average compensation. How the derived demand for labor and worker preferences between leisure and work might yield this result is left for future analysis. That the signs of the two coefficients are also statistically insignificant from one another, even as they both statistically significantly differ from zero, is reassuring.

Health and Safety

The magnitude of the coefficient on mortality suggests the typical female worker receiving the average wage of the industry would pay somewhat more than two yen over her period of employment in order to reduce the risk of mortality by 0.001; thus 1,000 workers in the same situation collectively paid 2,000 yen to save one life. Given that the annual wages of such workers were 40–50 yen, this could be construed as implying these workers placed a monetary value on life that exceeded the economic potential or human capital embodied in such a life.[4]

Off-work Environment

The remaining job characteristics, dormitory conditions and free time, are all statistically significant from zero. Workers implicitly paid for their dormitory accommodation and food, as well as tuition for the existence and quality of schools. At the same time, firms in 1897 implicitly compensated workers for the restrictions placed on their activities during their time off. Although restrictions on leisure were compensated, the worker apparently was not indifferent as to what she did while confined within the mill compound.

Inserting sample values for wages, the estimated coefficients on dormitory living implies an additional worker living in the dormitory would pay an implicit rent equivalent to 8.5 percent of actual wages. Such a share for rent in total expenditures is not out of line with budget data available for almost the same year (Yokoyama 1898).

Although the coefficient on hours of free time for workers living in dormitories is significantly different from zero, 17 is exceedingly small. The price for an extra hour of free time outside the mill compound is less than 1 percent of a day's wages for most mills. This somewhat surprising result may be rationalized in a number of ways. First, in this one instance, the data may be suspect. Sample information on the number of hours allowed outside daily was taken by Boren investigators from company regulations and not, as in the case of most of the information collected, from actual practice. Alternatively, assuming the data are correct, allowing that the typical worker already had two hours outside, she did not value additional freedom very highly.

Related to this, we know the runaway rate of mill recruits was so high for so long that mills almost certainly could have found ways to reduce it had they been so inclined. The mills chose not to do so, because they viewed workers' running away from the mill as an acceptable means of separation. Notice in table 9.2 that even mills with relatively high retention rates for newly recruited workers paid recruits no special premium. The mills were not interested in investing even the small resources necessary to build a work force composed primarily of long-term workers. The low implicit price for lessening mill workers' opportunities to run away is certainly consistent with this view.

---

[4] For other estimates of the value of human life, relying on observed behavior with respect to safety, see Smith (1976). The mortality data used in the analysis have been standardized for age. This standardization was accomplished using life-tables for the 1890s available in Yasukawa and Hirooka (1972).

In assessing health and safety conditions in mills and their supply and demand, the analysis here is hampered by multicollinearity. The coefficient on sickness and injury is insignificantly different from zero with the wrong sign. On the other hand, the coefficient on mortality is statistically significant from zero with the proper sign.

Table 9.2: The estimation of the off-the-job-consumption branch

Estimated expenditure elasticities	$\eta_{W_e E}$	1.02	
	$\eta_{W_F W}$	0.89	
Estimated Allen elasticity of substitution	$\sigma_{W_c W_f}$		4.78
Estimated price elasticities		W_c	W_f
	W_c	-0.012	1.02
	W_f	4.66	-0.236

The coefficient on food subsidies for workers in the wage-explaining regression implies a typical worker implicitly returned approximately 28 percent of this subsidy in the form of lower wages. This is yet another puzzling result. If the coefficient estimate is taken seriously, this result is prima-facie evidence arbitrage among job opportunities of varying characterics was really not possible. It seems reasonable that at the least there should have been a yen-for-yen substitution between wages and food subsidies. Perhaps because the mill was buying in bulk, the worker might have implicitly paid out more than it was costing the firm to provide the subsidized food. Overall, because packages of job characteristics cannot be untied, the result here is plausible. Given that workers lived in a mill dormitory compound with restricted access to the outside, the firm had to provide dining halls and prepare food. The inability to cater to individual tastes and problems inherent in mass preparation of food may have caused workers to place a low value on what the firm was providing, no matter how efficiently the firm might have been performing this function.

The coefficient on literacy is insignificantly different from zero. Although firms did not pay literate workers a premium, workers did implicitly pay for the quantity and quality of education offered. For example, if the mills had doubled the number of instructors, or halved the class size, in return for this opportunity workers would have implicitly paid 5.5 percent of the money wages they would otherwise have received. Finding evidence for such implicit payments is all the more surprising, as these classes were attended after the conclusion of a twelve-hour shift.[5]

Workers' Traits

While the Japanese cotton spinning mills of 1897 apparently paid no premium to workers for their literacy or for their initial desinclination to run away, the other traits are statistically significant from zero. The coefficient on the rate of

[5] In this instance, as in others, more interpretative weight than can be reasonably borne is placed on statistically significant regression coefficients. The majority of the Japanese mills in 1897 did not provide schools or instructional personnel. The presence or absence of compound schools may well just be a good proxy for overall mill quality.

absenteeism is, however, sufficiently small that it appears the typical mill provided little extra compensation for workers with good attendance. This is interesting, as already in 1897 quite a few mills were reporting programs of bonuses for workers with perfect attendance records. There is evidence such programs did not have a time-series impact, so it should not be surprising to find their cross-sectional impact also was limited.

If workers did not receive much of a premium for good attendance, age and increased experience do appear to have brought significant rewards. A 20-year-old worker with one and a half years' experience with a firm of some 200 workers could expect a 5 percent increase in wages, if she worked an additional year at her mill.[6]

Estimating Workers' Preferences: Procedures

Having briefly summarized what the estimation of equation (3) can tell about the implicit market prices for job characteristics and the manifestations of mill paternalism, we now look at the determinants of these market prices. Market price is determined by the interaction of supply and demand. But, as can be seen from equations (1) and (2), while it is possible to identify the demand for job characteristics using non-job firm characteristics which do not appear in equation (1), there are no variables in equation (1) available for use as exclusion restrictions in order to identify equation (2). Worker traits are assumed to affect both supply and demand functions. Thus, in what follows only demand functions for job characteristics will be estimated. With only one side of the market firmly identified, a full explanation of the determinants of the price of job characteristics cannot be given. Nonetheless, estimation of the demand function alone provides invaluable information regarding what workers in the early period of Japan's industrialization valued.

With ten job characteristics and five worker traits, the estimation of a system of demand functions which serves the purposes of our analysis is complex. It is desirable to allow interaction among the demands for job characteristics. With so many variables, unless considerable structure is imposed on the problem, there is

---

[6] Although multicollinearity hinders any effort at precisely distinguishing the separate impact of increased age from increased experience in this sample, separately they each significantly differ from zero with a 10 percent critical region; taken jointly, a small critical region will suffice to reject the null hypothesis.

In Saxonhouse (1976), using a comprehensive data set from the period 1897–1935, relationships between productivity and experience and wages and experience were found in a general setting to be significant. The coexistence between these relationships and high turnover and firm disinterest in cutting turnover can be understood if it is recognized that (1), technologically speaking, most Japanese mills were almost identical, and (2) most firms were reluctant to invest in improving the quality of their workers. The paper argues that the improvement in worker skills was worker financed.

little hope of feasible estimation. Thus, it will be assumed workers had trans-cendental logarithmic preference characteristics, a functional form offering very rich possibilities for interaction between various job characteristics (see Diewert 1974), and from which a system of demand equations can be derived. This preference function will be assumed to be a utility tree with four branches (the utility-tree approach is described in Strotz 1957).

It is hypothesized the worker, consciously or unconsciously, made decisions on how to allocate her income among four branches (grand categories) of off- and on-the-job expenditure. After the decision to allocate among these four, a decision was made within each category. The categories are the same ones used earlier in discussing wage-explaining relationships.[7]

W ≡ off-the-job consumption
W_c ≡ off-the-job consumption equal to money wages
W_f ≡ consumption out of bonuses paid at time of recruitment

Z_1 ≡ pace of work
Z_{1a} ≡ length of rest periods
Z_{1b} ≡ length of working shift

Z_2 ≡ health care
Z_{2a} ≡ incidence of sickness and injury
Z_{2b} ≡ incidence of mortality

Z_3 ≡ off-work environment
Z_{3a} ≡ percentage of workers living in dormitories
Z_{3b} ≡ number of hours allowed outside mill compound per day
Z_{3c} ≡ food subsidy per dormitory worker multiplied by Z_{3a}
Z_{3d} ≡ instructional personnel for company school per worker

Formally, the system being described here can be expressed as:

$$\ln U = \ln U(W_c, W_f, Z_{1a}, Z_{1b}, Z_{2a}, Z_{2b}, Z_{3a}, Z_{3b}, Z_{3d}; T)$$

$$= \ln U[W(W_c, W_f), Z_1(Z_{1a}, Z_{1b}), Z_2(Z_{2a}, Z_{2b}),$$

$$Z_3(Z_{3a}, Z_{3b}, Z_{3c}, Z_{3d}); T] \tag{4}$$

where, as before, **T** is the traits vector.

[7] Income is used here in Becker's sense: the sum of potential pecuniary and nonpecuniary compensation which might be received by the worker (Becker 1965).

The categories are arguably arbitrary, but given the functional form used here, some choice is necessary. A priori, it clearly makes no sense to estimate the health-care branch. In a two-attribute world, Z_{2a} and Z_{2b} can only be substitutes. This is beyond the realm of plausibility. In any event, because it is not possible to get statistically significant estimates of W_{Z2a}, it will be assumed that $Z(Z_{2a}, Z_{2b}) = Z_{2b}$.

Assume now that the worker is maximizing her instantaneous utility subject to the constraint:

$$W - \sum_{i=1}^{3} W_i Z_i = 0 \tag{5}$$

and that the form of the relationship used to approximate the negative logarithm of the utility function is given by:

$$-\ln U = \alpha_0 + \alpha_w \ln W + \sum_{i=1}^{3} \alpha_{Z_i} \ln Z_i + \sum_{i=1}^{3} \beta_w \beta_{Z_i} \ln W \ln Z_i$$

$$+ \sum_{i=1}^{3} \sum_{j=1}^{3} \beta_{Z_i Z_j} \ln Z_i \ln Z + \sum_{i=1}^{3} \beta_{WT_i} \ln W \ln T_j$$

$$+ \sum_{i=1}^{3} \sum_{j=1}^{3} \beta_{Z_i T_j} \ln Z_i \ln T_j \tag{6}$$

Using this form with the first-order conditions for the maximization of utility and rearranging, the following budget-share equations are obtained:

$$\frac{W}{W + \sum W_i Z_i} = \frac{\alpha_W + \Sigma \beta_{WZ_i} \ln Z_i + \Sigma \beta_{WT_j} \ln T_j}{[\alpha_w + \beta_{WZ_i} \ln Z_i + \Sigma \beta_{WT_k} \ln T_k + \Sigma(\alpha_{Z_i} + \beta_{WZ_i} \ln W + \Sigma \beta_{Z_i Z_j} \ln Z_j + \Sigma \beta_{Z_i T_k} \ln T_k)]} \tag{7}$$

$$\frac{W_i Z_i}{W + \sum W_i Z_i} = \frac{\alpha_{Z_i} + \beta_{WZ_i} \ln W + \Sigma \beta_{Z_i Z_j} \ln Z_j + \Sigma \beta_{Z_i T_k} \ln T_k}{[\alpha_w + \Sigma \beta_{WZ_i} \ln Z_j + \Sigma \beta_{WT_k} \ln T_k + \Sigma(\alpha_{Z_j} + \beta_{WZ_j} \ln W + \Sigma \beta_{Z_j Z_m} \ln Z_j + \Sigma \beta_{Z_m T_n} \ln T_K)]} \tag{8}$$

$(i = 1, 2, 3)$

The budget equations in (7) constitute the first level of the system of demand being estimated. Of the four equations in (7), because of the budget constraint only three are independent. In the empirical work presented, it is assumed the budget-share equations have additive disturbances with a joint normal distribution. Given the disturbances of any $n - 1$ of the budget-share equations, the disturbance of the remaining equation can be determined from the budget constraint. The budget-share equations are homogeneous of degree zero in the parameters; hence a normalization of the parameters is required for estimation. The normalization adopted is $\Sigma \alpha = -1$.

The estimation of the within-branch equations proceeds analogously with the first level of estimation. $W(W_c, W_f)$, $Z_1(Z_{1a}, Z_{1b})$, $Z_2(Z_{2a}, Z_{2b})$, and $Z_3(Z_{3a},$

Z_{3c}, Z_{3d}) are separately approximated by a transcendental logarithmic form analogous to equation (6) and separate blocks of budget-share equations analogous to equation (7) are derived. To estimate the unknown parameters of the within-branch share equations and the grand budget-share equations, the iterative Zellner estimation procedure is used. The interactive nonlinear estimation routine used in these procedures employs a combination of Gauss-Newton and steepest-ascent methods.

Workers Preferences: Implications

For our analysis, we have hypothesized the worker consciously or unconsciously decides how to allocate her income among four grand categories (branches) of off- and on-the-job expenditure. After that decision, an allocation is decided for the components of each branch. The categories are the same as in our discussion of wage-explaining relationships, except estimation is not possible for the health branch. Income used here includes nonpecuniary as well as pecuniary compensation (Becker 1965). The results for the estimation of the branches provide the demand part of the system, and from these results, a number of observations can be made.

Off-the-Job Consumption

Female workers viewed recruitment bonuses and wages as substitutes: a higher recruitment bonus today was a substitute for higher wages throughout the worker's period of employment. Also, the "expenditure elasticities" (really "receipt elasticities") suggest that as workers receive more in wages and recruitment bonuses, bonuses become much less preferred. This is entirely consistent with the expected relationship between resources and time preferences. Using the estimated parameters of the demand subsystem, a number of elasticities have been calculated and are presented in table 9.2.

Pace of Work

Late 19th century textile workers viewed rest periods during a shift and length of shift as very good substitutes. As a female worker had more resources to allocate to the improvement of the quality of her job, shortening the working shift was given priority over increased rest periods. This accords well with the historical experience of the cotton spinning companies after 1897, although, with persistent pressure from the International Labor Organization, it is hard to argue the shortening of shifts that did occur was largely a result of changing market phenomena. As indicated by the estimated expenditure elasticities taken from the fitted utility function, a 1 percent increase in the implicit price of either a change in the total length of the rest period or a change in the length of a shift led to an increase of more than 2 percent in the implicit expenditure on the other job characteristic (see table 9.3).

Table 9.3:   The estimation of the pace-of-work branch

Estimated expenditure elasticities	$\eta_{Z_{1a}(\Sigma W_{Z_{1i}}Z_{1i})}$		0.87
	$\eta_{Z_{1b}(\Sigma W_{Z_{1i}}Z_{1i})}$		1.24
Estimated Allen elasticity of substitution	$\sigma_{Z_{1a}Z_{1b}}$		4.3
Estimated price elasticities of demand	η_{ij}	Z_{ia}	Z_{ib}
	Z_{1a}	-2.03	2.42
	Z_{1b}	2.90	-3.35

Table 9.4:   The estimation of the availability and quality of off-the-job mill-compound experience branch

Estimated expenditure elasticities of demand	$\eta_{Z_{3a}(\Sigma W_{Z_{3i}}Z_{3i})}$		0.56	
	$\eta_{Z_{3b}(\Sigma W_{Z_{3i}}Z_{3i})}$		2.10	
	$\eta_{Z_{3c}(\Sigma W_{Z_{3i}}Z_{3i})}$		0.88	
	$\eta_{Z_{3d}(\Sigma W_{Z_{3i}}Z_{3i})}$		1.09	
Estimated Allen elasticities of demand	σ_{ij}	Z_{3a}	Z_{3b}	Z_{3c}	Z_{3d}
	Z_{3a}		-0.264	-0.381	4.21
	Z_{3b}			0.818	1.93
	Z_{3c}				0.975
	Z_{3d}				
Estimated price elasticities of demand	η_{ij}	Z_{3a}	Z_{3b}	Z_{3c}	Z_{3d}
	Z_{3a}	-0.717	0.0230	0.0768	0.5556
	Z_{3b}	0.6843	-0.0221	1.253	0.4694
	Z_{3c}	0.1859	0.1382	-0.7518	0.2409
	Z_{3d}	1.975	0.2451	0.8867	-18.40

Off-Work Environment

Unsupervised leisure time outside the mill was the preferred way for a worker to improve her off-the-job environment. Together with the price inelastic demand for free time, this suggests, even if it does not necessitate, that a bountiful, highly elastic supply of free time from the company side was responsible for the observed low implicit price of unsupervised time. As noted before, it seems firms just did not particularly care that workers had a high rate of absenteeism and ran away (see table 9.4).

That unsupervised free time and worker education should have relatively high elasticities, and shelter and food should have low elasticities of expenditure is entirely consistent in spirit with most demand and budget studies. Putting stereotypes of the susceptibility of young Japanese female workers to paternalistic blandishments aside, the same independence which resulted in high runaway rates also resulted in a high preference for free time outside the mill compound over organized activities provided by management. It is also most reasonable that the purchase of dormitory services should be complementary with free time outside the mill and with food subsidies. A substantial number of female workers bought no dormitory services and hence had little desire implicitly to purchase unsupervised leisure time and a diminished, if not negligible, desire to gain company-subsidized food.

Although it is in any case difficult to rationalize market prices, explicit, implicit, or otherwise, in the absence of information about the character of supply, the results on worker preferences for education are particularly puzzling. Recall that the implicit price of available education within the mill was estimated as being very large. Now if the quality of available education is measurable by the teacher-pupil ratio, it would seem the supply of more and better-quality primary and department education would be easy to accomplish. Given that the expenditure elasticity of demand for education is near unity and that education's own price elasticity of demand is evidently very high, it is hard to understand why the implicit price of education remained so high for so many workers. It would appear that Japanese cotton mills were specifically unresponsive to workers' interests in this area.

The Choice among Branches

The estimates of each of the branches of the demand subsystems allows for the condensing of nine attributes into four – off-the-job goods, pace of work, health, and dormitory life. The estimation of the demand system given in equation (7) describing the allocation of female workers' income to these four attributes, conditioned on five workers' traits, is given in table 9.5.

The expenditure elasticities of demand calculated from the estimated demand system suggests that at a very low Beckerian income, workers cared most about wages. As incomes increased, more priority was placed on reducing the risk of mortality and improving on-the-job conditions, and to a lesser extent improving dormitory life. Evidence from this cross-section also does well as an indicator of secular trends. Real wages rose after 1897 and, although the prices paid are not known, workers implicitly purchased more safety and improved on-the-job conditions. While some improvement in the quality of dormitory life did occur before the Pacific War, changes comparable to what happened in safety and shifts came only in the late 1950s.

Too much should not be made of the poor worker's strong preference for money wages. The results in table 9.5 on elasticities of substitution and price elasticities of demand are such that even at a low level of Beckerian income, workers were sensitive to opportunities to reduce the risk of mortality, slow the pace of work, and improve dormitory life.

Table 9.5:   The estimation of the full demand system — the choice among off-the-job goods, pace of work, health, and dormitory life

Estimated expenditure elasticities of demand					
		$\eta_{W(W+\Sigma W_i Z_i)}$	0.84		
		$\eta_{Z_1(W+\Sigma W_i Z_i)}$	1.38		
		$\eta_{Z_2(W+\Sigma W_i Z_i)}$	1.47		
		$\eta_{Z_3(W+\Sigma W_i Z_i)}$	1.12		

Estimated Allen elasticities of demand	σ_{ij}	W	Z_1	Z_2	Z_3
	W		1.899	3.302	2.851
	Z_1			1.919	1.670
	Z_2				1.141
	Z_3				

Estimated price elasticities of demand	η_{ij}	W	Z_1	Z_2	Z_3
	W	−0.1828	0.2523	0.1856	0.5129
	Z_1	2.374	−1.565	0.1477	0.4236
	Z_2	3.455	0.3121	−2.658	0.3627
	Z_3	2.875	0.2569	0.1012	2.2221

Traits and Preferences

In order to understand how preferences may vary among workers with different traits, the signs of the partial derivatives of each of the elasticities presented in table 9.5 with respect to each of the five worker traits are given in table 9.6.

The impact of traits on preference is complex. Workers with a relatively low Beckerian income and a high propensity to run away exhibit a greater preference for money wages than their more stable counterparts. The same result occurs with workers exhibiting a high rate of absenteeism. The short-term, frequently-absent poor worker cared relatively little for the mill environment. By contrast, older, more experienced workers, even when poor, showed relatively more interest in shortening the work day and improving the dormitory environment. Interestingly, this concern with the nonwage aspects of the job did not extend to lowering the risk of mortality. Older, more experienced workers, when poor, seemed less inclined to pay for safety than other workers; presumably they placed more reliance on themselves and less on the mill environment in the avoidance of risk. Similarly, older workers, being closer to retirement or natural death, might be viewed as having less to lose in human capital than their younger colleagues.

The findings on substitution and price elasticities are consistent with our interpretation of the expenditure elasticities. Workers with high absentee rates and a high propensity to run away found nonpecuniary benefits relatively poor substitutes for wages compared to other workers. For such workers, the share of wages in total Beckerian income is relatively insensitive to changes in implicit

Table 9.6:   The variation of preferences among workers

	T_1	T_2	T_3	T_4	T_5
$\eta_{w(w+\Sigma w_i Z_i)}$	−	+	+	−	−
$\eta_{Z_1(w+\Sigma w_i Z_i)}$	+	−	−	+	−
$\eta_{Z_2(w+\Sigma w_i Z_i)}$	+	+	+	−	+
$\eta_{Z_3(w+\Sigma w_i Z_i)}$	+	−	−	+	+
σ_{wZ_1}	−	+	+	−	−
σ_{wZ_2}	−	+	+	−	+
σ_{wZ_3}	−	+	+	−	−
$\sigma_{Z_1 Z_2}$	+	+	+	−	−
$\sigma_{Z_1 Z_3}$	+	−	−	+	−
$\sigma_{Z_2 Z_3}$	+	+	+	+	+
η_{ww}	−	+	+	−	−
$\eta_{Z_1 w}$	−	+	+	−	−
$\eta_{Z_2 w}$	−	+	+	−	−
$\eta_{Z_3 w}$	−	+	+	−	+
η_{wZ_1}	−	+	+	−	−
$\eta_{Z_1 Z_1}$	+	−	+	+	+
$\eta_{Z_2 Z_1}$	+	+	+	−	−
$\eta_{Z_3 Z_1}$	+	−	−	+	−
η_{wZ_2}	−	+	+	−	+
$\eta_{Z_1 Z_2}$	+	+	+	−	−
$\eta_{Z_2 Z_2}$	+	+	+	−	+
$\eta_{Z_3 Z_2}$	+	+	+	+	+
$\eta_{Z_1 Z_3}$	+	−	−	+	−
$\eta_{Z_2 Z_3}$	−	+	+	−	−
$\eta_{Z_3 Z_3}$	+	−	−	+	+

prices. Again, for older, more experienced and stable workers, the opposite is generally true. For these workers, most job characteristics are relatively good substitutes for each other and expenditure shares are relatively sensitive to price changes.

Summary

The preceding analysis finds workers during Japan's early industrialization chose their jobs for both pecuniary and nonpecuniary reasons. Workers exhibited a willingness to pay implicitly for dormitory space, for food subsidies, for more time outside the mill compound, and for educational opportunities. On the job, workers would trade cash pay for more safety, longer rest periods, and shorter shifts. Workers were clearly not indifferent to mill-compound and job conditions, but this does not mean a bundle of job characteristics weighted with nonpecuniary benefits was necessarily an efficient means of attracting workers. For example, the analysis suggests workers would have considered themselves better off if the resources which their employers devoted to food subsidies were given to them directly, even though they would probably have had to spend more on food. Moreover, reactions to job and compound amenities varied from worker to worker.

The less the Beckerian income (nonpecuniary as well as cash income) the worker received from the mill, the stronger the preference for pecuniary benefits. Also, the less a worker's attachment to her job, as manifested by high absenteeism and a high propensity to run away, the stronger her preference for cash wages. Such workers viewed nonpecuniary amenities as relatively poor substitutes for money. By contrast, older and more experienced workers seemed to place a relatively higher priority on nonpecuniary benefits and were more sensitive to relative prices in deciding between pecuniary and nonpecuniary benefits.

The association between the traits of stability and positive reaction to the mill and job environment suggest further changes in these variables might have been one way to obtain the more stable work force which was absent from the textile industry in the pre-Pacific War period. Instead, given the package of job characteristics offered during this period, the industry acquired a labor force which worked primarily for the wages they were receiving and which had little attachment to the jobs they were performing.

A Comparison with India

Employe turnover at Japanese mills remained high throughout the 1930s, but for the Japanese textile industry to have acquired a more stable labor force might have been a matter of winning the battle, but losing the war. With inexperienced, but relatively well-educated girls in dormitory settings, Japan achieved world dominance. The demographics of the Indian labor force and its modes of labor organization did not resemble those of Japan in the 20th century, though its machinery increasingly did. And its industries in the first decades of the 20th century lost what international competitive strength they had. These issues are explored in this section of the chapter.

The Indian industry began earlier than the Japanese, and in 1889 a working party of officials from the Japanese government and Boren (the then-infant All Japan Cotton Spinners' Association) visited India to collect information about the already substantial machine textile industry there, and published an extensive report (Boren n.d.). Productivity in the 1890s was higher in India than in Japan; in 1898, monthly output per worker was 297 pounds in Japan and 319 in India. But in the next ten years this was reversed; in 1909, daily output was 15.4 pounds in Japan, 12.9 in India (Takamura 1971, vol. 1: 33 and vol. 2: 143).

Gender of the Labor Force

In the late 19th century and early decades of the 20th, Japan and India present almost mirror images in the composition of their factory cotton spinning labor force. During this period, between 75 and 85 percent of cotton spinning mill labor in Japan was female and in India was male. In addition, whereas the Japanese industry relied primarily on young, unmarried women, what women the Indian industry did use were almost always married or widowed. For all the periods for which data are available, the role of female labor is relatively constant, except in Japan for the very first decade of the industry's experience. During the 1880s, males constituted as much as 40 percent of the industry's labor force, and in the highly successful Osaka Spinning Mill this proportion rose as high as 45 percent.

The rapid rise in the proportion of women has been linked to the adoption of ring spinning (see Takamura 1971). After the late 1880s, virtually all new spinning mills in Japan used ring spindles, which were first developed in the United States in the 1830s, and improved significantly in the 1870s. The ring substantially reduced the skill and strength required of workers in producing yarn, and this was generally known. But the adoption of this machine does not inevitably change the sex composition of the spinning industry labor force. Even in Japan, for the first two or three years after the introduction of ring spinning, the average proportion of female workers in the total workforce in ring mills was not significantly different from the average for mule mills. On the other hand, in Indian mills there are numerous examples of ring departments using relatively more women than mule departments of the same mill (Pearse 1930). Overall, in India, the use of the ring in no apparent way reduced the preponderance of males.

In some cases, choice of a male work force when introducing rings can be put down to poor management. For example, in 1889 Kanebo opened its first ring mill with an unusually high proportion of male workers; this is just one instance of the admittedly poor quality of the mill's first managers. After substantial early losses, new management was brought in and, among other changes, the composition of the labor force was altered.

Not all instances of the lack of perfect correlation between the use of rings and the make up of the labor force can be explained away so easily. Given the results of the previous section, it can be argued with considerable confidence that spinning technology by itself was not decisive in determining the quality of the labor employed, or for that matter the character of the job performed or the environment in which that labor worked. A range of market outcomes was possible in this industry. Given the Japanese wage rate, dormitory system, and other environmental variables, the Japanese management acquired one sort of labor force. In a different setting, the Indian spinners chose quite differently.

Absenteeism and Educational Background

The rate of absenteeism is one of the indexes of the motivation and quality of a mill's labor force. Motivation is affected by pecuniary incentives, intensity of work, and organizational amenities; the quality of the labor force reflects general education, vocational training, and nutrition, among other factors. The first systematic information on absenteeism is reported by Boren for 1897. Based on comprehensive mill data, the absentee rate for workers living in company-owned dormitories within the mill compound was over 8 percent. Such absenteeism may seem unremarkable, but consider the context in which it was recorded. These girls were being fed and housed at company expense. They were unable to leave the compound except under supervision and their leisure time activities were carefully controlled by mill matrons. Although it is conceivable living in such dormitories might have raised the incidence of sickness, one of the investigators employed by the industry in this survey doubts it. The famous journalist Yokoyama wrote in 1898:

> It is surprising that there are many absentees in cotton spinning factories. Although the percentage of absentees to the total number of workers varies from factory to factory, it is about 10 percent average, that is, if the total number of workers in a factory is 2,000, then the number of absentees is about 200 daily on average. In such a case, 20 to 30 absentees are due to illness, but the others are simply due to idleness. (Yokoyama 1898: 188)

In August 1904, an extremely comprehensive survey of ten mills was undertaken by Boren. The results are given in table 9.7. This survey is illuminating because the detail given suggests how attendance records were kept in the industry and how absenteeism rates reported for this and other years were actually calculated. What is especially interesting is the confirmation of the very high rates of absenteeism reported elsewhere for the spinning industry and the documentation taken from internal mill records that this absenteeism was directly linked to the difficulties mills faced in getting the full complement of labor needed. (1904 is during the Russo-Japanese War, but almost all the evidence indicates the war did little to disrupt textile-industry labor markets.)

Subsequent surveys do little to dispel the impression given by this survey. In 1912, Uno finds the rate of absenteeism among workers living in company-owned dormitories was 6 percent, married workers living in company-owned houses averaged 8 percent, and workers who commuted from their own living accommodation averaged 17 percent (Uno 1912). In 1919, a Boren survey again complains bitterly about the poor quality of Japanese textile workers and their insensitivity to pecuniary incentives. In this context, an absentee rate of 8.3 percent for dormitory workers is reported (Kamisaka 1919). Finally, in 1931,

Table 9.7: An investigation of absenteeism in ten Japanese cotton spinning mills

	Total workers (1)	Needed to operate (2)	Actually present (3)	Ill, accidents	Absent without leave	Total absent (4)	Percentage of labor force needed that is present (3)÷(2)	Percentage of labor force absent (4)÷(1)
Male workers	1,747	1,632	1,510	59	116	237	92.5	13.6
Dormitory females	4,598	8,911	4,097	291	139	501	91.8	10.8
Commuting females	4,831		4,086	255	349	745	86.7	15.4
Total	11.176	10,543	9,693	605	604	1,483		13.3

The total number of absent workers exceeds the sum of those ill, accidents, and absent without leave because of excused leaves

Source: Compiled by author from various primary sources

a widely respected observer of the Japanese textile industry and an otherwise unabashed admirer of the quality of Japanese labor writes: "Statistics show that the girls are subject to a good deal of malingering. Twenty percent of the female operatives living in dormitories absent themselves after they receive their monthly pay check" (Pearse 1929).

The absentee rate is only an imperfect index of worker motivation and only one of several which might be used. Nonetheless, the prevalence of high rates of absenteeism not only in the 1890s, but also through the 1930s does confirm the observations made in the first part of this chapter. The Japanese textile industry achieved world dominance in the first three decades of the 20th century using seemingly poorly motivated labor. The industry probably chose, perhaps reluctantly, to have such a labor force, and over time it increasingly learned how to make effective use of its unwilling employes.

From this perspective, the Indian contrast with the Japanese case is interesting. Absenteeism is one area where there is more information for India than for Japan. The 1889 Boren mission to India noted that absenteeism in Bombay mills varied from 5 to 14 percent, and behavior was not unlike Japanese mills in the late 19th century, particularly when differences in age, sex, and living situations are taken into account. As is clear from table 9.8, in the succeeding fifty years until the beginning of the Pacific War, Indian rates of absenteeism do not appear to change very much. For the forty years prior to the war, if anything, Indian absenteeism is less than Japanese. Thus, differences in worker motivation probably help little in explaining the comparative Japanese-Indian productivity performance.

If both Indian and Japanese textile workers differed little in motivation, they certainly appear to differ in educational background. Indian workers had relatively little exposure to primary education, whereas most Japanese mill hands had some. On the Indian side, supporting data are not as detailed as one might wish. Most observers flatly state almost all Indian textile workers were illiterate (see, for example, Pearse 1929). Such observations are consistent with such other sources as the Indian census of 1921, which found 93 percent of the Indian population to be illiterate. It should be noted, however, that in the late 1930s a study of family budgets of industrial workers for Madras and Ahmedabad reported 65 percent of heads of households to which textile workers belonged were literate (*Report* 1937: 12 and 1938: 35). What definition of literacy was used and what such a survey indicates about the textile workers themselves is difficult to say.

In contrast, as early as 1897, at least half the Japanese cotton spinning work force were considered literate. As compulsory education came to be enforced and improved between the mid-1890s and 1910, in part due to the urging of Boren, the textile industry's high labor turnover and use of young workers insured this change was rapidly reflected in its labor force. By 1924, 94 percent of the textile industry labor force had some exposure to formal education. Almost 80 percent had a six-year primary education. Some nine years later,

Table 9.8: Absenteeism in Indian mills

Year	Mill	Absenteeism (percentage)
1887	Buckingham Mills, Madras	7.39
1887	Carnatic Mills, Madras	6.1
1889	Bombay City	18.36
1897	Buckingham Mills, Madras	7.79
1897	Carnatic Mills, Madras	12.36
1902	Ahmedabad	16.61
1907	Bombay City	17.0
1907	Century Mills, Bombay	10.30
1907	Buckingham Mills, Madras	11.83
1907	Carnatic Mills, Madras	14.09
1923	Bombay	11.2
1923	Ahmedabad	8.7
1923	Sholapur	11.6
1926	Bombay	8.3
1926	Ahmedabad	7.7
1926	Sholapur	12.3
1934	Bombay	11.4
1934	Ahmedabad	9.1
1934	Sholapur	10.2
1938	Bombay	8.30
1938	Ahmedabad	3.29
1938	Sholapur	10.73
1939	Bombay	10.50
1939	Ahmedabad	3.30
1939	Sholapur	10.77

Source

1923: *Report on an Enquiry into the Wages and Hours of Labour in the Cotton Mill Industry* 1925
1926: *Report on an Enquiry into the Wages and Hours of Labour in the Cotton Mill Industry* 1930
1934: *General Wage Census*, pt I 1937
1938–39: *Report of the Textile Labour Inquiry Committee*, vol. II 1941
Other years: Das 1923

almost 95 percent were primary school graduates, and almost 30 percent had additional formal education.

Explicitly linking the different educational experiences of Japanese and Indian textile workers to differential productivity performance in the two countries is not a simple matter. Elsewhere it has been shown that the increasing incidence of primary education among Japanese textile workers can be linked directly to increases in productivity (Saxonhouse 1976). Literacy alone or the substantive results of educational experience are not thought to be primary vehicles by which productivity was influenced. Rather, it is the form by which Japanese primary education was imparted that is seen as important. Within the primary school, the future mill operative learned to respond to the discipline of a nonfamily adult. The demands for constant attention and regular attendance, the necessity of confronting new situations and skills, and mastering them – how similar this was to what life was to be like in the Japanese mill compound.

For all the cogency of these arguments, however, it remains puzzling why it is not possible to demonstrate econometrically that for 1897, everything else being equal, better-educated workers received superior rewards from the firms. It is equally puzzling why, if education was so beneficial, the mills allowed the implicit price of educational services offered within the mill in 1897 to remain so high. Perhaps analysis for later periods would show more consistent results.

Working Hours and the Double-Shift System

The results in the first part of this chapter suggest Japanese mill hands placed considerable priority on the improvement of working conditions and, in particular, on shorter work shifts. There is also considerable evidence such improvements directly increased worker productivity (Saxonhouse 1976; Toyo 1953: 212–15).

The double-shift system was well established in Japan by the late 1880s. Shifts were usually twelve hours, beginning at 6 a.m. and 6 p.m. One hour, typically spread over three breaks, was allowed for rest during each shift. It was not uncommon for overtime to be assigned to a fraction of the work force. In principle, workers had one day off a week. The double-shift system, as it came to be practiced in the late 1880s, continued with little change until 1916, when the Factory Act came into force. Mild limitations on the work of women and children were imposed by this legislation. Revisions in 1926 prohibited night work by women, beginning in 1929. By 1930, typical working hours were $8\frac{1}{2}$ hours on each of two shifts, with the first shift starting work at 5 a.m.

In India, factory legislation came much earlier, largely as a result of British pressure. After 1881, children were not supposed to work more than nine hours a day, and in 1891 this was reduced to seven hours. The limit for women was eleven hours. The next major change in factory legislation came in 1911, when men's hours were set at no more than twelve a day; this was reduced to eleven in 1922. In 1922, men and women were not supposed to work more than 60 hours a week, and children (under 12), six hours a day. In 1935, the daily limit for adults was dropped to ten hours and the weekly maximum to 54 hours. It is difficult to say whether this legislation was effective. For example, in the late 19th century, it is commonly observed that Indian mills worked a single shift from dawn to dusk, which was, for a large part of the year, almost 15 hours.

The Factory Labor Commission in 1908 pointed out that employes worked twelve to fourteen hours daily in many mills, with a holiday only once in two weeks. On the other hand, in 1921 working hours in the Bombay Presidency (province, which also included such textile centers as Ahmedabad and Sholapur) were reported to be 10 hours for men and $9\frac{1}{2}$ for women. In 1926, when 10 hours work was the standard, workers in the reeling and winding departments of Bombay mills were working only $9\frac{1}{4}$ hours. While there was periodic use of double shifts, it was only in the late 1920s that the Indian industry comprehensively introduced the system. At this time, shifts were typically seven or eight hours. It is puzzling why India did not adopt the double shift sooner; the factory legislation did not necessarily conflict with it. Perhaps it was a matter, as in so many other areas, of blindly following British textile practice and not adapting to Indian conditions.

Unlike Japan, India in the 1890s and early 1900s attempted to build a relatively high quality textile labor force. One component of this strategy was the payment of relatively good wages. Like so many other countries, India emerged after World War I with a highly inflated wage structure relative to prices and was under increasing pressure in its home markets from Japanese imports. Faced with this situation and the difficulties of cutting money wages, the addition of an evening shift without a premium in wages had the double benefit of cutting real wages while also cutting the cost of capital.

It is ironic that during the 1920s, when India was implicitly cutting income by making working conditions worse, Japan, facing the same inflated wage structure, was responding to international pressure to improve conditions in its mills. Thus the Japanese textile industry was being forced to raise income implicitly by cutting lengths of shifts and doing away with night work for women. It is thus all the more remarkable that, at the end of this period of adjustment, the Japanese industry emerged with far more competitive strength than the Indian industry.

Labor Turnover

The most striking contrast between the Japanese and Indian textile-industry labor forces, particularly after 1910, was in their turnover rates. The Japanese industry experienced high turnover rates and high labor productivity. The Indian industry experienced low rates of turnover and low labor productivity. This association is certainly not what normally would be expected, but it is consistent with the findings on absenteeism, education, and worker shifts.

As shown in tables 9.9 and 9.10 both industries suffered from labor-force instability in the early period of industrialization. Only the figure for Bombay in 1907, already a mature industry center, is particularly low. What is surprising is that the shift towards a lower labor turnover was much more marked in India than in Japan. While the Indian industry exhibited a very sharp drop in turnover rates between the turn of the century and the 1930s, the Japanese decline was

Table 9.9:   Labor turnover in the cotton textile industry in Japan and India

Year	Mill	Labor turnover *(percentage per year)*
	Japan	
1890	Kanegafuchi Spinning Mill	116
1897		86
1900	Osaka area mills	120
1904	Kanegafuchi Spinning Mill	108
1905	Kanegafuchi Spinning Mill	88
1906	Kanegafuchi Spinning Mill	68
1907	Kanegafuchi Spinning Mill	74
1908	Kanegafuchi Spinning Mill	66
1909	Kanegafuchi Spinning Mill	109
1910	Kanegafuchi Spinning Mill	72
1911	Kanegafuchi Spinning Mill	71
1912	Kanegafuchi Spinning Mill	80
1913	Kanegafuchi Spinning Mill	75
1914	Kanegafuchi Spinning Mill	61
1915	Kanegafuchi Spinning Mill	51
1920	Spinning and weaving	52
1921	Spinning and weaving	70
1922	Spinning and weaving	83
1923	Spinning and weaving	71
1924	Spinning and weaving	67
1925	Spinning and weaving	65
1926	Spinning and weaving	69
1927		61
1928		49
1929		49
1930		53
1932	Dai Nippon Spinning Mill	48
1933	Dai Nippon Spinning Mill	54
1934	Dai Nippon Spinning Mill	45
1934	Spinning and weaving	51
1935	Spinning and weaving	53
	India	
1905	Buckingham Mill, Madras	86
1905	Carnatic Mill, Madras	89
1906	Buckingham Mill, Madras	95
1906	Carnatic Mill, Madras	98
1907	Buckingham Mill, Madras	87
1907	Carnatic Mill, Madras	98
1907	Ahmedabad	89
1907	Bombay	38

Table 9.9 continued

Year	Mill	Labor turnover (percentage per year)
1907	Nagupur	85
1934	Bombay	28
1938	Bombay	21
1943	Bombay	25

Source: Compiled by the author for Japan from various primary sources, Fujibashi (1943), and Yokoyama (1898), and for India from Das (1923) and various government statistical series including *Report* (1946)

Table 9.10: Length of service in the cotton textile industries of Japan and India (percentage distribution)

A: Japan	1897	1918	1927	1936
Less than one year	46.2	50.3	18.3	29.5
From one to two years	23.3	18.4	19.8	20.5
From two to three years	13.3	11.1	17.2	15.4
From three to four years	7.7	9.3	11.9	14.9
From four to five years	4.7	9.3	7.9	14.9
Total less than five years	95.2	89.1	75.1	80.3
From five to ten years	4.6	7.0	17.5	11.9
More than ten years	0.2	3.9	7.4	7.8

B: Bombay, India	1890	1927–28	1940
Less than five years	72.2	37.6	29.5
From five to ten years	11.1	23.4	28.5
More than ten years	16.7	39.0	52.0

Sources

Japan: Saxonhouse 1976
India: Morris 1965

more gradual. As late as the onset of the World War I, Japanese rates were hardly different from those of the early 1890s. And turnover in the early and mid-1930s were hardly different from twenty years earlier.[8]

[8] Saxonhouse (1976) shows the time pattern of departure of new recruits in the spinning industry did not change between the 1890s and the 1930s. This suggests the turnover and experience rates derived are largely the function of elapsed time and current demand conditions.

The turnover rates of women workers living in dormitories were significantly higher than those of all other Japanese mill workers. Nonetheless, the sharp contrast in the level and movement of the overall turnover rate between the two countries cannot be explained only by the differing sexual composition of the labor force. Turnover rates of male Japanese workers were much higher than the rates in the Indian industry. In addition, the turnover rates of Japanese male workers, none of whom lived in dormitories, were not significantly different over the thirteen-year period examined from those of non-dormitory female textile workers. The rates for commuting men and women in Japan were comparable to and possibly higher than, depending on region and time period, the Indian industry's turnover rates. They were also significantly higher than the turnover rates in other Japanese industries. (Data are given in tables 9.9–9.11.)

The development of the dormitory system was part of a Japanese textile-industry management decision to use teenage girls from rural areas who would stay only briefly in mill compounds before leaving the industry. These workers typically entered employment in a mill with very limited objectives. Money was to be earned for a wedding, or the family budget was in need of a supplement. Such limited objectives are consistent with the relatively high absentee rates exhibited by dormitory workers and with the findings in the first part of the chapter on the implicit cost of recruitment bonuses.

The high turnover rates in the early days in both the Indian and Japanese industries have been linked to the methods used to recruit at least a portion of their workers. In Japan, workers were at first recruited from rural villages by

Table 9.11: Percentage annual turnover rates by sex and residence in the Kanegafuchi spinning mills, 1903–15

Year	Commuting men	Commuting women	Women resident in company dormitories
1903	83	138	63
1904	80	92	108
1905	68	84	88
1906	50	60	80
1907	65	54	85
1908	68	52	80
1909	95	79	111
1910	67	69	80
1911	67	65	76
1912	70	71	83
1913	73	65	78
1914	50	54	66
1915	43	51	63

acquaintances and relatives in the mills or by freelance recruiters. After the late 1890s, recruitment came increasingly under the direct supervision of the textile firms, and was limited to specially authorized company representatives. Hiring from rural villages has remained extremely important to the Japanese textile industry throughout the 20th century.

In India, recruitment in villages bears some resemblance to Japanese practice. An agent or jobber induced the worker to enter the industry, receiving a commission from the worker's ultimate employer. Unlike Japan, the Indian jobber retained considerable authority over his recruit even after employment, at least until the enactment of the Badli Control Act. Given the absence of a dormitory system, such a relationship is not unexpected. It is commonplace for analysts to link the jobber's continued authority over recruits with the high turnover and high absenteeism prevalent in the Indian industry, because another commission was earned by shifting the worker to another mill, or, by sending him home, a fee could be earned on the replacement. But in the perspective of the Japanese experience, where recruiters did not have such authority, these absentee and turnover rates seem unexceptional.

It is also commonplace to link turnover rates with the close connection mill hands maintained with their native villages. It is suggested that mill hands, particularly in India, left to participate in village activities such as festivals, planting, and harvesting. If this is true, regular seasonal patterns in monthly turnover rates should be observed. To test this, the Spearman's coefficient of rank correlation was calculated for monthly turnover for the Buckingham Mills and Carnatic Mills in 1905 and 1907 in Madras, a sample of ten Japanese mills for 1906-09, and Dai Nihon Boseki for 1932-34. The results show no regular changes in the turnover rates for Buckingham ($r_s = 0.28$) or for the Carnatic Mills. The Japanese results, however, are mixed. The data from the 1930s reveal some seasonal changes ($r_s = 0.874$) that are not in the earlier, larger sample ($r_s = 0.174$). Emphasis on the village nexus and the role of the recruiter in accounting for the instability of the industry's labor force is clearly overdone for both countries. More stress needs to be placed on the structure of incentives and opportunities workers faced on entering the mill.

Wage Structure and Labor Management

Some characteristics of the wage structure in both the Indian and Japanese industries may be viewed as reflecting differing labor management policies. In general, regional wage differentials and size-of-firm wage differentials in the Indian cotton textile industry were much larger than in Japan. Wage differentials by sex in Japan decreased continuously until the 1930s. By contrast, fragmentary information for the Bombay Presidency reveals the average wage rate for women workers was almost consistently half that of men from the 1910s to the 1930s.

The explanation of aggregate wage differentials by sex is complex. It is well known that sex was a prime determinant of the job assignments of new recruits.

Typical job assignments by sex in India and Japan are presented in table 9.12. The different opportunities afforded by these differing assignments certainly explains part of the differential. As a result of careful inspection of Kanegafuchi personnel records, it is evident in Japan, as in India, both men and women were present in many sections. These men and women have the same job titles, and in many instances the men are present in numbers sufficient to preclude their being in a supervisory role.

Even more interesting in Japan, wage differentials by sex for the same job vary between 30 and 80 percent. By contrast, in India, when men and women did the same job, they received almost the same pay. For example, in the reeling and winding departments, Indian differentials by sex were 10 percent during the interwar period (Labor Ministry 1953).

The presence of wage differentials by sex within the same job classification in Japan and their absence in India may relate to differences in wage payment systems in the two industries. As table 9.12 indicates, workers received their wages on a piece or time-rate basis, depending on the section to which they

Table 9.12: Stylized specification of jobs and modes of payment in Japanese and Indian textile mills

Department	Japan			India		
	Sex	*Mode of payment*	*Index of earnings*	*Sex*	*Mode of payment*	*Index of earnings*
Mixing and waste	M, W	T	}115	M, W	T	95
Scutching	M	T		M	T	100
Carding	M	T	110	M	T	90
Drawing	M	P	105	M	P	110
Slubbing	W	P		M	P	125
Intermediate frame	W	P	}110	M	P	115
Roving	W	P		M	P	110
Spinning	W	P, T	100	M, W	T	100
Winding	W	P	100	W	P	65
Reeling	W	P	100	W	P	60
Warping	W	P	115	M	P	215
Doubling	W	P	100	M	T, P	–
Sizing	M	T	110	M	P, T	255
Drawing-in	W	P	90	M	P	185
Weaving	W	P	120	M	P	175

Specification is based on various data from the 1920s and 1930s for both industries and simplified for some regional variation

T = time
P = piece rate

belonged. In the hopes of increasing labor productivity, both industries increasingly used piece rates. By the 1920s, about half the workers in the Indian cotton textile industry were paid piece rates.

The Indian piece-rate system linked daily effort with daily remuneration. While this certainly allowed pecuniary incentives full play, it has been alleged that it was also responsible for promoting poor discipline within the mills. Loitering and absenteeism were higher in piece-rate than in time-rate departments. Indian management in introducing the piece rate allowed workers considerable scope in the choice between leisure and money.

Japan adopted piece rates somewhat more broadly than did India, but the Japanese form of the system never reached the Indian extreme of linking daily remuneration to daily effort. In Japan, workers were given efficiency ratings on the basis of their previous productivity and length of service. Individual or group productivity was monitored daily and was a significant aspect of the regular review of a worker's efficiency rating.

Concluding Remarks

Changes in the quality and organization of the labor force in Japan's early industrialization in textiles appear to be responsible for the bulk of the improvement in this industry's total factor productivity at the end of the 19th century and during the first three decades of the 20th. A better-educated, more experienced labor force, working shorter hours, transformed an industry that initially could not compete with Indian yarns even in its home market into the major force in world textile markets. Most of these changes in the quality, morale, and organization of the labor force were exogenously determined. The incidence of exposure to government-sponsored primary education changed dramatically during the latter half of the Meiji period (1885-1911). Working hours were shortened, primarily because of international pressure. And worker experience increased because the industry matured; for the one or two workers from each entering cohort who stayed permanently eventually came a large corps of supervisory personnel.

The differences between the Indian and Japanese textile industry labor forces are remarkable. The Japanese labor force – largely female, highly productive, and, despite close supervision, exhibiting high rates of turnover and absenteeism – can be contrasted to the Indian labor force – mostly male, less productive, loosely supervised, and having high rates of absenteeism. It is evident that the acquisition of a mature, stable labor force does not necessarily result in industrial success.

References

Antos, Joseph R., and Sherwin Rosen (1975), "Discrimination in the Market for Public School Teachers," *Journal of Econometrics*, 3(2): 123–50 (May).

Becker, Gary (1965), "A Theory on the Allocation of Time," *Economic Journal*, 75: 493–517 (September).

Boren (Dai Nihon Boseki Rengokai) (n.d.), *Indo mensan oyobi bosekigyo hokokusho*; this has been reprinted in *Shibusawa Eiichi denki shiryo*, vol. 10: 267–328.

Boren (Dai Nihon Boseki Rengokai) (1897), *Boseki shokko jijo chosa gaiyo*.

Das, R. K. (1923), *Factory Labour in India*, Berlin.

Diewert, W. D. (1974), "Applications of Duality Theory," in Michael D. Intriligator and David A. Kendric, eds, *Frontiers of Quantitative Economics*, vol. 2, Amsterdam: North Holland.

Fujibayashi, K. (1943), "Meiji nijū-nen dai ni okeru bōseki rōdōsha no idō genshō ni tsuite," *Mita gakkai zasshi*, 37; reprinted in *Meiji zenki no rōdō mondai*, Tokyo (1960).

Kamisaka, S. (1919), *Cotton Mills and Workers in Modern Japan*, Osaka.

Koseisho (Ministry of Welfare, Government of Japan), *Koseisho rodosha boshu nenpo*.

Labor Ministry (Government of India) (1953), *Economic and Social Studies of Women Workers in India*, Delhi. (This contains information from the 1920s and 1930s on textile companies in the Bombay Presidency.)

Lucas, Robert E. B. (1977), "Hedonic Wages in the Returns to Schooling," *American Economic Review*, 67(4) (September).

Minami, Ryoshin (1973), *The Turning Point in Economic Development*, Tokyo: Kinokuniya.

Minami, Ryoshin, and Akira Ono (1979), "Wages," and "Factor Incomes and Shares," in Kazushi Ohkawa and Miyoha Shinohara, with Larry Meissner, eds, *Patterns of Japanese Economic Development*, New Haven, CT: Yale University Press.

Morita, Yuzo (1944), *Jinko ron hatten shi*, Nihon Hyoronsha.

Morris, Morris D. (1965), *The Emergence of an Industrial Labor Force in India*, Berkeley, CA: University of California Press.

Pearse, Arno S. (1929), *The Cotton Industry of Japan and China*, Manchester.

Pearse, Arno S. (1930), *The Cotton Industry of India*, Manchester.

Report on an Enquiry into the Conditions of Labor in the Cotton Mill Industry in India (1946), Delhi.

Report on an Enquiry into the Family Budgets of Industrial Workers in Madras City (1938), Madras.

Report on an Enquiry into Working Class Family Budgets in Ahmedabad (1937), Bombay. (This includes some non-textile factory workers.)

Sampei, T. (1936), "Meiji zenki ni okeru fujin oyobi yōnen rōdōsha no jōtai," *Rekishi kagaku*, 5.

Saxonhouse, Gary R. (1966), "Country Girls and Communication Among Competitors in the Prewar Japanese Spinning Industry," in Hugh Patrick, with Larry Meissner, eds, *Japanese Industrialization and Its Social Consequences*, Berkeley, CA: University of California Press.

Smith, R. (1976), *The Occupational Health and Safety Act*, Washington, DC: American Enterprise Institute.

Strotz, Robert H. (1957), "The Empirical Implications of a Utility Tree," *Econometrica*, 25: 269–80 (April).

Takamura, N. (1971), *Nihon bōseki gyōshi josetsu*, Tokyo.

Toyo boseki nanjunen shi (1953), Osaka.

Uno, Riemon (1912), *Shokkō jijo mondai shiryō*, Osaka: Nihon Kyoiku Kai.

Yasukawa, Masaaki (1971), "Nihon no moderu seimeihyo," *Mita Gakkai Zasshi*, 64 (May).

Yasukawa, Masaaki, and Keijirō Hirooka (1972), "Meiji-taishō nenkan no jinkō suikei to jinkō dōtai," *Mita gakkai zasshi*, 65 (February/March).

Yokoyama, Gennosuke (1898), *Nihon no kasō shakai*; 1949 reprint edn, Tokyo: Iwanami Bunko.

10 Technology Choice in Cotton Textile Manufacturing

GARY SAXONHOUSE

In his influential article, "Economic Development in Historical Perspective," William Parker observes:

> Nearly all the production and transport techniques developed between 1770 and 1870 promoted the geographical concentration of industry. Those developed since that time have, in contrast, favored deconcentration. At first sight it appears odd that the drift to technological change should have been so strongly in one direction in one period and the reverse in another. It suggests that some relatively simple principle may underlie the variety of changes in each period and that a fundamental shift occurred between say, 1870 and 1920, in the principle on which technology advanced. Our ignorance of the history of modern technology is so profound that it is not possible to work out the nature of this shift in detail from readily available material. (Parker 1961)

It was the fate of the cotton spinning industry to be the first industry of the Industrial Revolution whose technology followed its goods out of proximity to the North Atlantic to Eastern Europe and Russia, to Mexico and Brazil, to India and to Japan. By 1900, even as an enormous international trade in cotton goods continued, and even as the British industry remained dominant, major textile industries existed at numerous locations on three continents. In speculating on the reasons for a widening technological transfer after 1870, Parker emphasizes the relative decline of purely mechanical inventions and a redirection of invention into chemistry and subatomic physics. Although such changes might have been important after 1920, cotton textiles, relatively uninfluenced by such redirections in inventive activity, was the only industry to achieve global status in the fifty years after 1870.

Unhappily, the multinational comparative possibilities of this first major modern case of technological transfer have never been exploited. Where a frontal assault might have been made on the global economic watershed identified by Parker, there have been only binational or bi-regional comparisons. The experiences of Britain and America, of Japan and India, of New England and the American South with cotton textile production have all been the subject of extended bilateral comparison. Unfortunately, in the same way that a perfect least squares fit with a single independent variable is always achieved with a sample size of two, strictly binational comparisons run the risk of yielding facile, simplistic, and even fallacious interpretations of complex phenomena.

The historical laboratory, however, unlike the statistical services of 20th-century international institutions, does not yield large samples easily, and the economic historian is usually left with a choice between binational comparison or no contemporaneous comparison at all. This is all the more reason why the global experience of the cotton textile industry, of which there is a record, should not be ignored. In particular, this essay examines the global adoption pattern of two competing spinning processes during the fifty years after 1870. It is true the choice between ring and mule spinning during this period has already been subjected to British–American and Indian–Japanese comparisons (for example, Mehta 1954; Sandberg 1969; Takamura 1969; Kiyokawa 1976; Lazonick 1981a). Using entirely new sources of information, however, the British and Indian experiences are re-evaluated and set within an interpretive framework which includes as part of its historical sample Japan, the United States, Canada, France, Austria, Russia, Switzerland, Italy, and Brazil.

Mule and Ring Technology

Both mule and ring spinning are direct adaptations of and improvements on spinning processes dating from the earliest days of the Industrial Revolution. The mule is based on the principle of intermittent spinning, the same principle underlying both the spinning wheel and the famous Hargreaves jenny. Mule spindles rest on a carriage that travels on a track a distance of more than five feet, while drawing out and spinning the yarn. On the return trip, as the carriage moves back to its original position the newly spun yarn is wound onto a paper tube on the spindle to form a cone shape called a cop. The process of building up this cop is regulated by a wire which moves up and down to guide the yarn. The mule, as its name implies, is traditionally thought of as a hybrid machine. As the mule spindle travels on its carriage, the strands of loose cotton, called sliver, which it spins are fed to it through rollers geared to revolve at different speeds to draw out the yarn. Such rollers were a principle element of Arkwright's water frame, which was the early alternative to the spinning jenny. (More detailed descriptions are given by Copeland (1912) and Taggart (1920).)

The late 19th-century ring-spinning machine also rested on more than a century's development of continuous spinning processes. The mule spindle does not spin while yarn is being wound on the cop. By contrast, the ring, which is an immediate descendant of Arkwright's water frame, is spinning all the time. Again, unlike the mule, the frame on which ring spindles rotate is fixed in place.

On each ring spindle is a little wire, known as a traveller, and around each spindle is a C-shaped steel ring. After the thread is drawn through rollers similar to those used by the mule, it passes through the traveller onto a wooden bobbin which has been placed on the spindle. As the spindle revolves, the traveller is drawn around the outside of the ring, receiving its impetus from the yarn. Because the traveller is revolving a little more slowly than the bobbin, twist is put in the yarn. At the same time, the yarn is wound on the bobbin, and, in order to secure uniformity in winding, the frame of rings moves up and down slowly. (See Copeland (1912), Taggart (1920), or Jeremy (1973) for more detail.)

While both the late 19th-century ring and the mule are clearly recognizable descendants of 18th-century machines, the pace of their development in the intervening hundred years was quite uneven. The original Hargreaves spinning jenny and Arkwright's water frame were produced within a year or two of one another in the late 1760s. (These inventions are discussed in Mantoux (1961).) The yarn the water frame produced was strong, but rather coarse. In contrast, the drawing-out feature of the jenny produced yarn which was weak and broke easily, but which could be extremely fine. Yarn from the water frame was most suitable for warp, and yarn from the jenny was most suitable for weft, making these two early spinning machines complementary. The water frame, incorporating as it did hundreds of spindles at a time, made possible the factory production of cotton yarn at the same time it also enhanced the cottage production of weft yarn.

This complementarity between factory and cottage ended not long after the invention of mule spinning in 1779. Although the first mules were made of wood and their small size made them suitable for use in cottages, by 1790 large mule-spinning machines with metal rollers and wheels, fitted with hundreds of spindles and powered by waterwheels, were being used in large factories. Mule spinning meant the demise of Hargreaves' jenny, but it did not mean the end of spinning by continuous methods. While it is true that within 20 years of factory-usable mules becoming available over 80 percent of British cotton goods were produced from mule-spun yarn, spinners still found an important niche in the market for yarn best produced by methods of continuous spinning. The water frame, and later the throstle, by twisting and drawing the yarn simultaneously could not produce fine yarn, but they did produce coarse yarn faster and cheaper than did mule spinning, and thus they continued to dominate this segment of the yarn market.

The advantage in cost that continuous spinning maintained over mule spinning was threatened in the 1830s with the introduction of the self-actor. Until the development of this device, a good deal of strength had been required for pushing the mule spindles back and forth on their carriages. The self-actor removed this requirement, allowing a potentially more diverse, if still highly skilled, labor force and much larger individual frames.

Hardly had such dramatic improvements in mule spinning been accomplished when equally important improvements were made in continuous spinning.

Although the throstle spun coarse yarn faster than the mule, its cost advantage was limited because it was a heavy user of energy and because, at operating speeds of more than 3,000 rpm, the legs of the U-shaped flyer fixed at the top of the spindle were spread by centrifugal force, causing the flyer to distort and wobble.

The development of cap spinning and ring spinning at this time gave continuous spinning the means to achieve higher speeds by dispensing with the flyer. Instead of a flyer, cap spinning used a conical cap mounted over the top of the spindle to guide the yarn to the bobbin below. Ring spinning replaced the flyer with a C-shaped ring traveling at high speed around a grooved circular raceway mounted on a plate, which in turn traveled up and down the spinning bobbin. These improvements in continuous spinning meant dramatic increases in output per spindle with less labor and no increase in energy required. By the 1850s, average speeds on ring machines reached 5,000 rpm and there were reports at this time of successful ring spinning of coarse yarn at 9,000 rpm (Copeland 1909: 122). The achievement of such high average spinning speeds meant that, despite the tremendous significance of the self-actor for mule spinning, by the 1860s – at least in the United States – there were almost as many ring as mule spindles.

Following the introduction of the self-actor in the 1830s, there were only minor improvements in mule spinning throughout the rest of the 19th century. By contrast, in the early 1870s major improvements in ring spinning were made with the introduction of the Sawyer spindle. This new spindle was reduced in weight and its point of support was changed to an elevated holster. By these changes and improvements, energy requirements were reduced, the speed increased, and the quality of work improved. By the mid-1870s, the average speed of rings in operation reached 7,500 rpm. The late 1870s saw the development of the Rabbeth spindle and within a few years average spindle speeds were as high as 10,000 rpm.

By the late 19th century, as machine spinning of yarn was becoming truly global in location, the textile industry continued to face, as it had since the Industrial Revolution, two competing spinning technologies. Late 19th-century mule spinning continued to require a large number of highly skilled, if no longer necessarily brawny, operatives. By contrast, ring spinning remained a relatively unskilled task and, because it required no complicated rolling carriage, it took up two-thirds of the space of mules of comparable capacity.

The very simplicity of rings – spinning and winding yarn in one motion – placed special demands on the fiber being spun. In the absence of large inputs of labor in the preparatory stages, in contrast to mules, rings could successfully spin yarn for any given fineness from only a narrow range of cotton grades. Quite apart from limitations on the raw-cotton inputs, the strain on the yarn from the simultaneous spinning and winding also, with the constraints of late 19th-century technology, made it very difficult to spin fine yarns on ring machines.

Similarly, whereas the ring had to wind its spun yarn onto wooden bobbins, the mule wound its yarn onto a paper tube called a cop. Because a cop holds more yarn than a wooden bobbin, compared to ring spinning, mule spinning did not require as frequent labor-using removal of yarn from spindles. Moreover, if the yarn was being transported a significant distance before being woven, it was an important advantage to have the yarn on cops, at least for mule-spun weft yarn. Warp yarn, unlike weft yarn, needs to be rewound before weaving. If a ring mill did its own warping before shipping the yarn to a weaving shed, the initial spinning on bobbins was inconsequential (see Copeland 1909; Lazonick 1981a).

In the late 19th century, the differing characteristics of ring and mule-spinning machines meant that, within any one economy, the adoption of one rather than the other method led to a different set of labor, capital, energy, transportation, land, and raw-cotton costs. By the 1950s, some eighty years after the major improvements in ring-spinning machines, the ring had completely supplanted the mule worldwide. Is this a case of very slow diffusion of an important technology, or did the differing factor costs across economies lead to differing choices as to the appropriate technology across national and regional economies facing markedly differing endowments and institutions?

Was the final global victory of ring spinning only the result of later technological improvements such as high-draft spinning and massive changes in global resource endowment? Did the great global expansion of machine spinning in the late 19th and early 20th centuries come at a time when methods of intermittent and continuous spinning could continue to coexist successfully, as they had for the previous hundred years? Was the relatively slow diffusion of the ring a matter of lack of information and entrepreneurial failure, or another of Rosenberg's cases (1972) where a lag in diffusion is really the playing out of changing market circumstances in the presence of very good knowledge of local circumstances?

Previous Estimates of Ring Diffusion

The four countries for which substantial information has hitherto been available have previously suggested a rather simple interpretation of ring diffusion. The conventional wisdom is that in America, Japan, and India, the ring was rapidly adopted, and in England adoption was rapid for low-count yarn. Mules remained predominant in England, but only because so much high-count yarn was produced there. Similarly, the mule remained a major technology well into the 20th century, because England bulked so large in total world production.[1]

[1] Yarn is measured by weight, and yarn size by a measure relating weight to length. The metric unit is the tex, the weight in grams of 1,000 m of yarn. Count indicates the length of a pound of yarn. For cotton, one count is 840 yards (one hank). Most final-output yarn has several plys twisted together; hence 20/3 (read 20-count 3-ply), is a yarn 5,600 yards long per pound (20 times 840 divided by 3). Single-ply yarn is abbreviated as an "s" after the count number, so 16s is a 16-count single ply. A coarse yarn is up to 20s; medium is 21s to 40s; fine, 41s to 80s; and over 80s are superfines. Over half of the yarn spun is coarse, with

Table 10.1: Spindles in place, 1907

Country	Number of spindles	Country	Number of spindles
United Kingdom	43,154,713	United States	23,200,000
Germany	9,191,540	Russia	7,562,478
France	6,609,105	India	5,279,595
Austria	3,584,434	Italy	3,867,862
Spain	1,800,000	Japan	1,483,497
Brazil	1,000,000	Belgium	1,000,000
Canada	893,761	China	755,938
Mexico	693,843		

Sources

United Kingdom, United States, Italy, France, Germany, Russia, and Australia: Copeland 1909
Japan: Boren 1907
Spain, Brazil, Belgium, Canada, and Mexico: United States Department of Commerce *Special Agent Series*
China: Pearse 1931

Table 10.2: Spindles in the United States (millions)

Spindle	1870	1880	1890	1900	1905
Ring	3.7	–	8.9	13.4	17.9
Mule	3.4	–	5.4	5.6	5.2
Total	7.1	10.6	14.3	19.0	23.2

Source: Copeland 1909: 128

The United States

Reviewing the previously available spindle data, it is clear that the great American improvements in ring spinning in the 1870s led to rapid diffusion in New England and the South during the late 19th century. Even prior to the development of the Sawyer–Rabbeth spindle, census returns for 1870 indicate the ring was already the preferred machine.

Britain being the only pre-World War II exception among major spinners, although in physical amount the United States produced as much non-coarse yarn as Britain.

There are three main types of yarn: warp (also called twist), used as longitudal thread; weft (or filling), for cross-wise thread; and knitted, used in knitting. Warp yarns tend to be tightly twisted, wefts less so.

Japan

The Japanese spinning industry is, with the American case, another well-known example of the rapid diffusion of ring spinning. With the exception of two very minor instances, the Japanese cotton spinning industry's early mills, including the highly successful Osaka Spinning Mill, all used mules (Kinukawa 1937). The Japanese mule episode proved to be short-lived. By the mid-1880s, the first ring-spinning machines had been purchased as an experiment, and even prior to their success in 1889 new orders for mules had almost entirely stopped. In

Table 10.3: Spindle investments in Japan

Year	New mules	Mules scrapped	Total mules	New rings[a]	Total rings
1866	1,824	–	1,824	–	–
1871	2,000	–	3,824	–	–
1873	–	–	3,824	720	720
1875	2,000	–	5,824	–	720
1880	4,080	–	9,904	–	720
1881	10,000	–	19,904	–	720
1882	6,000	–	25,904	–	720
1883	14,500	–	40,404	1,152	1,872
1884	6,000	–	46,404	–	1,872
1885	24,800	–	71,204	4,020	5,892
1887	–	–	71,204	5,164	11,056
1888	13,500	2,000	82,704	36,272	47,328
1889	29,224	–	111,928	108,744	186,072
1890	11,664	–	123,592	94,953	251,025
1891	–	5,902	117,690	51,032	302,057
1892	–	4,560	113,130	6,872	308,929
1893	–	31,300	81,830	97,960	406,889
1894	2,000	4,000	79,830	156,742	563,631
1895	4,000	13,028	66,802	76,844	640,476
1896	46,140	16,820	96,122	265,180	905,656
1897	17,020	14,000	99,142	226,884	1,132,540
1898	11,620	9,800	100,962	83,000	1,215,540
1899	1,616	–	102,578	61,908	1,277,448
1900	–	2,000	100,578	1,796	1,275,652

In addition to rings and mules, some throstles were used in the early days of the Japanese cotton spinning industry. In 1866, the first spinning mill in Japan used 1,800 throstle spindles as well as 1,824 mule spindles. Another mill erected in 1880 included 448 throstles in addition to its 2,080 mule spindles

[a] This column is net ring investment

Source: Noshomusho 1901

Japanese eyes, the ring had come to dominate the mule to such an extent that virtually all the mule-spinning machines in use in 1889 were scrapped within the next few years. Spectacular fires of suspicious origin in the two largest Japanese mule mills contributed to this process; the mills claimed they were not insured (Saxonhouse 1974). Some new mules continued to be purchased, but where scrapped mules were designed to spin 10s, 12s, or 14s, the large mules purchased in 1896, 1897, and 1898 were designed to manufacture such fine yarns as, respectively, 80s, 80s, and 58s (Boren *Geppo* 1901 June).

India

In India, where a much larger mule-spinning industry had already been created in the 1870s, it has previously been suggested by many Indian economists and others that once a ring mill was actually erected in Bombay, the Indian response to the new technology matched the Japanese and quite probably exceeded the American examples (Wacha 1915; Harris 1925; Mehta 1954; Takamura 1969). After 1882, following experiments in the mills in Bombay controlled by J. N. Tata, the ring was reputedly universally chosen by promoters of new mills. Supporting evidence for this view comes from much-cited statistics in Bombay Millowners' Association sources. According to this material, after the introduction of the ring, some additional mules may have been purchased, but this was accompanied by a dramatic increase in the use of the ring, and in due course was followed by a decline in the use of the mule. Note, however, the following authorized description of the initial introduction of the ring into Bombay by Tata:

> [Tata's] readiness to give an immediate trial to any new machinery quickly placed him at an advantage. In America, where the spindle was invented, the trials had not given sufficiently successful results to justify extensive use of the machine. While experiments in Lancashire were still at a tentative stage, and nothing had been done upon a large scale, two frames at the Empress Mill were in daily use. For Mr Tata persevered, and insisted that the machines should run to their full capacity. The normal speed of 6,000 rpm was soon exceeded; at the Empress Mill 9,000 rpm was considered a fair average but 12,000 rpm were frequently obtained. . . . [On] account of this improvement, the output of the machines was so satisfactory that Mr Tata scrapped every other type. At first, his statistical results were received with incredulity even by the best English firms and he had great difficulty in persuading Messrs Platt Bros of Oldham, to take up the manufacture of the necessary plant. Their conservatism was at length broken down and in later years they supplied Mr Tata with several ring frames. (Harris 1925: 31)

This account of Tata's struggles is filled with major errors. In 1875, almost ten years before these experiments in Bombay took place, millions of American ring spindles were operating at an average speed of 7,500 rpm and, in the mid-1880s, speeds closer to 10,000 rpm were the norm (Copeland 1909). Similarly, although English machinery manufacturers were undoubtedly conservative, orders for at least hundreds of thousands of ring-spinning machines were taken by British manufacturers such as Howard & Bulloughs, Asa Lees, Dobson & Barlow, Brooks and Doxey, J. Hetherington, and even Platt Bros between 1880 and 1885. Indeed, prior to the onset of Platt's reputed refusal of Tata's request for rings and Tata's so-called experiments with spindles purchased from Brooks & Doxey, many orders for export of ring-spinning machines to India were booked by British firms. Platt's records indicate the firm supplied rings to at least five Indian mills in 1882, including three in Bombay, where Tata's Empress Mill was located. These gross inconsistencies suggest further examination of the diffusion of ring spinning is in order.

England

Unlike the American, Japanese, and Indian cases, it is widely agreed there was a predominance of mules in English cotton spinning well into the 20th century. Unfortunately, a continuing series on machinery purchases, however reliable, or even a good set of benchmarks, has not been available. However, working with data from the *Cotton Factory Times* and Robson (1957), a number of estimates have been constructed, including those by Sandberg (1979) and Lazonick (1981a), for the period between 1907 and 1913. Both these estimates, while covering only a very limited period of British textile history, suggest that a large stock of mules continued to grow through concentration on high-count yarn, and also that the ring industry, concentrating on lower-count yarns, made substantial inroads prior to World War I.

New Data Sources

Full discussion of the worldwide diffusion of ring technology has been hampered by lack of appropriate data. Beyond the four countries discussed above, there has been very little evidence about the timing of ring adoption. Indeed, even for these countries, only in the Japanese case has accurate and comprehensive data been available previously. Fortunately, these data limitations are now at an end. Unusually complete data on worldwide shipment of ring and mule-spinning machines between 1880 and 1920 have been obtained from six British textile machinery companies: Platt Bros, Dobson & Barlow, Howard & Bulloughs, Asa Lees, Tweedales & Smedley, and Taylor-Lang. Excluding the German, the American, and to a much lesser extent the French markets, these six English machinery-makers accounted for the vast majority of worldwide machinery sales. It is possible to obtain from each of these companies not only the quantity of each type of machine sold in each national market, but also the identity of each machine's purchaser, the count of yarn to be spun, and the grade of raw cotton to be used.

The compilation and analysis of this new data source indicate a striking alteration of previous understanding of the pace of ring diffusion. In consequence, a substantially new, richer interpretation of technology choice in low-income areas is needed.

England

It is now entirely clear that during the years after the improvements in ring spinning in the 1870s until as late as 1914, British spinners invested overwhelmingly in mule rather than ring spindles. The primary-source evidence collected here indicates investment in ring machinery comprised only 3.3 million spindles, and investment in mules comprised an extraordinary 10.0 million spindles during the reference period 1907-13. This is far more mule investment than previous work suggested, and indicates adoption of ring spinning by the British industry went much more slowly than was previously reported. Mules were the dominant English technology for all yarn counts prior to World War I, not just for higher-count yarn. Similarly, what use was made of rings was not confined to the lowest counts. The data are given in tables 10.4-10.6.

India

The Indian evidence (tables 10.7-10.8) is equally surprising. Bombay Millowners' Association (BMOA) data indicate that between 1884 and 1894 the Indian stock of spindles increased by 1.4 million, of which 0.2 million were a net increase in mule spindles and 1.2 million were a net increase in ring spindles. The newly available data confirm the increase of 1.4 million spindles during these ten years, but indicate a division of 0.9 million mule spindles and 0.5 million ring spindles. Between 1894 and 1914, the differences are equally striking. BMOA data indicate the stock of mule spindles declined by 0.4 million spindles, and the

Table 10.4: Purchase of cotton spinning machinery (spindles) by English firms, 1878-1914

Time Period	Mules		Rings		
	Number	Percentage	Number	Percentage	Total
1878–90	11,687,870	94	792,100	6	12,479,970
1891–98	5,813,819	87	860,215	13	6,674,034
1899–1906	13,659,835	84	2,670,776	16	16,330,661
1907–14	10,055,583	75	3,624,996	25	13,320,579

Table 10.5:   English orders of mule and ring spindles annually, 1878–1914

Year	Mules	Rings	Year	Mules	Rings
1878	49,252	0	1897	288,304	271,582
1879	208,994	0	1898	993,063	141,964
1880	808,513	20,060	1899	1,341,650	171,570
1881	847,352	46,474	1900	1,041,153	98,192
1882	920,527	45,741	1901	1,955,587	163,580
1883	1,396,242	39,656	1902	1,540,914	115,502
1884	2,076,166	211,216	1903	1,503,762	203,072
1885	1,325,271	130,193	1904	804,299	417,311
1886	916,529	63,436	1905	2,509,469	702,831
1887	752,958	37,366	1906	2,927,001	800,580
1888	834,970	58,160	1907	1,963,587	343,005
1889	940,346	90,986	1908	1,379,288	297,427
1890	1,373,350	48,922	1909	1,064,105	352,006
1891	880,097	80,554	1910	686,205	333,099
1892	1,161,972	65,326	1911	1,137,158	351,636
1893	828,200	90,650	1912	1,680,083	667,668
1894	666,612	8,442	1913	933,421	495,918
1895	604,712	55,726	1914	1,211,716	392,237
1896	391,483	145,347			

stock of rings increased by 5.2 million spindles. But with major mule orders coming into England from India throughout the 1900–14 period, it is hard to imagine the widespread scrapping implicit in the Indian economic historians' data on the types of spindles in use.

Table 10.7 also indicate the experience of the Indian spinning industry differs substantially from both the Japanese and American cases, on the one hand, and the British case, on the other, and is entirely contrary to previous belief. Unlike the Japanese and American cases, mule spinning remained important long after the early and very substantial adoption of ring spinning by some segments of the Indian industry. Indian spinners ordered many more mule spindles after 1884 than they did before. These mule spindles were predominantly to spin low-count yarn. Indeed, the median-count yarn for which new mule-spinning machinery was purchased was also lower than for ring-spinning machines throughout the period 1880–1920. Only after 1907 did ring spinning emerge as the dominant technology for all the relatively coarse yarn counts spun by the Indian industry.

Russia

The records of the British textile machinery manufacturers help describe a much different picture of ring–mule competition than had been previously understood,

Table 10.6: Distribution of English purchases by yarn count (spindles), 1878–1920

Time period	Count interval	Mules		Rings	
		Number	Percentage	Number	Percentage
1878–90	1–20	313,642	3.6	69,750	23.8
	21–25	190,686	2.2	56,420	19.3
	26–30	327,188	3.8	76,880	26.2
	31–35	1,496,312	17.3	57,660	19.7
	36–40	1,464,687	17.0	24,800	8.5
	41–60	3,580,312	41.4	34,410	11.7
	60+	1,157,662	13.4	4,030	1.4
	Total	8,639,222	100.0	292,950	100.0
1891–1900	1–20	589,536	9.9	149,800	17.6
	21–25	243,504	4.1	134,050	15.8
	26–30	506,232	8.5	113,750	13.4
	31–35	563,904	9.5	101,850	12.0
	36–40	1,126,740	19.0	86,100	10.2
	41–60	1,766,472	29.7	116,200	13.7
	60+	1,147,032	19.3	40,950	4.8
	Total	5,945,556	100.0	847,700	100.0
1901–10	1–20	902,538	5.9	263,720	14.2
	21–25	387,933	2.6	213,940	11.5
	26–30	490,854	3.2	348,080	18.7
	31–35	1,131,000	7.4	288,040	15.5
	36–40	2,033,538	13.4	427,120	23.0
	41–60	4,974,138	32.7	229,520	12.4
	60+	6,413,901	34.8	87,400	4.7
	Total	15,190,461	100.0	1,857,820	100.0
1911–20	1–20	411,600	8.5	213,096	12.0
	21–25	128,094	2.4	165,002	9.3
	26–30	341,584	6.3	213,095	12.0
	31–35	436,212	8.1	333,132	18.7
	36–40	1,050,140	19.3	588,064	33.0
	41–60	1,672,146	30.8	131,376	7.4
	60+	1,355,950	25.0	139,196	7.8
	Total	5,434,186	100.0	1,782,960	100.0

Table 10.7:   Indian orders for mule and ring spinning machines, 1880–1920

Time period	Mule machines	Median spindles per machine	Ring machines	Median spindles per machine	Percentage mule	Percentage ring
1880–90	1,615	733	3,209	286	56	44
1891–1900	1,914	747	3,877	322	53	47
1901–10	468	739	5,159	339	16	84
1911–20	510	719	4,322	331	20	80

Table 10.8:   Median counts for which Indian machines were rated

Time period	Mule	Ring
1880–90	18	19
1891–1900	14	18
1901–10	17	20
1911–20	13	20

Table 10.9:   Russian orders for mule and ring spinning machines, 1878–1916

Time period	Mule machines	Median spindles per machine	Ring machines	Median spindles per machine	Percentage mule	Percentage ring
1878–90	1,625	1,031	1,826	317	74	26
1891–1900	1,207	1,056	4,910	337	44	56
1901–10	472	1,112	1,923	376	42	58
1911–16	334	1,159	1,523	386	40	60

particularly for India and Britain. Other countries displaying more persistence for the mule than previously had been conventional include Austria, Switzerland, Belgium, and France. The newly available data also shed light on other very important cases which, as a consequence of limited evidence, had previously been little discussed. An example of this is the Russian experience. At the turn of the century, the Russian spinning industry was the fourth largest in the world

Table 10.10:   Median counts for which Russian machines were rated

Time period	Mule	Ring
1878–90	34	32
1891–1900	35	34
1901–10	35	34
1911–16	38	34

Table 10.11:   Brazilian machinery orders, 1880–1920

Time period	Number of mules	Number of rings	Percentage of mules	Percentage of rings
1880–90	1	257	0.4	99.6
1891–1900	1	374	0.3	99.7
1901–10	5	683	0.7	99.3
1911–20	6	664	1.0	99.0

Table 10.12:   Distribution of Brazilian ring machines, by count

Count interval	Number of machines, 1880–90	Percentage of machines
1–20	101	43
21–25	29	12
26–30	26	11
31–35	1	1
36–40	75	32
41–60	–	–
60+	2	1

after the United Kingdom, the United States, and Germany. In common with the revised view of the English and Indian cases, the Russian industry showed a surprising and long-lived preference for mule spinning. In the three decades between 1878 and 1916, 3.9 million mule spindles and 3.5 million ring spindles were purchased. Unlike all the other major spinning nations, preference for mules did not diminish decade by decade; almost the same proportion of mules was purchased by the Russian industry after 1911 as in the 1890s. (See tables 10.9 and 10.10.)

Brazil

In contrast, there are other newly discovered cases which closely follow the Japanese pattern of extremely rapid adoption and almost exclusive use of ring-spinning machines. Brazil is such a case. A substantial Brazilian industry developed in the 1880s which, with the exception of an order placed for a single mule-spinning frame in 1880, used only rings. The Brazilian industry's almost exclusive interest in using rings was complemented by an almost exclusive interest in spinning relatively coarse yarns. Note that all the ring-spinning machines used in Brazil in the 1880s from 1881 onward came entirely from the reputedly conservative, mule-oriented Platt Bros of Oldham. (Data are given in tables 10.11 and 10.12.)

Interpretation

The simple interpretation of the global pattern of the diffusion of spinning technology between 1870 and 1920 described earlier must now give way before new data which it cannot explain. The slow global diffusion of the ring is not simply an English adjustment to their own worldwide dominance in high-count yarns. After reviewing the global data, any simple linear association between the yarn count demanded and the choice between the ring and the mule is out of the question. The English used the mule to spin both high and low-count yarn, whereas the Japanese attempted to spin almost the whole spectrum using the ring. Many Indian manufacturers used the mule to spin coarser yarns, while reserving the ring for relatively finer work. The actual magnitude of the mule's persistence generally, and in particular with respect to low-count yarns, is now readily apparent.

If yarn count demanded, or position in the global yarn market, by themselves cannot provide a satisfactory explanation of the global pattern of ring and mule use, what other variables might have greater explanatory power? The earlier review of how the two spinning technologies work suggests that, in addition to the type (count) of yarn demanded, considerations such as quality of the labor supply (skilled/unskilled, male/female), quality of the raw material used (short staple/long staple), industrial organization (spinning and weaving separate or integrated), managerial quality (presence or absence of trained engineers, British advisers), import barriers (output or input protection), market institutions (presence or absence of spot markets in output and inputs), and character of the local power supply (availability of water) might be important.

There is considerable variation in each of these variables across the national cases that are available, so much so that no single variable can possibly be brought up to the pedestal from which yarn count demanded has been toppled. For example, England, with many highly qualified mule spinners, and India, with male labor cheap relative to female labor, long persisted with mules, but Russia, whose czarist labor force has been shown by Gerschenkron (1962) and

Rosovsky (1961) to have been unusually unskilled, also chose to use skill-intensive mule-spinning machines. Japan and China, with relatively poor-quality local cotton, adopted the ring quickly, whereas India, which also grew primarily short-staple cotton, continued to a significant degree with mules. Again, non-integrated spinners in England by and large used mules, whereas those in Japan used rings. India, with British spinners in dominant technical positions, persisted in its use of the mule, but Brazil, which for many years also had many British spinners, used rings.

If the degree of ring diffusion is not easily subject to single-variate explanation, it is hardly alone in this among economic processes! In this instance, given the character of both the dependent and independent variables, the risk of specification error and the lack of full quantitative information at present on all potential explanatory variables suggest the maintained hypothesis ought to be further explored by first examining how close each of a number of important spinning countries stand in relation to an implicitly derived multiple regression plane. Such an approach, if treated as exploratory, is very useful, but it should be recognized that subtly many of the degrees of freedom added by using a large cross-country sample for comparative analysis are being used up. This is tantamount to violating classical statistical canons by adding the higher-order terms of explanatory variables after observing the output of a multiple regression. Too much like the straight line regression between two points earlier derided, the fit may be excellent without there being any statistical evidence!

United States

Turning first to the American case, recall that with the cut in energy costs associated with using the Sawyer–Rabbeth spindle and the substantial increases in productivity made possible by increased speeds, the 1870s and 1880s saw a dramatic increase in the proportion of mills in the United States using rings. The paradigmatic American mill had weaving and spinning under one roof and sold cloth rather than yarn, and therefore did not suffer from using the expensive-to-ship wooden bobbins required by ring machines. Furthermore, the local availability and cost advantage of high-quality American raw cotton meant American spinners had relatively less need for a mule machine, one of the great virtues of which was its ability to make use of very short staple cotton. Finally, notwithstanding many decades' use of mules, skilled American mule spinners remained relatively scarce. The more rapid adoption of the ring in the late 19th century removed an important labor constraint on textile manufacturing in the United States. (A closely related discussion on the role of labor and choice of technique in American cotton spinning is contained in Lazonick (1981b).)

Japan

The first Japanese mills had been clustered around cotton-producing regions with the expectation they would provide a market for Japan's cotton growers, who had been hard hit by the collapse of hand-spinning in the face of competition from Indian cotton yarns. Japanese cotton is coarse and extremely short stapled, so it is not surprising the English engineers asked by the Ministry of Agriculture and Commerce and Yamabe Takeo, the celebrated president of the Osaka Spinning Mill, advised the use of mules. That the intended markets for such yarn were geographically dispersed handloom weavers, that water power was thought to be readily available, and that male labor was relatively abundant may also have influenced the English advisers' thinking. Turning to English machinery manufacturers for advice in the 1870s and 1880s made it highly probable mules would be the recommended technology. England was the home of the mule and the English machinery manufacturers were the pre-eminent producers of machinery. By contrast, all the great advances in ring-spinning technology in the 1870s were American in origin and development.

The switch from the virtually exclusive use of mules to the virtually exclusive use of rings in the space of four or five years went hand in hand with a number of other major adjustments in Japanese spinning. During the 1880s, where the Japanese cotton spinning industry relied primarily on poor-quality, short-stapled Japanese raw cotton, the switch to rings was accompanied by a large increase in the use of higher-quality Chinese cotton and the significant use by the industry for the first time of still higher-quality raw cotton imported from East India. The shift from domestic raw cotton to imports from East India was almost as complete and dramatic as the shift from ring to mules, and was facilitated by the removal of the 5 percent import duty on such cotton. Data on cotton imports are given in table 10.13 (also see Ranis and Saxonhouse 1978: 272).

The change in the type of machine and in the character of raw material was also accompanied by a change in the use of labor. Where the highly profitable, mule-using Osaka Spinning Mill operated in 1884 with equal numbers of male and female operatives, the largely ring-using industry by 1891 had a labor force that was more than 80 percent female (Kinukawa 1937: vol. 2: 193). The substi-

Table 10.13: Use of domestic and imported raw cotton in the Japanese cotton industry, 1883–98

	1883	1884	1887	1892	1893	1894	1895	1896	1897	1898
Percentage of domestic raw cotton used	94.3	87.6	86.5	29.1	25.9	23.3	14.8	9.1	6.8	6.0
Percentage of imported raw cotton used	5.7	12.4	13.5	70.9	74.1	76.7	85.2	90.9	93.2	94.0

Source: Noshomusho 1901

tution of rings for mules required a higher-quality imported raw material, but labor that required very little training. This gave the industry an opportunity to rely primarily on young girls who were not expected to remain for an extended period in the mills (Saxonhouse 1976).

The Japanese industry, even while improving the quality of raw-cotton input, was still spinning with rings a quality of cotton which even mule spinners in England and the United States rarely used. To counter this, the industry developed labor-intensive cotton-mixing methods which improved the quality of predominantly short-stapled raw cotton by a judicious blending of small amounts of longer-stapled cotton. Nevertheless, ring spinning with such cotton meant many more breaks than would have occurred had mules been used. However, the substitution of cheaper unskilled female for potentially skilled male labor allowed a significant decrease in the number of spindles a spinner tended. By assigning an unprecedentedly small number of spindles for each spinner to tend and using carefully mixed cottons, it was possible to operate ring spindles at the very fast speed of 10,000 rpm without frequent yarn breakages totally undermining efficiency (Nichimen 1957).

The increasing use of labor in the preparatory stages, in ring spinning, and in reeling the yarn off the wooden bobbin prior to shipment resulted in the total staff level in Japanese mills almost doubling, relative to the amount of machinery, between the late 1880s and the early 1890s (Boren *Geppo*, various issues).

India

To understand the persistence of mule purchases by Indian manufacturers it is instructive to view Indian criticism of the contrary Japanese practice. A lengthy translation of an article published in the respected *Indian Textile Journal* appears in the June 1892 Boren *Geppo*. The following is a short extract:

> The use of rings or so many ring spinning machines is one reason for the lack of sucess of the Japanese spinning industry. The Japanese industry *uses many kinds of cotton and the managers of the new companies are very inexperienced.* When asked why they use rings they reply that they are operated with success in the United States, England and India and with such reasoning it is no wonder they have met with little success. (Italics added.)

The article goes on to list seven factors which must be considered when deciding between the ring and the mule. (1) What raw materials are being used? (2) What is the technical skill of the workers? (3) What count yarn is being produced? (4) What is the climate? (5) When the yarn is not woven at the same mill, where will it be marketed? (6) What is the availability of repairs and new machines? (7) Is water available?

In fact, persistence of mules in India can be explained by most of the same factors that caused the Japanese initially to opt for mules. The relatively poor quality of the local cotton, and the far-flung handloom weavers to which the machine-made yarn would be shipped, doubtless made English textile machinery manufacturers urge the Indians, as they did the Japanese, to adopt the mule. Having adopted the mule, the Indians, unlike the Japanese, continued to make new purchases even after a ring section developed, in part because male mule spinners in India, unlike Japan, were relatively cheap, and because the Indian industry quickly developed major yarn markets at home and overseas which could not be serviced by wooden bobbin-using ring spinners.

Even more important than either of these considerations was India's difficulty in emulating Japanese cotton-mixing practices. Depending on country and count, raw cotton is from 75 to 85 percent of the cost of cotton yarn. It was only sophisticated cotton mixing which could undercut the mule's ability to spin a better quality of yarn for a given quality of raw cotton. Because of the natural protection afforded locally grown cotton, the Indians found it relatively difficult to spend resources on efficiently improving the quality of input as a substitute for improving the quality of the machinery. As India came to lose its overseas yarn markets and as power looms improved to the point where more effective competition against the protected domestic handloom weavers was possible, interest in the ring greatly increased. Nonetheless, it was well into the first decade of the 20th century before the Indian industry accepted the superiority of the ring-spinning machine for most of the yarn counts spun in India.[2]

England

The English spinning industry's massive continuing commitment to mules incorporates many of the same elements found in the Indian case. The widespread successful competition of handloom weavers again machine-made cloth in all but the few high-income areas of the world, at the same time as hand-spun yarn could not successfully compete with machine yarns, meant there were good-sized markets which could be served by an efficient English industry that did not use the wooden bobbin. Serving this huge overseas yarn market maintained a large army of non-integrated mule spinners with little incentive to consolidate with or independently add a weaving shed to their operations.

Quite apart from the needs of overseas markets, the presence of an extremely active and diverse spot market in raw cotton allowed English spinners much the same flexibility that investments in cotton-mixing allowed their Japanese counterparts. At one end of the quality spectrum, rings could not use sufficiently poor-

---

[2] Clark (1907) observed that in 1906 mules were preferred on Indian cotton for spinning yarns above 26s and even on the coarser counts. The preference for mules for counts above 26s continues to be reported in Odell (1917).

quality raw cotton for the spinning of very coarse yarns. At the other end, ring spinning was too stressful to spin quality yarn apart from very high-quality raw cotton. With the mule, English spinners had a machine which, because of its intermittent spinning method, could use a great variety of cotton to spin a given count of yarn.

The English mule-using industry proved to be a great stabilizing force in world cotton markets. By virtue of their technology, they sought low-cost solutions on extremely short notice for over 75 percent of their input cost. This flexibility in the use of raw cotton, together with the availability of a relatively large supply of high-quality spinners who could manage the complicated machinery, is what allowed mule spinning to remain not only competitive, but also dominant at all count levels in England for so long.

Russia

The Russian case shows elements from each of the previous cases, plus government intervention, which together produced the most remarkable case of mule persistence outside England. The Russian industry faced in its early days a larger handloom industry and a relatively short-staple cotton. Behind a barrier of high effective tariff protection, a large cotton industry staffed by British engineers and using mule machinery had developed by the 1840s. This was true despite the relatively poor quality of Russian labor. Quite like the Indian case, the relative availability of male labor to some extent compensated for this.

The improvements in rings in the 1870s and the successful large-scale importation of long-stapled American cotton, together with continuing problems in training mule spinners, created the first substantial interest in ring spinning. This interest was reflected in the sharp increase in ring spindleage in both the 1880s and 1890s. Following a shift in czarist policy toward aggressively encouraging Russian cotton growing, a stiff tariff was placed on imported raw cotton at the turn of the century. The tariff was extremely effective. In 1895, no more than a quarter of the raw cotton used by the industry was short-staple Russian cotton, but just fifteen years later it had supplanted the by now much higher cost, longer-staple American cotton. The raw-cotton tariff, combined with a newly higher tariff on fine cotton yarns, increased Russian textile manufacturers' satisfaction with mules in the period before World War I.

Brazil

In its exclusive use of rings, the Brazilian spinning industry seems quite close to the Japanese, but that is the extent of the similarity. In the first place, as late as 1910 most Brazilian room bosses and mill managers were displaced Lancashiremen. Given their technologically conservative reputation, it may seem surprising such a group ran an industry relying entirely on rings. However, the same conservatism that insisted short-staple raw cotton should be spun on mules also

Table 10.14: A stylized multivariate explanation of technology choice in the cotton industry

Country	Spinning machine	Raw-cotton staple length	Count spun	English presence	Import barriers	Labor supply	Spot markets	Integrated mills
England	mules	relatively short	median 20s	yes	no	high quality male	yes	no
Russia	mules	short	median 30s	yes	yes	poor quality male	no	yes
Japan	rings	short	low 20s	no	yes	poor quality female	cotton-mixing	no
USA	rings	long	–	no	no	poor quality	yes	yes
India	mules	short	low 20s	yes	no	–	no	no
Brazil	rings	long	mid 20s	yes	yes	poor quality	no	yes
Austria	mules	short	–	yes	yes	male	no	no
Switzerland	mules	long	high	no	no	poor quality female	no	yes
Italy	mules	relatively long	–	no	yes	poor quality female	no	no

felt for coarse and medium-grade yarns the high-quality raw cotton grown in Brazil could best be spun on rings!

Concluding Remarks

Table 10.14 summarizes information on the experiences of the countries covered above, as well as three other countries for which material is readily available. Together with the previous discussion, the table demonstrates that, even though a univariate explanation of technology choice in cotton spinning is not possible, it is not so difficult to explain the extremely heterogeneous national behavior with respect to ring diffusion. The observed behavior in each national case can be reasonably explained on the basis of quality of raw material available, industrial organization, managerial quality, quantity of labor supply, import barriers, and character of market institutions.

Great care must be taken not to confuse the explanation of why turn-of-the-century spinners behaved as they did with confirmation that such behavior was efficient. The preceding analysis confirms that spinning firms, regardless of national location, made decisions on the basis of rules of thumb pointed out by such contemporary observers as Ralph Odell, W. A. Graham Clark, Melvin Copeland, and writers in the *Indian Textile Journal*. Unfortunately, it does not fully answer whether such rules were leading spinners to efficient or inefficient behavior. That the mule ultimately disappeared does not mean that the rules of thumb were wrong to suggest its purchase in either 1875 or 1900.

Note in this connection that it is the Japanese case that is the outlier from the implicit multiple regression. The Japanese industry stands alone as a case of using relatively short-staple cotton exclusively with ring machines before World War I. When continued improvements in ring-spinning technology and changes in global factor prices made ring spinning the dominant technology for virtually all grades of cotton, Japan was well positioned, unlike most of its competitors, to take charge of large segments of the world textile market.

Japan came to be well positioned as a short-staple raw-cotton-using ring spinner because of its unique commitment to cotton mixing. Neither before nor after World War I were Japanese techniques emulated successfully, if such emulation was attempted at all. In the absence of cotton mixing as part of the technological choice set, most of the world's great spinning industries appear to have behaved sensibly. Further explanation is needed as to why Japanese cotton mixing could not diffuse more widely.

References

Boren *Geppo* (*Dai Nihon Boseki Rengokai Geppo*), a monthly journal published by the All Japan Cotton Spinners' Association.

Boren (Dai Nihon Boseki Rengokai) (1907), *Menshi boseki jiji sankosho Meiji 40-nen*.

Clark, W. A. Graham (1907), *Cotton Fabrics in British India and the Philippines*, Washington, DC.

Copeland, M. T. (1909), "Technical Development in Cotton Manufacturing since 1860," *Quarterly Journal of Economics*, 24: 109–59 (November).

Copeland, M. T. (1912), *Cotton Manufacturing Industry of the United States*, Cambridge, MA: Harvard University Press.

Gerschenkron, Alexander (1962), *Economic Backwardness in Historical Perspective*, Cambridge, MA: Harvard University Press.

Harris, Frank (1925), *Jin Tata: A Chronicle of His Life*, London: Blackie.

Jeremy, D. (1973), "Innovation in American Textile Technology during the Early Nineteenth Century," *Technology and Culture*, 14: 40–75.

Kinukawa, Taichi (1937), *Hompo menshi boseki shi*, vol. 2, Osaka: Nihon Mengyo Kurabu.

Kiyokawa, Yukihiko (1976), "Indo menkogyo ni okeru gijutsu to shiba no keisei ni tsuite," *Keizai kenkyu* (July).

Lazonick, William H. (1981a), "Factor Costs and the Diffusion of Ring Spinning in Britain Prior to World War I," *Quarterly Journal of Economics*, 96: 89–109 (February).

Lazonick, William H. (1981b), "Production Relations, Labor Productivity and Choice of Technique: British and US Cotton Spinning," *Journal of Economic History*, 41(3) (September).

Mantoux, Paul (1961), *The Industrial Revolution in the Eighteenth Century*, New York: Harper and Row.

Mehta, S. D. (1954), *The Cotton Mills of India 1854–1954*, Bombay: Textile Association.

Nichimen (1957), *Nichimen 70-nenshi*, Osaka.

Noshomusho (1901), *Nihon menshi boseki kiju*, Tokyo.

Odell, Ralph M. (1917), *Cotton Goods in British India*, part II, Washington, DC.

Parker, William N. (1961), "Economic Development in Historical Perspective," *Economic Development and Cultural Change*, 10: 1–7 (October).

Pearse, Arno S. (1931), *Japan and China: Cotton Industry Report*, Manchester: International Federation of Master Cotton Spinners' and Manufacturers' Association.

Ranis, Gustav, and Gary Saxonhouse (1978), "Technology Choice, Adaptation and the Quality Dimension in the Japanese Cotton Textile Industry," in *Papers and Proceedings of the Conference on Japan's Historical Development Experience and the Contemporary Developing Countries*, Tokyo: International Development Center of Japan.

Robson, R. (1957), *The Cotton Industry in Britain*, London: Macmillan.

Rosenberg, Nathan (1972), "Factors Affecting the Diffusion of Technology," *Exploration in Economic History*, 10(1): 3–33 (Fall).

Rosovsky, Henry (1961), *Capital Formation in Japan*, Glencoe, IL: Free Press.

Sandberg, Lars (1969), "American Rings and English Mules: The Role of Economic Rationality," *Quarterly Journal of Economics*, 83(1): 25–43 (February).

Sandberg, Lars (1979), *Lancashire in Decline*, Columbus, OH: Ohio State University Press.

Saxonhouse, Gary R. (1974), "A Tale of Technological Diffusion in the Meiji Period," *Journal of Economic History*, 34(1): 149–65 (March).

Saxonhouse, Gary R. (1976), "Country Girls and Communication among Competitors in the Japanese Cotton-Spinning Industry," in Hugh Patrick with Larry Meissner, eds, *Japanese Industrialization and Its Social Consequences*, Berkeley, CA: University of California Press.

Taggart, W. Scott (1920), *Cotton Spinning*, London: Macmillan.

Takamura, N. (1969), *Nihon bosekigyo shi josetsu*, Tokyo.

United States, Department of Commerce, *Special Agent Series*.

Wacha, D. E. (1915), *The Life and Work of J. N. Tata*, Madras: Granach.

11 Borrowed Technology in Iron and Steel: Brazil, India, and Japan

AKIRA ONO

Technology transfer enables less developed countries (LDCs) to attain higher rates of economic growth. Often, this is simply the importation of capital-intensive methods without modification, called nonadapted borrowed technology. Nonadaptive technology tends to lower labor's relative share, and to restrict employment opportunity in the modern sector. Adaptive borrowing involves modification to reflect domestic factor prices. Besides avoiding unfavorable effects on labor's relative share and employment opportunity, this process promotes learning-by-doing and thereby increases technological capability. The raw silk industry in prewar Japan provides an outstanding example of adapted borrowed technology. Domestically-produced reeling equipment modified the imported models by using wooden frames instead of iron, making the machines less capital-intensive (Ono 1968).

One objective of this essay is to ascertain the extent of adaptation of borrowed technology in Japan's prewar iron and steel industry. Adaptation was done by a private ironworks in the early Meiji period, but later it shifted to nonadapted technology. There was also a change from using scaled-down to scaled-up equipment. (Scaling down is selecting technology at the lower end of the plant-capacity range, and is done to acquire technical, organizational, and operational experience with the modern technology.)

Borrowed technology often simply means a borrowed production method. But, as discussed later, the fact early government-run ironworks in Japan failed to produce pig iron with imported modern equipment suggests the absence of experience can be an obstacle. Thus, the term technology involves not only a method of production embodied in equipment, but also the experience (or skill) necessary for operating the equipment or processing the materials and fuels.

An essentially similar version of this essay has been published in the *Hitotsubashi Journal of Economics* (February 1981), and excerpts have been used in this chapter with permission.

The author is indebted to Professors Kazushi Ohkawa and Miguel Urrutia for their useful comments on the original version of this paper. Thanks are also due to Miss Gwendolyn R. Tecson for her editing of the English in earlier versions.

Borrowing technology successfully usually involves either acquiring methods not far beyond present capability, or else importing the experience as well as the production method. Thus, government-run ironworks in Japan tried to introduce the necessary experience by hiring English technicians and skilled workers. However, this did not succeed, partly because they had no specific knowledge of the characteristics of Japanese coal and iron ore. In other words, foreign technicians' experience is not always relevant to the conditions in another country.

A second objective is to find the extent of similarity between Japanese and LDC experiences. Brazil and India have been chosen mainly because of the availability of information. Nonadapted importation prevailed for steel mills established with assistance from advanced countries. However, scaling down of equipment is found in Brazil and India in the postwar period, and mixing charcoal with coke to feed blast furnaces in Brazil may be considered a technology adaptation.

Why LDCs tend to select capital-intensive production methods is also discussed. This is the factor-proportion problem. Several elements are examined, such as technological fixity, inefficient choice of technology by government enterprises, availability of capital from abroad, weak market pressures, and factor-price distortions. The existence of scale economies is important in the case of iron and steel. LDCs tend toward large-scale equipment, because even if not adapted to domestic factor prices, it enables LDCs to achieve a substantial reduction in production costs.

The next section describes technology adaptation in Meiji Japan. This is used as a basis for a simple model of adaptation and the shift to nonadaptive borrowing. Using the Japanese experience and the model as a framework, Indian and Brazilian experiences are examined and compared to the Japanese experience. The final section of the chapter looks further at several causes of nonadaptive borrowing.

Technology Adaptation in Japan

Tatara-buki, refining iron sand in furnaces using charcoal, was the prevalent process in Japan before the Meiji era. However, by the mid-19th century, this method could not meet demand, in quantity and in quality. To satisfy the demand, expanding mainly because of military needs, the Tokugawa government and several clans imported modern methods. It was from a Dutch book, written in 1826 by Huguenin, that early 19th-century Japan learned new iron-making technology. Japanese technicians constructed furnaces from the book's description. These new reverberating furnaces for making steel and the blast furnaces for pig iron were quite different from the traditional methods of making iron and steel. The experience laid the foundation for the skills needed to modify equipment imported from England in the early Meiji period.

Ambitious attempts were made by the Meiji government to transplant modern techniques with the intention of building a richer nation and a stronger army. Government-run ironworks were established at Kamaishi (on the Pacific coast of northern Japan) and Nakaosaka (in modern Tochigi prefecture). However, both were closed in 1882, shortly after their establishment, and in 1885 were sold to private investors. The Nakaosaka works still did not succeed, but Tanaka Chobei, who bought Kamaishi, successfully ran that works.

It was partly because of the success of private ironworks that government officials, despite their earlier failures, decided to try again, establishing the Yawata works in norther Kyushu. When its furnaces were fired in 1901, some of the skilled workers at Kamaishi were sent to help. After the Russo-Japanese war, many private firms were established that made steel solely with open hearths. Thus, the rapid expansion of the industry can be attributed to the growth of both private and government enterprises.

Tanaka, originally an iron dealer, installed a small blast furnace at Kamaishi, because the 25-ton furnace the government had imported from England was too large for him to operate. The small furnace was producing pig iron by 1886. This encouraged Tanaka to establish a private iron-manufacturing company (Tanaka Ironworks at Kamaishi; by merger, it is today part of Shin Nippon Seitetsu). In 1892, he had five blast furnaces, each with a capacity of less than 6 tons per day.

A reduction in furnace size from 25 tons to less than 6 tons enabled modification of ancillary equipment, generally lowering the capital–labor ratios. Whereas government mills used an iron blower driven by steam, Tanaka's air blast was produced by a method similar to the traditional one, but was modified to include stoves for preheating the blast. Water wheels were gradually replaced by steam boilers, but at the Kurihashi branch, where charcoal was available, they were still used in the early 1900s. When the government built Kamaishi, rails and steam locomotives were imported to transport coal and iron ore. When Kamaishi closed, these were sold for a railway between Osaka and Sakai. Tanaka constructed transport facilities using horse tramways and carts. Table 11.1 summarizes the differences between Tanaka's ancillary equipment and those at other mills.

A Model of Adaptation and the Shift to Nonadaptation

Having outlined Japan's experience, it can be used to illustrate a simple model and my basic hypothesis. The curves α and β in figure 11.1 are isoquants corresponding to different output levels. For a given factor proportion, capital and labor employed on the α curve are γ times those on the β curve, and output on α is γ^n times that on β, where n is greater than unity because of scale economies. (A blast furnace is an example of increasing returns to scale, because the furnace's volume increases more rapidly than the enclosing surface.)

Table 11.1: Differences in ancillary equipment between Tanaka and other ironworks

	Source of power	Blowing equipment	Hot-blast stove
Before the Meiji restoration			
Traditional method (*Tatarabuki*)	man power cattle water wheels	wooden bellows	not used
Western small-scale blast furnace	water wheels	wooden bellows	not used
Government-run ironworks at Kamaishi	steam engines	iron blower	used
Tanaka ironworks at Kamaishi (between 1885 and 1891)	water wheels[a]	wooden bellows	used

[a] A steam boiler was used at the Suzuko branch of Tanaka Ironworks.

Sources: Fuji Seitetsu KK 1956 and 1957; Nippon Kogakukai 1929; Saigusa and Iida 1957

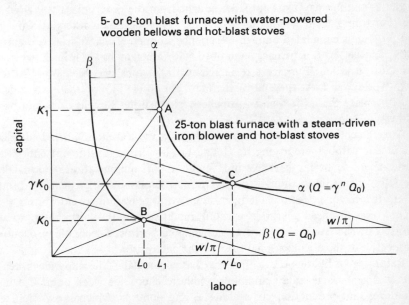

Figure 11.1: Adaptation of borrowed technology

Point A on α indicates an imported 25-ton blast furnace equipped with a steam-driven iron blower and hot-blast stoves. Such a furnace was beyond the experience of early Meiji ironworkers. At the Tanaka works, therefore, furnaces were scaled down to a size within previous experience. Point B on β indicates a 5- or 6-ton furnace.

The hypothesis here is that large-scale equipment requires experience or skill to operate because of the technical, organizational, and operational characteristics specific to it; that is, the α curve presupposes a greater body of experience than the β curve. So long as experience and skills remain at original levels, only the β curve is available to entrepreneurs.

Point B was chosen along β to minimize the cost per unit of output by taking the domestic-wage–rental ratio (w/π) into consideration. This production method was different from both the imported and the traditional. Hot-blast stoves, which were not used until they were available from England, were combined with a traditional method of producing a blast, water-powered wooden bellows. Point B is adapted borrowed technology.

The Tanaka Works at Kamaishi is an example of adapted borrowed technology in the period 1885–91. But in subsequent years, it shifted to nonadapted borrowing. This shift is demonstrated by several changes in Tanaka's technology. In its early days, the charge of coke and ore was brought to the furnace mouth by hand, but later steam and electric power were used (Fuji Seitetsu 1956: 206). Wooden bellows were gradually replaced by iron blowers; this allowed higher working temperatures in the furnaces (Saigusa and Iida 1957: 95). In 1893, one of the 25-ton per day blast furnaces bought from the government was fired for the first time since it was acquired in 1887. This suggests workers at Kamaishi had by then accumulated enough experience to operate a large-scale furnace. In 1901, another 25-ton furnace, equipped with a steam-driven iron blower, was put into operation. Furnace size increased to 60 tons in 1904, and 120 tons after World War I. At the end of the Meiji period (1911), railroads were being laid to replace the less expensive, smaller-scale facilities such as carts and horse tramways.

Government-run ironworks at both Kamaishi and Yawata imported advanced equipment without modifying it. Unlike private firms, government enterprises could afford to be more or less indifferent to cost minimization, and installed the latest plants, even though they were more capital-intensive than warranted by relative factor prices in Japan. In other words, government enterprises were apt to use advanced methods without modification. But ultimately, so did privately-owned Tanaka. A shift to nonadapted borrowed technology occurred irrespective of the organizational form of the enterprise.

Returning to figure 11.1, a firm that has accumulated the experience necessary to operate large-scale equipment is able to choose between point C, which minimizes unit production costs along α, and point A, which is an imported, capital-intensive method. Under specified factor prices, the unit cost at C, $(w\gamma L_0 + \pi\gamma K_0)/\gamma^n Q_0$, is less than at A, $(wL_1 + \pi K_1)/\gamma^n Q_0$. Point C is risky, however, as it has not been done, and thus may not be practical. In contrast, point A is known to be feasible, and is thus a quick, riskless way of expanding, even though the unit production cost is higher at A than at C.

When there is substantial scale economy, that is, when n is very large, a firm may shift from B to A rather than C, because A is less risky than C, and A has lower unit costs than B. The unit costs at A, $(wL_1 + \pi K_1)/\gamma^n Q_0$, will be far smaller than at B, $(wL_0 + \pi K_0)/Q_0$, if n is very large. When scale economies are limited, a shift from B (adapted technology) to A (nonadapted) does not profit a firm, so further adaptation of the technology to domestic factor prices should be made, and C should be chosen.

Indian and Brazilian Experience

India and Brazil also have long metallurgical traditions. In India, smelting and fashioning iron was known from early times. Diminutive furnaces produced small blooms of soft iron, used chiefly for ax heads and plowshares. Even in the 1910s, this method was practiced in widely scattered areas. In the Central Provinces alone, nearly 4,500 tons of iron ore were smelted in 1916 in as many as 300 native furnaces. The technique is wasteful of ore and fuel compared to modern methods. In Brazil, which possesses the rich ores of Minas Gerais, small furnaces producing forgeable iron have been operated since the beginning of the 17th century, but even in the early 20th century most of the demand was satisfied by imports. Interruption of imports by World War I spotlighted the need for domestic production. In 1921, a Belgian established an ironworks with charcoal-fired furnaces, Companhia Siderurgica Belgo-Mineira (CSBM).

India

The first effort to produce steel along modern lines was made by J. M. Heath in 1830, with financial aid from the East India Company. Until the Tata Iron and Steel Company (TISCO) was founded in 1907, attempts to introduce modern techniques mostly failed. Causes for the failures include insufficient government protection, charcoal shortages, and high costs from using charcoal. (See Hata et al. 1943: 8; Dey (1933) is another source on the early period.)

In prewar India, most attempts to borrow advanced iron-making technology were made by private enterprises. The discovery of the Iron Belt (in eastern India) in 1905 led to formation of two big companies, TISCO (1907) and IISCO (Indian Iron & Steel, 1918). TISCO was the first successful Indian steel mill; it produced profits immediately after beginning operations in 1911. The company was financed by private money and managed by Indians, but skilled workers and supervisors were Americans and Europeans. This dependence, together with the quality of Indian ores (60 percent iron), can explain why TISCO achieved early profitability.

When TISCO started operations, it was larger, more capital-intensive, and had more up-to-date machinery than Yawata in 1901. For example, Yawata started with coke ovens of the obsolete beehive type. Initially, TISCO also tried to minimize investment in machinery by using coolie labor, especially in materials handling, but it quickly discovered coolie labor did not substitute for machinery. The equipment then adopted was extraordinarily capital-intensive.

In the prewar period, TISCO employed a large number of foreign skilled workers. This, however, cannot justify the importation of capital-intensive methods, as, in 1925–26, it was estimated that to replace foreigners with Indians would save only 15 percent of the total wage bill. As the number of foreign workers decreased, the equipment became increasingly capital-intensive, which further demonstrates high-salaried foreigners were not a decisive reason for nonadapted borrowed technology.

Japanese ironworks in the Meiji era can be characterized by a short period of dependence on foreign technicians and skilled workers, who were involved primarily in helping to establish mills. They may have been discharged too soon, as it took ten years after kindling the first blast furnace at Yawata in 1901 for the mill to record profits.

While the government of India was keenly interested in the growth of TISCO, the overall attitude was one of simple approval and moral support. It was difficult for the Indian government to take active measures, as the British government initially adhered to *laissez-faire* as a colonial policy. Only in the 1920s was protection provided. (Dey (1933) and Fraser (1919) discuss TISCO's history.)

During the post-colonial period, the Indian government has been committed to growth through central planning, and has been intent on importing advanced technology through formation of government-run ironworks. However, in India, as in Japan, successful government-run mills were preceded by private ones. Just as Yawata benefited from the supply of skilled workers from Tanaka, new public-sector mills in India drew on TISCO and IISCO. Private mills also participated in attaining government production targets. Three public-sector mills were established during the second five-year plan, which began in 1956 and gave high priority to heavy industry. They were Rourkela, Bhilai, and Durgapur. They received financial and technical assistance from West Germany, the Soviet Union, and the United Kingdom, respectively, including from 37 to 65 percent of the foreign-exchange requirements. Interest rates were low, only 2.5 percent for Bhilai from the Soviet Union, and 4.75 percent for private IISCO from the World Bank.

The Indian government gave financial assistance to private mills. For example, about a quarter of TISCO's 1952 expansion was funded by the government without interest during the construction period. However, in the third five-year plan, the government did not allow private ironworks to expand capacity, because of a new government mill at Bokaro. (See Johnson (1966) for more on the post-war Indian industry.)

In 1960 TISCO had accumulated the skills to operate a 1,650-ton blast furnace, almost five times the size of its first furnace. In contrast, blast furnaces installed in 1959–60 in a new public sector mill had capacities between 1,000 and 1,250 tons of pig iron. However, blast furnaces in these Indian mills were of a similar size to an average-sized furnace in an advanced country. Throughout the 20th century, equipment and designs for the main production processes have been imported with little or no modification. Any adaptation of technology has been confined to subsidiary processes such as mining, transportation, material handling, construction, and so on.

Brazil

For LDC economies, including Meiji Japan, establishment of a steel mill is to some extent a manifestation of economic nationalism. The Companhia Siderurgica Nacional (CSN), which was founded in 1941 by the government and started operations in 1946, is the first coke-using steel mill in Brazil. Getulio Vargas, then dictator, emphasized national unity and pushed a vigorous program for economic development. The technical and economic planning and construction of the CSN plant were carried out and financed by Americans. Other ironworks with coke blast furnaces, such as USIMINAS (Usinas Siderurgicas de Minas Gerais) and COSIPA (Companhia Siderurgica Pautista), were founded after World War II with the assistance of Japanese and European firms. The top three Brazilian companies (CSN, USIMINAS, and COSIPA) are owned by the government.

The size of blast furnaces at major government mills has increased throughout the postwar period. Generally, Latin American countries import equipment. To take USIMINAS as an example, coke ovens, sintering machines, blast furnaces, blooming mills, plate rolling mills, and continuous casting equipment have been imported from Japan without modifying them for the factor prices prevailing in Brazil, except that the capacity of blast furnaces was kept to the average size in Japan. USIMINAS furnaces were thus of 700-ton per day capacity in 1962, less than half the size that Yawata operated at its largest branch in 1959.

The larger the furnace size, the more difficult it is to operate. While USIMINAS scaled down, there was no adaptation made to Brazilian factor prices, in contrast to Tanaka's technology adaptations in the 1880s. The reduction of furnace size lowered initial costs, but scaling up soon began, as it had for Tanaka. The largest daily capacity of a USIMINAS blast furnace was 700 tons in 1962, 900 in 1966, 1,500 in 1973, and 4,300 in 1974.

In the case of Brazil, a protracted dependence on foreign workers was also indispensable. In establishing USIMINAS, for instance, up to 200 Japanese technicians and skilled workers helped with construction and subsequent operation, and a few have remained to provide technical instruction. Whereas CSN and USIMINAS invited technicians and skilled workers from the United States and Japan, respectively, COSIPA sent Brazilian workers to Europe for training. This does not seem to have been successful. In 1973, there was only a minor difference in rated capacity between COSIPA and USIMINAS, but production of steel ingots by COSIPA was only half that of USIMINAS.

The Brazilian industry produced pig iron in charcoal-fed furnaces longer and in greater proportion than either Japan or India. This is due to the favorable natural environment, where eucalyptus trees grow quickly. The use of charcoal as fuel restricts the size of the blast furnace, and a charcoal furnace is thus generally smaller and simpler than a coke-fed one. This means a technology adaptation was made to suit Brazilian factor prices. Firms using charcoal have lower labor productivity, but low Brazilian wages allow such low-productivity, less capital-intensive firms to exist. They have, however, been losing market share. (See Greene (1967) for more on Brazil.)

Causes of Nonadapted Borrowing

There are several reasons why LDCs tend to employ highly capital-intensive methods of production, in spite of resource endowments characterized by an abundant supply of labor and a scarcity of capital. These include (1) technological fixity, (2) inefficient choice of technology by government enterprises, (3) availability of capital from advanced countries, (4) lack of competitive market pressures, and (5) factor-price distortions. Let us look at each reason in turn.

Technological fixity is often mentioned as a key factor. From an engineering viewpoint, factor substitution is thought to be limited to a narrow range. According to Eckaus (1955), entrepreneurs in LDCs are apt to believe the western way of producing, which involves high ratios of capital to labor, is the best, if not the only, way, so there is no room for adjusting to factor prices prevailing in their countries. In other words, whatever the actual characteristics of the production function may be, they believe the production function they face is a limitational one in which no substitution is possible.

In this chapter, the ironworks at Kamaishi and the many charcoal furnaces still operating in Brazil have been cited as examples of technology adaptation in which capital–labor ratios are lowered to a considerable extent, compared to the unmodified imported advanced technology. Thus, the problem is why entrepreneurs in LDCs tend to switch from labor-intensive methods of production, suited to domestic factor prices, to capital-intensive methods not suited to them.

It is often claimed that governments, which are more or less indifferent to cost-minimization, tend to employ capital-intensive equipment irrespective of factor price ratios. This tendency is believed to be strengthened by the ability of governments to mobilize large amounts of capital. However, Tanaka Ironworks, which was privately owned, changed from small to large furnaces that were quite capital-intensive by the standard of the day. Another example is TISCO in prewar India. Also a private enterprise, it installed the most-up-to-date equipment. Adoption of capital-intensive methods cannot be attributed solely to inefficient choice of techniques by government enterprises.

Investment capital available to LDCs is not limited to domestic sources: funds can be borrowed abroad. Because interest rates are lower in advanced countries, LDCs can justify using more capital-intensive methods than otherwise. Under the second five-year plan, public-sector mills in India borrowed between one and two-thirds of the foreign-exchange requirements from advanced countries. The same is true of Brazil.

However, despite access to foreign capital markets, the percentage of interest payments in the total cost of steel produced was 11 percent in 1966 in Brazil, much higher than in Europe (4 percent) and the United States (1 percent) (Ohara 1972: 299–302). This was partly due to a high rate of interest (22 percent in 1967) on loans by BNDE (National Bank for Economic Development), which is the principal financial institution for the iron and steel industry in Brazil.

Another argument is that while competitive market pressures push producers to minimize costs, a lack of pressure can result in nonadapted borrowing, that is, a failure to choose efficient production methods. LDCs typically protect domestic markets. But ironworks in prewar Japan were exposed to foreign competition. This was especially severe for pig iron, because imposition of a tariff was seen as an obstruction to the growth of domestic metal-using industries. (Much of the pig iron came from India.) Nevertheless, production methods were not adapted to factor prices in most of the prewar years, and became more and more capital-intensive. Therefore, adoption of highly capital-intensive methods in Japan is not attributable to weak competitive pressures in product markets.

Capital subsidies, interest rates pegged artificially low, duty-free importation of capital equipment, the minimum wage, and so on, tend to cheapen capital and make labor more expensive, inducing entrepreneurs in LDCs to choose more capital-intensive methods of production. These policy measures for distorting factor prices were emphasized by Mason (n.d.) in his discussion of the factor-proportions problem. But TISCO and Tanaka in the prewar period seem to be exceptions. Self-reliance of private enterprises was the basic doctrine followed by the Indian government until the necessity of protecting the iron and steel industry was recognized by the British government in the 1920s. Although Tanaka bought iron-making equipment from the government at cheap prices and received military orders, expansion was undertaken without direct government aid until the Steel Industry Promotion Act in 1918.

These exceptions may not be sufficient to deny the general validity of the factor-distortions hypothesis, for other examples can be shown in which the choice of capital-intensive methods in LDCs was closely associated with distorted factor prices. It should be noted, however, that factor-price distortions presuppose more basic causes, which can be traced to, say, general backwardness. These are, in the context of this analysis, a lack of the scientific knowledge indispensable to the search for production techniques suited to LDCs, and a deficiency of funds necessary to develop these techniques to the level of practical use. These factors cause LDCs to distort factor prices so capital-intensive equipment can be chosen.

Borrowing advanced technology has the advantage of saving the time and money required if LDCs were to try to develop their own production methods. It also enables LDCs to avert the risk of failure involved in such research and development activities. Even if not adapted to domestic factor prices, modern technology lowers the cost per unit of output. Especially in the case of iron and steel, the existence of scale economies leads to adoption of capital-intensive methods, as these bring about a substantial reduction in unit production cost. This has an important implication.

If technology adaptation is made, it is in industries where scale economies do not exist or are slight. Iron and steel and other scale-sensitive industries cannot be expected to increase employment opportunity or moderate a decline in labor's relative share of income. LDCs need to be aware of the importance of the choice of industry.

References

Dey, H. L. (1933), *The Indian Tariff Problem in Relation to Industry and Taxation*, London: George Allen and Unwin.

Eckaus, R. S. (1955), "The Factor-Proportions Problem in Underdeveloped Areas," *American Economic Review*, 45: 539–65 (September).

Fraser, L. (1919), *Iron and Steel in India: A Chapter from the Life of Jamshedji N. Tata*, The Times Press.

Fuji Seitetsu KK, Kamaishi Seitetsujo (1956), *Kamaishi seitetsujo schichijunenshi.*

Fuji Seitetsu KK, Kamaishi Seitetsujo (1957), *Kindai tetsu sangyo no seiritsu − − Kamaishi Seitetsujo Zenshi.*

Greene, D. G. (1967), *Steel and Economic Development. Capital–output Ratios in Three Latin American Steel Plants*, East Lansing, MI: Michigan State University.

Hata, T. et al. (1943), *Indo oyobi goshu tekkogyo no kaibo*, Minzoku Kagakusha.

Johnson, W. A. (1966), *The Steel Industry of India*, Cambridge, MA: Harvard University Press.

Mason, R. H. (n.d.), *The Transfer of Technology and the Factor Proportions Problem: The Philippines and Mexico*, United Nations Institute for Training and Research Report No. 10.

Nippon Kogakukai, ed. (1929), *Meiji kogyo shi, kahei tekko hen.*

Ohara, Y., ed. (1972), *Keizai to toshi kankyo; Buraziru*, Tokyo: Aiya Keizai Kenkyujo.

Oishi, M. (1974), "Buraziru no tekkogyo," mimeo.

Ono, A. (1968), "Gijutsu shinpo to Borrowed Technology no ruikei," in J. Tsukui, and Y. Murakami, eds, *Keizai seicho riron no tenbo*, Iwanami Shoten.

Saigusa, H., and K. Iida, eds (1957), *Nippon kindai seitetsu gijutsu hattatsushi*, Tokyo: Toyo Keizai Shimposha.

PART IV   Intersectorial Resource Flows and Finance

12 Changes in Intersectoral Terms of Trade and their Effects on Labor Transfer

SUSUMU HONDAI

Modern economic growth involves the flow of capital and labor between the agricultural and nonagricultural sectors. The topic of this chapter is how the terms of trade between the two sectors affect that flow. To find the role of the terms of trade in economic development, I have analyzed its effect on the transfer of labor between agriculture and nonagriculture, and the factors affecting changes in the terms of trade, from the perspective of economic development in Japan and Taiwan.

The analysis is in terms of a two-sector economy, where the output and inputs of both sectors are exchanged in a market. Terms of trade are defined as the ratio of agricultural product prices to nonagricultural product prices. In other words, it is a relationship between two sectors. When analysis is of a single sector, and is concerned with profit-maximizing behavior within the sector, terms of trade are defined as the ratio of the sector's output prices to its input prices, which is the basis of the farmer's parity issue in several countries, including the United States.[1]

The concern here is with the allocation of resources between two sectors, hence the use of the definition of terms of trade as the price of one sector's output relative to that of the other. A decline in prices for agricultural products relative to nonagricultural prices is a movement of the terms of trade against agriculture. On the other hand, an increase in agricultural prices relative to those of nonagriculture is a movement of the terms of trade towards agriculture.

In a less developed economy, financial institutions which channel savings from the agricultural to the nonagricultural sector are incompletely developed. As major savers, landlords and farmers thus are often a significant source of direct investment in industry in the early stages of development. A premise of

---

[1] In chapter 13 below, Mody, Mundle, and Raj also discuss the relationship between the agricultural and nonagricultural sectors. Because the two chapters are looking at different aspects of the relationship, they use a different definition of terms of trade.

this essay is that, because they are making investment decisions and receiving income in both sectors, landlords and farmers are likely to be responsive to changes in market conditions throughout the economy. For example, over-production of agricultural products and the consequent decline of agricultural prices will lead them to invest more in industry.

Farm household responsiveness to changes in market conditions is partly indicated by Japanese data. When the terms of trade were in favor of agriculture in the years 1894–1900 and 1917–28, the amount invested in agriculture by the entire farm household sector grew at 2.1 and 3.5 percent annually, respectively. The picture is quite different in periods when the terms of trade were against agriculture: during 1900–17, investment rose only 1.7 percent annually, and the level actually fell at a 1.4 percent rate between 1928 and 1935. Moreover, although the data are sketchy, because the transactions took place outside formal capital markets, there is significant anecdotal evidence landowners financed small-scale manufacturing and service activities in the rural areas in which they lived.

More generally, when the terms of trade are favorable to the agricultural sector, it attracts more capital investment, its production function shifts upwards, and labor productivity increases. This expansion of production increases the marketable surplus of agricultural products and turns the terms of trade against the sector. Agriculture can then release labor to the nonagricultural sector.

It is commonly believed that agricultural price policies and marketing controls turn the terms of trade in favor of nonagriculture and increase the marketable agricultural surplus available to finance industrialization. While pricing policies and marketing controls may influence short-run fluctuations in the terms of trade, I hypothesize they are not likely to influence the long-run movement significantly. Instead, domestic economic factors are the major determinants of long-run movements of the terms of trade. Specifically, changes in terms of trade relate to agriculture's growth rate relative to nonagriculture's. The terms of trade move against agriculture when the sector's growth is relatively close to that of the nonagricultural sector. Conversely, they move toward agriculture when that sector's growth is slow compared to the growth of non-agriculture.

In a market economy, expansion of production in one sector tends to turn the terms of trade against that sector. Any actual deterioration in the terms of trade induces investors to allocate a larger share of investment to the other sector; but that in time leads to relative overproduction and consequent deterioration of that sector's terms of trade. Such investment behavior, respon-sive to changes in market conditions throughout the economy, has therefore caused relatively faster growth of one sector in one period, and of the other sector in the next.

In both Japan and Taiwan, the movement in terms of trade correlates well with the relative growth rates of the two sectors. Agriculture's terms of trade improved when the sector's growth was relatively slow compared to non-agriculture, and declined when growth was relatively fast. There is a clear three-stage pattern in both countries: initial improvement in agriculture's terms of trade was followed by a period of movement against agriculture, and then a second turn toward agriculture. The next section discusses these historical changes, and provides a test of the hypothesis. Labor productivity is the principal factor in changes in the terms of trade. Other contributors include demand growth and foreign trade, both of which consistently worked to move the terms of trade against agriculture; this phenomenon is demonstrated in the second part of the chapter.

Empirical Observations and Hypothesis

Although terms of trade are defined as the ratio of agricultural product prices to nonagricultural product prices, such data are not actually available. As the best proxies, ratios of price indexes are used. For the period before World War II, the terms of trade for Japan are the ratio of an index of prices received by farmers to the price index of manufacturing and mining products, and for Taiwan they are the index of the price of agricultural goods divided by the price index of manufactured goods. For the postwar period in both countries, the terms of trade are the ratio of the index of prices received by farmers to the wholesale price index of manufacturing and mining products. Changes in the terms of trade are given in tables 12.1 and 12.2.

Japan's Terms of Trade

The terms of trade fluctuated in the process of Japan's economic development, as shown in figure 12.1. They were favorable for agriculture and rose by almost 20 percent between 1885 and 1895, a period during which the general price level rose by about 30 percent. After 1895, the terms of trade declined slightly and fluctuated just below the 1895 level until 1915. During the decade from 1895 until the end of the Russo-Japanese War in 1905, the general price level rose by about 50 percent. There was then some slackening in inflation.

During the 1895–1910 period, several policies were implemented to raise agricultural prices, mainly the rice price. Until 1894, rice was an export commodity, representing about 10 percent of total exports, and rice imports were not taxed. After the turn of the century, rice exports declined rapidly, but rice remained a duty-free import. A 5 percent *ad valorem* duty on rice imports was imposed in 1904, but this was to raise money for the Russo-Japanese War, and thus cannot be considered a protective measure. In 1906, this was changed to 64 sen per 60 kilograms, which gave it the character of a protective duty (see Ogura 1967: 169–79). Before 1910, imports were less than 10 percent of national income, and the relative insignificance of imported goods explains why

Table 12.1:   Relative sectoral growth and the trend in agriculture's terms of trade, Japan, 1885–1969

| Period | Growth rate[a] in | | Trend in agriculture's terms of trade (P_a/P_m) |
	Agriculture	Nonagriculture	
1885–97	1.5	3.2	toward
1897–1904	1.5	1.9	against
1904–18	2.4	3.4	against
1918–30	0.9	2.3	toward
1930–37	0.9	5.0	toward
1951–59	4.6	9.6	stable
1960–70	2.9	10.4	sharply toward

[a] Percent per annum

Sources

Growth rates: LTES vol. 1
Movement in the terms of trade was determined from the following data: P_a and P_m for the pre-World War II period, LTES (vol. 9: 160 and vol. 8: 192, respectively); for the postwar period, various issues of the *Statistical Yearbook of Japan*

Table 12.2:   Relative sectoral growth and the trend in agriculture's terms of trade, Taiwan, 1920–77

| Period | Growth rate[a] in | | Trend in agriculture's terms of trade (P_a/P_m) |
	Agriculture	Nonagriculture	
1920–40	na	na	toward
1954–57	4.6	6.4	against
1957–70	3.6	12.4	toward
1970–77	2.2	12.0	sharply toward

[a] Percent per annum
na Not available

Sources

Growth rates: *Statistical Yearbook of the Republic of China*, 1981 edn
Movement in the terms of the trade was determined from the following data:
P_a before 1940, Ishikawa (1967); 1952–57, Ho (1978: 424); 1958–80, *Statistical Yearbook of the Republic of China* (1981 edn: 466)
P_m before 1940, Shinohara (1967); 1952–58, *Taiwan Statistical Data Book* (1969 edn: 120); 1954–61 and 1962–73, *Statistical Yearbook of the Republic of China* (1978 edn: 283 and 1981 edn: 458, respectively); 1974–75 and 1976–80, *Commodity Price Statistics Monthly, Taiwan Area, the Republic of China* (1977 July: 62 and 1981 Nov.: 60, respectively). (The last-named is published by the Provincial Bureau of Accounting and Statistics; title varies)

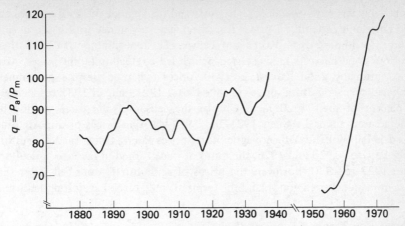

Figure 12.1: Changes in the terms of trade, Japan.

A seven-year moving average was used in the period preceding World War II (1934–36 = 100) and a five-year moving average in the period after World War II (1965 = 100).

Sources
Prewar: P_a: LTES vol. 9: 160; P_m: LTES vol. 8: 192.
Postwar: *Statistical Yearbook of Japan* various issues.

the terms of trade did not reflect the world trend of foodstuffs and manufactured goods prices.

During World War I, many countries of the Far East turned to Japan for manufactured goods that could no longer be supplied by the Western countries. Exports of finished manufactured goods, particularly cotton goods, rose substantially, and Japan's balance of trade became very favorable. The prices of manufactured goods rose significantly, whereas those of agricultural products rose moderately, causing the terms of trade to turn further in favor of non-agriculture from 1910 until the end of World War I.

In 1918, partly due to production shortages and increases in consumption, the price of rice rose suddenly, doubling and tripling from the previous year's level. The sudden rise in the price of rice led to riots in Toyama prefecture, and eventually rioting spread throughout the country. This led to a policy of substantial imports of rice from Korea and Taiwan. Together with the agricultural price index, the index for mining and manufacturing products rose to its highest level in 1920. Then, in 1921, it dropped by 23 percent. The worldwide depression following World War I also brought a marked decline in the prices of rice and silk. Under these circumstances, there was a strong demand by farmers for a comprehensive policy to maintain the price of rice. This led to the enactment of the Rice Act in 1921, which gave the government the power to adjust supply and demand by storing rice when prices fell very low, and by selling it when prices rose.

The recurrence of several poor harvests and the absence of any exceptionally good ones kept agricultural prices from declining very much until 1927, in spite of large rice imports from Korea and Taiwan. Then, beginning with 1927, there were four good harvests in succession, which led to steadily falling prices. After an exceptionally good harvest in 1930, prices collapsed despite government purchases. Nonagricultural prices declined after 1921, and in 1931 reached just 58 percent of their 1920 high. One of the causes of the price decline for manufactured goods between 1921 and 1932 was that prices of imported raw materials fell by half. With nonagricultural prices falling faster than agricultural prices between 1920 and 1926, the terms of trade turned in favor of agriculture. From 1927 to 1930, however, the prices of agricultural goods fell faster than those of manufactured goods, and the terms of trade turned against agriculture.

Influences on Taiwan's Terms of Trade

Under Japanese rule, Taiwan was developed to complement Japan, with the colonial government devoting large amounts of effort and money to transform agriculture. This included building a transportation and communication system. As Taiwan's agricultural production expanded in the 1920s, exports to Japan increased. Imports of Taiwanese rice to Japan increased from 1.6 percent of Japan's domestic production in 1916-20, to 2.4 percent in 1920-25, 3.9 percent in 1925-30, and 7.1 percent in 1930-38. In the 1935-40 period, half of Taiwan's rice production went to Japan. This export demand pushed up domestic prices for agricultural products. Most of the manufactured products available were Japanese-produced. Thus prices in both sectors were heavily influenced by Japanese prices, which explains the similarity in movement of the two countries' terms of trade (see Ishikawa et al. 1969).

In the 1950s, foreign exchange and rice marketing controls depressed agricultural prices and promoted import substitution. Agricultural products were the principal export, and sellers were paid at exchange rates much less favorable than the rates applied to importers of producer goods. In addition, farmers were required to sell rice to the government at prices substantially below market, and chemical fertilizers were obtainable only from the government by barter. In 1949, 1 kilogram of ammonium sulfate was set at 1.5 kilograms of rice. This fell to 0.9 in 1960 and was 0.53 in 1972, when the system was abolished. (See Sasamoto and Kawano 1968; Saito 1972; Hsu 1974.) In the 1950s and 1960s, the government was taking more than 50 percent of total rice production; compulsory sales and barter each accounted for about half of this.

The Three Stages

In both countries, the long-run movement shows a clear three-phase pattern. Although there were short-run fluctuations and reversals in each phase, the overall trend in the terms of trade in Japan moved in favor of agriculture before 1895, against agriculture until 1917, and then, again, in favor of agriculture until prewar data end in 1937. For Taiwan, the lack of data during the war and early post-colonial period leaves a gap. Before 1940, movement was in favor of agriculture. In the 1950s, government control of rice marketing was relaxed slightly, but the terms of trade moved sharply against agriculture between 1952 and 1958. In the 1960s, control was gradually further reduced and the terms of trade began moving rapidly in favor of agriculture.

From agriculture's point of view, the phases can be called a gestation stage, a rapid increase stage, and an appendage stage. Consistently favorable terms of trade in the gestation stage induces a channeling of investment into agriculture. Worsening of the terms of trade in a rapid increase stage is traceable primarily to a large increase in agricultural productivity. Ultimately, the sector plays a passive role, reduced to being an appendage of nonagriculture.

When the terms of trade moved in favor of agriculture in the first stage in Japan, agriculture was growing slowly (1.5 percent annually), whereas non-agriculture was growing rapidly (3.2 percent). In the first part of the second stage, agriculture maintained the same growth rate, but nonagricultural growth slowed to 1.9 percent. Then, in the later part of the second stage, both sectors had sharp rises in their growth rates, to 2.4 percent for agriculture and 3.4 percent for nonagriculture. In the third stage, when the terms of trade again moved in favour of agriculture, the nonagricultural sector initially grew at 2.3 percent and then at 5.0 percent, whereas agriculture grew at 0.9 percent through-out the period. In the period after World War II, agriculture and nonagriculture grew at almost the same rate during the 1940s and early 1950s, but then agricultural growth slowed, while nonagriculture started to expand at about 10 percent annually.

During stage one in Taiwan, rice exports to Japan grew very rapidly and the terms of trade moved significantly in favor of agriculture. During stage two (1952–58), agriculture grew quickly (4.6 percent annually), but more slowly than nonagriculture (6.4 percent). However, in the 1960s, agricultural growth slowed, while nonagriculture's growth rate shot up. Growth in both sectors declined in the 1970s, but the gap between the two rates widened. This disparity favored further movement in the terms of trade toward agriculture.

The data reviewed in this section support the hypothesis that the main factor changing the terms of trade was domestic economic conditions. Rapid growth in agricultural productivity could increase the marketable agricultural surplus to support industrialization, turning the terms of trade in favor of nonagriculture. Next, the hypothesis is assessed quantitatively.

Analysis of Changes in the Terms of Trade

When the terms of trade are favorable to the agricultural sector, the sector attracts more capital investment. As it accumulates capital, the sector's produc-tion function shifts upwards and labor productivity increases. This expansion of production increases the marketable surplus of agricultural products and ulti-mately turns the terms of trade against the sector. Agriculture can release labor to the nonagricultural sector, which can absorb the labor without turning the terms of trade against itself. If agriculture cannot raise its labor productivity, the marketable surplus of agricultural products will not increase, and agriculture cannot release labor. In this case, if labor is drawn from agriculture, the terms of trade will move against nonagriculture and industrialization will be hindered because the supply price of labor rises in terms of industrial products.

The model for analyzing changes in the terms of trade is based on supply and demand equilibrium. For simplicity, it is assumed the supply of products depends on the price levels of the previous year. Equilibrium conditions in both agriculture (subscript a) and nonagriculture (subscript m) can be expressed as:

$$S_a = f(P_a, I, N) \tag{1}$$

$$S_m = f(P_m, I, N) \tag{2}$$

where P represents prices; I, per-capita gross national product; N, population; and S, total supply. Supply can be expressed explicitly as:

$$S_a = A P_a^{-\alpha_a} I^{\beta_a} N \tag{3}$$

$$S_m = B P_m^{-\alpha_m} I^{\beta_m} N \tag{4}$$

where α and β are price and income elasticities of demand, respectively.

From equations (3) and (4), the terms of trade can be written as:

$$q = C \frac{S_m^{1/\alpha_m} I^{\beta_a/\alpha_a}}{S_a^{1/\alpha_a} I^{\beta_m/\alpha_m}}$$

where $q = P_a/P_m$. Because supply consists of domestic production and net imports, S can be written:

$$S_a = (1 + M_a) Q_a \tag{5}$$

$$S_m = (1 + M_m) Q_m \tag{6}$$

where Q is domestic production and M is the ratio of net imports to domestic production.

Using equations (5) and (6), and expressing domestic production in terms of labor productivity,

$$q = C \frac{L_m^{1/\alpha_m} (Q_m/L_m)^{1/\alpha_m} (1 + M_m)^{1/\alpha_m} I^{\beta_a/\alpha_a}}{L_a^{1/\alpha_a} (Q_a/L_a)^{1/\alpha_a} (1 + M_a)^{1/\alpha_a} I^{\beta_m/\alpha_m}} \tag{7}$$

where L is the number of workers employed in each sector.

Differentiating equation (7) totally with respect to t,

$$G(q) = \frac{1}{\alpha_m} G(L_m) - \frac{1}{\alpha_a} G(L_a) + \frac{1}{\alpha_m} G\left(\frac{Q_m}{L_m}\right) - \frac{1}{\alpha_a} G\left(\frac{Q_a}{L_a}\right)$$

$$+ \frac{1}{\alpha_m} G(1+M_m) - \frac{1}{\alpha_a} G(1+M_a) + \frac{\beta_a}{\alpha_a} G(I) - \frac{\beta_m}{\alpha_m} G(I) \qquad (8)$$

where G indicates the annual growth rates of the respective variables.

In equation (8), changes in the terms of trade are decomposed to changes in nonagricultural labor, agricultural labor, labor productivities in each sector, shares of net imports of agricultural products and nonagricultural products, and demand for agricultural and nonagricultural products.

The results of applying equation (8) to time-series data for 1885–1937 and 1951–70 for Japan, and for 1952–77 for Taiwan, as well as price elasticities, are shown in tables 12.3 and 12.4. The signs in the last two columns of tables 12.3 and 12.4 are the same in each period, as expected.

Implications

The analysis shows large changes in nonagricultural labor productivity and a slowdown in the increases in agricultural labor productivity were the main contributors to raising the terms of trade. Rapid increases in agricultural labor productivity in 1895–1917 in Japan and in 1954–57 in Taiwan account for the turning of the terms of trade against agriculture in those periods. This made it possible to release labor from agriculture and allowed a rapid increase in non-agricultural labor. Conversely, especially slow increases in agricultural labor productivity in 1918–30 in Japan and in 1970–77 in Taiwan account for the turning of the terms of trade in favor of agriculture. Even in these periods, however, a rapid expansion of imports of agricultural products permitted the release of labor from agriculture to continue.

The growth of demand also significantly influenced the terms of trade. Because the income elasticity of demand for nonagricultural products exceeded that for agricultural products throughout the period, the net effect was always against agriculture, particularly after World War II. The total effects of imports on the terms of trade in Japan were negative, except in the 1960s, because imports of agricultural products were growing more rapidly than those of non-agricultural products. But the effects were rather small compared to other variables, except in the 1918–30 period of increasing rice imports from Taiwan and Korea. For Taiwan, foreign trade had positive effects in 1954–57, reflecting the expansion of agricultural exports, but by the 1960s trade had negative effects due to the increase in food imports and exports of manufactured goods.

The combined effect of demand and imports was always against agriculture. Thus, changes in relative labor productivity between the two sectors, and the

Table 12.3: Annual rates of change in variables, Japan[a]

(1) Period	(2) + $\dfrac{1}{\alpha_m} G(L_m)$	(3) − $\dfrac{1}{\alpha_a} G(L_a)$	(4) + $\dfrac{1}{\alpha_m} G\left(\dfrac{Q_m}{L_m}\right)$	(5) − $\dfrac{1}{\alpha_a} G\left(\dfrac{Q_a}{L_a}\right)$	(6) − $\dfrac{1}{\alpha_a} G(1+M_a)$	(7) + $\dfrac{1}{\alpha_m} G(1+M_m)$	(8) + $\dfrac{\beta_a}{\alpha_a} G(I)$	(9) − $\dfrac{\beta_m}{\alpha_m} G(I)$	(10) G(s)	(11) G(q)
1885–95	3.78	0.10	4.14	1.89	1.06	0.04	2.76	5.73	1.94	1.74
1895–1905	2.24	0.27	2.77	3.34	1.66	0.05	0.69	1.52	−0.88	−0.74
1905–17	4.11	−1.30	2.25	5.57	1.02	0.03	2.39	4.24	−0.74	−0.78
1918–30	2.99	−0.62	1.66	1.82	2.02	0.12	0.55	1.27	0.83	0.92
1930–37	3.36	−0.69	4.08	3.43	1.04	0.21	2.80	5.59	1.08	1.84
1951–59	7.33	−4.20	7.44	13.85	0.67	0.39	9.10	13.33	0.61	0.56
1960–70	4.40	−10.92	9.44	18.40	−0.42	−0.01	9.37	12.75	3.75	3.90

[a]Percent per annum

Columns (2)–(9) are values of the terms in equation (8); $G(s)$ is the result of substituting these values in equation (8). $G(q)$ is the annual rate of change in the terms of trade; $q = p_a/p_m$

Elasticities used:

Years	1885–95	1895–1905	1905–18	1918–30	1930–37	1951–59	1960–70
Price elasticity							
agriculture	−0.59	−0.55	−0.52	−0.50	−0.48	−0.48	−0.45
nonagriculture	−0.50	−0.55	−0.60	−0.66	−0.72	−0.72	−0.75
Income elasticity							
agriculture	0.70	0.55	0.55	0.36	0.36	0.68	0.45
nonagriculture	1.15	1.21	1.15	1.10	1.05	1.50	0.98

Sources

The values have been computed by the author from data in the following:

Before World War II: L_m and L_a, PJED: 392; Q_m, LTES vol. 1: 226; Q_a, LTES vol. 9: 152. Postwar, for these four variables, various issues of the *Statistical Yearbook of Japan* M_a and M_m, LTES vol. 14: 184–91; I, LTES vol. 1: 237 Price elasticities have been estimated based on cross-country demand studies by Lluch and Williams (1975). Income elasticities of agricultural products have been obtained from a consumption pattern study by Kaneda 1969 for the pre-World War II period, and other income elasticities are calculated from consumption data in LTES and PJED

Table 12.4: Annual rates of change in variables, Taiwan[a]

(1) Period	(2) + $\frac{1}{\alpha_m} G(L_m)$	(3) − $\frac{1}{\alpha_a} G(L_a)$	(4) + $\frac{1}{\alpha_m} G\left(\frac{Q_m}{L_m}\right)$	(5) − $\frac{1}{\alpha_a} G\left(\frac{Q_a}{L_a}\right)$	(6) − $\frac{1}{\alpha_a} G(1+M_a)$	(7) + $\frac{1}{\alpha_m} G(1+M_m)$	(8) + $\frac{\beta_a}{\alpha_a} G(I)$	(9) − $\frac{\beta_m}{\alpha_m} G(I)$	(10) $G(s)$	(11) $G(q)$
1954-57	8.55	1.00	2.02	7.16	−1.86	−1.45	2.73	7.68	−2.13	−2.83
1957-70	10.57	0.57	8.20	6.14	1.78	−1.46	4.16	11.25	2.18	2.17
1970-77	8.66	−1.90	7.80	5.69	3.90	−1.77	6.02	10.64	2.38	3.30

[a] Percent per annum

Columns (2)–(9) are values of the terms in equation (8); $G(s)$ is the result of substituting these values in equation (8). $G(q)$ is the annual rate of change in the terms of trade; $q = p_a/p_m$.

Elasticities used:

Years	1954-57	1957-70	1970-77
Price elasticity			
agriculture	−0.56	−0.53	−0.49
nonagriculture	−0.60	−0.63	−0.70
Income elasticity			
agriculture	0.40	0.40	0.40
nonagriculture	1.20	1.15	1.05

Sources

The values have been computed by the author from data in the following:
The Statistical Yearbook of the Republic of China (1981 and 1980 edns), except as noted. L_m and L_a, 1952-66, Galenson (1979: 387); Q_m, 1952-62, Ho (1978: 368); O_a, 1952-74, Ho (1978: 340); M_a and M_m, *Taiwan Statistical Data Book* (1980 edn: 183–89); price indexes of exports and imports, *National Income of the Republic of China* (1980 edn: 170–73).
Price elasticities have been estimated based on cross-country demand studies by Lluch and Williams (1975). Income elasticities of agricultural products have been obtained from a consumption pattern study by Ozaki (1973) and those for nonagricultural products are approximated from those of Japan

relative size of their labor forces, determined whether agriculture's terms of trade improved. If the growth of agricultural labor productivity is relatively faster than that of nonagriculture, the terms of trade move further against agriculture, and resources, including labor, are transferred to nonagriculture. In short, domestic economic conditions influencing labor productivity determine the trend in the terms of trade.

Agricultural Productivity and Labor Allocation

In an economy that is closed and has no technological progress or capital accumulation in agriculture, industrialization and economic growth will eventually lead to a shortage of labor as defined by Fei and Ranis (1964). Japan was able to postpone the arrival of that point by rapid expansion of agricultural production before World War I, and industrial development was supported by a very elastic supply of labor from the agricultural sector. When agriculture was stagnant in the 1920s and 1930s, imports of agricultural goods created a marketable agricultural surplus, which seems to have postponed further the arrival of the shortage point, and released a large number of workers from agriculture. This flow of labor from agriculture made industrialization easier by keeping the industrial wage low and the competitive position of industrial products strong in international markets.

Taiwan was also able to create a marketable agricultural surplus through extremely rapid expansion of agricultural production from 1952 to 1958. While rice had been the principal prewar crop, sugar was the major postwar export crop. When agricultural growth slowed slightly in the 1960s, agricultural exports declined, but Taiwan remained a net exporter. As agriculture stagnated further during the 1970s, the island finally became a net importer. As in Japan, the arrival of the shortage point was delayed, and release of labor from the agricultural sector continued because of food imports.

If Japan and Taiwan had been unable to expand imports, what would have been the effect on labor allocation and output of the two sectors? To find out, the question can be rephrased as follows. For Japan in the 1920s and 1930s, and for Taiwan in the 1970s, what pattern of labor allocation and sectoral output was necessary to maintain the terms of trade as they actually were, if (case one) imports had been held at the 1915–17 and 1970 levels, respectively, and if (case two), in addition, agricultural production had progressed at the 1905–18 (1953–70) growth rates?

The notation is the same as earlier, with hypothetical values identified by a prime ($'$). The model is basically the same as equation (7). Because both the actual conditions and case one lead to equivalent terms of trade, they can be written:

$$q = C \frac{L'^{1/\alpha_m}_m (Q'_m/L'_m)^{1/\alpha_m}(1+M'_m)^{1/\alpha_m}I^{\beta_a/\alpha_a}}{L'^{1/\alpha_a}_a (Q'_a/L'_a)^{1/\alpha_a}(1+M'_a)^{1/\alpha_a}I^{\beta_m/\alpha_m}} \qquad (9)$$

Assuming a typical constant-elasticity production function:

$$Q_a = Q_{oa} L_a^{\epsilon_a} \tag{10}$$

$$Q_m = Q_{om} L_m^{\epsilon_m} \tag{11}$$

where ϵ is the production elasticity of labor, and capital and other production factors are included in Q. The relation between Q and Q' is:

$$Q'_a = Q_a (L'/L_a)^{\epsilon_a} \tag{12}$$

$$Q'_m = Q_m (L'/L_m)^{\epsilon_m} \tag{13}$$

Substituting equations (12) and (13) in (9), and then equating equations (7) and (9) yields:

$$\frac{L'_m{}^{\epsilon_m/\alpha_m}}{L'_a{}^{\epsilon_a/\alpha_a}} = \left(\frac{1+M'_a}{1+M_a}\right)^{1/\alpha_a} \frac{L_m^{\epsilon_m/\alpha_m}}{L_a^{\epsilon_a/\alpha_a}} \tag{14}$$

Following the same steps, case two is:

$$\frac{L'_m{}^{\epsilon_m/\alpha_m}}{L'_a{}^{\epsilon_a/\alpha_a}} = \left\{\frac{(1+M'_a)(1+g')}{1+M_a}\right\}^{1/\alpha_a} \frac{L_m^{\epsilon_m/\alpha_m}}{L_a^{\epsilon_a/\alpha_a}} \tag{15}$$

where g' is the hypothetical growth rate of agricultural output.

The results of applying this model are given in tables 12.5 and 12.6. The comparison of the actual cases with case one indicates that if agricultural output expands very slowly and there are no imports of agricultural products, the marketable surplus of agricultural products is not sufficient to release the labor needed for rapid expansion of the industrial sector. To avoid an extreme movement of the terms of trade against nonagriculture, a large share of the labor force has to remain in the agricultural sector. A massive drive toward industrialization in the face of stagnant agriculture inevitably results in an increased industrial wage, and brings about continuous worsening of the nonagricultural terms of trade. Such a rise in industrial wages leads to a reduction in the demand for labor in the nonagricultural sector and industrial growth will be slowed substantially.

In Japan's case two, reduction of agricultural imports is more than offset by rapid agricultural growth until about 1930. Thereafter, however, fast growth alone cannot produce enough agricultural surplus to maintain the terms of trade as they actually were, and the size of the agricultural sector's labor force had to expand by reducing that of nonagriculture. In Taiwan's case two, agricultural growth in the 1950s and 1960s is just fast enough to offset the absence of

Table 12.5:   Actual and hypothetical distribution of output and labor, Japan (1934–36 prices)

	Q_a $(10^6 yen)$	Q_m $(10^6 yen)$	L_a $(1,000)$	L_m $(1,000)$	$(1+M'_a)$	$(1+g')$[a]
Actual						
1920	3,062	7,837	14,139	12,986	–	–
1925	3,073	9,918	13,735	14,370	–	–
1930	3,390	10,355	14,131	15,488	–	–
1935	3,145	13,500	13,932	17,279	–	–
Case 1						
1920	3,076	7,743	14,300	12,825	1.22	–
1925	3,263	8,938	15,955	12,150	1.21	–
1930	3,564	9,553	16,019	13,600	1.19	–
1935	3,500	11,322	18,200	13,011	1.21	–
Case 2						
1920	3,099	7,872	14,045	13,080	1.22	1.015
1925	3,300	9,369	14,015	13,110	1.21	1.015
1930	3,859	10,606	13,469	16,100	1.19	1.015
1935	4,024	13,094	14,761	16,450	1.21	1.015

[a] The actual growth rate is already included in Q_a for the actual case and hypothetical case 1. For hypothetical case 2, the 1.5 percentage-point difference between the actual growth rate (0.9 percent annually) and the hypothetical growth rate (2.4 percent annually) is shown in this column in the form it appears in equation (15) $(1 + g')$

Sources: For the analysis, the production elasticities of labor adopted are 0.62 for non-agriculture (Ohkawa and Rosovsky 1973) and 0.40 for agriculture (Hayami et al. 1975)

agricultural imports, so the size of the sector's labor force does not have to be expanded to maintain the terms of trade as they actually were.

Both cases show imports of agricultural products had sizeable impacts on the transfer of labor, and accelerated national income growth. Imports postponed the arrival of the labor-shortage point, and made the progress of industrialization easier. Even had growth of agricultural output in the 1930s in Japan continued at the fairly fast rates attained in 1905–18, not enough labor would have been released from the sector to sustain the expansion of nonagriculture that actually occurred. When agriculture was relatively stagnant, both countries relied on imports to depress agricultural prices. Moreover, even with rapid agricultural growth, imports were inevitable to sustain the rate of industrial growth in the 1930s in Japan and 1970s in Taiwan.

Table 12.6: Actual and hypothetical distribution of output and labor, Taiwan (1976 prices)

	Q_a (NT$ million)	Q_m (NT$ million)	L_a (1,000)	L_m (1,000)	$(1+M'_a)$	$(1+g')^a$
Actual						
1971	73,202	371,864	1,666	3,138	–	–
1974	74,368	500,137	1,651	3,737	–	–
1977	79,843	718,302	1,670	4,388	–	–
Case 1						
1971	73,707	368,544	1,709	3,095	1.00	–
1974	77,958	477,502	1,966	3,480	1.00	–
1977	85,511	665,867	2,153	3,905	1.00	–
Case 2						
1971	74,294	371,632	1,669	3,135	1.00	1.014
1974	81,472	495,165	1,708	3,680	1.00	1.014
1977	89,779	714,252	1,708	4,350	1.00	1.014

[a] The actual growth rate is already included in Q_a for the actual case and hypothetical case 1. For hypothetical case 2, the 1.4 percentage-point difference between the actual growth rate (2.18 percent annually) and the hypothetical growth rate (3.58 percent annually) is shown in this column in the form it appears in equation (15) $(1 + g')$

Source: For the analysis, the production elasticities of labor adopted are 0.65 for non-agriculture and 0.27 for agriculture; estimated by the author from national income statistics

Concluding Remarks

Japan's agricultural sector created a marketable surplus because of the rapid increase in its labor productivity until 1917, and it transferred that surplus to nonagriculture partly through a turn in the terms of trade against agriculture. When agriculture was technologically stagnant, Japan relied on imports from Taiwan and Korea to depress agricultural prices, and thereby maintain the transfer of labor to nonagriculture. The technologically dynamic agriculture of Taiwan also attained a rapid increase in labor productivity, especially in the 1950s, and transferred resources through declining terms of trade. As crop yields increased, the terms of trade tended to turn against agriculture. But the decline in relative prices did not discourage agricultural production, because technology was also reducing costs. It is, however, difficult to achieve a continuous transfer of resources out of agriculture when the sector is technologically stagnant.

In the gestation period of both countries (1885–97 in Japan, and before 1940 in Taiwan), the terms of trade moved toward agriculture, and this provided incentives for landlords and farmers to invest more in the sector, which set the stage for growth in labor productivity.

In the third stage, agriculture is passive, an appendage of nonagriculture. The improvement in agriculture's terms of trade is due primarily to the scarcity of natural resources available to agriculture. Because both Taiwan and Japan are resource-poor, agricultural goods will become relatively more expensive through time, at least in the absence of foreign trade. In Japan, government protection of farmers has in any case kept food artificially expensive in most of the postwar period.

It is in the second stage that agriculture plays a dominant and positive role in growth. The terms of trade moved consistently against agriculture, because of the sector's increased labor productivity. This allowed labor to shift to non-agriculture rapidly without turning the terms of trade towards agriculture.

Continuous technological change in agriculture means that the net transfer of resources and labor from agriculture is sustained and the sector can meet an expanding demand for agricultural products without turning the terms of trade in favour of agriculture. Moreover, technological change in agriculture, by moving the terms of trade against agriculture, directly accelerates growth in national income, as shown by comparing actual cases with hypothetical cases. The decline in agriculture's terms of trade induces resource flows that encourage industrial development. If these resources are then actually used constructively in nonagriculture, rapid growth of the economy can be achieved.

References

Fei, John C. H., and Gustav Ranis (1964), *Development of the Labor Surplus Economy: Theory and Policy*, Homewood, IL: Richard D. Irwin.

Galenson, Walter (1979), "The Labor Force, Wages and Living Standards," in Walter Galenson, ed., *Economic Growth and Structural Change in Taiwan*, Ithaca, NY: Cornell University Press.

Hayami, Yujiro, in association with Masakatsu Akino, Masahiko Shintani, and Saburo Yamada (1975), *A Century of Agricultural Growth in Japan*, St Paul, MN: University of Minnesota Press.

Ho, Samuel P. S. (1978), *Economic Development of Taiwan, 1860–1970*, New Haven, CT: Yale University Press.

Hsu Wen-Fu (1974), "Prices and Pricing of Farm Products," in Tsung-han Shen, ed., *Agriculture's Place in the Strategy of Development: The Taiwan Experience*, Taipei: Sino-American Joint Commission on Rural Reconstruction.

Ishikawa, Shigeru (1967), *Taiwan nogyo seisangaku no suikei 1905–1967*, Keizai Kenkyusho Tokeigakai, Kako Tokei Serizu no. 6 (February), Tokyo: Hitotsubashi University.

Ishikawa, Shigeru, Miyohei Shinohara, and Tohiyuki Mizoguchi (1969), "Senzen ni okeru Taiwan no keizai seicho," *Keizaikenkyu*, 20: 49–60 (January).

Kaneda, Hiromitsu (1969), "Long-Term Changes in Food Consumption Patterns in Japan," in Kazushi Ohkawa, Bruce F. Johnston, and Hiromitsu Kaneda, eds, *Agriculture and Economic Growth: Japan's Experience*, Tokyo: University of Tokyo Press.

Lluch, Constantino, and R. Williams (1975), "Cross-Country Demand and Saving Patterns: An Application of the Extended Linear Expenditure System," *Review of Economics and Statistics*, 57: 320–28 (August).

LTES (*Estimates of Long-Term Economic Statistics of Japan*), series edited by Kazushi Ohkawa, Miyohei Shinohara, and Mataji Umemura, Tokyo: Toyo Keizai Shimposha.

vol. 1, *National Income* (1974), Kazushi Ohkawa, Nobukiyo Takamatsu, and Yuzo Yamamoto.

vol. 8, *Prices* (1967), Kazushi Ohkawa, Osama Noda, Nobukiyo Takamatsu, Saburo Yamada, Minoru Kumazaki, Yuichi Shionoya, and Ryoshin Minami.

vol. 9, *Agriculture and Forestry* (1966), Mataji Umemura, Saburo Yamada, Yujiro Hayami, Nobukiyo Takamatsu, and Minoru Kumizaki.

vol. 14, *Foreign Trade* (1979), Ippei Yamazawa and Yuzo Yamamoto.

Ogura, Takekzau (1967), *Agricultural Development in Modern Japan*, Tokyo: Fuji Publishing Co.

Ohkawa, Kazushi, and Henry Rosovsky (1973), *Japanese Economic Growth: Trend Acceleration in the Twentieth Century*, Stanford, CA: Stanford University Press.

Ozaki, Chujiro (1973), "Report of Survey on Changes in Food Habits in Relation to Food Production Pattern," in *Changes in Food Habits in Relation to Increase of Productivity*, Asian Productivity Organization.

PJED (*Patterns of Japanese Economic Development*), Ohkawa, Kazushi, and Miyohei Shinohara, with Larry Meissner, eds (1979), New Haven, CT: Yale University Press.

Saito, Kazuo (1972), *Taiwan no nogyo ge*, Tokyo: Azia Keizai Kenkyusho.

Sasamoto, Takeharu, and Shigeto Kawano (1968), *Taiwan keizai sogokenkyujo*, Tokyo: Azia Keizai Kenkyusho.

Shinohara, Miyohei (1967), *Taiwan kokogyo seisangaku no suikei, Taisho 1-nen-Showa 15-nen*, Keizai Kenkyusho Tokeigakai, Kako Tokei Serizu no. 4, Tokyo: Hitotsubashi University.

Thorbecke, Eric (1979), "Agricultural Development," in Walter Galenson, ed., *Economic Growth and Structural Change in Taiwan*, Ithaca, NY: Cornell University Press.

13 Resource Flows from Agriculture: Japan and India

ASHOKA MODY, SUDIPTO MUNDLE, and
K. N. RAJ

This paper analyzes and compares the experiences of Japan after the Meiji
Restoration and of India after Independence with regard to one major facet of
agriculture's contribution to industrial development: resource flows from
agriculture. To this end, we have pulled together different estimates and sources
of piecemeal data to present a more carefully cross-checked and comprehensive
treatment of the problem than has been available hitherto.

The political and administrative changes ushered in by the Meiji Restoration
of 1868 brought in their wake a profound reordering of Japan's economic
arrangements, setting the stage for modern economic growth (MEG) in Kuznets's
sense. This transitional period appears to have reached completion with the end
of the Matsukata deflation policy in 1885 (Ohkawa and Shinohara 1979). The
following half-century saw the transformation of Japan from an agrarian economy
to a modern industrial power at a pace till then unknown in human history. The
post-Independence period in India is roughly comparable to the post-Restoration
period in Japan as a development stage.

There are, however, significant differences in the two countries' heritages
and in the growth processes in the periods compared here. Two dissimilarities
are particularly important in our analysis. The first is the institutional and
technological change within agriculture in Japan during the Tokugawa period,
which made possible significant increases in output through intensive application
of human labor, for which there is no parallel during the colonial period in India
(see Smith 1959). Second, population growth in India since Independence has

In the preparation of this paper, the authors have greatly benefited from the help and
suggestions of Professors Kazushi Ohkawa, Simon Kuznets, and Shigeru Ishikawa (who was
the main discussant of the paper at the 1982 CA Conference). Helpful comments were also
made by other conference participants, especially Professors Gustav Ranis, Hugh Patrick,
John C. H. Fei, Juro Teranishi, Nobukiyo Takamatsu, and Yujiro Hayami. Dr Mundle would
like to acknowledge a grant from the Japan Foundation. This made it possible for him to
visit Tokyo to collaborate with Professor Ohkawa and other members of staff at the International Development Center of Japan in constructing resource-flow time series for Japan.

been much higher than in Japan in the late 19th century, and, again in contrast with Japan's experience, the bulk of the increment has had to be absorbed in agriculture.

We begin by outlining concepts and definitions used in measuring intersectoral resource flows. This framework is then used to analyze Japan and India. Data limitations prevent our drawing firm conclusions. To facilitate further research, these data problems are discussed in some detail for the Indian case. Similar discussion of the Japanese data are available in Mundle and Ohkawa (1979) and the LTES volumes from which the Japanese estimates have been computed. Lack of data also means that for both countries we must take the nonagricultural sector as a whole, rather than only the industrial sector, even though our concern is with agriculture's contribution to industrialization.

Measuring Intersectoral Resource Flows

One facet of agriculture's contribution is its financing of nonagricultural investment. Conceptually, this is equivalent to the excess of total savings in the agricultural sector over and above the total investment in that sector. We refer to this as the savings surplus transferred from agriculture to nonagriculture. There is, however, an altogether different sense in which agriculture may contribute to development of the nonagricultural sector, arising from the intersectoral flow of commodities. The flow of investment leads to a growing stock of physical capital. To set this plant and machinery in motion requires a flow of materials, including agricultural raw materials. There also is a need for labor, which in turn requires wage goods, especially food. In a closed economy, this growing flow of commodities – food and raw materials – must be supplied by the domestic agricultural sector.

Purchases of one sector's products by another can be analyzed in terms of trade between the sectors. Imports from agriculture by the nonagricultural sector (purchases of agricultural products by nonagriculture) can be paid for with exports of the nonagricultural sector's products, such as farm machinery, fertilizers and pesticides, and manufactured consumer items. To the extent the value of exports from agriculture exceed its imports, there is a net transfer of resources out of agriculture. This export surplus is the excess of aggregate expenditure by nonagriculture over and above the value added or income originating in that sector. This is partly reflected in the savings surplus, partly in a net flow of factor incomes and other current transfers, partly even in unilateral nonmarket deliveries of, say, food from a farm household to members who have migrated to cities.

This kind of resource contribution is a balance of trade surplus between agriculture and nonagriculture. We refer to this resource flow as the trade surplus, to distinguish it from the savings surplus. The concept of resource transfer in this sense was first articulated in modern development literature by Ishikawa (1967), though a very similar concept is evident in the classical literature in Preobrazhensky's notion of primitive socialist accumulation (Preobrazhensky 1965). For a full discussion of the concept, and its relationship to the savings surplus, in the context of the intersectoral balance of payments, see Ishikawa (1967), Lee (1971) and Mundle and Ohkawa (1979).

Because peasant households are usually the units of consumption as well as of production, a farm household sector (henceforth, farm sector) is analytically meaningful. Data on disposable income, consumption, and savings can be put together for this sector without much difficulty. On the other hand, data on output, costs of production, value added (income by sector of origin), and capital formation are usually available only by sectors of production; here agriculture appears as a natural boundary. Thus our empirical analysis will be of the farm sector in some places, and of the agricultural sector in others. This procedure is unavoidable, though it does raise some difficult problems of interpretation.

Resource Flows in Japan, 1887–1937

For our purpose, three features of the Japanese growth experience are important. The trend of the rate of growth increased progressively, irrespective of the method used to measure it; there were, however, long alternating phases of upswings and downswings. The trend acceleration in output growth was accompanied by rising growth rates of investment as well as by a larger share of investment in value added; investment also exhibited up- and downswings. Growth was accompanied by a major shift in industrial structure.

The share of agriculture in net product declined from 42 percent in 1887 to 18 percent in 1938. If the nonagricultural sector is divided into industrial and services sectors, only the industrial sector increased its share of NDP (net domestic product) (from 20 percent in 1887 to over 50 percent in 1938); the share of the services sector actually declined marginally. Services were initially dominant in the nonagricultural sector, accounting for nearly two-thirds of value added in the sector, and over a third of total domestic product. Within the industrial sector, it was manufacturing, rather than the construction and the facilitating industries (transportation, communications, public utilities, etc.), that recorded the main thrust of expansion, rising from 13 percent of NDP in 1887 to 35 percent in 1938. (See Ohkawa and Rosovsky 1973; Ohkawa and Shinohara 1979.)

The Trade and Savings Surpluses of Agriculture

For Japan, estimates of the savings surplus are available for both the farm and the agricultural sectors. However, in the case of the trade surplus, reliable estimates for the farm sector are lacking, as crucial data on costs of production, particularly relating to purchased and self-supplied components, are not available for the nonagricultural activities of farm households. The available estimates of trade surplus are presented in table 13.1.

In the period 1882–92, the estimated market surplus of the agricultural sector was nearly one-half of value added in agriculture; agricultural imports formed an equally high proportion of value added in agriculture, indicating the two sectors were already fairly integrated and interdependent. This also means nonagriculture was by and large paying for its purchases from agriculture with its own sales to the latter, so the net resource contribution – the trade surplus – of the agricultural sector was marginal.

Data on the savings surplus have been summarized in table 13.2 for the agricultural sector and the farm sector. The savings surplus of agriculture (K_a) was positive throughout the period 1888–1938, but, until the turn of the century, it was at the modest level of only about a tenth of gross value added in agriculture.

Table 13.3 relates the trade surplus (B) to income originating in the non-agricultural sector (Y_{na}), and thereby to the size of that sector's market, and also relates the savings surplus (K_a, K_f) to the magnitude of aggregate saving in the agricultural sector as well as to aggregate investment in the nonagricultural sector.

Prior to the turn of the century, agriculture's trade surplus (B) was less than 1 percent of income originating in nonagriculture (Y_{na}); it subsequently rose to a high of 6 percent in the period 1908–17, but then turned negative in the 1920s. This cannot be regarded as a major transfer of resources for industrialization. However, the picture is different when we turn to the savings surplus in agriculture (K_a or K_f). With direct taxes treated as compulsory savings and thus included in the sector's total savings, over 40 percent of agricultural savings were being transferred out of the sector toward the end of the 19th century. At the beginning of the 20th century, this proportion was more than 50 percent and, by World War I, it exceeded 70 percent. In short, less than one-third of agricultural savings was being put back into agriculture; the rest was evidently channeled into industrialization.

The proportions are almost identical for the farm sector up to 1913–17, and differ significantly only in the interwar period, when the transfer was lower, though still substantial. Until the end of the 19th century, 90 percent or more of the transferred savings was through taxation. Thereafter, the proportion of taxes declined significantly, although in 1913–17 it was still 50 percent.

Interpretation of the Japanese Experience

It would not be surprising if the transfer of such a large part of agricultural savings had adverse consequences on agricultural development. This has been suggested as an important factor in the sector's stagnation in the 1920s (see Mundle and Ohkawa 1979). Oshima (1965) has pointed out that the squeeze on agriculture contributed significantly to agrarian unrest during this period, and thus had important political consequences. The focus of this chapter, however,

Table 13.1: Average annual trade surplus of agriculture, Japan, 1888–1937[a]

Time period	X_a	C_s	R_s	I_s	E	C_p	R_p	I_p	M	G_a	B	Y_a
1888–92	473	210	51	24	188 (47.0)	104	61	23	188 (47.0)	1	−1	400
1893–97	645	276	66	33	270 (48.8)	147	81	34	262 (47.4)	1	7	553
1898–1902	948	373	94	41	440 (53.7)	249	108	48	405 (49.5)	2	33	819
1903–07	1,237	498	115	49	575 (54.3)	296	144	59	499 (47.2)	2	74	1,058
1909–12	1,544	551	124	53	816 (61.8)	416	190	71	677 (51.3)	5	134	1,320
1913–17	1,850	770	135	55	890 (56.8)	317	249	80	646 (41.3)	6	238	1,566
1918–22	4,205	1,193	275	111	2,626 (73.5)	1,656	567	186	2,409 (67.5)	22	195	3,571
1923–27	4,005	1,002	228	133	2,642 (76.7)	1,901	569	214	2,684 (77.9)	59	−101	3,444
1928–32	2,844	665	174	105	1,900 (79.0)	1,435	454	177	2,066 (85.9)	68	−234	2,404
1933–37	3,331	782	192	86	2,271 (81.6)	1,502	505	177	2,184 (78.5)	62	25	2,782

[a] In million yen at current prices; numbers in parentheses are percentages

X_a	Value of agricultural production
subscript s	Components supplied from within the sector
subscript p	Components purchased from outside the sector
C	Consumption
R	Current inputs
I	Investment goods
E	Marketed surplus (exports) of agriculture
M	Total imports (purchases) by agriculture on private account ($M = C_p + R_p + I_p$)
G_a	Central and local government investment expenditure in agriculture (including forestry and fisheries, but the value of these components is so negligible that it makes little difference). Includes items such as riparian public works, agricultural capital formation, and natural disaster reconstruction other than buildings
B	Trade balance (surplus) of agriculture ($B = E − M − G_a$), with any difference due to rounding
Y_a	Gross value added in agriculture

Source: Mundle and Ohkawa 1979

is on the impact of savings transferred from agriculture on accumulation outside the sector, and on industrialization. Consequences within the sector are not analyzed, but two will be raised as part of the context.

The financial outflow to the government cannot be interpreted as having played the same role as private savings transfers, and some authors, such as Teranishi (1976), have argued that the net outflow as taxes ought not to be counted at all as part of agriculture's contribution to financing industrial growth. The case for exclusion is essentially that a substantial part of the land tax financed current government expenditure rather than capital expenditure. However, government investment was a substantial part of aggregate investment, and was mainly used for building infrastructure essential for industrialization. Because the land tax provided a large part of revenue, we can regard it as a contribution made by agriculture, even though it was not wholly (or even largely) used directly for industrial investment.

When the tax component is added to Teranishi's estimates in table 13.4 (lines 4 and 5), the results are broadly similar to our estimates in table 13.3. Moreover, as a cross-check against our first set of estimates, two estimates are given in table 13.3 for the proportion of nonagricultural investment financed by agriculture, as explained in the notes to this table. These estimates suggest that after the turn of the century, 20–30 percent of nonagricultural investment was financed by savings transferred from agriculture.

In the case of private savings taken by itself, our estimates show there was actually a net inflow to the farm (agricultural) sector up to the end of the 19th century. However, from the beginning of the 20th century, and especially after the end of the Meiji period (1911), the net outflow was quite substantial until the 1920s, when there was again a net inflow. Teranishi's estimates also show net lending by the farm sector via the capital market was substantial only between 1913 and 1917, when it accounted for nearly 18 percent of the sector's total savings, and during 1918–22, when it was over 31 percent. This decade was the key period in Japan's industrialization drive, prior to World War II.

Net lending, however, is not a full measure of the total private savings flow out of agriculture, as it excludes direct private investment by farm households in nonagricultural activities. Going by the different estimates of net lending and total private savings transfers presented in tables 13.2, 13.3, and 13.4, it appears that such direct investment across sectors, not reflected in transactions through the capital markets, was indeed quite substantial. Most likely, it financed small-scale manufacturing or service activities in the rural or traditional sector. However, we leave this as a hypothesis for further research.

Our entire discussion has been confined so far to flows measured at current prices. In terms of actual purchasing power, we need to look at the index for the terms of trade in the final column of table 13.3 (P_f). It fluctuated around a trend in favor of agriculture at least up to the end of the 1920s. Our estimates of the resource transfer out of agriculture must therefore be interpreted in the context of a secular pattern, where, say, a yen's worth of purchasing power

Table 13.2: Average annual savings surplus of agriculture and farm sector, Japan, 1888–1937[a]

(a) Agricultural sector

Time period	Y_a	T_a		C_a	S_a	I_a	G_a	$S_a - I_a - G_a$	K_a
1888–92	400	59	(155.3)	314	27	47	1[b]	−21	38
1893–97	553	65	(104.8)	423	65	67	1[b]	−3[b]	62[b]
1898–1902	819	97	(91.5)	622	100	89	2[b]	9	106
1903–07	1,058	114	(74.0)	794	150	108	2	40	154
1908–12	1,320	154	(68.0)	967	199	124	5	70	224
1913–17	1,566	167	(49.4)	1,087	312	135	6	171	338
1918–22	3,571	288	(41.7)	2,849	722	297	22	403	691
1923–27	3,444	310	(69.7)	2,903	541	347	59	135	445
1928–32	2,404	213	(127.6)	2,100	304	282	68	−46	167
1933–37	2,782	198	(53.4)	2,284	498	263	62	172	371

(b) Farm sector

Time period	Y_f	T_f		C_f	S_f	I_f	G_f	$S_f - I_f - G_f$	K_f
1888–92	555	59	(115.7)	478	58	65	1	−8	51
1893–97	724	65	(108.3)	572	87	91	1	−5	60
1898–1902	1,079	97	(68.9)	818	164	118	2	44	141
1903–07	1,390	114	(57.0)	1,046	230	142	2	86	200
1908–12	1,737	154	(52.2)	1,273	310	164	5	141	295
1913–17	2,202	167	(35.2)	1,531	504	191	6	307	471
1918–22	4,843	288	(56.1)	3,904	651	404	22	225	513
1923–27	4,526	310	(164.0)	3,820	396	458	59	−121	189
1928–32	3,203	213	(−407.3)	2,799	191	377	68	−254	−41
1933–37	3,502	198	(127.1)	2,816	488	332	62	94	292

[a] In million yen at current prices; figures in parentheses are percentages

[b] Correction of misprint in source

subscript a   Agricultural sector
subscript f   Farm sector
Y Income
T Direct taxes paid, assumed to be the same for both the agriculture and farm sectors, and interpreted as a forced savings transfer
C Consumption
S Savings ($S_a = Y_a - T_a - C_a$ and $S_f = Y_f - T_f - C_f$)
I Private investment
G Government investment
K Savings surplus transferred from the sector ($K_a = T_a + S_a - I_a - G_a$ and $K_f = T_f + S_f - I_f - G_f$)

Sources: For agricultural sector: Mundle and Ohkawa 1979; for farm sector: Ohkawa, Shimizu, and Takamatsu 1978

Table 13.3: Relative size of the trade surplus and the savings surplus of the agricultural and farm sectors, Japan, 1888–1937[a]

Time period	Y_a	B/Y_a (%)	Y_{na}	B/Y_{na} (%)	$K_a/(S_a + T_a)$ (%)	$K_f/(S_f + T_f)$ (%)	I_{na}
1888–92	400	0.3	577	0.2	41.9	43.6	100
1893–97	553	1.1	875	0.7	46.9	39.5	201
1898–1902	819	4.0	1,447	2.3	53.8	54.0	290
1903–07	1,058	7.0	1,998	3.7	58.3	58.1	374
1908–12	1,320	10.2	2,673	5.0	63.5	63.6	603
1913–17	1,566	15.2	4,012	5.9	70.6	70.6	920
1918–22	3,571	5.5	9,780	2.0	68.4	54.6	2,692
1923–27	3,444	−2.9	11,259	−0.9	52.3	26.8	2,363
1928–32	2,404	−9.7	10,978	−2.1	32.3	−10.1	2,002
1933–37	2,782	0.9	13,927	0.2	53.3	42.6	3,256

Time period	$F_a(1)$ (%)	$F_a(2)$ (%)	S_{na}	S_{na}/Y_{na} (%)	I_{na}/Y_{na} (%)	K_a/Y_{na} (%)	P_f
1888–92	−14.0	−13.0	114	19.8	17.3	6.6	100.0
1893–97	10.9	−23.9	194	22.2	23.0	7.1	112.1
1898–1902	21.0	6.2	225	15.5	20.0	8.3	124.5
1903–07	26.7	5.3	177	8.9	18.7	7.7	128.7
1908–12	23.5	23.5	393	14.7	22.6	8.4	135.6
1913–17	28.4	9.4	997	24.9	22.9	8.4	124.0
1918–22	30.9	32.0	2,101	21.5	27.5	7.1	148.6
1923–27	14.5	30.2	1,642	14.6	21.0	4.0	148.0
1928–32	7.4	20.2	1,848	16.8	18.2	1.5	118.2
1933–37	25.4	39.5	2,421	17.4	23.4	2.7	133.7

[a] In million yen at current prices, except where percentages are noted

Y_a Income of the agricultural sector

Y_{na} Income of the nonagricultural sector, Mundle and Ohkawa 1979

I_{na} Investment in the nonagricultural sector; derived by subtracting $(I_a + G_a)$ (given in table 13.2) from gross fixed capital investment for the whole economy (which is inclusive of military investment, and adjusted for duplication of construction estimates) as indicated in PIED: table A-38 col. 28

S_{na} Savings in the nonagricultural sector; derived by deducting agricultural savings S_a from total savings of the economy, from PJED: table A-5 column 1

F_a (1) and (2) are alternative estimates of the percentage of nonagricultural investment financed by agriculture; $F_a(1) = I_{na} - S_{na}$ — net borrowing from abroad, from PJED: table A-5 column 2; $F_a(2) = I_{na} - S_{na}$ — long-term capital inflows from abroad, from PJED: table A-31 column 10

P_f Terms of trade between the farm sector and the nonfarm sector, from Ohkawa, Shimizu, and Takamatsu 1978: Statistical Appendix table 4

Sources: Sources are included with the explanation of variables

Only variables not explained in tables 13.1 and 13.2 are explained here:

Table 13.4: An alternative estimate of financial resource flow from the farm sector, Japan, 1899–1933[a]

	1899–1902	1903–07	1908–12	1913–17	1918–22	1923–27	1928–33
(1) Net increase in financial assets of farm sector (K)	1	13	4	43	208	24	−11
(2) Investment in farm sector + $K (=S)$	121	159	105	240	658	524	403
(3) K/S (%)	0.8	8.2	2.3	17.9	31.6	4.6	−2.7
(4) Net outflow through direct tax from agriculture net of subsidies (T)	104	115	154	166	290	291	188
(5) $S + T (= S')$	225	274	259	406	948	815	591
(6) $(T + K)/S'$ (%)	46.7	46.7	61.0	51.5	52.5	38.7	62.1

[a] In million yen at current prices, unless a percentage

Source: Teranishi 1976: tables 1 and 6

transferred to the nonagricultural sector in 1916 secured only two-thirds the volume of agricultural commodities it had bought at the end of the Matsukata deflation, 30 years earlier. In other words, the resource transfer in real terms did not increase as dramatically as the current price estimates indicate. Moreover, the generation of a savings surplus in agriculture was itself facilitated by this shift in terms of trade.

Nevertheless, whether measured in real terms or in current prices, the savings transfer out of agriculture forms a considerable part of total investment in non-agriculture. As a proportion of total savings in agriculture itself, it was even higher. Because, according to our estimates in tables 13.1 and 13.3, there was no trade surplus of comparable magnitude, the balance of payments on current and capital account implies there were substantial flows to agriculture in the form of factor payments and other transfer payments on current account. This is another tentative inference which we will leave for further investigation.

Resource Flows in India, 1951–71

Post-Independence in India is the period roughly comparable to the half-century of industrialization following the Meiji Restoration in Japan. First, the rates of growth recorded by the Indian economy during those years were substantially higher than those recorded during the colonial period, and compare favorably to the rates attained in Japan during the late 19th century. Second, the rate of investment rose sharply.[1]

However, the pace of structural change appears to have been much slower than in Japan. As a consequence, the weight of the agricultural sector in the total economy, much greater in India even at the outset (about 54 percent of NNP in India in 1951/52, compared to 42 percent of NDP in Japan in 1887), remained considerably larger than during the comparable periods in Japan.

Agriculture's Trade Surplus

The earliest attempt to estimate the intersectoral balance of trade for India was by Ishikawa (1967) for the year 1951/52. Subsequently, Thamarajakshi (1969) computed terms of trade between agriculture and industry, and to compute the base-year weightings, she calculated intersectoral commodity flows in the base

[1] Official estimates of Indian national income prepared on a systematic basis begin with 1948–49. For the earlier period, some estimates of individual researchers are available, and Mukherjee (1969) has collated some of this material to put together a national-income series starting in 1857. We have relied on his estimates for the period before 1948–49, and on the official series for the period thereafter.

Gross capital formation as a proportion of gross domestic product (both valued at current prices) rose from about 10 percent in the early 1950s to more than 20 percent in the late 1970s. However, gross fixed capital formation in real terms did not rise as fast.

year. From these, we get balance of trade estimates for 1951/52 and 1960/61 at 1960/61 prices. The only available time-series of intersectoral commodity flows is that computed by Mundle (1981b) for the period between 1951/52 and 1970/71.

Ishikawa's estimate is not comparable to the other two, as it pertains to the farm households sector rather than to agriculture as a branch of production *vis-à-vis* nonagriculture, which is the demarcation used in the Thamarajakshi and Mundle estimates. Moreover, Ishikawa had to rely on the All India Rural Credit Survey of 1951/52, which (as Ishikawa points out) is a weak data base for his exercise, and in any case quite different from the sources available later to Thamarajakshi and Mundle. Although the two latter exercises are more similar, even they have differences. Both used the same National Sample Survey series of consumer expenditure to measure the consumer goods flows, but their sources of data and methods of estimating the intersectoral flow of producer goods are different. Also, there are some differences in the classification of commodities, agricultural and nonagricultural populations, etc. Thus, none of the three balance-of-trade estimates are fully comparable.

For 1951/52, all the estimates show a net inflow (trade deficit) for agriculture. Ishikawa's estimate is only at current prices and shows a smaller net commodity inflow than Mundle's current price estimate. Thamarajakshi's is only at constant prices, and shows a smaller net inflow than Mundle's constant price estimate. However, for 1960/61, Mundle shows a net commodity outflow (a trade surplus) for agriculture, whereas Thamarajakshi indicates a trade deficit.

We primarily use Mundle's series for analyzing the movement of the balance of trade, and Thamarajakshi's for the movement in sectoral terms of trade, as they are the only time-series so far available. It is important to remember that both the balance of trade and terms of trade series have had to be constructed by putting together different sources of data, of varying reliability, which are sometimes also conceptually incompatible. These problems are discussed by Mody (1979 and 1980) and Mundle (1980a and 1980b).[2]

The most significant problem for our purposes is the choice of prices. Both Thamarajakshi and Mundle used the NSS series for calculating consumer-goods flows; this series uses purchase prices. However, the intersectoral flow of producer goods is given at producers' prices. The complete balance-of-trade estimate, which puts together these two sets of data, is therefore either an underestimate or an overestimate, depending on which set of prices is considered appropriate.

---

[2] The NSS (National Sample Survey) series is the only available time-series on patterns of consumption expenditure. Compiled by the National Sample Survey Organization, the samples are designed to minimize estimation bias, but it has been claimed that the survey underrepresents upper-income consumption brackets. If this is true, the estimates overstate expenditure on necessary items such as food grains, while understating items like manufactured consumer durables. Thus intersectoral commodity-flow estimates based on the NSS overstate agriculture's exports and understate its imports. However, both the fact of the bias as well as its magnitude remain controversial questions.

If, in keeping with the social accounting convention adopted in industrial economies, distribution margins are treated as value added in nonagricultural activities the Thamarajakshi and Mundle estimates of agriculture's exports are overestimates, as they include the trade margin on outflows of consumption goods. If, on the other hand, the traders' margin is treated, along with landlords' rent and moneylenders' interest, as claims on the income originating in agriculture, then these estimates understate agriculture's exports, as they do not include the trade margin in the export of producer goods. The choice depends on how one views the formation of prices and income distribution in agrarian economies like India.

The time-series of the trade surplus of agriculture (taken from Mundle) is given in table 13.5. At current prices, the agricultural sector had an initial trade deficit, but moved to a surplus by the mid-1950s; in absolute terms, the surplus peaked in the mid-1960s, and then declined. At its peak, the trade surplus was a little over 10 percent of value added in agriculture, larger than in Japan at any time in the period 1888–1937, but it declined rapidly, to around 3 percent, by 1970/71. The turn in the balance of trade from the mid-1960s is sharper in the constant-price series.

This raises two questions: first, as to the factors underlying the movements in the trade balance, particularly the upward turn from the mid-1950s, and the downward turn a decade later; and second; whether this indicates a savings flow from agriculture during the earlier phase, more or less as in Japan between 1903 and 1922. We start with an analysis of the underlying factors, and then consider the estimates of the intersectoral savings, before offering an answer to the second question.

Interpretation of Movements in the Trade Balance

Estimates of exports and imports at constant prices (using Thamarajakshi's deflators) are given in table 13.6 The effects of changes in the terms of trade are eliminated when constant prices are used; these are discussed later. It is evident from the sale and purchase ratios in the table that agriculture has been closely linked with the nonagricultural sector since Independence, in terms of commodity flows. In most years, half or more of agriculture's net output (value added) was delivered to nonagriculture as food or raw materials (column 6). This ratio was a little higher than the import (purchase) ratio (final column), except at the beginning and end of the period. Both ratios are lower than for Japan, though not much lower than Japan in the decade 1888–97. The main difference is that in Japan, both the sale and purchase ratios have a clear secular tendency to rise, whereas for India, no uniform trend appears. With regard to commodity composition, in the Indian case, agriculture has throughout been a net importer of consumer goods (columns 2 and 7), whereas it was a net exporter of producer goods (columns 3 and 8).

Table 13.5:   Intersectoral balance of trade and the terms of trade, India, 1951–74

| | Trade surplus of agriculture (in Rupees crore) | | Terms of trade | |
| | | | | |
Year	At current prices	At constant (1960/61) prices	Thamarajakshi series (1960/61 = 100)	Kahlon–Tyagi series (1970/71 = 100)
1951/52	−926.3 (−22.6)	−787.6	100.7	
1952/53	−789.7 (−18.4)	−952.6	99.1	
1953/54	−205.0 (−4.4)	−353.5	103.7	
1954/55	−7.7 (−0.2)	70.5	97.0	
1955/56	−5.4 (−0.1)	151.6	94.8	
1956/57	488.0 (9.0)	475.7	102.5	
1957/58	289.3 (5.6)	367.9	98.5	
1958/59	334.4 (5.2)	314.1	101.7	
1959/60	533.6 (8.3)	515.1	101.7	
1960/61	695.4 (9.9)	695.4	100.0	
1961/62	775.9 (10.7)	751.8	100.7	
1962/63	816.9 (11.0)	848.7	99.1	
1963/64	902.7 (10.5)	946.1	97.4	
1964/65	816.9 (7.8)	358.6	108.7	
1965/66	1,014.9 (9.9)	256.9	114.5	
1966/67	900.3 (7.4)	−34.9	123.1	
1967/68	662.7 (4.4)	−544.8	125.0	115.6
1968/69	641.0 (4.3)	−524.2	116.3	105.1
1969/70	763.9 (4.6)	−713.9	125.7	101.8
1970/71	602.9 (3.4)	−762.9	127.3	100.0
1971/72			120.1	97.5
1972/73			118.9	103.6
1973/74			136.9	108.3
1974/75			133.9	99.6

The figures for the trade surplus have been reached after adjusting the export and import values of table 13.6 for international trade; for details, see Mundle 1981b
Figures in parentheses denote percentages of net value added in agriculture for the period 1951/52–1959/60, and of gross value added in agriculture for the period 1960/61–1970/71
The constant price estimates are based on the same deflators used by Thamarajakshi for computing her terms of trade series
One crore is ten million

Sources

Trade surplus of agriculture: Mundle 1981b: tables 5.5 and 5.6 respectively
Terms of trade: Thamarajakshi 1977: table 2; Kahlon and Tyagi 1980: table 6

Table 13.6:   Commodity exports and imports of agriculture in India, 1951/52–1970/71[a]

Year (1)	Export of consumer goods (2)	Export of producer goods (3)	Total exports from agriculture (4) (5)	Import of consumer goods (6)	Import of producer goods (7)	Total imports by agriculture (8) (9)
1951/52	1,518	729	2,248 (42.3)	2,328	408	2,736 (51.5)
1952/53	1,670	762	2,431 (43.6)		356	3,721 (58.6)
1953/54	1,899	818	2,716 (45.2)	2,786	306	3,092 (51.4)
1954/55	1,902	917	2,819 (46.6)	2,512	324	2,836 (46.9)
1955/56	2,061	1,036	3,097 (51.2)	2,715	341	3,056 (50.5)
1956/57	2,115	1,152	3,267 (51.4)	2,603	349	2,952 (46.4)
1957/58	2,063	1,235	3,298 (54.5)	2,700	291	2,992 (44.6)
1958/59	2,130	1,357	3,487 (52.0)	2,857	296	3,153 (47.7)
1959/60	2,157	1,499	3,655 (55.3)	2,871	266	3,137 (47.4)
1960/61	2,303	1,680	3,983 (56.8)	2,933	256	3,189 (45.5)
1961/62	2,381	1,719	4,100 (57.9)	3,024	349	3,373 (47.7)
1962/63	2,398	1,767	4,165 (60.3)	2,968	352	3,320 (48.1)
1963/64	2,517	1,816	4,333 (61.0)	2,965	411	3,376 (47.5)
1964/65	2,487	1,848	4,336 (56.0)	3,382	503	3,885 (50.2)
1965/66	2,453	1,823	4,276 (63.7)	3,412	500	3,912 (58.3)
1966/67	2,480	1,802	4,282 (64.6)	3,491	599	4,050 (61.1)
1967/68	2,703	1,789	4,492 (58.4)	4,180	702	4,882 (63.4)
1968/69	2,729	1,790	4,519 (57.9)	4,187	792	4,979 (63.8)
1969/70	2,826	1,785	4,611 (55.7)	4,381	926	5,307 (64.1)
1970/71	2,943	1,732	4,675 (52.5)	4,387	1,073	5,459 (61.3)

Figures in parentheses denote the sales ratio (middle column) and purchase ratio (right-hand column) expressed as percentages of value added in agriculture

[a] In Rupees crore, at 1960/61 prices; one crore is ten million

Source: Mundle 1981b: tables 3.13, 4.7 and 4.8

To explain the changes that produced a sharp turn in the overall balance of trade of the agricultural sector in the mid-1960s, we divide the 20-year reference period into two subperiods at 1964/65, and, in table 13.7, compare growth rates for agricultural imports and exports, and a number of variables that could have affected them.

It was the increase in the growth rate of consumer-goods imports that really accounted for the greater part of the increase in the overall rate of growth of imports into agriculture. The sharp acceleration in imports of producer goods was only a minor factor, as the weight of producer goods was small even toward the end of the period. There is some controversy about whether the agricultural growth rate declined, but there has been no claim the rate increased. The increase in the rate of consumer-demand growth is therefore probably accounted for by the positive income and substitution effects of a shift in the terms of trade in

Table 13.7: Intersectoral community flows and related variables in India, growth rates, 1951–71

Variables	Annual compound rates of growth		Direction of change
	1951/52– 1964/65	*1964/65– 1970/71*	
Gross product in agriculture	2.9	2.4	decrease
Input/output ratio (nonagriculture to agriculture)	−1.6	11.3	increase
Agriculture's imports of consumer goods	2.9	4.4	increase
Agriculture's imports of producer goods	2.7	13.5	increase
Total imports by agriculture	2.7	5.8	increase
Gross product in nonagriculture	5.8	3.9	decrease
Input/output ratio (agriculture to nonagriculture)	1.6	−4.8	decrease
Agriculture's export of consumer goods	3.9	2.9	decrease
Agriculture's export of producer goods	7.4	−1.1	decrease
Total exports by agriculture	5.2	1.3	decrease

Annual compound growth rates r have been calculated using the formula $Y_t = Y_0 b^t$ where $b = 1 + r$
All variables are at constant prices

Source: Mundle 1981b: tables 3,7, 3.13, 4.6–4.8

favor of agriculture, as shown by the Thamarajakshi series in table 13.5. But the series constructed by Kahlon and Tyagi (1980), also given in table 13.5, does not show such a sustained shift. Our explanation must thus be treated as tentative. The higher growth rate of imports by agriculture on account of consumer demand was of course reinforced by the increase in the rate of growth of producer-goods imports, which largely reflected the spread of biochemical technology in agriculture, beginning in the mid-1960s, and the consequent increase in the nonagricultural inputs required per unit of agricultural output.

The growth rate of agriculture's exports of both consumer and producer goods declined sharply. The slower growth of consumer-goods exports, which was the larger of the two components, is explained partly by the slower growth of gross value added in nonagriculture in the late 1960s, reflecting, among other things, some deceleration in the industrial growth rate, and partly, if the Thamarajakshi series is accepted, by the negative income and price effects of the shift in terms of trade. In the case of producer goods, an important additional factor explaining the slower growth of exports is the structural change within the nonagricultural sector: the relative share of agro-based industries, and hence of agricultural inputs into nonagricultural production as a whole, declined (see Mundle 1981a and 1981b).

Table 13.7 shows that the values of almost all the variables that could affect agriculture's imports increased between the two periods, whereas values of all the variables affecting agriculture's exports decreased. The net effect is reflected in the overall balance of trade in real terms shown in table 13.5 (trade surplus of agriculture, at constant 1960/61 prices). It should be emphasized that what is important here is not the absolute value or sign of this variable (these could change with a change in the deflator base year), but the direction of change of the balance over time. From the early 1950s until 1963/64, the entire balance appears to have been moving clearly in favor of agricultural exports; then the balance began to move in the opposite direction.

This turn also appears in the estimates of agriculture's trade surplus at current prices (table 13.5). It does not, however, come out so sharply, because of changes in the price level, particularly the rise in the relative price of agricultural commodities after the mid-1960s, reflected in the Thamarajakshi terms of trade series.

Agriculture's Savings Surplus

Was agriculture's trade surplus, particularly between the mid-1950s and the mid-1960a, indicative of a savings flow from agriculture, as in Japan during the first two decades of the 20th century? This is the question we now address. A major difficulty in answering it is that there are no estimates of savings of either agriculture or the farm sector for the period under review (1951–71). The available estimates are for the rural sector as a whole, and thus include savings from nonfarm business.

A series covering 1950/51–73/74 has been constructed by Krishna and Raychaudhuri (1980: 33) for rural savings and private investment in agriculture. These estimates suggest there was a net excess of rural savings over agricultural investment up to 1955/56, and a net deficit thereafter, except in 1966/67 1967/68, and 1969/70. The excess in the first few years of the 1950s was in the range of 1.5–2.2 percent of the net value added in agriculture but was negligible in the late 1960s (table 13.8).

One has to be careful drawing inferences from these estimates (Desai 1981). The estimates of rural savings are derived from balance sheets for the rural household sector constructed on the basis of surveys conducted by the Reserve Bank of India for 1951/52, 1956/57, and 1961/62. In these surveys, there has been an obvious underestimation of the financial assets of rural households, and consequently of their net savings. In addition, although the estimate of private investment in agriculture includes physical assets created through use of family labor (following the methods used by India's Central Statistical Organization for the purpose), no allowance has been made for this in the estimates of rural saving (see Panikar 1970; Bhalla 1976).

If the underestimation of the financial assets of rural households was confined to currency or gold holdings (which are notoriously difficult to quantify), one could adjust for year-to-year changes in currency holdings and just ignore

Table 13.8:　Rural savings and private investment in agriculture in India, 1951–74[a]

Year	Rural savings	Private investment in agriculture	Year	Rural savings	Private investment in agriculture
1950/51	166	59	1962/63	248	303
1951/52	171	100	1963/64	284	348
1952/53	164	57	1964/65	327	434
1953/54	181	100	1965/66	468	559
1954/55	148	105	1966/67	650	630
1955/56	154	136	1967/68	629	623
1956/57	188	233	1968/69	603	672
1957/58	180	182	1969/70	834	820
1958/59	212	246	1970/71	865	968
1959/60	213	248	1971/72	869	934
1960/61	225	296	1972/73	1,125	1,152
1961/62	196	265	1973/74	1,279	1,407

[a]In Rupees crore; one crore is ten million

Source: Krishna and Raychaudhuri 1980: 33, table 13

changes in holdings of gold. But the underestimation we have in mind is more difficult to allow for, as what has been largely left out is informal lending between households within the rural sector. Even as late as 1962, informal (in the sense of being noninstitutional and not government-regulated) intrasectoral loans from landlords, agricultural moneylenders, and friends and relatives accounted for over half of rural borrowings (Mody 1981). Borrowing households are more likely to report the liability than lending households are the asset, and the difference gets treated as an inflow of savings from outside the sector.

Rural household savings could therefore have been in excess of private investment in agriculture in the early 1950s by larger margins than indicated by the series in table 13.8. There could also have been such an excess in subsequent years. On the other hand, the savings estimates pertain to all rural households, whereas the estimates of investment relate to agriculture alone. Whether there would be an overall savings surplus for agriculture, or even the farm sector, taken independently after the necessary adjustments in the savings estimates is difficult to say.

However, Mody has made partial estimates of some major components of the net savings flow into agriculture that adjust for the effects of underreported informal lending within the sector, and for savings in the form of currency. The first of two sets of estimates presented by Mody (1981) is based on data from sample surveys of farm households conducted by the NCAER (National Council of Applied Economic Research) for the years 1962, 1968/69, 1969/70, and 1970/71, adjusted to incorporate currency holdings. The adjustment was based on an earlier NCAER estimate that savings in the form of an increase in currency stock constituted about 30 percent of the change in financial assets of the rural sector in 1962. Mody found very large inflows of saving to the farm sector (table 13.9).

Mody's second set of estimates allows for internal transfers of savings that are not fully reported by lending households. These estimates are based on survey data for farm households collected by the RBI (Reserve Bank of India) for 1951/52, 1961/62, and 1971/72, and the annual balance sheets of cooperative and commercial banks. This set represents estimates of changes over a decade, based on comparisons of the stock of assets and liabilities. The estimate for the decade 1952-62 is open to serious question, as the 1952 survey was not based on random sampling. There are also wide differences between the estimates based on NCAER data and those based on RBI data.

The adjusted estimates based on the RBI surveys for 1961/62 and 1971/72 provide as firm a basis as possible for judging the order of magnitude of net borrowing by the farm household sector. This works out to approximately 830 million rupees per annum over the decade 1962-72. Of this, about 800 million rupees is accounted for by an upward adjustment of the survey estimate of household borrowings to cover the discrepancy between this estimate and the figure reported in the accounts of cooperative and commercial banks. Even the unadjusted survey estimate indicates some net borrowing by the farm sector.

Table 13.9:   Estimates of net financial lending by the farm sector in India[a]

	Period (1)	Change in financial assets (2)		Change in financial liabilities (3)	Miscellaneous capital transfers (4)	Net borrowing by households (5)
Ishikawa (RBI)	1951/52	15		307	–	292
Ishikawa (RBI)	1956/57	17		183	–	166
Mody (NCAER)	1962	102	(39)	172	25	95
Mody (NCEAR)	1968/69	49	(20)	699	4	654
Mody (NCAER)	1969/70	682	(220)	792	−41	69
Mody (NCAER)	1970/71	288	(81)	829	−40	561
Mody (RBI)	1952-62	650		1,463	–	813
Mody (RBI)	1962-72	903		1,731	–	828

Figures in parentheses denote net acquisition of currency holdings

Miscellaneous capital transfers refer to acquisition of financial and physical assets such as through gifts not included under change in financial assets (column 2) in the NCAER surveys

RBI   Reserve Bank of India
NCAER   National Council of Applied Economic Research

[a] In Rupees crore; one crore is ten million

Sources: Ishikawa 1967: table 4.2; Mody 1981: tables 2 and 14

Whichever source we use, and whatever adjustment we make, the farm sector thus appears to have been a net borrower.

A second aspect of the financial transactions is the changing composition of the sources of credit for farm households. Though sources internal to the farm sector still account for a very large part of rural credit, their share came down from 54 to 44 percent over the decade 1962-71. The share of credit from outside the farm sector has gone up substantially, whereas that of traditional external sources, like professional moneylenders and traders, has either not changed much or declined. The increase in external sources during the decade is accounted for by the modern sector doubling its share from 16 to 32 percent. Within the modern sector, the bulk of the expansion is by cooperatives, which raised their share from 10 to 22 percent and have now come to compete with agricultural moneylenders (at 23 percent) as the largest source of rural credit (Mody 1981: table 6). What is significant about these changes is that the modern sector is entirely dependent on the government. All the components, commercial banks, cooperatives, and insurance companies, are either owned or controlled by the government.

There is substantial evidence from RBI data to indicate the bulk of the finance made available to farm households through these agencies is absorbed by the wealthier 10 percent of farm households (Mody 1981). It is possible a high proportion of the loans is used for nonagricultural activities. To that extent, it is doubtful whether there has been a net inflow to finance agricultural investment, particularly as the estimated flow is not large. Moreover, the proportion of cultivators in the RBI survey reporting capital expenditures fell from two-thirds in 1961/62 to one-half in 1971/72. Real investment declined in most states and, in some, even nominal investment fell. Questions have been raised as to the comparability of the surveys, but the relationship between credit flows and the investment behavior of farm households does need to be examined more carefully.

Our effort to judge from partial indicators the direction and magnitude of savings flows into and out of agriculture has so far considered only credit flows on private and public account. The budgetary operation of the government also could be an important channel. Estimates of the resource flows on government account in India *vis-à-vis* the farm sector are available (Shetty 1971; Mody 1981). Unlike data for Japan, however, Indian estimates include indirect tax revenue collected from the sector, and the current and capital expenditures of the government in agriculture. Despite the inclusion of indirect tax revenue in the flow out of agriculture, the estimates indicate a significant overall inflow. Though the annual rate appears to have declined after 1965/66, the flow has nevertheless continued to be into agriculture, not out of agriculture as in Japan (table 3.10).

The evidence we have put together suggests that there is a substantial flow of savings into the farm sector in India, particularly through public credit agencies, though how much actually was invested in agriculture is difficult to say. In any

Table 13.10: Net resource flows on government account into agriculture in India[a]

Time period	Annual tax burden on farm sector	Average annual public expenditure in the farm sector	Average annual net flow of funds on government account
1951/52–1955/56	52	99	47
1956/57–1960/61	84	186	103
1961/62–1965/66	161	343	182
1966/67–1968/69	395	470	75

[a] In Rupees crore; one crore is ten million
Sources: Shetty 1971; Mody 1981

case, there is no evidence of a net savings outflow from agriculture during the 1950s and 1960s.

One further problem remains. The large trade surpluses of agriculture, particularly before the mid-1960s, have to be reconciled with the net flow into agriculture suggested by the different partial estimates of savings flows. The most obvious explanation is that a part of the income originating in agriculture was actually accruing outside the sector by way of rent, interest, and trading profits. To that extent, the estimated trade surpluses are offset by the flow of such factor incomes away from the sector, and do not show up as part of the savings surpluses of agriculture. If this explanation is valid, and the Kahlon and Tyagi (1980) terms of trade series in table 13.5 is correct, the proportion of income flowing away from agriculture in the form of trading profits was rising between 1967/68 and 1973/74, as the margin between farm gate and wholesale prices evidently was widening.

Concluding Observations

It is obvious that savings flows from agriculture made a significant contribution to industrial capital accumulation in Japan, particularly in the early decades of the 20th century, but there is no evidence of a similar savings contribution in India during the corresponding period of the 1950s and 1960s. The scale of savings flow to the nonagricultural sector may have had adverse effects on the development of agriculture in Japan. Similarly, it is possible, given the conditions of Indian agriculture in the 1950s that some flow of savings into the sector was essential to promote agricultural growth. Without that growth, industrialization would have strained the economy more severely, and run into serious bottlenecks, including the lack of demand for industrial products, even sooner than it has. This is especially so in view of the evidence that a significant portion of the income originating in agriculture has in fact not accrued to that sector, thereby diminishing its capacity to self-finance needed investment.

Compared to Japan, allowance must also be made in India for the large call on resources made by irrigation, based on construction of extensive reservoirs and canals (Vaidyanathan and Jose 1978); and for a much higher population growth in India, particularly in the rural sector, attributable to the impact of public-health measures on mortality rates. It is thus hazardous to draw any unqualified conclusions about the desirability of what has happened in intersectoral resource flows in either country during the periods under review.

At the same time, it is apparent that institutional factors, such as the size-distribution of operational holding in Japan and India, also contributed significantly to differences in bias in the technology adopted for increasing agricultural output, and thereby to differences in resource requirements. It is well known there was a strong bias toward labor-intensive techniques in Japan and, with the population dependent on agriculture not growing significantly in the 20th century, a shortage of labor and a rise in wage rates favored a structure of small farms based mainly on the labor of peasant nuclear families. Thus, while ownership holdings were concentrated in a small proportion of agricultural households, operational holdings were relatively evenly distributed, as large holders normally let out their lands in small parcels. This stands in contrast to the size-distribution of operational holdings in India, where, in many regions, the skewness in the distribution is very nearly the same as the distribution of ownership holdings (Raj 1970).

Such contrasts in the conditions of agricultural growth, and consequent differences in the resource requirements of the sector, are reflected in sharply differing savings-allocation policies by the governments. In Japan, the high land tax served as the major instrument of savings transfer from agriculture, especially during the Meiji period (1868-1911).

In India, the national government has also intervened actively in the inter-sectoral transfer of savings, but the thrust has been in the opposite direction. Taxation of land has almost been abandoned since Independence, whereas government expenditure on irrigation and other agricultural projects has been substantial. The bulk of external credit to the farm sector – over half in the early 1980s – has come from government institutions. Indeed, it needs to be emphasized that most of the evidence indicating a net flow of funds into Indian agriculture relates to flows from government sources; relatively little is known about private flows, particularly direct private investment across sectors. It is even possible part of the credit extended from government sources to farm households is used for nonagricultural purposes such as agro-processing factories, warehousing and cold storage, truck fleets, etc.

Ishikawa (1981) has drawn attention to two phases in Japan's agricultural growth before World War II; these are distinguished by differences in technology. In the first phase, up to about 1911, increased output was associated with technological changes centered on conversion of wet paddy fields to dry fields and the associated use of animal power instead of human labor for plowing. The increase in use of purchased manufactured inputs like chemical fertilizers or capital goods such as farm machinery was minimal. In the phase after 1911, a biochemical technology similar to the contemporary Green Revolution, along with some mechanization, increased purchases from nonagriculture. (For a somewhat different view, see Hayami et al. (1975).)

While this change in the role of manufactured inputs in agriculture bears some resemblance to the two phases in Indian agricultural growth before and after the mid-1960s, what is of note in the Japanese case is the element of genuine technological progress in both phases. This made possible a certain degree of balanced expansion of agriculture's export surplus, even with the sector's increased import requirements after 1911. As Ishikawa puts it,

[that] technological progress accounted for more than half the rate of growth of agricultural output is one of the most essential aspects of the

contribution that agriculture made to the success of industrialization. If the rate of technological progress had been very low, the amount of agricultural products which agriculture was able to supply the emerging industrial sector under the given prices would have been much smaller. (Ishikawa 1981: 184)

(Technological progress here refers to an upward shift of the production function, as distinguished from a movement along a production function.)

What perhaps makes Indian agricultural growth since Independence qualitatively different is the absence of genuine technological progress in the phases both before and after the Green Revolution. In the 1950s and early 1960s, there was on the whole no change of technology at all, only the application of old technology on a wider land base. The subsequent technological change, a shift to the new biochemical mix of inputs, has been without technological progress in the sense defined here. The use of fertilizers and pesticides increased, together with the use of high-yield variety seeds. The beginning of mechanization also occurred. But acreage expansion has leveled off, and productivity increased much less than the use of the new inputs. Hence, agricultural output growth did not rise and the growth of the sector's exports actually slowed, which led to the shift in the sector's trade balance.

Genuine technical changes similar to Japan's second phase did not take place in India. Why? A proper exploration of the reasons requires a probe deep into questions not only of the social and political biases of the particular features of land structure and education in the Indian context today, but also the differences in the conditions of international technology transfer experienced by Japan and India. Although this is beyond the scope of this essay, we can suggest one aspect of the answer.

In India, the new technology has been embodied largely in imported fertilizers and pesticides, or in imported technologies for producing these inputs, and partly in the research and development work of universities and research centers set up under the same broad stimulus. The learning-by-doing factor, adaptation of new techniques through the feedback received from farmers' experience, has been relatively weak. In Japan, the leading agents of technological change were the farmers; imports played a relatively minor role (Ishikawa 1981). The initiative in Japan was local and was thus much more responsive to local needs, and the manner of adaptation of the new technology ensured maximum efficiency.

There remain a number of issues, analytical as well as empirical, which must be resolved before we can offer clear answers to questions of agricultural surpluses. At the empirical level, we need, for both India and Japan, estimates that distinguish between flows through government and private channels, as well as between different strata or groups within each sector. Especially important here are the trader's margins and other components of factor income payments or current transfers between sectors. The net-income transfer, conceptually equal to the difference between the trade surplus and the savings surplus, was generally very large in both countries. Yet no attempt has been made so far to measure this flow, or its components, except as a residual balancing item. If we can learn a little more about these important gaps in data, the contrasting experiences of India and Japan could lead to useful insights into the role of agricultural surpluses under Asian conditions of development.

References

Bagchi, Amiya (1970), "European and Indian Entrepreneurship in India, 1900–1930," in E. Leach and S. N. Mukherjee, eds, *Elites in South India*, Cambridge: Cambridge University Press.

Bagchi, Amiya (1972), *Private Investment in India, 1900–1939*, Cambridge: Cambridge University Press.

Bhalla, Surjit S. (1976), "Aspects of Savings Behavior in Rural India," mimeo, Princeton University and Brookings Institution.

Bhatia, B. M. (1967), *Famines in India*, Bombay: Asia Publishing House.

Blyn, George (1966), *Agricultural Trends in India, 1891–1947: Output, Availability and Productivity*, Philadelphia: University of Pennsylvania Press.

Gadgil, D. R. (1942), *Industrial Evolution of India*, Bombay: Oxford University Press.

Gupta, K. L. (1970), "On Some Determinants of Rural and Urban Households Saving Behavior," *Economic Record*, 46(116): 578–83 (December).

Hayami, Yujiro, in association with Masakatsu Akino, Masahiko Shintani, and Saburo Yamada (1975), *A Century of Agricultural Growth in Japan*, St Paul, MN: University of Minnesota Press.

India National Account Statistics, Central Statistical Organisation, Department of Statistics.

Ishikawa, Shigeru (1967), *Economic Development in Asian Perspectives*, Tokyo: Kinokuniya Bookstore.

Ishikawa, Shigeru (1981), *Essays on Technology, Employment and Institutions in Economic Development*, Tokyo: Kinokuniya Bookstore.

Kahlon, A. S., and D. S. Tyagi (1980), "Inter-sectoral Terms of Trade," *Economic and Political Weekly*, 15(52): A-173 to A-184.

Krishna, Raj, and G. S. Raychaudhuri (1980), "Trends in Rural Savings and Private Capital Formation in India," *World Bank Staff Working Paper No. 382*, Washington: World Bank.

Lee, Teng-hui (1971), *Inter-sectoral Capital Flows in the Economic Development of Taiwan 1895–1960*, Ithaca, NY: Cornell University Press.

Mody, Ashoka (1979), "Resource Flows between Agriculture and Non-agriculture: Critique of an Estimate," *Indian Journal of Agricultural Economics*, (October–December).

Mody, Ashoka (1980), *Inter-sectoral Resource Transfers: A Reply to a Reply*, Trivandrum: Centre for Development Studies Working Paper No. 113.

Mody, Ashoka (1981), "Resource Flows between Agriculture and Non-agriculture in India, 1950–1970," *Economic and Political Weekly*, annual number, March.

Mukherjee, M. (1969), *National Income of India: Trends and Structure*, Calcutta: Statistical Publishing Society.

Mundle, Sudipto (1980a), *Inter-sectoral Resource Transfers: Reply to a Critique*, Trivandrum: Centre for Development Studies Working Paper No. 105.

Mundle, Sudipto (1980b), *Inter-sectoral Resource Transfers: Some Further Remarks*, Trivandrum: Centre for Development Studies Working Paper No. 119.

Mundle, Sudipto (1981a), "Growth, Disparity and Capital Reorganization in Indian Economy: Some Speculations," *Economic and Political Weekly*, annual number.

Mundle, Sudipto (1981b), *Surplus Flows and Growth Imbalances*, New Delhi: Allied Publishers.

Mundle, Sudipto, and Kazushi Ohkawa (1979), "Agricultural Surplus Flow in Japan 1888–1937," *The Developing Economies*, 17 (September).

Ohkawa, Kazushi, and Henry Rosovsky (1973), *Japanese Economic Growth: Trend Acceleration in the Twentieth Century*, Stanford, CA: Stanford University Press.

Ohkawa, Kazushi, Yutaka Shimizu, and Nobukiyo Takamatsu (1978), "Agricultural Surplus in an Overall Performance of Savings and Investment," in *Papers and Proceedings of the Conference on Japan's Historical Development Experience and the Contemporary Developing Countries*, Tokyo: International Development Center of Japan.

Oshima, Harry T. (1965), "Meiji Fiscal Policy and Agricultural Progress," in W. W. Lockwood, ed., *The State and Economic Enterprise in Japan*, Princeton, NJ: Princeton University Press.

Panikar, P. G. K. (1970), *Rural Savings in India*, Bombay: Somaiya.

PJED (*Patterns of Japanese Economic Development: A Quantitative Appraisal*, Kazushi Ohkawa and Miyou Shinohara, with Larry Meissner (1979), New Haven, CT: Yale University Press.

Preobrazhensky, Eugenii (1965), *The New Economics*, English translation by Brian Pearce, London: Oxford University Press.

Raj, K. N. (1970), "Ownership and Distribution of Land," *Indian Economic Review*.

Sivasubramoniam, S. (1977), "Income from the Secondary Sector in India," *Indian Economic and Social History Review* (October–December).

Shetty, S. L. (1971), "An Inter-sectoral Analysis of Tax Burden and Taxable Capacity," *Indian Journal of Agricultural Economics* (July–September).

Shetty, S. L. (1978), *Structural Retrogression in the Indian Economy*, Bombay: States' People Press; also in *Economic and Political Weekly*, annual number (February).

Smith, Thomas C. (1959), *The Agrarian Origin of Modern Japan*, Stanford, CA: Stanford University Press.

Teranishi, Juro (1976), "The Pattern and Role of Flow of Funds between Agriculture and Non-agriculture in Japanese Economic Development," reprinted in Kazushi Ohkawa and Yujiro Hayami, eds, *Papers and Proceedings of the Conference on Japan's Historical Development Experience and the Contemporary Development Countries*, Tokyo: International Development Center of Japan.

Thamarajakshi, R. (1969), "Inter-sectoral Terms of Trade and Marketed Surplus of Agricultural Produces, 1951–52 to 1965–66," *Economic and Political Weekly*; also reprinted in P. Chaudhuri, ed., *Readings in Indian Agricultural Development*, London: George Allen and Unwin.

Thamarajakshi, R. (1977), "Price Incentives and Agricultural Production," in D. Ensminger, ed., *Food Enough or Starvation for Millions*, New Delhi: Tata McGraw Hill.

Tyagi, D. S. (1979), "Farm Prices and Class Bias in India," *Economic and Political Weekly* (September 29).

Vaidyanathan, A., and A. V. Jose (1978), "Absorption of Human Labor in Agriculture: A Comparative Study of Some Asian Countries," in *Labor Absorption in Indian Agriculture, Some Exploratory Investigations*, Bangkok: Asian Regional Team for Employment Promotion, International Labor Office.

14 Government Credit to the Banking System: Rural Banks in Nineteenth Century Japan and the Postwar Philippines

JURO TERANISHI

Modern finance has penetrated rural areas of the Philippines, and rural banks (RBs) have been crucial in this process. This essay first looks at the development and role of RBs, and compares RBs and Philippine government credit policy to the Japanese experience in the late 19th and early 20th centuries, a similar period in Japan's banking development. A major contrast between what has happened in the Philippines and what occurred in Japan is the withdrawal of extensive government credit to the banking system in Japan. The second half of this chapter analyzes the effects of this, concluding that the policy of gradually decreasing government credit was effective in bringing about deposit banking, by making it more profitable for banks to seek deposits by offering higher interest rates.

Comparison is handicapped by the absence of a Japanese counterpart to RBs. Closest are the prefectural *noko ginko*, but they were for long-term financing of both agriculture and rural industry, using funds from the sale of debentures. RBs are short-term lenders to agriculture, and collect deposits. Thus the comparison here is to the entire Japanese commercial banking system. This system was established when there were no other modern financial intermediaries, in sharp contrast to Philippine RBs, which were introduced on the fringe of a well-established commercial bank system. Notwithstanding their negligible share in

The author is very grateful to those institutions and people who extended warm support during his research trip to the Philippines, especially the Department of Rural Banks and Saving & Loan Associations (RB & SLA) in the Central Bank, the Economics Department at the International Rice Research Institute, and several rural banks where interviews were conducted. The Director of the RB & SLA, C. V. Odra, kindly read a draft of this essay and offered clarifications.

This chapter is complementary with chapter 15 of this volume by Patrick and Moreno; the latter is more of an overview of the entire financial system and an analysis of the commercial banks. Hugh Patrick provided comments on my research.

the financial aggregates, outside Metro Manila (where the commercial banks are concentrated), RBs are the principal nongovernment modern financial institutions.

The Role and Characteristics of RBs

RBs are private local banks supplying credit mainly to small farmers. Their development has been remarkable, partly owing to substantial government credits. The number of RBs increased from 18 in 1953 to 1,032 in 1980, at which point virtually every significant rural area was served. Government statistics show financing from informal sources (that is, sources outside the formal, government-regulated system such as landlords, moneylenders, and family) decreased from about 90 percent of farm liabilities in the late 1950s, to less than 30 percent in the early 1970s (*Action Program* 1977), although a survey by the Presidential Committee on Agricultural Credit (1981) suggests a smaller decline.

The late 19th century is a comparable period in Japan's banking development. The number of private commercial banks increased from four in 1872 to over two thousand in 1901, reaching virtually every town. Traditional credit's share of agricultural liabilities declined from 93 percent in 1888 to 64 percent in 1911. Initially, Japanese banks were also heavily reliant on government credit (half of their financial resources in the mid-1870s), but by 1900 such support was less than a tenth of resources.

RBs are considered by many observers as mere conduits for government credit to agriculture. Initially, RBs were supported by government equity investment. The government provided up to half the capital in exchange for nonvoting preferred stock with a 2 percent maximum yield; private investors held common stock and managed the bank. The older RBs have redeemed much of this preferred stock, and the government stopped taking equity positions in new banks in 1958. But Central Bank (CB) credit has increased, particularly since 1973. At the end of 1980, CB credits were 30.7 percent of RBs' total resources. Of this, about one-sixth were STD (special time deposits, which are CB advances against agricultural lending and anticipated rediscounting), and the balance was rediscounting.

Over 90 percent of RB lending is directed to agriculture, and RB loans are over 17 percent of total lending to agriculture by various institutions (table 14.1; 1971–75 data). Although the Philippine National Bank (PNB) provides over half the total, the bulk of its loans are to the sugar industry, mainly in Western Visayas. Commercial bank loans, over a quarter of the total, are mainly to processing firms. The Development Bank of the Philippines (DBP) loans long-term to large-scale farmers. The Agricultural Credit Administration (ACA) and (LBP) are small-farmer oriented, but provide less than 1 percent of credit. RBs are by far the most important institutional source of credit for small farmers.

Table 14.1: Distribution of agricultural lending by institutional source in the Philippines, 1971–75

	Percentage share of total lending to agriculture	Lending to agriculture as a percentage of total lending by the institution	Medium and long-term loans as a percentage of total agricultural lending by the institution, in 1975
Government institution			
Philippine National Bank (PNB)	52.7	51.2	0.0
Development Bank of the Philippines (DBP)	2.5	26.7	91.2
Agricultural Credit Administration (ACA)	0.7	100.0	1.8
Land Bank of the Philippines (LBP)	0.1	42.0	66.4
Private institutions			
Commercial Banks (KBs)	25.1	4.4	0.0
Rural Banks (RBs)	17.2	91.2	7.1
Private development Banks (PDBs)	0.7	50.0	87.6
Savings and Mortgage Banks (SMBs)	0.1	2.9	0.0
Stock Savings and Loan Associations (SSLAs)	0.5	18.4	0.0
Non-banks	0.4	–	–

Source: Action Program 1977: 20, 22, 31, 33

RB loans are mostly secured by real-estate mortgages, and have six- to twelve-month terms; longer-term loans are only 7 percent of loans. In the mid-1960s, a no-collateral policy was tried, and in the early 1970s, a joint-liability system was introduced. Both failed, because of abuse by borrowers. Saito and Villanueva (1978) have calculated the effective interest rate to be between 19.3 and 20.8 percent. This includes a basic rate of 12 percent, to which is added a 2 percent service charge, a 3 percent compulsory donation to the Barrio Savings Fund, and a contribution to the Barrio Guarantee Fund of 55 pesos per hectare. However, this range is disputed by the Central Bank's Director of RBs, who tells me that the 12 percent basic rate includes the service charge, and the other items are collected only from those who benefit from the programs financed by the contributions. Traditional sources charge 50 to 90 percent (*Action Program* 1977: 13), and one study found rates up to 320 percent (Kikuchi et al. 1977).

Almost all RBs are unit banks (that is, they have no branches). This is considered a special merit, as each RB is thus considered to be in close contact with its borrowers, which helps lower information costs (*Action Program* 1977: 68).

Philippine government data divided the country into twelve regions throughout the 1960s, then into ten. Significant variation is found in the regional density of RBs, measured by the number of farms per RB. Central Luzon and Southern Tagalog, the two densest regions for RBs, are also well-developed in other ways, including commercial banking and manufacturing, and this regional difference in the development of banks still existed in 1980. The two have been combined in the analysis as CL&ST, covering Manila and central Luzon north to Dagupan and San Jose and southwest through Quezon province. The ten remaining regions have been consolidated as Others. RBs share certain characteristics according to when they were founded, so my analysis also groups banks by age: old (1953–58), new (1959–63), and young (1964–68). Table 14.2 gives the number of banks in each region by when they were founded.

Because of changes in the way data are collected and presented in the *Annual Report on Rural Banks*, time-series and cross-section analysis using data on individual RBs can be done only through 1968. A few RBs that ceased to exist before then have also been eliminated. Several interesting points emerge from the data, which are summarized in table 14.3.

Over the ten years for which there are data (1958–68), the average size of accounts at new RBs in the CL&ST region was somewhat smaller than at old RBs, and new RBs relied more on equity than the older RBs; young RBs had even smaller accounts. In the other regions, relative to old RBs, new banks relied even more on equity than in the CL&ST region, and both old and new raised a larger share of their funds from equity than their CL&ST counterparts. One explanation is that newer RBs opened in poorer areas.

While, on average, an old RB in the CL&ST region increased its deposits and equity half as much again as a new RB did in the 1963–68 period, in the other regions the two groups averaged the same. This suggests that in the CL&ST region new RBs had limited success getting depositors to switch, and their customers who were new to banking were poorer than old RB customers. In the absence of the shift to small savers, inflation (for which no adjustment has been made) would increase the average account size.

In less-banked areas, both new and old RBs drew new depositors from the same pool. This last point suggests an institution-elasticity – that is, deposits in RBs increase with the geographical spread of RBs. One reason for this is the extremely poor condition of the roads; half of all rural barrios have farm-to-

Table 14.2: Number and density of banks by region in the Philippines

| | Region | | | | | | | | | | | | |
	I	II	III	IV	V	VI	VII	VIII	IX	X	XI	XII	Total[a]
Number of RBs in 1968	39	15	93	129	28	48	14	4	6	11	9	13	413
O	15	5	28	38	8	12	4	1	4	6	5	4	130
N	11	5	40	57	12	12	3	3	2	0	2	3	150
Y	13	5	25	34	8	24	7	0	0	5	2	6	129
Number of RBs in 1975	82	42	118	185	59	97	46	22	9	39	35	32	766
Number of KBs in 1975	74	18	90	490	33	75	57	22	14	39	57	18	989
Number of SBs in 1975	5	—	3	64	2	4	6	—	1	1	4	1	91
Number of PDBs in 1975	7	3	27	51	7	10	7	5	5	7	10	3	142
Number of farms (thousand, 1971)	215	172	169	270	223	191	222	200	153	167	179	194	2,355
Area of cultivated land (thousand ha, 1971)	380	581	540	1,074	921	782	479	674	632	727	898	806	8,494
Average farm size (ha)	1.8	3.4	3.2	4.0	4.1	4.1	2.2	3.4	4.1	4.3	5.0	4.2	3.6
Farms per RB (thousands)[b]	5.5	11.5	1.8	2.1	8.0	4.0	15.9	50.0	25.5	15.2	19.9	14.9	5.7
Cultivated land per RB (thousand ha)[b]	9.7	38.7	5.8	8.3	32.9	16.3	34.2	168.5	105.3	66.1	99.8	62.0	20.6

Regions

I	Ilocas	IV	Southern Tagalog
II	Cagayan Valley	V	Bicol
III	Central Luzon	VI	Western Visayas
VII	Central Visayas	X	Northern Mindanao
VIII	Eastern Visayas	XI	Southeast Mindanao
IX	Western Mindanao	XII	Southwest Mindanao

[a] The actual number of RBs in 1968 was 411. However, two were created by merger. They are treated as four separate banks to preserve consistency of the data

[b] Calculated using the number of RBs in 1968 and the data for 1971 on farms and cultivated land. In 1980, 332 RBs were located in regions III and IV (CL & ST) and 700 in the other regions. Data on the number of farms and cultivated area are not available for 1980. Using the number of farms and cultivated area in 1971 and the number of RBs in 1980, there were 1,493 farms with 5,882 cultivated hectares per RB in the CL & ST area and 2,941 farms with 9,091 cultivated hectares (about 35 square miles) in other regions

Sources: Number of RBs is from various issues of the *Annual Report on Rural Banks*; other data are from *Action Program* 1977

Table 14.3:   Mobilization of private funds by old and new RBs, by region

(a) $(\Delta D + \Delta E)$/number of RBs (thousand pesos)

Age of bank	Time period	CL & ST	Others	Total
O	1958–63	479	229	356
	1963–68	474	205	472
N	1963–68	305	205	270

(b) $\Delta D/(\Delta D + \Delta E)$ (percentage)

Age of bank	Time period	CL & ST	Others	Total
O	1958–63	80.6	70.6	77.5
	1963–68	85.6	77.0	83.1
N	1963–68	71.5	54.6	66.9

(c) D/number of accounts (pesos)

Age of bank	Year	CL & ST	Others	Total
O	1958	211	147	191
	1963	269	228	256
	1968	259	226	249
N	1963	251	128	205
	1968	237	191	225
Y	1968	182	258	207

D = saving deposits; E = common stock

Source: *Annual Report on Rural Banks* 1959, 1964, 1968

market roads that are impassable during parts of the rainy season (World Bank 1976: 182). This also helps explain the one possible anomaly: young RBs in the other regions had an average deposit size as high as that for old RBs in the CL&ST region.

This analysis suggests a general pattern in the mobilization of financial resources: as RBs have become established, the source of funds generally has shifted from equity to deposits, and from large to small depositors.

RBs draw funds from three other ways in which potential depositors can hold financial assets: cash, nonagricultural investments (including commercial bank deposits), and capital involved in traditional agricultural lending. In addition, banks seek to have depositors reinvest earnings, and increase their savings rate.

Which of these sources of funds is mobilized is important. Thus, Tobin and Brainard (1963) emphasize that the mobilization of cash has the greatest impact on the enonomy. It directly increases the supply of investment capital (several-fold with fractional reserves), and thus lowers the required return on investment. To the extent commercial bank deposits are shifted to RBs, there is a shift of real resources from large-scale nonagriculture to small-scale agriculture.

It is difficult to say anything definite about the sources of deposits, but what data there are suggests cash has been the principal one. This is reached largely by elimination. The growth rate of commercial bank deposits has not fallen when RBs have been established in an area, as one would expect if funds were being shifted. Deposits are not attractive to traditional lenders, as the returns are so much lower. Therefore, when the first RB opens in an area, the accumulated cash of small savers is the only place initial deposits can come from. This is also the impression of the rural bankers I interviewed in October 1981. The pattern of later accounts tending to be smaller suggests as the RB becomes accepted in the community, the poorer members are willing to trust their cash to it. Once the one-time effect of depositing cash hordes has been exhausted, deposit growth must come from increased savings or institutional changes, such as enforced usury laws, flushing traditional lenders into becoming bankers or depositors.

Equity for RBs has come mainly from nonagriculture. Most stockholders are businessmen, lawyers, professors, doctors, and government officials (Ishikawa 1970), presumably investing from commercial bank deposits or current savings. Government regulation prohibits a single family from owning more than 35 percent of an RB at the time it is established. Sources of RB funds are summarized in tables 14.4 and 14.5. The relative size of lending and of deposits of RBs and commercial banks are compared by region in table 14.6.

Table 14.4: Percentage distribution of rural bank liabilities, 1955–80

			Capital accounts	
Year	Deposits	Borrowings[a]	Common stock	Others[b]
1955	8.9	11.4	38.0	35.4
1960	32.8	14.9	27.4	19.9
1965	28.2	24.4	18.9	24.7
1970	39.7	25.0	14.4	20.1
1975	24.7	54.2	8.0	7.5
1980	30.8	50.6	7.3	6.3

[a] Almost all from the Central Bank
[b] Almost all government-held nonvoting preferred stock

Source: Annual Report on Rural Banks 1980

Table 14.5: Philippine Central Bank credit to rural banks, 1970-80[a]

Year	CBCI outstanding	CBCI held by KBs	Borrowings of RBs	Total resources of RBs
1970	68	–	164	655
1971	422	293	202	784
1972	957	418	331	983
1973	2,641	1,620	545	1,383
1974	4,582	2,200	1,024	2,111
1975	7,111	3,372	1,490	2,749
1976	8,141	3,919	1,532	3,018
1977		5,232	1,581	3,328
1978		6,909	1,938	4,037
1979		6,888	2,401	4,921
1980		6,170	2,797	5,524

CBCI are Central Bank certificates of indebtedness

[a] In million pesos

Source: Central Bank Statistical Bulletin various years

Looking at data for the entire banking system, there is a flow of funds through commercial banks into Metro Manila from the rest of the country. To offset this, the government channels funds to RBs through CBCI (central bank certificates of indebtedness). Commercial banks are required to devote at least 25 percent of their resources to agriculture, either as direct lending or by buying CBCI. Most buy CBCI, receiving 8 percent interest. The money is lent to RBs at 3 percent.

Most of the funds available to commercial banks to buy CBCI are from the nonagricultural sector, so the program is a subsidized transfer between the sectors. Nonagriculture is also heavily subsidized, directly and indirectly. Nevertheless, excluding all subsidies, it is possible that there is a net flow of funds into agriculture. This seems particularly likely for sugar (an export crop) and livestock and poultry (for urban consumption), which offered good returns at least in the 1970s.

When commercial banking began in Japan, initial deposits and equity can be considered to have come from the cash holdings of merchants and landlords. Most of the cash was in the hands of merchants, who had accumulated it during the fifty years of inflation that began around 1820 (see Teranishi 1982: ch. 3). The change in composition of private assets is shown in table 14.7.

Agriculture was a net borrower from the national banking system until around 1900, in all regions of the country. In the 1880s, much of the net lending

Table 14.6: **RBs and KBs compared (at the end of 1980)**

	CL & ST			Others	Total
	Total	*Metro Manila*	*Other*		
(1) Lendings and investments					
(2) RBs (million pesos)	2,008	112	1,895	2,692	4,699
(3) KBs (million pesos)	36,883	34,019	2,864	12,456	49,684
(4) RBs/KBs (percentage)	(5.4)	(0.3)	(66.1)	(21.6)	(9.4)
(5) Deposits					
(6) RBs (million pesos)	983	105	878	716	1,699
(7) KBs (million pesos)	26,120	23,048	3,072	9,073	35,414
(8) RBs/KBs (percentage)	(3.8)	(0.5)	(28.6)	(7.9)	(4.8)
(9) = (2)/(6)	2.04	1.07	2.16	3.76	2.77
(10) = (3)/(7)	1.41	1.48	0.93	1.37	1.41

Metro Manila is one of the ten administrative regions that replaced the twelve regions used during most of this study. It was part of Central Luzon, and covers the city of Manila's metropolitan area

Source: Various Central Bank material, including unpublished data on KBs

was by the former ruling elite, who had received government bonds commuting the annual stipends they previously had received. No artificial measures were taken to promote the flow; it simply followed the rule of profit maximization. In both the Philippines and Meiji Japan, traditional moneylending decreased as financial institutions developed. However, because the data for agricultural lending in the Philippines include processors and large plantations, it is difficult to say just how much less dependent small farmers are on traditional sources.

Government Policy

While Philippine RBs have continued to be dependent on subsidized government credit, first as equity and now as rediscounts and CBCI, Japanese banks became steadily less dependent. Philippine government policy has been to aid small farmers, and this has required subsidies. Part of the motivation is to prevent political unrest, and after martial law was imposed in 1973, Central Bank credits to RBs increased substantially. The government says this was coincidence; there were destructive floods in central and southern Luzon in 1972. There is also a fundamental economic reason.

The growth of RBs and improvements in rural life have been the result of moving cash hordes into RBs and of Central Bank credits. The interest-rate regulation accompanying this has made the mobilization of nonagricultural financial resources more or less artificial. These two processes have limits, and thus cannot be used indefinitely to increase the supply of funds available for investment.

Recently the Central Bank has encouraged RB-credits aimed at technical progress in farm production. These programs are supervised by government

Table 14.7: Percentage composition of private assets, Japan, 1874–1915

Year	Cash	Deposits	Insurance and trust funds	Securities
1874	75.1	1.9	–	23.0
1875	71.9	1.5	–	26.6
1876–80	47.4	2.7	–	49.9
1881–85	29.9	12.4	0.0	57.6
1886–90	21.6	18.6	0.1	57.5
1891–95	21.1	20.9	0.2	51.7
1896–1900	15.6	26.2	0.5	50.2
1901–05	10.3	30.6	0.9	47.1
1906–10	8.0	33.9	1.1	43.2
1911–15	6.2	33.5	1.9	42.6

Source: Teranishi 1982

officials, equipped with detailed procedural manuals. There is also discussion of integrating programs that finance agricultural diversification, and removing the requirement RBs specialize in servicing small farmers and rural businesses.

In July 1981, controls were removed on deposit interest rates, allowing them to float. The Meiji government in Japan also allowed floating rates, which contributed to deposit growth. It is not clear whether the policy will work in the Philippine RB case, given the fragility of the rural economy and the lack of infrastructure.

The Role of Government Credit in Japan

There was a close relationship between fiscal and credit policy in Meiji Japan. The process of establishing a modern financial system was closely entwined with establishment of the governmental fiscal system and the extent of the government's budget surplus or deficit. However, development of the fiscal system was usually given priority over the financial system (see Teranishi 1982: ch. 2).

At least ex post facto, government credit policy was remarkably consistent. Price (the interest rate) was the principal tool for changing credit supply. At first, funds were available at almost no cost. Subsequently these programs were replaced with credit sources at higher interest rates. The initial supplying of cheap funds made banking highly profitable, inducing the establishment of a large number of banks. Patrick (1966) has treated this as one component in a supply-leading approach to financial development: the government promotes banking services ahead of demand.

Government credit is composed of national bank-note issue, government deposits, and central bank loans, and, as used here, refers to all credit from monetary authorities, including the central bank. Data on these three components are given in table 14.8. Government bonds in bank asset portfolios are not subtracted, because I assume they are held as investments on their own merit and not as the result of guidance from government authorities. The Bank of Japan (the central bank) did not hold reserves for deposits or bank-note issue during this period.

Under the National Bank Act of 1876, a national bank could issue bank notes up to 80 percent of its equity capital, and the 20 percent reserve could be held in government paper currency rather than specie. Moreover, government bonds, including pension bonds issued to the deposed ruling elite, could be used for 80 percent of equity. It is reasonable to classify the right to issue currency, normally reserved for the government and central bank, as a form of government credit, the equivalent of an interest-free loan. This was a major part of government credit in the first half of Meiji (Patrick 1966 and 1967). The 1876 Act made banking a very lucrative business and the number of national banks increased from 4 in 1875 to 151 in 1879. Following revision of the National Bank Act in 1883, national bank notes were gradually redeemed.

Table 14.8: Percentage composition of government credit to the private banking system, Japan, 1874–1912

Time period	National bank notes (1)	Borrowing from the Bank of Japan (2)	Government deposits (3)
1874–78[a]	38.7[b]	11.7[c]	49.6
1879–82	84.9	2.9[c]	12.5
1883–87	75.7	7.5[c]	16.8
1888–92	36.4	40.9	22.6
1893–97	17.9	69.2	13.0
1898–1902	0.4	87.0	12.8
1903–07	0.0	86.8	13.2
1908–12	0.0	82.3	17.7

Before 1887, only national banks; after 1888, all banks

For the period 1888–92, government credit to quasi-banks is assumed to be zero

All figures are based on annual averages

After 1888, borrowing from the Bank of Japan is the sum of lendings to the private sector and special loans for national bank note redemption, as compiled by Goto (1970: table 88(1))

[a] At the end of June

[b] Based on amount of national bank notes actually in circulation

[c] Based on figures of borrowings from the liability side of the national bank balance sheets, composed of loans from the government and from other banks, including the Bank of Japan following its establishment; in principle, loans from other commercial banks should be excluded

Sources: Goto 1970; annual issues of *Ginko Kyoku Nanpo*

Deposits by the government were another important form of government credit. They did not receive interest; in fact, fees were paid for such services as transfers. Most national and large private banks were heavily dependent on these deposits, especially initially. In 1875, they comprised 30 percent of national bank deposits, and 56 percent for the Yasuda Bank. For Mitsui Bank, they were 40 percent in 1880 and 20 percent in 1891, which reflects the gradual reduction of deposits in the hands of the private banking system as time went on. One of the original purposes of the Bank of Japan was to serve as a repository for government deposits, and as a fiscal agent.

The Bank of Japan (BOJ) became an important source of funds soon after its founding. At first some of the loans were interest-free, with the rest at relatively low rates. It was thus profitable for banks to lend borrowings from the Bank of Japan, a practice called margin banking (*sayatori ginko*). The banks became quite reliant on BOJ loans, and this became a serious policy issue in the late

1890s, when the authorities tried to decrease dependence on government credit. In 1897, BOJ began direct loans to private business, and after 1899 these loans bore the same interest rate as loans to banks. Bank dependence on BOJ loans decreased rapidly thereafter.

Government credit can be considered a form of subsidy. In 1880, the government had provided 49 million yen, interest-free. The cost of the funds as deposits, using 6 percent, meant a 2.9 million yen subsidy. For comparison, industry received explicit subsidies of 2.6 million yen. Besides the financial subsidy, the very extension of government credit to banks enhanced public confidence in these new institutions.

Meiji banking is a story of the creation of a self-sustaining banking system through manipulation of government credit. A more important factor in the development of deposit banking, however, was the growth of the corporate business sector and the development of a close relationship between banks and businesses (see Teranishi 1982: ch. 1). The financial intermediation role of banking became substantial only after 1895, when the larger part of bank liabilities had become private deposits. Table 14.9 shows the changes in composition of Japanese bank liabilities.

The gradual withdrawal of government credit had its own set of effects. As demonstrated econometrically in the appendix my conclusion is that the policy of gradually decreasing government credit was effective in bringing about deposit banking, by making it more profitable for banks to see deposits by offering higher interest rates.

Appendix: The Effects of Withdrawing Government Credit

To test the conclusion, it is restated as two hypotheses: (1) the withdrawal of government credit caused a rightward shift of the deposit-supply function of banks; and (2) through market forces, the equilibrium quantity of deposits was increased as government credit decreased. (The deposit-supply function measures the amount of deposits banks want against the interest rate they will pay for that amount; a rightward shift means the banks are more willing to pay higher interest to get a given level of deposits.)

The rightward shift represents a substitution of deposits for government credit in the subjective equilibrium of banks. This can easily be demonstrated. Assume a bank maximizes its profits subject to its balance-sheet constraint; this can be written as:

$$\pi = rL - iD - c_1(L, X) - c_d(D, X)$$

where π is profits, r is the rate of return on L (loans and other invested assets), and i is the rate of interest on D (deposits); c_1 and c_d are administrative cost

Table 14.9: Percentage composition of bank liabilities, Japan, 1874–1913

Year	Private deposits	Government credit	Paid in capital and reserves	Year	Private deposits	Government credit	Paid in capital and reserves
1874	24.0	56.2	19.8	1896	41.2	22.6	36.2
1875	19.3	51.3	29.4	1897	46.5	19.4	34.1
1876	28.6	41.7	29.7	1898	49.3	15.0	35.7
1877	7.3	30.3	62.4	1899	54.3	14.6	31.1
1878	9.5	41.2	49.3	1900	53.8	12.0	34.2
1879	12.8	42.0	45.2	1901	55.6	6.8	37.6
1880	12.0	40.8	47.3	1902	59.4	5.6	35.1
1881	13.4	41.0	45.6	1903	61.3	4.9	33.9
1882	12.9	41.0	46.2	1904	61.2	6.9	31.9
1883	16.3	39.0	44.8	1905	62.9	8.7	28.4
1884	13.6	38.8	47.7	1906	69.6	6.7	23.7
1885	19.0	35.5	45.5	1907	65.1	8.2	26.7
1886	21.6	34.9	43.5	1908	65.6	5.7	28.7
1887	22.4	34.4	43.2	1909	69.2	3.4	27.5
1888	24.2	32.5	43.3	1910	68.6	5.7	25.7
1889	25.3	30.7	44.0	1911	68.1	6.6	25.3
1890	26.2	29.0	44.8	1912	67.9	6.8	25.3
1891	27.6	26.8	45.7	1913	68.8	5.4	25.9
1892	32.6	23.5	43.9				
1893	36.4	25.1	38.6				
1894	39.4	22.9	37.7				
1895	43.2	23.6	33.3				

Source: Teranishi and Patrick 1978: 354, where this is graphed as figure 1

functions for L and D, respectively; X is a market-size index, on which cost is dependent. The balance-sheet constraint is:

$$L = D + G + E$$

where E is the bank's equity capital and is constant.

Assuming the linear homogeneity of c_l and c_d with respect to their variables, we can reformulate the problem as:

$$\text{maximize } \frac{\pi}{X} = rl - id - c_l(l) - c_d(d)$$

subject to $l = g + d + e$, where

$$l = L/X, \quad g = G/X, \quad d = D/X, \quad e = E/X, \quad c_l = \bar{c}_l/X, \quad \text{and} \quad c_d = \bar{c}_d/X.$$

It is reasonable to assume the derivatives c'_l, c'_d, and c''_d are greater than zero, and c''_l is greater than or equal to zero. The first-order maximization is given by:

$$r - i - c'_l - c'_d = 0$$

Differentiating with respect to g yields:

$$-1 \leqslant \frac{\partial d}{\partial g} = \frac{-c''_l}{c''_l + c''_d} \leqslant 0 \quad \text{and} \quad 1 \geqslant \frac{\partial l}{\partial g} = \frac{c''_d}{c''_l + c''_d} \geqslant 0$$

Thus, an increase (decrease) in g causes a decrease (increase) in deposit supply by banks and a less-than-proportionate increase (decrease) in loans. In a perfect deposit market (in the sense of a constant marginal cost of deposits),

$$\frac{\partial d}{\partial g} = -1 \quad \text{and} \quad \frac{\partial l}{\partial g} = 0$$

which means in this polar case that a change in g is completely substituted for by a change in deposit supply, without any effect on loans.

The second part of the hypothesis – the substitution between government credit and private deposits in the market equilibrium – is not so easily demonstrated, as it requires, at the least, a general equilibrium analysis of asset markets, which I have undertaken elsewhere (see Teranishi 1982). However, the main point can be understood by reference to figure 14.1.

The larger the shift of deposit supply (the more perfect the deposit market), the larger the amount of deposits in equilibrium. The condition of a market-determined deposit interest rate is crucial to this analysis. If the rate is regulated,

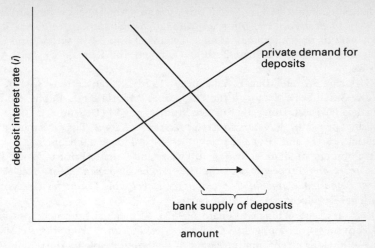

Figure 14.1:   The effect on deposits of a decrease in *G*

and set below its competitive equilibrium level, the equilibrium amount of deposits is determined irrespective of deposit-supply conditions. In other words, banks simply accept (supply) deposits up to the amount demanded at the ceiling rate. In this situation, there is no substitutability between deposit supply and government credit, and thus government credit cannot be manipulated to affect bank deposit supply. Changes in credit are simply reflected in changes in bank loans and other investments.

References

Action Program (1977), (Republic of the Philippines) Presidential Committee on Agricultural Credit, *Financing Agricultural Credit, The Action Program*, Manila.

Annual Report on Rural Banks, prepared by the Central Bank of the Philippines.

Goto, Shinichi (1970), *Nihon no kinyu tokei*, Tokyo: Toyo Keizai Shimposha.

Ishikawa, Shigeru (1970), *Agricultural Development Strategies in Asia*, Asian Development Bank.

Kikuchi, Masao, L. Banbo, and Yujiro Hayami (1977), "Evolution of the Land Tenure System in a Laguna Village," International Rice Research Institute, paper no. 77(11).

Patrick, Hugh (1966), "Financial Development and Economic Growth in Under-developed Countries," *Economic Development and Cultural Change*, 14: 174–89 (January).

Patrick, Hugh (1967), "Japan 1868–1914," in Rondo Cameron, ed., *Banking in the Early Stages of Industrialization*, New York: Oxford University Press.

Presidential Committee on Agricultural Credit (Republic of the Philippines) (1981), *A Study on the Informal Rural Financial Markets in Three Selected Provinces of the Philippines*, Manila: Technical Board for Agricultural Credit.

Sai Jun Mei (1980), "Japanese Trading Companies in Korea," *Chosun*, August: 70–88.

Saito, Katrine A., and Dan P. Villanueva (1978), "Transaction Costs of Credit to the Small-Scale Sector in the Philippines," World Bank, Public and Private Finance Division, Domestic Finance Studies, no. 53 (December).

Teranishi, Juro (1982), *Nihon no Keizai Hatten to Kinyu*, Tokyo: Iwanami.

Teranishi, Juro, and Hugh Patrick (1978), "The Establishment and Early Development of Banking in Japan: Phases and Policies Prior to World War I," in *Papers and Proceedings of the Conference on Japan's Historical Development Experience and the Contemporary Developing Countries*, Tokyo: International Development Center of Japan.

Tobin, James, and William Brainard (1963), "Financial Intermediaries and the Effectiveness of Monetary Controls," *American Economic Review*, 53: 383–400 (May); reprinted in *Essays in Economics*, vol. 1, Amsterdam: North Holland (1971).

World Bank (1976), *The Philippines: Priorities and Prospects for Development* (a World Bank Country Study), Washington, DC: World Bank.

Yamaguchi, Kazuo, et al. (1974–75), "Mitsui bussan kabushiki kaisha hyakunen-shi," mimeographed, Tokyo.

Yamamura, Kozo (1976), "General Trading Companies in Japan — Their Origins and Growth," in Hugh Patrick with Larry Meissner, eds, *Japanese Industrialization and its Social Consequences*, Berkeley, CA: University of California Press.

Yamazawa, Ippei, and Hirohisa Kohama (1978), "Trading Companies and the Expansion of Japan's Foreign Trade," in *Papers and Proceedings of the Conference on Japan's Historical Development Experience and the Contemporary Developing Countries*, Tokyo: International Development Center of Japan.

15 Philippine Private Domestic Commercial Banking, 1946-80, in the Light of Japanese Experience

HUGH PATRICK and HONORATA A. MORENO

Introduction

The Philippines represents a fascinating case of the complex evolving interactions between the financial system and the economic development process. However, the causal relationships between the two are obscure: financial and other data are not available; and differences between appearance and reality abound. We focus on the development of the private domestic commercial banking system from independence in 1946 to 1980, in the light of Japan's historical experience.

Although a few banks had been established in the colonial period, independence inaugurated a new era in financial development. The major policy-induced changes in financial structure and liberalization of interest rates in 1980, and the structural effects of the unexpected and generally unrelated financial crisis of 1981, may herald the beginning of a new era in Philippine financial development.

As in other nations, commercial banks play a key role in Philippine financial development. Our main emphasis is the evolving structure of the banking system in the context of its dynamic, but rather unstable and uneven growth. We are concerned both with issues of industrial organization – the nature of competition, the structure of ownership, the degree of specialization of function, relations with borrowers – and with bank performance. Of particular interest is the role of

We are indebted to various leading members of the public and private financial community for their insights provided in interviews, and to Lerma Moreno and Ellen Rose Payongayong for research assistance. We have benefited from discussions with Professor Edita Tan and her research on Philippine finance (see especially Tan 1979 and Tan et al. 1981). Patrick is mainly responsible for the interview data and the drafting of this essay, and Moreno for the tabular data. Financial support for this study was provided by the International Development Center of Japan through its Comparative Analysis Project.

The Philippine currency is the peso, abbreviated as P. in the text. The value of the peso against the dollar declined steadily in the 1970s, reaching about 7.5 pesos to 1 dollar in 1977.

banks as part of family-owned groups of companies, analogous to prewar Japan's *zaibatsu*. Government policy has been of paramount importance in shaping the structure and growth of the banking system, and indeed of specific banks. The government regulates entry requirements, types of financial services allowed, minimum capital requirements, and the like, and maintained nominal interest-rate ceilings on deposits and loans. Inflationary pressures in this restrictive policy environment substantially affected bank behavior and performance. Beyond this, government emphasis on import-substituting economic development has determined the overall economic environment.

This study is based on a variety of Philippine sources, published and unpublished. We have benefited from some access to materials of the Central Bank, Securities Exchange Commission, and other government agencies. We have learned much about the actual nature and behavior of the private commercial banking system through extensive interviews with experts in the financial community. The Philippines is a country where much is known by a relatively small elite, but little is published, particularly during the institution of martial law between September 1972 and January 1981.

Comparison with Japanese Financial Development

The development and growth of banking face common isues and problems in all market-oriented economies. As a former colony, the Philippine financial system has been based on the American model of specialized types of financial institutions engaged in a variety of specialized financial activities. Comparative analysis of the Philippine financial system and the commercial banking system has thus been mainly in terms of United States practice and experience. However, there are also substantial differences between the respective processes and patterns of economic and financial development. And, there are certain striking Philippine similarities with the financial development of Japan.[1]

Between 1868 and 1905, Japan experienced the initial creation and integration of a financial system under government sponsorship (termed supply-leading). From 1905 to 1937, development, growth, and increasing diversification of the financial system was in a relatively free market environment (demand-following). Throughout the prewar period, the family-owned industrial, financial, and commercial conglomerates (the *zaibatsu*) and their relations with large banks were increasingly significant.[2]

---

[1] Recently the IMF and World Bank staff have prepared a series of studies including the Philippines in comparative analysis of financial markets and institutions in developing countries; see, for example, Khatkhate and Villanueva (1979) and Saito and Villanueva (1978a).

[2] The dating of periods if somewhat arbitrary. For a more detailed discussion of the Japanese financial system from the 1880s to the 1970s, see Teranishi and Patrick (1977 and 1978), and Patrick (1967, 1980, and 1984).

In many respects, postwar Philippine financial and economic development is similar, with some time compression, to Japan's two prewar phases. The 1946–80 period may be divided into two sub-eras. The first two decades remind one of Meiji Japan in the ease of creating new banks and other financial institutions and consequent expansion in their numbers; the opting for specialized rather than general-purpose institutions; and government and central bank stimulus, including government deposits and other official credit. Since the mid-1960s, Philippine development is similar to Japan's second phase: the growing role of industrial activity; the rise in family-owned groups of companies; the growth and diversification of the financial system, even as financial dualism persisted, but decreased; bank runs, panics, and failures; efforts to strengthen the banking system by increasing minimum capital requirements, making new entry difficult, and encouraging bank mergers; and the development of fairly widespread branch banking on a national basis.

Still other features appear more like Japan's post-World War II phase – notably the significant amount of central bank credit directly to the banks; and the maintenance of low interest-rate ceilings which resulted, among other things, in a high concentration of Japanese major bank loans to large enterprises, some degree of erosion of national interest rates by compensating balances and other means, and retarded growth of the bond market. In contrast to the Philippines, financial intermediation has been quite successful in postwar Japan, *despite* the system of interest-rate controls, because the Japanese financial system was highly developed and its structure very stable, personal saving rates became extremely high, low-risk assets alternative to saving deposits were not readily available to the predominantly urban population, and business investment demand was far stronger than could be financed from internal or private sources.

The level of financial development in the Philippines, as measured by the ratios of financial assets to GNP and M_2 to GNP, in the late 1970s was below that of Japan at the turn of the century – although the levels of income per capita may have been roughly comparable. A major contrast is between Japan's prewar policy of free interest rates and market-clearing financial markets and the Philippine policy of regulated interest rates and credit rationing to clear markets. We hypothesize that this policy difference has been a major cause of lagging Philippine financial development relative to Japan's historical experience.

Comparison between earlier Japanese experience and the contemporary Philippine commercial banking system must be done flexibly. The Philippine era considered here combines both supply-leading and demand-following elements, and in some respects combines the experience of Japan's first two phases. In this spirit, Japan's successes and failures in financial policy and in the development of the financial system can provide insights for Philippine policy-makers. Further, as discussed below, the similarities between Philippine financial–commercial–industrial family groups and Japanese prewar *zaibatsu* are notable; their implications for financial and economic development are less clear, although certainly they have served to concentrate economic and political power.

Table 15.1:   Economic overview

(a)   Basic indicators

Population (millions, mid-1980)	49.0
Area (1,000 km^2)	300
GNP per capital (US dollars, 1980)	690
Growth rate per capita (real, average annual, percentage, 1960–80)	2.8
Inflation rate (average annual, percentage)	
1960–70	5.8
1970–80	13.2

(b)   Growth rates (real, average annual, percentage)

	1960–70	*1970–80*
Gross domestic product	5.1	6.3
Agricultural production	4.3	4.9
Manufacturing	6.7	7.2
Gross domestic investment	8.2	10.5
Merchandise trade		
Exports	2.2	7.0
Imports	7.1	3.4
Population	3.0	2.7

(c)   Structure of production and demand (share of GDP, percentage)

	1960	*1980*
Agriculture	26	23
Manufacturing	20	26
Consumption	84	75
Gross domestic investment	16	30
Gross domestic savings	16	25
Exports of goods and non-factor services	11	20

Source: World Bank 1982, *Annex*

The Financial Environment

The development of the financial system has been concomitant with that of the Philippine economy. Indicators of the performance of the Philippine economy are provided in table 15.1.[3]

[3] For good studies of Philippine economic performance, see Ranis et al. (1974), Bautista (1970), and Bautista and Power (1979), and the periodic publications ("Executive Briefing Pamphlets" and others) of the Center for Research and Communications, Manila.

Balance of payments problems and excessive rates of inflation, especially in the oil crises of 1974–75 and 1979–80, have on occasion forced the Central Bank to take restrictive credit policies which have resulted in very tight domestic financial markets (Bautista 1980). While production, finance, and financial institutions occur throughout the Philippines' many islands and their major regional subcomponents, the predominance of Metro Manila is striking. This highly congested metropolitan area contains 13 percent of the nation's population, yet produces one-third of the gross national product, and contains more than half the nation's industrial activity. The bulk of commercial bank activities, including virtually all head offices, is in Metro Manila.

Over most of the postwar period the government has pursued an economic development strategy based mainly on import-substituting industrialization and the continued development of traditional exports, crops (sugar, copra, timber), and mining. In the early 1980s, the government began moving toward a more export-oriented industrialization policy. The degree of government intervention in the economy is substantial; instruments include direct controls (over imports, prices of key domestic consumption goods, interest rates), as well as subsidies and other preferences (such as credit allocation at low interest rates) to priority sectors and activities. These policies, together with fundamental features of the economy, such as surplus labor and capital market dualism, mean that relative prices for many goods and factors of production differ substantially from world prices or shadow prices in equilibrium.

The Group Form of Industrial Organization

One of the most important, and fascinating, aspects of Philippine economic structure is the group form of organization of large-scale business. The turbulent rise and spread of successive waves of Philippine groups over the past three decades is reminiscent of Japanese *zaibatsu* between the early 1900s and World War II. This "Japanese phenomenon" seems to be an important, if poorly studied, characteristic of the industrialization process in many developing countries.[4]

Typically, a group is owned by one family, often including various branches with different names; however, in the Philippines, some groups are owned and controlled by several closely associated individuals or families. Whether personally managed by members of the owning family or by hired professional managers, close personal relationships – based in part on ethnicity or region of birth – are a central feature of Philippine groups. Unfortunately even imprecise data about groups are scanty. One of the few quite open about its membership is the First

---

[4] Relatively few empirical studies are available; the Nicaraguan case has been analyzed by Strachan (1976), Pakistan by White (1974), and Korea by Jones and Sakong (1980). Our study focuses on Philippine commercial banks and hence the operations of domestic groups. Many groups, especially the largest, have substantial ties with foreign firms, mainly based in the United States or Japan. For a description of Japanese involvement, as well as brief descriptions of most of the Filipino groups, see Tsuda (1978).

Holdings Group; it listed its member companies in newspaper advertisements in February 1980, giving information about telephone numbers and office location. This group was established in the early 1970s by taking over the operations and various subsidiaries of Meralco (Manila Electric Company) from the Lopez family.

There are alternative forms of group-centralization organizations: holding companies; operating conglomerates; management companies; or in-house management groups. In the Philippines, the predominant forms are management companies and in-house management groups. (For a brief description, including a listing of the top 13 management companies, see SEC-Business Day (1978: 173–81).)

SEC-Business Day (1978) has identified some 47 private business groups as of 1977. Doherty (1979) and (1980) has identified some 89 major individuals and families who form the basis of the main groups. By listing the interlocking directorates of banks and companies, he concludes that alliances comprising "ten groups connected with the commercial banks dominate the Philippine business world" (Doherty 1980: ch. 5). Some 23 of the 28 domestic commercial banks (including the two government commercial banks) are members of these ten groups. One problem with using interlocking directorships to define and classify groups, as Doherty recognizes, is that control cannot be inferred. However, it is reasonable to assume patterns and channels of cooperation, at the least.

The families and their economic groups are involved in a dynamic process. There have been several waves entering the oligarchy, and a few washed out The oldest and most established - such as the Zobel-Ayala and the Soriano - date back to the Spanish era. Others became important during the early American period. Still others emerged following independence, as the government encouraged import-substituting industrialization. And a new wave emerged under martial law in the 1970s. Before World War II, families were based mainly in agriculture, mining, and associated commerce, whereas more recently industry and finance have become important. Beginning with the Spanish, there has been a close, two-way relationship between economic and political power; government and big business (that is, major families) have been closely intertwined.

Doherty (1980, ch. 5) classifies the major families into three groups.

Among the 89 families, some exercise much greater control than others. Among these are the new elite who have risen to prominence since the declaration of martial law. They are Disini-Velayo, Benedicto, Conjuangco-Enrile, Silverio, Cuenca, Abello, Oreta, Tantoco, Ozaeta and Floirendo. . . . Others, though considered among the premartial law traditional elite, have also grown significantly under martial law due to connections. . . . Among them would be Sycip, Yuchengco, Yulo, Elizalde, Aboitiz, Alcantara, J. B. Fernandez, Nubla, Siguion-Reyna, S. Valdez, Palanca and Jose Concepcion.

There is a third group. They are also part of the old traditional elite.... Though they are still a significant group and in general have managed to hold their own under martial law, they have done so despite periodic harassment. This group would include such names as Soriano, Zobel-Ayala, J. A. Araneta, Cabarrus, J. P. Fernandez, Madrigal-Olondriz, C. Ledesma, Laurel and Ortigas. Though they may not be happy with developments at present, they know that if they express this unhappiness too freely, they can go the way of the Lopezes and find their investments expropriated.

The groups are important for our analysis because of their close, complex, rather heterogeneous sets of relationships with the commercial banks. These involvements can be viewed from the perspective of either the banking system or the group system. Some groups grew out of family-owned banks; others started banks; some have no direct ownership-control relationship. The 21 largest groups were affiliated with ten banks; five were identified as having no close bank affiliation. Several banks are identified with two or more groups, in particular Far East Bank and Trust Company (FEBTC). Almost all banks were started by one or two families; almost all those families appear in the list of 47 groups. Gregario Licaros, governor of the Central Bank at the time, may have been only mildly exaggerating when he said "the average Filipino banker is in the banking business not for banking profits; he uses his bank for allied business" (*FEER*, April 7, 1978: 80).

The Financial System

Table 15.2 provides a summary description of the organized financial system before the 1980-81 reforms had substantial effect.[5] As in the US, the system was founded on specialization: there were different types of financial institutions, under different laws and regulations, to meet specific financial functions. In practice, in both countries commercial banks, directly and through subsidiaries or affiliates, provide a wide range of services. Thrift banks collect savings and time deposits, and make commercial and mortgage loans; they have had no demand deposits. Rural banks collect time and saving deposits and make loans predominantly for agriculture. Mainly unit banks, they are widely dispersed throughout the country, are heavily subsidized by the Central Bank, and are little more than conduits for Central Bank and government credit. Their development resembles that of Japanese local banks initially (see chapter 14 above).

Government financial institutions are important; they hold about two-fifths of the total assets of the financial system. Their lending activities are widespread;

[5] Emery (1970), IMF/World Bank Mission (1979), and Tan et al. (1981) provide good general descriptions of the financial system. For more detailed quantitative data, see Hooley and Moreno (forthcoming), and the annual reports and other publications of the Central Bank of the Philippines. An important analytical review of the literature is provided by Tan (1979).

Table 15.2: The Philippine financial system: institutions and total assets

	1980 Head offices	1980 Total offices	Total assest 1974	Total assest 1980	Percentage of total assets 1974	Percentage of total assets 1980	Percentage ratio to GNP 1974	Percentage ratio to GNP 1980
Banking institutions	1,209	3,419	54,142.8	193,599.2	72.3	79.9	54.2	71.8
Commercial banks	32	1,501	42,424.8	144,428.0	56.7	59.6	42.5	53.5
Government[a]	2		13,154.3	41,395.0	17.6	17.1	13.2	15.3
Private domestic	26		23,133.0	84,275.1	30.9	34.8	23.1	31.2
Private foreign branches	4		5,605.4	18,730.9	7.5	7.7	5.6	6.9
Thrift banks	144	671	1,666.9	10,547.1	2.2	4.4	1.6	3.9
Private development banks	43	154	296.3	1,618.3	0.4	0.7	0.3	0.6
Savings and mortgage banks	10	266	1,159.9	7,352.6	1.6	3.0	1.2	2.7
Stock savings and loan associations	91	251	210.7	1,576.2	0.3	0.7	0.2	0.6
Rural banks	1,030	1,155	2,110.7	5,524.2	2.8	2.3	2.1	2.0
Specialized banks[a]	3	92	7,940.4	33,099.9	10.6	13.7	7.9	12.3
Development Bond of the Philippines[a]			6,758.0	27,088.0	9.0	11.2	6.7	10.0
Land Bank[a]			1,182.4	6,056.0	1.6	2.5	1.2	2.2
Philippine Amanah Bank[a]			—	—	—	—	—	—

Nonbank financial institutions	1,178	1,475	20,714.2	48,604.5	27.7	20.1	20.7	18.0
Investment houses	12	62	3,839.9	8,607.3	5.1	3.6	3.8	3.2
Finance companies	342	531	2,306.7	11,902.1	3.1	4.9	2.3	4.4
Investment companies	62	62	689.0	4,979.7	0.9	2.1	0.7	1.8
Securities dealers/brokers	141	141	882.1	1,035.5	1.2	0.4	0.9	0.4
Pawnshops	544	598	100.8	290.5	0.1	0.1	0.1	0.1
Fund managers	12	12	1,951.5	1,658.1	2.6	0.7	1.9	0.6
Lending investors	57	61	24.9	50.2	–	–	–	–
Nonstock savings and loan associations	72	72	71.2	299.4	0.1	0.1	0.1	0.1
Mutual building and loan associations	7	7	24.7	18.7	–	–	–	–
Private insurance companies			3,468.0		4.6		3.4	
Specialized nonbank[a]	4		7,355.4	19,763.0	9.8	8.2	7.3	7.3
GSIS (Government Service Insurance System)[a]			4,144.5	9,245.5	5.5	3.8	4.1	3.4
SSS (Social Security System)[a]			2,388.9	8,220.7	3.2	3.4	2.4	3.0
ACA (Agricultural Credit Administration)[a]			451.5		0.6		0.5	
NIDC (National Industrial Development Corporation)[a]			370.5		0.5		0.4	
Total			74,857.0	242,203.7	100	100	74.9	89.8

Commercial bank data by category are slightly different from the total, since the data are from a different source; accordingly ratios are slightly different as well

[a] Indicates government financial institutions

Sources: IMF/World Bank 1979: tables 1 and 2, commercial bank by category, appendix tables; Central Bank Factbook 1980: Philippine Statistical Yearbook 1981

they are heavily involved in lending to priority sectors, however defined. Most of their funds, including deposits, come from governmental sources. The main government institutions are the Philippine National Bank (PNB), the Development Bank of the Philippines (DBP), the Land Bank, the Government Service Insurance System (GSIS), and the Social Security System (SSS).

The Development Bank of the Philippines has a significant role, not just because of its size, but also because it has few substitutes. It provides 47 percent of the long-term loans and 15 percent of medium-term loans in the Philippines; 71 percent of its loans are to industry (IMF/World Bank 1979: 43–45). DBP is essentially a conduit for government domestic funds, and for loans from such international agencies as the World Bank and the Asian Development Bank.

The Philippine National Bank is by far the largest commercial bank; in 1980, it held 31 percent of the commercial banking system's assets and 16 percent of the entire financial system's assets. Established in 1916, it earlier had some Central Bank functions, including currency issue and acting as the fiscal agent for the government. In part because of overdue loans to government corporations, PNB was in serious trouble in the early 1970s. A special governmental study by the Joint IMF-CBP Banking Survey Commission concluded PNB should be assisted in order to "perform its role as a tool of government policy" (1972: 106). PNB plays "a special role not performed by private commercial banks, that of an instrument of national monetary policy. It is also called upon to finance highly risky ventures, to provide loans for food production, agricultural production, and industry, and to make loans to the government, its political subdivisions and instrumentalities" (ibid.: 105–6). Although the structure of costs and net returns on loans and investments evidently do not differ significantly from private commercial banks (Saito and Villanueva 1978a), PNB apparently lends particularly to those industrial groups which have risen in power over the past decade. It, together with the DBP, lent actively to them in 1981, and took substantial equity and operating control of a number of their companies in the 1981 financial crisis.

Commercial banks hold almost three-fifths of the assets of the financial system, a ratio comparable to Japan in the 1920s. The system has three elements: two government commercial banks; branches of four foreign banks (Citibank, Bank of America, Hong Kong and Shanghai Bank, and Chartered Bank); and 26 private domestic banks. The main focus of this study is the private domestic banks, which together comprise one-third of the entire financial system.

Citibank, with a long history in the Philippines, was second in size only to PNB until 1978; but by 1980 three private domestic commercial banks had more assets. Although foreign banks are not allowed to open new branches, they have been innovative in developing finance companies, leasing companies, and other financial subsidiaries. They have superior access to foreign funds within the policy constraints of swap limits set by the Central Bank. Generally subject to the same domestic regulatory environment as the private domestic banks, they are also subject to the US Foreign Corrupt Practices Act. They have tended to finance foreign trade, multinational companies, and the 300 largest industrial corporations.

Financial intermediation has grown over time, absolutely and, more importantly, relatively. Assets of the entire financial system were 48 percent of GNP in 1960, 72 percent in 1970, 86 percent in 1977, and 90 percent in 1980.[6] Similarly, relative to GNP, the total assets of commercial banks were 16 percent in 1950, 17 percent in 1960, 34 percent in 1975 and 52 percent in 1980; their time and saving deposits relative to GNP rose similarly, but less sharply – from 4 percent in 1950, 7 percent in 1960, 13 percent in 1970, 12 percent in 1975, to 23 percent in 1980. Demand deposits moved erratically downward, from 8 percent in 1950, 6 percent in 1960 and 1970, to 5 percent in 1980. The substantial difference between asset and deposit ratios reflects the use of deposit substitutes, Central Bank credit, and foreign-currency swap arrangements, as well as net worth. The ratios of commercial bank assets to GNP for Japan were substantially higher: 24.6 percent in 1885, 34.6 percent in 1900, 53.1 percent in 1913, 63.7 percent in 1920, and 107.3 percent in 1930.

The Philippines now has a sophisticated system of commercial banks and other financial institutions, with highly sophisticated and responsive short-term money markets. The system is innovative and on the whole well-developed. Yet this is too sanguine. The financial system itself has been subject off and on to serious difficulties. Emery noted of the late 1960s, "the Philippines has probably had more financial scandals or financial institutions in distress than any other Southeast Asian country" (Emery 1970: 482). Problems were particularly severe in the 1960s and early 1970s, and again in early 1981. Open-end mutual funds were started, and then collapsed. A number of savings and loan associations, finance companies, insurance companies, and investment houses have been in trouble at one time or another. The commercial banking system has been particularly vulnerable and unstable, with several bank runs, and a few bank failures.

Perhaps more serious, the financial system has not developed fully or evenly, either in the provision of medium-to-long-term credit for investors or credit to small borrowers in agriculture, commerce, and industry. Financial dualism persists. The clearest indicators of this are in access to funds by category of borrower (such as the size or nature of enterprise), and differentials in interest rates on borrowed funds substantially in excess of administrative costs and default risks. Teranishi's research suggests government-subsidized credit programs have substantially reduced the role of traditional finance in agriculture (see chapter 14 above). However, most small-scale producers, especially outside agriculture, continue to rely on family, friends, moneylenders, and other traditional forms of credit. In Japan, financial dualism persisted, even as it diminished, until after World War II (Teranishi and Patrick 1977; Patrick 1982). The speed

[6] See IMF/World Bank Mission (1979: 1), table 15.2, and for 1970, Ranis et al. (1974: 229), (the latter has been adjusted to exclude Central Bank assets). The comparable ratios for prewar Japan were 37 percent in 1885, 64 percent in 1900, 110 percent in 1913, 133 percent in 1920, and 240 percent in 1930.

with which dualistic differentials decrease depends on interest-rate policies and on the development of a modern financial system.

The Role of the Monetary Authorities

The financial environment is very much determined by the policies and regulations of the monetary authorities, notably the Central Bank of the Philippines. Like central banks in many developing countries, it has three main goals. The first is the macro stabilization of the economy, using control of high-powered money, the money supply, credit availability, and interest rates. A second objective is long-run economic development. To this end, the Central Bank allocates credit to priority sectors through preferential terms (availability and low interest rates) for the rediscount of certain types of paper, restrictions on commercial bank portfolios, and provision of credit to government financial institutions, rural banks, and the like. The third objective is the healthy growth of the financial system and its constituent individual institutions through regulation, control, and inspection. Under the financial reforms proposed to the legislature in 1972 and subsequently implemented under martial law, a great deal of discretionary power devolved on the Central Bank.

One persistent feature of the past two decades has been the substantial amount of credit provided by the Central Bank to commercial banks through loans and rediscounts. This has its analogy in postwar Japan, where city banks engaged in substantial "overloan" from the Bank of Japan. Loans and rediscounts are part of a complex pattern of credit flows with the commercial banks, involving also reserve requirements, commercial bank purchase of Central Bank Certificates of Indebtedness (CBCIs, analogous to Treasury bills), and required holdings of governments bonds in asset portfolios.

One key issue has been the allocation of Central Bank credit, in its various forms, among the commercial banks. One important, and at times highly profitable, source of borrowed funds has been through swap arrangements. A commercial bank obtains a foreign-currency loan or deposit, converts the currency (typically dollars) into pesos, and purchases forward dollars at a favorable rate from the Central Bank. These transactions must be approved by the Central Bank. Control over large amounts of rediscounts and even modest amounts of swaps has been centralized at the highest levels; apparently Gregario Licaros, who headed the Central Bank until his resignation in early 1981, personally approved every swap transaction over $1 million. While stated criteria exist, the actual rules and procedures for allocation of credit have not been clear. The amounts obtained by individual banks have varied widely. Favoritism, rather than equal opportunity of access to Central Bank credit by objective criteria, seems important.

The type of interest-rate system – market-determined or controlled – has profound implications for implementation of stabilization policy, promotion of saving and channeling it to the most productive investment uses, and for the development of a healthy and effective financial system. The theoretical case for market-determined interest rates is strong. Nonetheless, one of the most important policies pursued by the Central Bank until 1981 was to set maximum interest rates on time and savings deposits, loans, discounts, and money-market instruments (deposit substitutes). A government study in 1972 made a sensible, sophisticated analysis of the problems caused by a system of rigid, low interest rates and the misallocations of credit that result, and made a strong argument for a flexible interest-rate policy (Inter-Agency Committee on the Study of Interest Rates, 1972: 17). Finally, in July 1981 such a policy was partially adopted. Until then, and exacerbated during periods of rapid inflation, the interest-rate ceiling had strongly negative effects on regular financial markets.

Market rates for loans and discounts were below ceiling rates until about 1960. Since then, however, it appears that most of the time the equilibrium rate has been higher than the ceiling for loans, and at times substantially higher. While data on profits and profitability of investment are poor, a real return of 15-20 percent seems likely (see Ranis et al. 1974; Tan 1979). However, with inflation accelerating in the 1970s, especially in the 1970-74 and 1979-80 periods, actual real return on deposits and some loans were lower, at times even negative (table 15.3).

The capital market has remained undeveloped, despite the early creation and active role of investment houses designed to make medium and long-term placements and to underwrite new securities issues. Although some 5,000 new companies register with the SEC (Securities and Exchange Commission) each year, virtually none are public. Only 58 of the top 1,000 industrial corporations are listed on stock exchanges, and a dozen of those listed issues are not traded. New issues do not average more than 30 per year. The stock market is small, natural-resource (oil and mining company) oriented, and speculative. Bond issues have been virtually non-existent in the erratically inflationary environment, and there is no secondary market.

Short-term financial markets for large transactions have been much more active. Philippine bankers, financiers, and big businessmen are very sophisticated. The gap between ceiling and market-equilibrium rates has been sufficiently large that considerable, at times unconventional, financial innovation has taken place in efforts to avoid or evade the official ceilings (Khatkhate and Villanueva 1979). It is impossible to obtain accurate, comprehensive data on effective interest rates. A probably reasonable generalization is that, particularly in periods of monetary tightness, virtually all private financial institution loans, except those either eligible for preferential rediscount or to related business interests, have been at effective interest rates above the ceiling. And large holders of financial assets have received yields substantially in excess of the maximums on deposits. (See Tan (1979: 49); for the only comprehensive empirical study of the Philippine money market, see Tan et al. (1981: ch. 7).)

Evolution of the money market has been in large part in response to interest-rate ceilings and Central Bank regulations. A liquidity tightness in the mid-1960s

Table 15.3: Inflation, interest rates and real interest rates

	Rate of inflation[a]	Savings deposits		Time deposits		Money-market rates[d]		Ceiling lending rate[e]	
		Interest rate[b]	Real interest rate[c]	Interest rate[b] (360 days)	Real interest rate[c]	Nominal interest rate	Real interest rate[c]	Nominal	Real
1959	−0.9	3.0	3.9	3.5	4.4			14	14.9
1960	4.2	3.0	−1.2	3.5	−0.7			14	9.8
1961	1.6	3.0	1.4	3.5	1.9			14	12.4
1962	5.8	3.0	−2.8	3.5	−2.3			14	8.2
1963	5.6	3.5	−2.1	4.5	−1.1			14	8.4
1964	8.2	3.5	−4.7	4.5	−3.7			14	5.8
1965	2.6	4.0	1.4	5.0	2.4			14	11.4
1966	5.4	5.75	0.35	6.5	1.1			14	8.6
1967	6.3	5.75	−0.55	6.5	0.2	11.6	5.3	14	7.7
1968	2.4	5.75	3.35	6.5	4.1	12.1	9.7	14	11.6
1969	2.0	6.0	4.0	7.0	5.0	13.7	11.7	14	12.0
1970	14.3	6.0	−8.3	7.0	−7.3	13.6	−0.7	14	−0.3

Year								
1971	14.7	6.0	−8.7	7.0	−7.7	12.7	−2.0	14	−0.7
1972	10.3	6.0	−4.3	7.0	−3.3	14.3	4.0	14	3.7
1973	11.0	6.0	−5.0	7.0	−4.0	9.2	−1.8	14	3.0
1974	34.5	6.0	−28.5	9.5	−25.0	17.6	−16.9	14	−20.5
1975	8.2	6.0	−2.2	9.5	1.3	15.0	6.8	14	5.8
1976	6.1	7.0	0.9	10.0	3.9	12.9	6.8	14	7.9
1977	7.9	7.0	−0.9	10.0	2.1	12.6	4.7	14	6.1
1978	7.6	7.0	−0.6	10.0	2.4	10.7	3.1	14	6.4
1979	18.8	7.0	−11.8	10.0	−8.8	12.9	−5.9	16	−2.8
1980	17.8	9.0	−8.8	14.0	−3.8	13.3	−4.5	16	−1.8

[a] Measured by changes in the consumer price index
[b] Rates offered by commercial banks; rates by other financial institutions were generally 0.5 percent higher since July 29, 1974
[c] The real interest rate is defined as the nominal interest rate minus the rate of inflation
[d] These are the published rates; actual rates are considerably higher. In relatively thin markets, interest rates fluctuate widely; for this reason monthly averages, much less the annual average given in this table, are somewhat misleading
[e] The maximum rate for unsecured loans under the Usury Law until repealed, then Central Bank ceiling

Sources: IMF/World Bank 1979: tables 13, 31; Tan 1979: tables 6, 7; Central Bank *Statistical Bulletin* and *Philippine Financial Statistics*

led to the emergence of a commercial paper market (though not called that) with higher interest rates than on deposits. To compete, banks began issuing bankers' acceptances, trust certificates, repurchase agreements, and other deposit substitute instruments. Deposit substitutes flourished; with effective interest rates up to 30 percent, depending on market tightness, they amounted to some four-fifths of time and savings deposits by 1974–75 (IMF/World Bank 1979: 26, 61). It should be noted that commercial bank reliance on money-market instruments as a source of funds vitiates the significance of M_2 (as traditionally defined) as a measure of financial development.

Dynamic, Unstable Growth of the Private Domestic Banking System

Despite a long history, the commercial banking system has grown rapidly, albeit turbulently, only since the mid-1950s. Postwar development until 1980 can be divided at 1965, when new entry was discouraged. The number of banks quadrupled between 1950 and 1965.

Over the period there were several bank runs, which were relatively well contained by the Central Bank. Between 1968 and 1977, three banks failed, but all later reopened under new names and management; various others have been in trouble from time to time, two or three almost perennially. In response to the increase in capital requirements to P.100 million in 1973, in 1974–76 some thirteen banks merged (into six) and eight took in foreign partners. Between 1975 and 1978, three other banks changed ownership and their names were altered. In 1980, there were several further changes in ownership and, in 1981, additional mergers as the new era dawned – in part, in response to new opportunities for large-scale (universal) banking, in part, in response to the banking crisis of spring 1981. This history is briefly summarized in table 15.4, which lists all the banks of the postwar period and ranks them by size of assets as of 1980.

The 1946–65 period can be characterized as follows. Entry into commercial banking was easy and encouraged. Minimum capital requirements were low; the monetary authorities in effect subsidized the banks through government deposits, later withdrawn, and cheap Central Bank credit. The economy was going through import-substituting industrialization. Wealthy families began to move into industrial activities, and they recognized the benefits of controlling a bank. In other instances a banking family moved into industry. Almost all bank owners are involved in one of the industrial groups. This is not surprising. Capital is needed to start a bank; perhaps equally important were built-in depositor and lending relationships. As a consequence, between 1950 and 1955, five new banks were established; between 1955 and 1960, four; and between 1961 and 1965, some eighteen.

By the mid-1960s, the monetary authorities were concerned about the small size of banks, mismanagement, and the possibility (and actuality) of bank runs and financial crisis – concerns continuing to this day. The authorities essentially prohibited new bank entry, raised minimum capital requirements from P.8 million to P.20 million in 1965, and then to P.100 million in the 1973 reforms, and from 1973 have encouraged bank mergers and the inflow of foreign equity capital.

Despite the scandals and difficulties, Philippine banking history between 1965 and 1980 is less turbulent than that of Japan in the 1920s. Japan faced essentially the same problems, and also restricted entry, raised capital requirements, and forced mergers. The Philippines has not had a banking crisis as severe as that of Japan in 1927. It is unclear in the 1965–80 period whether the net flow of Central Bank credit was to or from the private commercial banks. It is clear that Central Bank credit was increasingly distributed differentially – not just to weak banks in periodical or perennial trouble, but also to favored stronger banks.

The 1970s was a period of shake-out and consolidation, much like Japan in the late 1920s and early 1930s. This process continues in the early 1980s. Of the 33 private commercial banks operating in 1973, 13 merged between 1974 and 1976, mainly in response to the fivefold increase in minimum capital requirements. Two involved large banks, BPI and PCIB, absorbing small banks. In two instances, Filmanbank (now Filipinas) and Associated Citizens, merger did not bring substantially improved performance.

Although a number of banks have been in sufficient difficulty to require emergency loans from the Central Bank, only three have been closed by the Central Bank: the Overseas Bank of Manila in August 1968, the Continental Bank in June 1974, and the General Bank and Trust Company (Genbank) in March 1977. All three subsequently reopened, albeit under new names and owners. These cases provide insights into the instability of the system. While not among the top banks in size, none was among the smallest. Lack of capital *per se* did not cause failure. The common pattern was one of bank owners making short-term loans to finance fixed (long-term) investments in affiliated companies, as well as unsecured loans to themselves. In some cases, there were other financial irregularities, but it is not clear whether they were the main cause of failure. In each instance, there was a heavy run on the bank when it became known some of the affiliated companies were in difficulty.

The failure of Continental in 1974 was particularly dangerous, because it precipitated a run on the entire system. Continental Bank was borrowing deposit substitutes heavily in the money market, and lending long-term through its affiliate Continental Finance to other business affiliates and to finance real-estate projects. When the bank's President was arrested and charged with alleged misappropriation of deposits and other financial irregularities, an immediate run on Continental Bank ensued and the Central Bank closed it. Concerns about the Continental failure spread to other banks; deposits started moving to the four foreign bank branches. The Central Bank averted a crisis by making emergency loans and assuring the financial community that it would cover all problems of liquidity drain.

Table 15.4: The private domestic banks: establishment, assets, branches, group affiliation

Name of bank (by size of total assets), 1980	Common abbreviation	Bank history	Controlling group (latest available data)	Foreign equity		
				Name of foreign investor	Equity (percentage)	Nationality
1 Allied banking Corporation	Allied	Takeover of assets and liabilities of General Bank & Trust Co.; opened June 1, 1977 after Genbank was declared insolvent and ordered closed by the Central Bank on March 25, 1977	Lucio Tan Willy Co			
General Bank & Trust Company	Genbank	Established September 7, 1963	Clarencio Yujuico	Grindlays (subsequently sold)	40.0	UK
2 Bank of the Philippine Islands	BPI	Established August 1, 1851; merged with People's Bank May 20, 1974	Ayala-Zobol	Morgan Guarantee Trust Co. (New York)	20.6	American
People's Bank & Trust Company	People's	Established November 1, 1926	J. Antonio Araneta			
3 Metropolitan Bank & Trust Company	Metrobank	Established September 7, 1962	George S. K. Ty			
4 Republic Planters Bank	RPB	Formerly Republic Bank; name changed after equity acquired by sugar bloc May 16, 1978	(Elizalde) Benedicto			
Republic Bank	Republic	Established January 5, 1961	Pablo Roman, Chairman			

5	Philippine Commercial & Industrial Bank	PCIB	Merger of PCIB, Merchants Banking Corporation and Philippine Bank of Commerce, March 23, 1976; PCIB established February 8, 1960	First Holdings		
	Merchants Banking Corporation	Merchants	Established September 3, 1963	Ruffino		
	Philippine Bank of Commerce	Commerce	Established July 8, 1938	Juan Cojuangco		
6	United Coconut Planters Bank	UCPB	Formerly First United Bank; name changed to UCPB August 12, 1975 after the Philippine Coconut Producers Federation acquired equity in the bank pursuant to Presidential Decree no. 755	Ramon Cojuango		
	First United Bank	FUB	Established May 16, 1963	Jose Cojuangco		
7	Far East Bank & Trust Company	FEBTC	Established April 4, 1960	Jose B. Fernandez, Jr. Barcelon Gokongwei Yulo Palanca Quimson Bancom Soriano Trinidad Sixto Roxas	Chemical Bank of New York	12.6	American
					Mitsui Bank of Japan	12.6	Japanese

Table 15.4 continued

Name of bank (by size of total assets), 1980	Common abbreviation	Bank history	Controlling group (latest available data)	Foreign equity		
				Name of foreign investor	Equity (percentage)	Nationality
8 Traders Royal Bank	Traders	Formerly Traders Commercial Bank; name changed to Traders Royal Bank, April 1, 1974 after Royal Bank of Canada acquired equity in the bank	Benedicto Africa	Royal Bank of Canada (subsequently sold)	30.0	Canadian
Traders Commercial Bank	Traders Commercial	Established June 18, 1963	Jose Africa, Chairman Montelibano			
9 Rizal Commercial Banking Corporation	RCBC	Established January 20, 1963	Yuchengco Valdez Siguion-Reyna SyCip Tantoco	Continental International Financial Corp. Ltd.	30.0	American
				Sanwa Bank of Japan	10.0	Japanese
10 China Banking Corporation	China	Established August 16, 1920 Reopened July 23, 1945	Deck-Chiong SyCip	Sanwa Bank of Japan	33.0	Japanese
11 Pacific Banking Corporation	Pacific	Established June 23, 1955 Merged with Progressive Commercial Bank, December 24, 1975	Babst Chua			
Progressive Commercial Bank	Progressive	Established May 3, 1962	Pastor Endencia Jorge Araneta			

12	The Manila Banking Corporation	Manilabank	Established January 20, 1961	Cabarrus Jose P. Fernandez Puyat			
13	Consolidated Banking Corporation	Solidbank	Established July 19, 1963	Madrigal			
14	Equitable Banking Corporation	Equitable	Established September 20, 1950	Trinidad Tomulo	Citibank	40	American
15	Philippine Bank of Communications	PBCom	Established September 4, 1939	Nubla-Ang Beng Uh			
16	Insular Bank of Asia and America	IBAA	Merger of Bank of Asia and First Insular Bank of Cebu, January 1, 1974	Kalaw	Bank of America (subsequently sold)	21.6	American
					Dai-ichi Kangyo Bank	10.0	Japanese
	Bank of Asia	Asia	Established October 15, 1963	Kalaw			
	First Insular Bank of Cebu	First Insular	Established January 23, 1961	Avoitiz			
17	Security Bank & Trust Co.	Security	Established June 18, 1951	Cy, Ang	The Bank of Nova Scotia	29.5	Canadian
18	Commercial Bank & Trust Co.	Comtrust	Established September 20, 1954	Ayala (purchased from Marquez)	The Chase Manhattan Bank, N.A. (subsequently sold)	30.0	
19	Philippine Banking Corporation	Philbanking	Established September 2, 1957	Laurel Ortigas-Villanueva			
20	Prudential Bank	Prudential	Established July 2, 1952	Santos			

Table 15.4 continued

Name of bank (by size of total assets), 1980	Common abbreviation	Bank history	Controlling group (latest available data)	Foreign equity		
				Name of foreign investor	Equity (percentage)	Nationality
21 International Corporate Bank	Interbank	Formerly Continental Bank Reopened September 19, 1977	Herdis Group			
Continental Bank	Continental	Established April 17, 1963, its closure was authorized by the President of the Philippines upon Central Bank recommendation on June 24, 1974 with takeover of its assets by the Central Bank	Munoz, Chairman			
22 Associated Citizens	Associated Citizens	Merger of Associated Banking Corp. and Citizens Bank, October 14, 1975	Leonardo K. Ty			
Associated Banking Corporation	Associated	Established February 8, 1965	Ty. Recto			
Citizens Bank & Trust Company	Citizens	Established October 4, 1962	Arambulo, President			
23 City Trust	City Trust	Formerly Feati Bank & Trust Co.	Madrigal Brimo	Citibank	32.3	American

	Feati Bank & Trust Company	Feati	Established November 7, 1961	Araneta
24	Producers' Bank of the Philippines	Producers	Established July 6, 1971	Co Bun Chun Henry L. Co.
25	Filipinas	Filipinas	Merger of Filipinas Bank and Manufacturers Bank December 29, 1975; name changed May 7, 1980 from Filipinas Manufacturers	Silverio; PNB majority shareholder from 1980
	Filipinas Bank & Trust Co.	Filipinas	Established October 5, 1964	Echaus, Chairman
	Manufacturers Bank & Trust Co.	Manufacturers	Established August 30, 1957	De las Alas, Chairman
26	Philippine Trust Company	Phil. Trust	Established June 1, 1964	Emilio Yap Ramos
27	Overseas Bank of Manila	Overseas	Established January 6, 1964 under Central Bank supervision starting November 1967 until operations suspended by CB Monetary Board August 1, 1968	

Sources: SGV annual *Study of Commercial Banks in the Philippines; Central Bank Factbook; The Philippine Financial System 1978*, 4th Q. Dosdos, Eisogio; SGV 1976; SEC-Business Day 1978; Lava 1976; Doherty 1979

Bank Typologies

The banks can be classified by distinctive economic, sociological, political, and institutional features. Table 15.5 groups them by management style and type of ownership. The foreign bank branches are generally regarded as the most professionally, and best, managed. They, especially Citibank, have been a training ground for young Filipinos who have subsequently moved into domestic bank management. Some family-managed banks are well managed, so inclusion in any particular category is not direct evidence on bank management.

Classification by ownership type is common in the Philippines. The main distinction is between banks controlled by indigenous Filipinos and by Filipino-Chinese. Almost all the joint-venture banks are in fact controlled domestically; foreign ownership is limited to 40 percent. Although Chinese ownership is involved in two of the joint-venture banks (RCBC and Security), neither is classified as typically Chinese.

Since there are considerable differences in the degree to which Chinese individuals and families have been integrated into the mainstream of Philippine life and culture, classification as Chinese is somewhat arbitrary. The stereotype is a bank started and owned by Chinese, receiving most of its deposits from Chinese people and companies, lending mainly to Chinese individuals and their companies, conservative in both assets and liability management, and unwilling to use much Central Bank credit. Within the Chinese business community, a good word-of-mouth reputation for creditworthiness is essential. It is not possible to provide quantitative evidence regarding the stereotype; it certainly does not apply equally to all the banks under Chinese-Filipino ownership.

The 1973 reforms made it possible for foreign banks to invest in domestic banks for the first time since 1947. Foreign investment was limited to a maximum of 40 percent, of which only 30 percent could be held in voting shares by one foreign owner. The liberalization was designed to attract foreign equity and loans, while retaining domestic control. Eight banks took foreign partners (table 15.4), for various motives (Lava 1976: 35–39). The record of these alliances is mixed. In six cases, the major foreign bank subsequently pulled out, usually by selling to the domestic owners. Foreign involvement appears to be extensive only in Citytrust, infused by Citibank with able staff and good banking practices. Though small, Citytrust is regarded as one of the best-managed banks.

Another classification is in terms of closeness to the present government. The phrases "political banks" or "quasi-governmental banks" are used, but their meaning is not entirely clear, and it is not possible to determine the precise operational significance of this classification. Those in control of these banks are typically members of the "new elite" of groups. Data on relationships and degree of closeness are not readily available; certainly it varies by bank. The main criterion is that each is under the effective control of persons close to the present government. In most instances, control passed to members of the "new

Table 15.5: Private commercial banks classified by management style and type of ownership, 1978

Management style[a]	Ownership type
Owner-managed	Anakbayan[b]
Associated Citizens	Comtrust[g]
China Bank	Filmanbank[g]
Equitable	Interbank[f]
Filmanbank	Manilabank
Philbanking	Philbanking
Phil. Trust[f]	PCIB[f]
Producers	Prudential
Prudential	Traders Royal[e, f, g]
Republic Planters[e]	Solidbank
Traders Royal[e]	
UCPB[e]	Filipino–Chinese
	Allied[f]
Intermediate	Associated Citizens
Allied	China Bank
Comtrust	Equitable
IBAA	Metrobank
Interbank	Pacific
Manilabank	PBCom[f]
Metrobank	Producers
Pacific	
PBCom	Joint ventures[c]
Security	BPI
	Citytrust
Professional management	FEBTC
BPI	IBAA[g]
Citytrust	RCBC
FEBTC	Security[g]
PCIB	
RCBC	Quasi-governmental[d]
Solidbank	Republic Planters[e, f]
	UCPB[e, f]

[a] This is a loose classification indicating roughly the degree to which the bank is managed in a traditional, often family style by owners, by professional managers hired by the owners, or in some intermediate position

[b] "The Anakbayan banks ... are where the Filipino families can trace their heritage and families way back" in the Philippines

[c] Banks which have a minority foreign ownership; China Bank and Equitable also have foreign participation (see table 15.6)

[d] This heading considers Republic Planters Bank and the United Coconut Planters Bank as quasi-government banks, apparently due to their sources of funds

[e] Apparently controlled by a single individual

[f] "Political banks," considered close to the government

[g] Remaining foreign interest subsequently sold

Sources: The "management style" classification is based on interviews in 1979 and 1980. Some informed observers would place certain banks in a different category. Ownership type: Katigbak, "3 Classes of Banks," *Times-Journal* April 2, 1979

elite" during the 1970s. Republic Planters and UCPB are special cases of private ownership with special monopoly powers. Each is involved heavily in the finance of a traditional export crop – sugar and coconut respectively – and each, rather than the Treasury, receives as deposits the export levies on these crops (Tan et al. 1981: 40–41).

The Structure of the Commercial Banking Industry

One striking feature of the Philippine banking system is the widely differential performances of banks – in growth, in profitability, in changes in relative position. Data are presented in table 15.6.

The concentration ratio in terms of the asset share of the top five private domestic commercial banks has been remarkably constant, around 35 percent since the mid-1960s. However, this is not a good measure of market power, because it excludes PNB, which is larger than the five private banks combined, and the four foreign banks. PNB, the five largest private domestic banks, and the two largest foreign bank branches (Citibank and Bank of America) together had 56 percent of total commercial bank assets in 1980.

More important, market shares and relative rankings have changed dramatically over time. Only one (BPI) of the top five banks in assets in 1965 was in the top five in 1980, and only four of the top ten. China Bank declined significantly, from first to tenth. Four increased their relative position sharply, from the bottom third to top positions including Allid (the successor of Genbank) from twenty-fourth to first and Metrobank from twenty-first to third. Republic Planters declined sharply over most of the period, but rebounded under its new "quasi-governmental" status in the late 1970s.

The coefficient of rank correlation between bank size and profitability (as of 1979) is 0.67, not particularly high. Of the six banks in the top quartile in profitability, two are also in the top quartile in both asset and deposit growth – UCPB and Metrobank. UCPB is a special case, since it receives low-cost deposits from the copra levies. Metrobank has expanded its branches aggressively, evidently with considerable success. Neither relied particularly heavily on Central Bank rediscount or swap facilities. Interestingly, the four top-rankers in profitability had below-average growth both of assets and deposits. Their performance may well be explained by a combination of careful management policy and limited growth possibilities in their traditional market areas.

In several instances, the Central Bank has successfully restored troubled banks to reasonably good operations without closing them, by changing management and providing bridging credit. However, a few banks remained chronically weak. The Central Bank has preferred to keep them afloat, rather than forcing closure and thereby possibly causing a bank panic. Filmanbank, one of the weaker, was finally taken over by PNB, which provided it with an infusion of capital, management, and a Central Bank emergency loan. Associated Citizens has also been regarded as weak, due to poor profit performance and ongoing managerial problems between its two ownership groups.

Four banks grew particularly rapidly from 1965 to 1980: Allied, Metrobank, UCPB, and RCBC. Four banks grew particularly rapidly between 1974 and 1980: again Allied and UCPB, and also Republic Planters (RPB), and Traders Royal. Neither merger nor foreign-capital partners were of lasting importance. Beyond that, few generalizations are possible. Metrobank, Chinese-Filipino owned, has quietly, but steadily grown over the years, has expanded branches rapidly, has been very profitable, and has not been closely involved with the government. RCBC, owned by the Yuchengco family, had its main growth spurt from 1965 to 1973, when an innovative management worked closely with the investment house Bancom. Conflict in 1973 between the bank owners and the Bancom group ended the connection, but RCBC has continued to do well under professional management.

The other four banks that have grown rapidly are all in the political bank category. As already noted, UCPB and Republic Planters benefit from special privileges. Traders Royal has combined exceptionally rapid deposit and asset growth, moving from among the smallest to eighth rank. Its profit record, poor overall, improved significantly between 1978 and 1980. Little is known about its sources of deposits or its clients, but it is not highly regarded by the financial community.

The most remarkable success story in the late 1970s was Allied Bank. Allied has risen like the legendary phoenix from the ashes of Genbank, which was closed in March 1977. The Central Bank found in Lucio Tan (chairman) and Willy Co (vice-chairman) new owners able and willing to infuse large amounts of capital, and to assemble a vigorous management team headed by an experienced banker, Romeo Co. Apparently Tan, of Fortune Tobacco, is the dominant owner. Not earlier identified as one of the 48 major groups, Tan has risen to considerable prominence since 1977. The Central Bank, with P.310 million in advances to Genbank, continued a strong package of support. Allied has grown remarkably rapidly. In just two and a half years, it became the largest private domestic commercial bank.

Allied has been aggressive in opening branches and seeking new business clients for loans, in part by highly competitive lending terms. It concentrates particularly on medium-size businesses – not the SEC-Business Day top 300, but the next 700. It has been highly responsive to the incentives built into government programs to provide funds for priority uses. But this is not the full story. Considerable interest has focused on how Allied has been able to raise substantial funds so quickly. One answer is that it has had great access to Central Bank credit (see table 15.7). At the end of 1978, Allied had outstanding P.889 million in loans and advances from the Central Bank, nearly twice that of the second largest borrower. This was equivalent to 24 percent of Allied's total assets, and 321 percent of its net worth. Moreover, it had P.665 million in foreign-currency

Table 15.6: Bank assets, liabilities, deposits and net worth: amounts and rank, selected years

(a) Total assets

Name of bank	Rank					Amount (in million pesos)				
	1980	1978	1973	1968	1965	1980	1978	1973	1968	1965
Private domestic										
1 Allied	1	3				7,256.9	3,709.3	670.5		
Genbank			14	26	24				93.8	55.9
2 BPI	2	1	2	4	4	6,441.7	4,442.0	1,262.2	398.9	221.5
People's				14	10				190.6	141.4
3 Metrobank	3	2	8	16	21	5,506.4	4,072.8	883.0	173.1	64.4
4 RPB	4	23				4,880.5	745.4			
Republic			19	13	5			270.9	224.8	219.8
5 PCIB	5	5	1	3	2	4,781.2	3,236.4	1,307.8	448.3	298.8
Merchants			20	25	29			269.5	95.0	35.4
Commerce			18	11	9			440.4	236.2	159.0
6 UCPB	6	4				4,644.9	3,436.9			
FUB			21	21	20			228.6	103.3	77.8
7 FEBTC	7	6	9	10	14	4,344.7	3,202.3	861.1	238.4	108.8
8 Traders Royal	8	16	29			3,757.9	1,801.8	136.5		
Traders (Commercial)				28	23				81.3	57.9
9 RCBC	9	7	3	20	25[a]	3,720.1	3,092.3	1,153.3	113.4	51.9
10 China	10	8	4	1	3	3,541.8	2,814.8	1,122.1	505.3	287.4
11 Pacific	11	9	10	9	12	3,344.7	2,544.4	801.9	263.8	129.6
Progressive			30	31	31			75.3	66.1	32.1

#	Bank									
12	Manilabank	12	7	15	17	3,204.4	2,207.0	969.1	183.5	101.1
13	Solidbank	10	6	7	19	2,978.7	2,524.2	1,005.9	269.5	78.7
14	Equitable	11	5	2	1	2,889.7	2,443.6	1,022.4	467.3	310.4
15	PBCom	18	16	8	7	2,744.6	1,410.3	501.8	265.6	179.9
16	IBAA	15	15		7	2,720.3	1,114.4	638.1		
	Asia			22	25[a]				102.5	51.9
	First Insular			23	26				101.6	47.0
17	Security	19	17	12	11	2,587.2	1,369.4	500.7	228.0	140.3
18	Comtrust	13	11	6	8	2,412.7	1,984.9	703.4	274.1	163.8
19	Philbanking	14	13	17	13	2,203.8	1,952.6	690.8	146.5	116.5
20	Prudential	17	12	5	6	2,177.5	1,603.8	700.2	324.7	210.7
21	Interbank	21				1,641.4	976.3			
	Continental				28				78.0	45.4
22	Assoc. Citizens	20		29		1,624.4	1,110.3			
	Associated	25	25	24	30			188.1	100.4	32.2
	Citizens	24	24	27	22			195.0	89.5	61.4
23	Citytrust	22	22	30	27	1,481.7	824.2	228.4	68.3	46.5
	Feati		23					211.9		
24	Producers	25	23			1,416.7	682.0			
25	Filmanbank	24				1,053.8	709.7			
	Filipinas		28	32	32			158.2	52.6	17.3
	Manufacturers		27	18	18			164.7	146.1	85.3
26	Philtrust	26	26	19	15	917.4	561.0	173.4	140.9	103.7
	Overseas				16					103.2
	Total private domestic					84,275.1	55,272.2	17,535.2	6,271.9	3,837.0

[a] The total assets of RCBC and Asia were equal

Table 15.6 continued

(b) Total liabilities

Name of bank	Rank				Amount (in million pesos)			
	1980	1978	1973	1968	1980	1978	1973	1968
Private domestic								
1 Allied	1	3			6,801.9	3,423.4		
Genbank			14	25			625.6	80.1
2 BPI	2	1	9	4	5,924.3	4,041.3	695.5	345.6
People's			17	14			417.1	167.4
3 Metrobank	3	2	7	16	5,152.5	3,837.8	826.4	157.5
4 RPB	4	13			4,628.4	653.0		
Republic			21	12			241.3	209.9
5 PCIB	5	5	1	3	4,398.8	2,997.7	1,213.0	381.3
Merchants			22	26			240.2	78.4
Commerce			19	11			403.7	210.9
6 UCPB	6	4			4,136.0	3,109.9		
FUB			24	23			203.2	84.7
7 FEBTC	7	6	8	10	4,016.1	2,944.9	759.5	214.2
8 Traders Royal	8	15			3,552.1	1,663.8		
Traders (Commercial)			32	28			113.8	68.6
9 RCBC	9	7	2	20	3,472.3	2,891.3	1,093.2	97.8
10 China	10	8	3	1	3,159.4	2,526.2	990.7	433.2
11 Pacific	11	9	10	8	3,125.3	2,372.8	733.9	236.4
Progressive			33	31			51.3	54.6

12	Manilabank	12	6	15	2,945.9	2,009.3	904.5	162.2
13	Solidbank	10	4	6	2,716.5	2,298.1	929.2	244.6
14	Equitable	11	5	2	2,544.3	2,175.8	918.9	419.2
15	PBCom	18	15	9	2,482.7	1,224.2	452.6	235.4
16	IBAA	16			2,455.8	1,611.6		
	Asia		20	22			340.1	86.4
	First Insular		23	21			238.9	80.0
17	Security	19	16	13	2,405.2	1,210.4	447.7	199.4
18	Comtrust	13	12	7	2,217.7	1,800.8	639.3	243.7
19	Philbanking	14	13	18	2,029.1	1,794.8	627.5	125.0
20	Prudential	17	11	5	1,977.3	1,426.7	639.7	287.3
21	Interbank	21			1,492.1	864.2		
	Continental		18	29			413.1	61.6
22	Assoc. Citizens	20			1,472.8	974.9		
	Associated		28	24			157.5	83.1
	Citizens		27	27			167.2	74.1
23	Citytrust	22			1,307.3	696.4		
	Feati		25	30			197.5	55.0
24	Producers	25	26		1,241.4	546.7	172.8	
25	Filmanbank	24			732.1	617.4		
	Filipinas		31	32			136.2	42.0
	Manufacturers		29	17			146.6	129.9
28	Philtrust	26	30	19	742.4	424.8	142.2	118.3
	Overseas							
	Total private domestic				77,281.3	50,146.6	16,274.9	5,477.8

Table 15.6 continued

(c) Total deposits

Name of bank	Rank					Amount (in million pesos)				
	1980	1978	1973	1968	1965	1980	1978	1973	1968	1965
Private domestic										
1 Allied	1	7				4,647.8	2,733.6			
Genbank			17	22	28			143.2	51.8	33.4
2 BPI	2	1	1	3	3	3,948.0	3,001.4	913.9	303.9	174.7
People's				13	11				123.5	77.3
3 Metrobank	3	3	9	15	18	3,559.9	2,616.0	473.2	104.5	39.1
4 RPB	15	23				1,518.5	313.6			
Republic			19	14	6			160.0	110.0	104.9
5 PCIB	6	4	5	5	4	2,758.5	2,142.3	586.7	223.6	155.0
Merchants			18	23	31			157.3	48.9	12.2
Commerce			13	10	8			249.7	154.1	92.4
6 UCPB	4	2				3,188.1	2,733.6			
FUB			21	21	21			143.2	51.8	33.4
7 FEBTC	5	5	8	12	14	2,922.7	1,889.7	475.0	130.0	58.1
8 Traders Royal	7	12				2,654.0	1,293.8			
Traders (Commercial)			28	31	22			39.2	18.8	30.4
9 RCBC	8	8	4	24	29	2,390.7	1,517.2	611.5	48.4	17.1
10 China	14	11	6	1	2	1,689.2	1,317.9	491.0	324.8	194.8
11 Pacific	9	10	10	9	13	2,363.8	1,351.7	472.1	157.2	66.8
Progressive			29	32	30			35.2	18.6	14.9

12	Manilabank	10	13	11	17	16	2,173.8	1,261.6	434.8	94.8	50.4
13	Solidbank	11	6	2	6	17	2,086.9	1,778.1	666.8	170.7	50.1
14	Equitable	12	9	3	2	1	1,818.4	1,460.5	636.4	309.4	229.1
15	PBCom	18	19	18	7	7	1,336.5	575.7	162.5	166.2	103.0
16	IBAA	19	17	13			1,332.6	878.4	319.3		
	Asia				28	27				37.2	19.0
	First Insular				19	23				78.5	28.2
17	Security	15	18	16	11	10	1,666.9	710.2	244.0	139.6	80.7
18	Contrust	13	14	12	8	9	1,769.7	1,257.1	350.5	163.5	86.1
19	Philbanking	20	16	14	18	15	1,215.6	910.0	275.6	82.7	56.9
20	Prudential	17	15	7	4	5	1,370.9	1,089.7	478.8	227.9	135.8
21	Interbank	23	26				581.5	231.6			
	Continental				27	25				37.6	22.1
22	Assoc. Citizens	21	20				842.6	504.4			
	Associated			26	25	32			73.1	42.1	8.2
	Citizens			25	29	24			77.9	33.5	24.7
23	Citytrust	24	22	22	26	26	531.5	369.6	105.1	38.1	20.8
	Feati										
24	Producers	22	25	30			599.4	264.5	27.8		
25	Filmanbank	26	21				387.6	383.3			
	Filipinas			27	30	33			63.8	27.0	6.7
	Manufacturers			24	20	20			89.9	62.1	36.7
26	Philtrust	25	24	23	16	12	519.6	311.2	91.1	101.4	73.5
	Overseas					18					38.6
	Total private domestic						49,031.2	31,888.4	9,143.3	3,681.4	2,159.2

Table 15.6   continued

(d) Total net worth

Name of bank	Amount (in million pesos)					Rank				
	1965	1968	1973	1978	1980	1965	1968	1973	1978	1980
Private domestic										
1 Allied				276.9	455.0				4	3
Genbank	12.0	13.7	44.9			20	27	17		
2 BPI	33.8	53.3	149.6	400.7	517.4	3	3	1	1	1
People's	23.5	23.2				8[a]	13			
3 Metrobank	8.0	15.6	45.5	234.9	353.9	28	23	14	8	6
4 RPB				92.4	252.1				25	14
Republic	26.9	14.9	29.6			6	26	23		
5 PCIB	45.8	67.0	94.8		382.4	2	2	5	7	4
Merchants	11.1	16.6	29.3	238.7		22	19	24		
Commerce	22.4	25.3	36.7			9	10	19		
6 UCPB				327.0	508.9				2	2
FUB	16.4	18.6	25.4			15	27	26		
7 FEBTC	17.1	24.2	101.6	257.4	328.6	13	12	4	6	8
8 Traders Royal				138.0	205.8				19	17
Traders (Commercial)	8.4	12.7	22.7			27	29	29		
9 RCBC	10.5	15.6	60.1	201.0	247.8	23	24	12	11	15
10 China	48.7	72.1	131.4	288.6	382.4	1	1	2	3	5
11 Pacific	18.2	27.4	68.0	171.7	219.2	12	9	7	16	16
Progressive	6.9	11.5	24.0							
12 Manilabank	15.5	21.3	64.6	197.6	258.5	16	16	8	12	12
13 Solidbank	12.9	24.9	76.7	226.1	252.2	19	11	6	9	13
14 Equitable	32.7	48.1	103.5	267.8	345.4	4	4	3	5	6

15 PBCom	11	13	16	7	7	261.9	186.1	49.2	30.2	23.9
16 IBAA	10	10	13			264.5	202.8	59.1		
Asia				22	21				16.1	11.2
First Insular				30	29				11.6	7.9
17 Security	20	17	15	8	10	182.0	158.9	53.0	28.6	21.5
18 Comtrust	19	14	9	6	8ᵃ	195.0	184.1	64.1	30.4	23.5
19 Philbanking	23	18	10	15	14	174.7	158.3	63.3	21.5	16.8
20 Prudential	18	15	11	6	5	200.2	177.1	60.5	37.4	28.7
21 Interbank	26	24				149.3	112.1			
Continental				20	25				16.4	9.9
22 Assoc. Citizens	25	21				151.6	135.4			
Associated			22	18	24			30.6	17.3	10.3
Citizens			25	25	18			27.8	15.4	13.2
23 Citytrust	24	23	21			174.4	127.8	30.9		
Feati			28	28	26			39.1	13.3	8.8
24 Producers	21	22				175.3	135.3			
25 Filmanbank	9	26				321.7	92.3			
Filipinas			30	32	31			22.0	10.6	6.5
Manufacturers			20	21	17			23.1	16.2	14.1
26 Philtrust	22	20	20	14	11	175.0	136.2	31.2	22.6	18.7
Overseas										18.7
Total private domestic						6,993.8	5,125.2	1,673.4	794.1	604.5

ᵃ The net worths of People's and Comtrust were equal

Sources

Data for 1980: *Central Bank Factbook* 1980: 40
Data for 1978: *Central Bank Factbook* 1978: 40
Data for 1973: SGV 1974: tables G, H; SGV 1973: tables O_1–O_3
Data for 1968: SGV 1969: tables E, F; SGV 1968: tables O_1–O_3
Data for 1965: SGV 1966: tables F and K

swaps, equivalent to 18 percent of its total assets, 36 percent of its total deposits, and 240 percent of its net worth. Central Bank support was undoubtedly essential in 1977 to ensure Allied's solid beginning. The support was received in 1978 and 1979 went far beyond those requirements, and was also substantially above average rediscount privileges relative to paid-in capital and priority program loans.

How do the profitability and growth indicators of differential bank performance compare with the managerial, ownership, and political criteria discussed earlier? Three of the six banks identified as professionally managed are in the top six in profitability, but two are below average. Of the three banks in the top quartile in profitability, growth of assets, and deposits – UCPB, Metrobank, and FEBTC – one is in each management category. At the other extreme, four of the six least profitable banks were in the owner-managed category. No clear association between management style and performance emerges.

For the eight political banks, the record is mixed, but on average favorable. Half are in the top half ranked by profitability. But five are in the top six in assets growth, and four in the top six (and six in the top eight) in deposits growth. UCPB and Allied have done extremely well by all criteria. Only PCIB ranks in the bottom quartile in profitability and growth.

Thus, there is no single, or simple, explanation for the large differences in growth rates and profit rates among banks. Size is no answer; some small banks do very well, some large banks do poorly. Good aggressive, innovative management – whether professional or family – obviously has been important; but it is difficult to obtain independent measures of management capabilities. Membership in the "new elite" has benefited some banks. Success has been achieved by several routes.

Commercial Bank Assets and Liabilities

As discussed above, commercial banking has grown rapidly, but there have been wide differences in the performances of individual banks. In this section, we look more closely at the banks' management of their liabilities and assets. The focus is the decade of the 1970s, and the way banks have responded to external opportunities (such as Central Bank credit or swaps) and constraints (such as interest-rate ceilings). Detailed portfolio data by bank are not available.

Bank Liabilities Management

The essence of commercial banking is the acquisition of deposits and deposit-substitutes from private sources, and the lending or investing of those funds. Financial intermediation occurs most effectively through leverage.

In 1980, the average net worth of banks was 8.5 percent of total assets. On average, about 94 percent of total liabilities (excluding net worth) have been either deposits or borrowed funds. Borrowings include Central Bank rediscounts and advances as well as private funds. With occasional specific exceptions, deposits by the government in the private commercial banks have been negligible in the 1970s. Foreign-currency swaps also enter the deposit base.

Reflecting the growth and relative decline of deposit substitutes, the share of deposits in total liabilities has ranged widely over time for the system and for some banks. The average ratio for all banks in 1980 was 63 percent, indicating considerable reliance on borrowed funds. Some banks have developed strong deposit bases – BPI especially, but also Solidbank, Prudential, Metrobank, and (based on the copra levy) UCPB. The average varies substantially by bank, with no clearly discernible explanation, except that banks regarded as weak have a higher proportion of demand deposits.

A basic liabilities management choice is the extent to which a bank relies on borrowed funds, which are a quick, easy way to growth. However, borrowed funds have been substantially more costly than deposits, because their market is competitive, while the ceiling on deposit interest rates constituted a subsidy by depositors to bank stockholders. Only when the marginal effective lending rate (adjusted for risk) is higher than the deposit substitute rate is it profitable for banks to borrow. Moreover, deposit substitutes may be more volatile, with shorter effective maturity, which makes them a riskier source of funds. The most profitable banks are divided almost equally between those relying substantially more or substantially less than average on borrowed funds; one strategy has not clearly dominated the other.

The Central Bank's stated rule has been to allow discount of eligible paper up to 50 percent of paid-in capital, plus paper eligible under Central Bank priority allocations (exports, small business, agriculture, etc.). Because the spread between the rediscount rate and the banks' effective lending rate has been substantial, one would expect that, in the absence of informal rules, all banks would continuously borrow almost to their limit. In practice, that has not been the case; table 15.7 provides the available data for the end of 1978, 1979, and 1980.

During the years 1978–80, provision of Central Bank credit was somewhat greater than the net worth of the banking system (table 15.7). This lending has been more than double the regular ceiling; special rediscounting for priority or other purposes was of greater importance than general rediscounting. What is startling is that seven banks in at least one of these three years had borrowings more than double their net worth, and three for all three years. Republic Planters is a special case, because it could rediscount its sugar bills, its main business.

A similar pattern of great variance appears in swap arrangements. For the 1978–80 period, swaps were slightly more important than Central Bank loans and advances; they financed about 12 percent of bank total assets. Seven banks had access to swap facilities in excess of their net worth in 1978, and fourteen in 1980. Not all banks with large Central Bank borrowings had large swap arrangements. Adding swaps and loans, reliance on Central Bank-related credit

Table 15.7:   Commercial bank reliance on Central Bank credit and swap arrangements (outstanding balances, December 31, 1978, 1979, 1980)

Name of bank	Central Bank credit (in million pesos)			Foreign exchange futures bought (in million pesos)		
	1978	1979	1980	1978	1979	1980
Private domestic	5,142.1	8,283.7	11,299.0	3,849.4	8,100.5	14,672.7
1 Allied Bank	888.7	850.6	542.7	664.6	1,412.2	1,461.6
2 BPI	207.6	506.6	904.8	62.9	345.5	756.0
3 Metrobank	271.9	461.8	464.9	257.1	607.1	1,138.0
4 RPB	213.7	1,494.8	2,545.1	–	–	71.7
5 PCIB	249.7	165.3	682.0	403.0	1,102.4	3,640.8
6 UCPB	157.2	305.7	366.0	–	187.8	829.8
7 FEBTC	146.4	337.5	308.6	356.1	399.2	953.1
8 Traders Royal	30.9	185.8	287.5	32.0	29.2	29.9
9 RCBC	448.2	439.9	374.3	689.6	1,696.7	1,095.6
10 China	327.5	471.5	724.1	272.8	439.9	769.2
11 Pacific	359.1	289.9	279.8	71.4	105.9	229.5
12 Manilabank	194.1	401.2	299.9	235.0	489.3	924.6
13 Solidbank	62.0	223.9	241.1	46.1	46.9	124.8
14 Equitable	40.4	142.6	283.4	131.4	75.7	201.3
15 PBCom	30.5	75.3	108.2	103.7	305.5	515.1
16 IBAA	110.7	109.5	515.9	117.8	199.9	66.2
17 Security	62.8	104.4	288.7	13.4	33.5	1,160.9
18 Comtrust	139.1	231.3	57.7	17.7	–	–
19 Philbanking	376.4	384.4	403.4	61.8	135.8	63.8
20 Prudential	25.4	100.5	220.5	–	1.5	46.1
21 Interbank	381.6	354.3	375.3	67.1	183.3	249.9
22 Associated Citizen	104.8	141.8	237.1	65.9	46.4	36.7
23 City Trust	119.0	159.5	275.6	148.3	109.8	177.2
24 Producers	153.1	163.7	266.4	70.1	93.7	135.5
25 Filmanbank	34.0	175.8	165.4	51.9	50.5	53.2
26 Philtrust	7.4	6.1	79.7	9.6	3.0	2.4
Government	7,850.5	9,162.4	12,342.3	1,310.5	1,412.7	2,329.2
PNB	7,725.4	9,025.0	12,293.3	1,278.7	1,384.4	2,320.5
Veterans	125.1	135.8	49.0	31.8	28.3	8.7
Foreign	483.1	902.0	2,018.6	2,214.8	3,964.0	3,900.4
Citibank, N.A.	242.4	503.6	973.0	1,814.8	3,074.6	3,483.6
Bank of America, NT & SA	165.9	278.5	749.1	165.3	585.5	102.7
HSBC	36.8	107.5	108.9	3.7	45.1	127.8
Chartered	38.0	12.4	187.6	231.0	258.8	186.3
All banks	13,475.7	18,348.1	25,659.9	7,374.6	13,477.2	20,902.3

Table 15.7: continued

| | Central Bank credit | | | | | |
| | Total assets (percent) | | | Total capital accounts (percent) | | |
Name of bank	1978	1979	1980	1978	1979	1980
Private domestic	9.3	12.02	13.41	100.32	140.23	158.08
1 Allied Bank	23.95	14.23	7.47	320.94	212.35	118.42
2 BPI	4.67	9.68	14.05	51.80	111.57	174.88
3 Metrobank	6.67	8.80	8.44	115.69	159.22	131.56
4 RPB	8.67	52.41	52.15	231.34	977.24	1,046.61
5 PCIB	7.71	4.49	14.26	104.58	58.52	193.64
6 UCPB	4.40	7.76	7.80	48.06	78.71	71.59
7 FEBTC	4.47	9.67	7.10	56.87	118.18	93.93
8 Traders Royal	1.71	7.63	7.65	22.38	112.37	139.91
9 RCBC	14.49	11.75	10.06	223.01	195.82	148.07
10 China	11.63	14.49	20.44	113.49	138.03	189.36
11 Pacific	14.11	9.01	8.37	209.14	159.55	133.01
12 Manilabank	8.79	14.18	9.36	98.22	185.31	116.08
13 Solidbank	2.45	8.14	8.09	27.41	89.85	91.96
14 Equitable	1.65	5.80	9.81	15.07	46.00	81.22
15 PBCom	2.16	3.66	3.94	16.37	33.91	41.47
16 IBAA	6.10	5.44	18.96	54.58	45.73	194.13
17 Security	4.58	7.21	11.16	39.52	62.37	158.13
18 Comtrust	7.00	10.46	2.39	75.55	121.73	27.32
19 Philbanking	19.27	19.68	18.30	237.79	231.99	230.66
20 Prudential	1.58	4.96	10.13	14.34	54.67	101.23
21 Interbank	39.08	30.65	22.86	340.41	291.58	251.93
22 Associated Citizen	9.44	11.49	14.60	77.41	107.50	156.42
23 City Trust	14.43	13.68	13.60	93.05	105.62	157.97
24 Producers	22.45	18.22	18.80	113.16	110.24	153.54
25 Filmanbank	4.79	17.56	15.70	36.87	204.94	95.33
26 Philtrust	1.31	0.91	8.69	5.41	3.96	45.11
Government	31.21	27.41	29.81	396.61	415.53	493.15
PNB	33.11	29.29	31.80	426.61	450.00	537.05
Veterans	6.84	5.18	1.79	74.24	68.09	22.93
Foreign	4.35	5.72	10.78	129.42	240.80	529.22
Citibank, N.A.	3.42	3.98	7.70	242.40	503.60	973.00
Bank of America NT & SA	7.30	7.42	20.80	–	–	–
HSBC	3.59	8.87	6.70	27.91	81.07	81.26
Chartered	5.16	1.43	21.68	26.87	8.73	127.26
All banks	14.72	15.53	17.77	180.20	215.10	255.79

Table 15.7   continued

	Foreign exchange bought					
	Total assets (percent)			Total capital accounts (percent)		
Name of bank	1978	1979	1980	1978	1979	1980
Private domestic	6.96	11.76	17.41	75.10	137.20	205.29
1 Allied Bank	17.91	23.62	20.14	240.03	352.55	348.94
2 BPI	1.41	6.60	11.74	15.68	76.09	146.12
3 Metrobank	6.31	11.57	20.67	109.43	209.32	322.04
4 RPB	–	–	1.47	–	–	29.48
5 PCIB	12.45	29.93	76.15	168.81	309.27	1,033.75
6 UCPB	–	4.77	17.86	–	48.35	162.30
7 FEBTC	11.11	9.67	21.94	138.31	139.78	290.10
8 Traders Royal	1.78	1.20	0.80	23.19	17.60	14.55
9 RCBC	22.30	45.30	29.45	343.17	755.72	433.42
10 China	9.69	13.52	21.72	94.54	128.77	201.16
11 Pacific	2.80	3.29	6.82	41.57	58.28	109.10
12 Manilabank	10.64	17.29	28.85	118.92	226.00	357.89
13 Solidbank	1.82	1.71	4.19	20.38	18.82	47.60
14 Equitable	5.37	3.08	6.97	49.04	24.42	57.69
15 PBCom	7.35	14.85	18.77	55.71	137.56	197.43
16 IBAA	10.57	10.11	2.43	58.09	83.48	24.91
17 Security	0.97	2.31	44.87	8.41	20.01	635.86
18 Comtrust	0.89	–	–	9.62	–	–
19 Philbanking	3.16	6.95	2.89	39.04	81.96	36.48
20 Prudential	–	0.07	2.12	–	0.82	21.16
21 Interbank	6.88	15.85	15.22	59.92	150.85	167.75
22 Associated Citizen	5.93	3.76	2.26	48.67	35.18	24.21
23 City Trust	17.99	9.42	11.96	115.99	72.71	101.57
24 Producers	10.27	10.43	9.56	51.77	63.10	78.10
25 Filmanbank	7.27	5.05	5.05	56.24	58.87	10.85
26 Philtrust	1.70	0.45	0.26	7.03	1.95	1.36
Government	5.21	4.23	5.63	66.20	64.07	93.07
PNB	5.48	4.49	6.00	70.61	68.03	101.38
Veterans	1.73	1.08	0.32	18.85	14.17	4.08
Foreign	19.93	25.12	20.82	593.33	1,058.22	1,022.58
Citibank, N.A.	25.63	30.47	27.57	1,814.80	3,074.60	3,483.60
Bank of America, NT & SA	7.27	15.61	2.85	–	–	–
HSBC	0.36	3.72	7.86	2.81	34.01	95.37
Chartered	26.70	35.40	21.53	163.34	182.26	126.38
All banks	8.05	11.41	14.47	98.61	158.86	208.36

The monetary authorities changed the commercial bank balance sheet reporting requirements in the late 1970s. Thus data on Central Bank rediscounts and swap arrangements are not readily available for 1979 and subsequent years

Source: Central Bank Factbook various issues

ranged from 46 percent of assets to 2 percent in 1978, and from 90 percent to 8 percent in 1980.

Part of the explanation for the disparities lies in the policy decisions and behavior of individual banks. Some banks prefer not to be involved with the Central Bank any more than is necessary, and some banks may not meet Central Bank standards. Nonetheless, the extraordinarily large amounts of Central Bank credit going to a few banks are difficult to justify by economic criteria. Interviews indicate a widespread perception that banks have not had equal access to Central Bank support; however, as a group, the political banks have not benefited disproportionately. Nonetheless, case-by-case approval of even relatively small swap contracts has lent itself to misuse, and opportunities for personal gain by administrators. One member of the financial community commented on the personal influences on Central Bank credit allocation decisions: "Each bank tries to have a friend in court to help out with specific projects or needs; having the right connection makes a lot of difference."

Nonetheless, it is difficult to generalize; each bank's situation must be considered separately; the quantitative data are merely guideposts to what is actually going on. For example, in 1978, RCBC was the largest user of swap facilities; presumably this is the continuation of a strategy and pattern initiated in the late 1960s. Although RCBC's large Central Bank loans were because of a lending policy which generated preferential paper for rediscount, it was unusually well treated. By 1980, PCIB also was being particularly well treated, and Allied had become less of an outlier. There is no general pattern whereby banks with foreign partners are larger-than-average users of swap facilities. The two weakest banks did not receive a great deal of Central Bank support between 1978 and 1980.

Bank Asset Portfolio Management

Interest-rate ceilings have distorted incentives and biased lending toward the most creditworthy – large firms, those with excellent collateral – and away from the more risky; toward large and against small transactions, where administrative costs are relatively higher; toward known, established borrowers and against those where costs of evaluation are greater; and toward the short term. The group ownership pattern provides another set of distortions, more difficult to determine.

Because so few data are available on bank asset portfolios and credit allocation, much less the explicit or implicit rules governing bank behavior, it is possible to evaluate the efficiency of the allocation process only in general terms. (For a more detailed discussion, see IMF/World Bank (1979).) Separate data are not available for the private domestic banks, but probably the general patterns would not differ greatly from that shown in table 15.8 for all commercial banks. The table's interest-rate data are difficult to interpret: effective interest rates are higher; some lower-rate loans may be under Central Bank

Table 15.8:   Commercial bank credit outstanding, selected features (September 1978, 1979, and 1980)[a]

	September 1978	September 1879	September 1980
Distribution by sector			
All industries	100.0	100.0	100.0
Agriculture, fishery and forestry	10.7	11.9	15.1
Mining and quarrying	6.7	8.1	8.7
Manufacturing	32.3	32.4	35.2
Electricity, gas and water	0.6	1.1	1.0
Construction	2.9	3.0	3.2
Trade	26.2	20.6	15.6
Transport, storage and communi- cation	2.0	2.6	2.9
Financing, insurance and business services	6.1	9.0	10.3
Real estate	3.8	3.8	3.1
Community, social and personal services	8.8	7.6	5.0
Distribution by maturity			
Short term	82.2	70.8	76.3
Intermediate term	10.2	13.7	10.6
Long term	7.6	15.5	12.9
Distribution by stated interest rate[b]			
More than 14%	5.5	6.5	37.9
14%	31.9	27.7	18.0
12–13%	33.9	40.6	17.0
Less than 10%	12.2	14.1	16.6
Other features			
Unsecured	31.8	36.2	39.7
Private corporations	66.1	73.7	67.6
Individuals	23.0	16.1	19.8
Single proprietors	5.5	2.8	3.1
Public sector	2.8	4.9	7.6

Data include government and foreign as well as private domestic commercial banks

[a] All figures are percentages
[b] The interest-rate ceiling was 12 percent on secured loans, 14 percent on unsecured

Sources: Central Bank of the Philippines, *Statistical Bulletin*, and *Philippine Financial Statistics* 1978, 1979, and 1980

priority lending programs, others may be at preferential terms to owners and related interests.

The top tier of borrowers are the largest 300 industrial corporations. Almost all are affiliated with a family group, or are foreign-owned, or government corporations. The second and third tiers comprise mainly the next 700. Below these are the small units which in fact produce nine-tenths of Philippine GNP. For most banks, the main choice is the degree to which they concentrate lending on the first tier, relatively to the second and third tiers. The first-tier market is highly competitive, with net spreads as low as 0.5 percentage points. First-tier firms obtain a substantial share of commercial bank loans, and probably most of the long-term credit. Major foreign banks lend primarily in this market.

The second and third tiers are much more lenders' markets. Borrowers are more concerned about access to and availability of funds than marginal cost. Collateral is important; so too are long, well-established ties. Net spreads to banks are up to 3 percentage points. The delineation between second and third tiers is somewhat arbitrary, as firms are spread over a multidimensional continuum. One criterion is that the second tier includes firms able and willing to borrow in the P.5–20 million range, whereas third-tier firms typically need loans under P.5 million.

Philippine bankers respond to interest-rate ceilings in the same way they have in postwar Japan or other countries where ceilings prevail. (For an analysis of some adjustment techniques in Japan, see Patrick (1965).) Much of the adjustment is through assets portfolio management. They seek both to minimize costs and to increase effective yields. Cost minimization is achieved by lending in large amounts (reducing transactions costs), to well-known companies (reducing information costs), and under the least risky conditions (top-tier companies or excellent collateral). Effective interest rates are raised in various ways. Service fees and commissions are charged; these, together with interest, are deducted in advance. Such fees are supposedly limited to 2 percentage points; in fact they can be considerably higher. Other business, such as letters of credit and foreign-exchange transactions, is important. Import and export financing are particularly attractive, in part because exchange between pesos and foreign currency can be at bank-determined spreads. Requiring compensating balances is illegal, but as one financial specialist put it, "it is not illegal for the companies to offer to hold deposit balances and for the banks to accept." Banks also increase effective yields by establishing finance companies, lending companies, and similar non-bank financial institution subsidiaries. The banks lend to them at rates within the ceiling; they in turn finance activities, or engage in direct investment, at higher yields.

Thus, data are not available on effective lending rates. Katigbak (October 29, 1979) suggests a cost of borrowing by clients as 18–24 percent, depending on the degree of compensating business provided by the client. Money-market rates would be a reasonable proxy, but evidence on actual rates (substantially above formal ceiling rates) is fragmentary. Regulation has made the money market less visible, less efficient, but nonetheless quite competitive. The best study of the money market appears in Tan et al. (1981). They obtained detailed data on money-market transactions, but note that their interest-rate data are probably below actual rates. (See also Tan 1979; Roxas 1976.)

The family (group) ownership of banks is certainly an additional factor in determining the portfolio composition of banks. It has been an accepted practice to lend to one's own group, just as *zaibatsu* banks did in prewar Japan and *keiretsu* banks have done in postwar Japan. Economic theory does not provide an unambiguous answer as to whether the financing of groups by their affiliated banks results in more or less efficient credit allocation than a system based on more arm's-length transactions; it is an empirical issue. Although lending to one's own businesses may well lead to greater *de facto* term transformation and risk-taking, it probably also impairs bank safety, as all the bank failures demonstrate. Efficiency is not the only criterion; such a system tends to maintain and enhance the concentration of wealth in a small number of families.

How extensive is lending to directors, officers, stockholders, and related interests (DOSRI), which is the main channel to affiliated (group) activities? Only the owner-managers of the banks really know. The Central Bank has set ceilings on DOSRI loans to an amount not exceeding their respective outstanding deposits and book value of their share of paid-in capital of the bank. Central Bank data indicate that as of December 31, 1978 DOSRI loans comprised 8.1 percent of commercial bank portfolios, 4.6 percent for savings banks, 10.4 percent for investment houses, and 1.7 percent for financing companies. The monetary authorities and private bankers agree that Central Bank data on DOSRI greatly understate the actual credit relationships. One rule of thumb has been that all unsecured loans, about one-third of the total, are DOSRI.

One issue is whether there has been political pressure on banks to make loans for particular projects or to particular companies or individuals. The general consensus of those interviewed is that such political pressures on most banks have been relatively modest, certainly far less than during the politically decentralized, convoluted period of the late 1960s and early 1970s, when many politicians were able to force banks into loans that at times were little more than payments to the politicians. During martial law, there were fewer politicians, political power was more centralized, and the economic environment less politicized. Equally important, politically-generated needs have been met through the various government financial institutions and to some degree the political banks. Those interviewed pointed out that, unlike the earlier period, during the 1970s real investment was financed – hotels, roads, sugar mills, cement factories, housing – and that demand does eventually catch up with capacity. Perhaps the main issue is the degree to which politically-motivated loans are accepted or at least tolerated as an inherent fixed cost of the socio-political-economic system, and to what degree they are variables subject to policy change.

Financing Development

There is widespread agreement that the pattern of credit allocation has not been optimal for Philippine economic development. Part is due to the development strategy itself, which pushed import substitution too far at the expense of exports and which did not create as vigorously competitive an industrial structure in domestic markets as has occurred in Japan. Part lies in government policies, which have distorted incentives in finance – the inability to control inflationary surges, the interest-rate ceilings. And part lies in the structure of the financial system itself, though probably less than criticisms would suggest. The commercial banks, given their structure and the environment in which they operate, have not surprisingly provided financial services mainly to urban areas, and lent short-term to large, usually safe and often affiliated, industrial and commercial enterprises. In general, the financial system gives preference to the financing of commerce, especially imports and exports, and to large firms.

In contrast, it is generally agreed that the financial system as a whole, and certainly its private component, has provided inadequate credit to small-scale farmers (especially for non-export crops) and to small businesses. Moreover, it is seen as not carrying out sufficient term transformation (providing sufficient medium and long-term credit). The monetary authorities have sought to redress these imbalances. Priority sectors have been identified and low-cost credit has been provided. The Central Bank provides commercial banks' preferential rediscounts for selected priority purposes – exports, certain types of agricultural loans, and the like – and also attempts to redirect their loan portfolios through various regulations. The government financial institutions provide two-fifths of total credit (see table 15.2). They obtain resources from social security revenues and other governmental sources; from international lending institutions such as the World Bank and the Asian Development Bank and foreign capital markets; and from the Central Bank.

The financing of agriculture is important, but detailed consideration is beyond the scope of this study (see chapter 14 above). Economic and financial dualism are pronounced; large landowners, corporate or family, produce commercial export crops, often on plantations, and raise funds through the modern financial system. Small farmers, typically rice-growers rely much more on traditional sources of agrarian credit (moneylenders, friends, and relatives) or government-subsidized credit programs (which barely reach the very small, especially landless, producers). A recent study of rural finance by the Presidential Committee on Agriculture Credit (1981) reports the average interest rate in the informal (traditional) market was 55.5 percent, and on loans from all sources (i.e. including formal institutions) was 45.0 percent.

Commercial banks are required to lend one-quarter of their incremental loanable funds over their May 1975 base for agricultural purposes. However,

Central Bank certificates of indebtedness can be held to meet this requirement in part; they are preferred since they are riskless, have low transaction costs, their yield is determined by market auction, and they simultaneously can be used to meet deposit reserve requirements. Central Bank programs have not been particularly successful in significantly increasing private domestic commercial bank lending to small farmers. As table 15.8 indicates, agricultural loans have remained substantially below target.

The situation for small businesses is similar, though much less well studied. In periods of credit stringency, as in 1979, even though total credit increased, the amounts to the smallest enterprises declined absolutely while that to the large firms increased substantially (table 15.9).

The basic cause of commercial banks' aversion to lending to agriculture and to small businesses is that such lending has not been profitable. Lending has been squeezed between high transaction costs and the interest rate ceilings Studies by Saito and Villanueva (1978a and 1978b) for various types of financial institutions suggest transaction costs (administrative plus default loss-risk) for loans to small-scale agriculture in the order of 5.5–7.3 percent, to small-scale enterprises 5.5–

Table 15.9: Total credits outstanding of private commercial banks, classified by size of firm

Size of firm[a]	Amount as of October 31 (million pesos)		Distribution (percentage)	
	1979	*1978*	*1979*	*1978*
Total	43,227.2	34,268.0	100.0	100.0
Cottage industry (less than 100 employees)	1,267.2	2,099.7	3.0	6.1
Small-scale enterprises (100–1,000 employees)	3,019.0	4,256.1	7.0	12.4
Medium-scale enterprises (1,000–4,000 employees)	4,205.0	4,066.5	9.7	11.9
Large-scale enterprises (more than 4,000 employees)	27,464.9	15,353.7	63.5	44.8
Others — unknown	7,271.1	8,492.0	16.8	24.8

Excluding PNB, past due items, items in litigation, domestic and foreign bills — clean

[a] Amount of assets, in 1,000 pesos

Source: Central Bank unpublished data

6.7 percent, and to large enterprises 1.8–2.5 percent (2.1 percent for commercial banks).

A major policy concern has been the shortage of medium and long-term credit to finance fixed investment. The data understate actual maturities, as most short-term loans are renewed (rolled over). Rollover is adantageous to banks, since they can regularly add service fees to raise effective yields. Data on credit granted by term are weak. Loans outstanding by financial institution as of 1977 are presented in table 15.10.

The share of intermediate and long-term loans is quite large substantially higher than for either prewar or postwar Japan. However, demand is not satisfied for any term. Government financial institutions, particularly DBP, made 72 percent of the long-term and 24 percent of the medium-term loans. Commercial banks, which includes PNB, provided just one-fifth of the term credit. A large and increasing proportion of new long-term credit – rising from 42 percent in 1975 to 72 percent in 1978 – came from foreign sources.

Medium- to long-term financing has not been economically attractive to lenders, and perhaps not to potential borrowers either. There have been three main causes: the high and erratic rates of inflation during the 1970s, especially in 1979- 80; the interest-rate ceiling system; and low interest rates on many foreign loans.

In our view, the basic culprit has been the interest-rate ceiling system. It has prevented the emergence of a normal term structure of interest rates; the available evidence suggests the persistence of an inverse term structure of interest rates, implausible for other than relatively short periods of time in free financial markets. An informal private market in term loans has developed parallel to the money market, presumably at interest rates appropriately higher than effective short-term rates; however, no data are available on amounts or effective interest rates.

The official data on longer-term interest rates reflect the fact that the cost of foreign borrowing, longer-term as well as short, has been significantly cheaper than domestic borrowing (IMF/World Bank 1979: 34). The low rates (relative to domestic Philippine rates) on World Bank and similar official loans in many instances are passed on as a form of indirect subsidy. Only after all such possible opportunities are exploited does it make sense for the enterprise, almost always large-scale, to turn to the domestic market. For efficiency in credit and capital allocation, and for encouragement of the domestic market for term credit, it would be preferable for the monetary authorities to charge domestic interest rates on foreign loans. It is more efficient to subsidize directly projects with high social benefit, but low market profitability.

Unfortunately, at times the government has established as priority projects a number that have performed badly, through poor project selection (such as cellophane and hotels), major cost overruns, where the causes are not completely clear (the Westinghouse nuclear electric power project, the Manila convention

Table 15.10: Credits outstanding of financial institutions by maturity, as of December 31, 1977

	Short term		Intermediate term		Long term	
	Amount (million pesos)	Percentage of total	Amount (million pesos)	Percentage of total	Amount (million pesos)	Percentage of total
Commercial banks	34,256.7	87.1	4,233.6	35.1	1,682.6	10.8
Savings bank	485.7	1.2	650.3	5.4	586.7	3.8
Stock S & L associations	389.6	1.0	48.7	0.4	33.0	0.2
LBP and PAB[a,b]	482.6	1.2	88.5	0.7	501.4	3.2
DBP[b]	563.9	1.4	1,794.9	14.9	7,356.0	47.0
PDBs	76.6	0.2	234.8	1.9	122.8	0.8
Investment houses	414.6	1.1	378.9	3.1	733.1	4.7
Financing companies	1,553.8	4.0	2,660.7	22.1	16.6	0.1
Investment companies	280.0	0.7	256.5	2.1	313.1	2.0
Securities dealers	450.1	1.1	9.1	0.1	20.7	0.1
GSIS[b]	—	—	917.2	7.6	2,477.7	15.8
SSS[b]	369.9	0.9	66.2	0.6	972.4	6.2
Private insurance companies	—	—	707.5	5.9	823.5	5.3
Total	39,323.4	100.0	12,047.6	100.0	15,639.6	100.0
Percentage of total credits	58.7		18.0		23.3	

Although data are not fully consistent, the following definitions are used: short term, up to one year; intermediate term, from one to five years; long term, five years or more

[a] Land Bank of Philippines and Philippine Amanah Bank
[b] Government financial institutions, but not including the two government-owned commercial banks

Source: IMF/World Bank 1979: 43, table 22

center, airplane purchases), or the creation of overcapacity (sugar mills, cement). It would be useful to have an analysis of the criteria the government uses to determine projects, the entrepreneurs to carry them out, the funding arrangements, the actual costs and expenditures involved, and the resultant social benefit. Data are not available. Perhaps it should be expected that priorities are shaped by political as well as economic considerations.

Dawn of a New Era?

Only time will tell whether our delineation of 1980–81 as a major turning-point in Philippine financial development is correct. The government has instituted major reforms in both the institutional framework of the financial system and its interest-rate ceiling policy. The main purposes are to increase competition among all kinds of financial institutions and to increase the availability of long-term funds for investment. In addition, the financial system was subjected to a major crisis in spring 1981, triggered by the flight of a highly respected business leader who left large debts behind.

In April 1980, the government passed a series of laws that enabled various financial institutions to engage in a wider range of functions, thereby reducing market segmentation. Functional differences among various types of thrift institutions were eliminated, and they were allowed to compete directly with commercial banks for domestic demand deposits; in effect, they have become deposit-creating (that is, commercial) banks. Other financial institutions are also allowed to convert to commercial bank status on meeting the P.100 million net worth requirement. Mergers among various types of financial institutions are encouraged. At the same time, minimum capital requirements have been increased, reducing entry opportunities by small institutions.[7]

The most visible, and most controversial, change has been the authorization of expanded banking activities by very large commercial banks (with net worth of P.500 million). This is termed unibanking in the Philippines, based on the German model of universal banking. The most important new function is that unibanks may engage in investment banking, both underwriting of new security issues and direct equity participation in industrial enterprises. In addition, they receive favorable tax treatment and other incentives, possibly including preferred access to Central Bank Credit.

Potentially the most profound reform was to shift from a ceiling interest-rate system to a market-determined system, effective on July 1, 1981, for time and savings deposits and term loans. At the same time, the monetary authorities made it clear that they would not tolerate "excessive competition" for deposits

[7] A good general description of the new laws is "Unibanking," *Business Day*, August 28, 1980, III: 17–32. Unibanking is discussed by the IMF/World Bank (1979) and Patrick and Moreno (1980), and in a broader context in Khatkhate and Riechel (1980).

that hurt smaller banks and thrift institutions. It seems possible that price leadership or other forms of oligopolistic behavior will occur. It is premature to judge whether a market-determined financial system with flexible interest rates will prevail. Interest-rate ceilings on loans with a maturity of less than two years were not removed, on the grounds that this would provide an upper limit to interest-rate competition for deposits. The monetary authorities have indicated that they plan to move gradually to a completely market-determined system. That would presumably result in a more efficient allocation of credit and greater rewards to savers.

Conclusions

In the 1955–80 period, the Philippines has undergone financial development similar in kind, though not in degree, to that in Japan from the 1870s to the 1930s. Like Japan, it created a dynamic system of commercial banks and a variety of specialized institutions for the collection of savings, financing of agriculture, and provision of long-term credit. The facilitating role of the government has been important, both in the first phase, when entry was easy and banks received government deposits, and subsequently, when entry was restricted, merger encouraged, and minimum capital size raised. A further important, and in some respects disturbing, similarity was the recurrent instability of the two banking systems.

By standing criteria, Philippine commercial bank lending appears reasonable; the average term is short, liquid asset ratios are relatively high, there is considerable diversification among sectors. But actual risks are probably substantially higher. Sectoral diversification masks what is substantially less diversification by group or DOSRI borrowers; moreover, such borrowers tend to engage in risky, at times speculative, investment activities. Nor is fraud unknown. And the still-underdeveloped state of the economy means increased risks as well as opportunity.

Riskiness on the loan (asset) side is matched by the insecurity of depositors. While the core of deposits for the commercial banking system as a whole may be relatively stable, as the IMF/World Bank (1979) alleges, that has certainly been far less true for individual banks, especially the weaker banks. Moreover, it does not take into account the important share of deposit substitutes in the liability structure of many banks; they are quite volatile, and too large to be covered by the relatively modest amounts of deposit insurance. As in the first sixty years of Japanese banking history, in the Philippines the monetary authorities have had to step in time and again to stop bank runs or contain their spread.

Perhaps the most important lesson to be learned from the Japanese experience of financial development is concerned with interest-rate policy. The lesson is twofold. First, from the 1870s to the eve of World War II, a flexible, free, market-determined interest-rate system contributed significantly to the rapid growth and relatively high level of financial intermediation, the increasing role of the modern financial sector and the decline in financial dualism, the allocation of credit among various types of users (while also biased toward large firms, apparently less so than in the Philippines), and the healthy growth of a strong capital market, including bonds and term loans. Second, the imposition of a controlled interest system with credit rationing, instituted during World War II and maintained in the postwar period, has probably had few advantages and has not had major deleterious effects only because the rate of private saving became so high, alternative saving (investment) opportunities were limited for the increasingly urban population, business investment demand was high, and economic growth was so rapid.

The adverse impacts of the controlled interest-rate system included redistributing income from the average Japanese (who saved in deposit form at low real interest rates) to the already wealthier stockholders and employees of the large firms receiving credit at low interest rates; and that the capital market, especially the bond market, did not develop and contribute significantly to the financing of long-term investment. It is noteworthy that relative to GNP per capita, financial development in Japan's repressed postwar financial system was substantially below that of Japan's market-oriented prewar system (Patrick 1984). The Philippine monetary authorities have known this lesson of the benefits of a market-oriented interest-rate system since the early 1970s, but began implementing it only in 1981.

One of the most striking similarities between the contemporary Philippines and prewar Japan is the emergence of family-owned financial–industrial–commercial groups of affiliated companies under central control (family-based groups, or *zaibatsu*). Because there are far fewer banks in the Philippines, the concentration of bank ownership to major wealth units seems substantially greater than in prewar Japan.

The relative economic effectiveness in the economic development process of the (family) group form of industrialization cannot be determined a priori. As Japan's experience as well as other cases suggest, there are both economic benefits and costs. (See Leff 1976 and 1979.) On the benefit side, the group may be able and willing to innovate, to search out foreign technology (frequently through joint ventures), to pool and otherwise take risk; to reduce risk and increase profits by internalizing to the group economies external to the individual firm; to economize on scarce entrepreneurial, managerial, marketing, and technical skills; and to offset imperfections in financial markets. On the cost side, the group may exploit market power not only of individual firms in oligopolistic markets, but of its entire operations; divert scarce capital and other resrouces to to its own, less efficient, activities; reduce the general competitive environment; and so forth.

The major criticisms of the group form are not simply in terms of standard economic criteria. The group perpetuates and enhances the concentration of income, wealth, and economic power. That economic power spills over into political power. They do not have to take as given the rules of the economic game as determined by government.

The "lessons" from the prewar Japanese experience of the *zaibatsu* form of industrial and financial organization are complex, mixed, and not yet fully evaluated by economic, political, or social criteria. It is our guess that, on grounds of pure economic efficiency, the *zaibatsu* (and the new *zaibatsu* of the 1930s, in some respects analogous to the Philippine new elite of the 1970s) were a net contributor to Japan's *economic* development prior to World War II. Despite some static misallocation of resources through exploitation of oligopoly market power, as entrepreneurs they may have imported technology and allocated resources reasonably well in a dynamic context. However, the political and social costs of the *zaibatsu* probably outweighed their efficiency benefits. There are few apologists for the *zaibatsu*.

This group form of industrial organization seems a significant characteristic in many latecomer developing countries with a capitalist system of private ownership of property. This phenomenon suggests a number of important theoretical and empirical issues: to what extent is the group form of industrial organization inevitable? To what extent will family-controlled groups evolve into management-controlled organizations? To what extent can the nature, growth, and function of groups be controlled by government policy? What are the interrelationships between economic and political power?

We cannot pretend to answer these questions in the Philippine context. No economic analysis has been carried out of the role of family groups; indeed the data are not available. However, the highly respected economist, technocrat and, since 1981, Prime Minister, Cesar Virata, has said: "Each of these family groups has its own conglomerate . . . these types of development have not produced an efficient industrial system. We cannot allow small cement plants to proliferate, for example, just because each family would like to have one" (*Business Week*, May 17, 1982). Inefficiently small-sized plants have been more likely under the Philippines' import-protection policies; in prewar Japan's more open trade context, the *zaibatsu* behaved differently. Interestingly, several of the "new elite" groups that flourished most in the 1970s were in the greatest trouble in the 1981 crisis; indeed, government financial institutions had to assume at least temporary control of the Herdes Group's Interbank and Commercial Bank (the 1981 reopened successor to the Overseas Bank), and the Silverio Group's Filipinas Bank.

Inevitably, the study of the commercial banking system becomes, implicitly at least, in part a discourse upon economic power in the Philippines. Ongoing economic and political changes have created opportunities for entry into the elite, despite the great importance of inheritance. Nonetheless, economic wealth and power remain highly concentrated (see Mangahas and Barros 1979). The relationships between and among the groups are variegated, situational, and certainly complex; they involve elements of friendship, hatred, alliance, competition, and *ad-hoc* arrangements. The Philippine rules of the game at the top are different from those of Japan or the United States, and certainly the game is played as toughly in the Philippines. There are major differences in "revealed" cultural norms shown in the behavior of those in power. Practices regarded as unacceptable in the United States or Japan are apparently tolerated in the contemporary Philippines. The relationships among financial, commercial, and industrial power, and their implications for development in the broadest sense, have yet to be understood fully – in the Philippines, in Japan, and indeed in any nation in the world.

References

Bautista, Romeo M. (1980), "Structural Change in the Philippines," in Lawrence B. Krause and Sueo Sekiguchi, *Economic Interaction in the Pacific Basin*, Washington: Brookings Institution, ch. 6.

Bautista, Romeo M., John H. Power, and associates (1979), *Industrial Promotion Policies in the Philippines*, Manila: Philippine Institute for Development Studies.

Business Week (1982), "Manila Moves in on the Family Conglomerates," May 17, 1982: 51–52.

Center for Research and Communications (CRC), Executive Briefing Pamphlet, series. See especially: "Regional Dimensions of Philippine Economic Growth," no. 11 (1979); and "Economic Aspects of Metro Manila and the Other Tagalog Areas," no. 12 (1979).

Central Bank of the Philippines, *Annual Report*, various years, Manila: CBP.

Central Bank of the Philippines, *Central Bank Factbook*, annual, various years, Manila: CBP.

Central Bank of the Philippines, *Statistical Bulletin*, annual, statistical appendix to the *Annual Report*, various years, Manila: CBP.

Doherty, John F. (1979), *A Preliminary Study of Interlocking Directorates Among Financial, Commercial, Manufacturing and Service Enterprises in the Philippines*, Manila.

Doherty, John F. (1980), "A Study of Interlocking Directorates among Financial, Commercial, Manufacturing and Service Enterprises in the Philippines," manuscript, Manila.

Emery, Robert F. (1970), *Financial Institutions in Southeast Asia*, New York: Praeger.

FEER (*Far Eastern Economic Review*), Hong Kong, weekly. Contains occasional articles on Philippine banking and finance.

Hooley, Richard W., and Honorata A. Moreno (forthcoming), *A Study of Financial Flows in the Philippines*, Manila: School of Economics, University of the Philippines.

IMF/World Bank Mission (1979), *The Philippines – Aspects of the Financial Sector*, report no. 2546-PH, October 1.

Inter-Agency Committee on the Study of Interest Rates (Republic of the Philippines) (1972), *Report*, Manila.

Joint IMF–CBP Banking Survey Commission (1972), *Report*, August.

Jones, Leroy P., and Il Sakong (1980), *Government, Business and Entrepreneurship in Economic Development: The Korean Case*, Cambridge, MA: Harvard University Press.

Katigbak, Norberto, "Financial Markets," (title varies), a column in the *Times-Journal of Manila*, various dates; this newspaper is now the *Manila Journal*.

Khatkhate, Deena R., and Klaus-Walter Riechel (1980), "Multipurpose Banking: its Nature, Scope, and Relevance for Less Developed Countries," IMF *Staff Papers*, 27(3) (September).

Khatkhate, Deena R., and Delano P. Villanueva (1979), "Reposit Substitutes and their Monetary Policy Significance in Developing Countries," *Oxford Bulletin of Economics and Statistics*, 41(1) (February).

Lava, Horacio C. (1976), "Transnational Banking Corporations in the Philippine Commercial Banking System," mimeographed; University of the Philippines, College of Business Administration.

Leff, Nathaniel H. (1976), "Capital Markets in the Less Developed Countries: The Group Principle," in Ronald I. McKinnon, ed., *Money and Finance in Economic Growth and Development*, New York: Dekker.

Leff, Nathaniel H. (1979), "Monopoly Capitalism and Public Policy in Developing Countries," *Kyklos*, 32(4): 718–38.

Mangahas, Mahar, and Bruno Barros (1979), *The Distribution of Income and Wealth: A Survey of Philippine Research*, Working Paper 7091, Manila: Philippine Institute for Development Studies.

Patrick, Hugh T. (1965), "Interest Rates and the Grey Financial Market in Japan," *Pacific Affairs*, 38(3 and 4): 326–44 (1965-66 Fall & Winter).

Patrick, Hugh T. (1967), "Japan," in Rondo Cameron et al., eds, *Banking in the Early Stages of Industrialization*, New York: Oxford University Press.

Patrick, Hugh T. (1980), "The Evolution of Japan's Financial System in the Interwar Period," Yale Economic Growth Center Discussion Paper, no. 345 (March).

Patrick, Hugh T. (1984), "Japanese Financial Development in Historical Perspective, 1868–1980," in Gustav Ranis et al., eds, *Comparative Development Perspectives*, Boulder, CO: Westview Press.

Patrick, Hugh, and Honorata A. Moreno (1980), "The Evolving Structure of the Philippine Private Domestic Commercial Banking System: An Overview," mimeographed.

Ranis, Gustav, et al. (1974), *Sharing in Development: A Programme of Employment, Equity and Growth for the Philippines*, Geneva: International Labor Organization; see especially ch. 7.

Presidential Committee on Agricultural Credit (Republic of the Philippines) (1981), *A Study on the Informal Rural Financial Markets in Three Selected Provinces of the Philippines*, Manila: Technical Board for Agricultural Credit.

Richard, Denis, and Delano P. Villanueva (1980), "Relative Efficiency of Banking Systems in LDCs: The Philippine Experience," *Journal of Banking and Finance*, 4(4).

Roxas, Sixto K. (1976), *Managing Asian Financial Development*, Manila: Sinagtala Publishers.

Saito, Katrine Anderson, and Dan P. Villanueva (1978a), "Portfolio Determinants of Commercial Bank Earnings in Selected Asian Countries," World

Bank, Public and Private Finance Division, Domestic Finance Studies, no. 49 (March).

Saito, Katrine Anderson, and Dan P. Villanueva (1978b), "Transactions Costs of Credit to the Small-Scale Sector in the Philippines," World Bank, Public and Private Finance Division, Domestic Finance Studies, no. 53 (December); a summary with the same title is published in *Economic Development and Cultural Change*, 29(3) (April 1981).

SEC-Business Day (1978), *1000 Top Corporations in the Philippines, 1977*, Business Day; published annually since 1969, covering years since 1968.

SGV (SyCip, Gorress, Velayo, and Co.), *A Study of Commercial Banks in the Philippines*, annual; also quarterly.

SGV (1976), *Key Officials and Board Members: Commercial Banks and Investment Houses*, Manila.

Strachan, Harry W. (1976), *Family and Other Business Groups in Economic Development: The Case of Nicaragua*, New York: Praeger.

Tan, Edita A. (1979), *Philippine Monetary Policy and Aspects of the Financial Market: A Review of the Literature*, Philippine Institute of Development Studies, Working Paper 7904 (May); prepared with the collaboration of Clodualdo R. Francisco.

Tan, Edita A., et al. (1981), "The Structure and Growth of the Philippine Financial Market and the Behavior of its Major Components," mimeographed.

Teranishi, Juro, and Hugh Patrick (1977), "Financas, Dualismo e Estrutura Industrial Differential do Japao" (Financial Dualism and Differential Industrial Structure of Japan), in Adolpho Ferriera de Oliviera et al., eds, *Mercado de Capitais e Desenvolvimemto Economico*, Rio de Janeiro: Instituto Brasileiro de Mercado de Capitais.

Teranishi, Juro, and Hugh Patrick (1978), "The Early Establishment and Development of Banking in Japan: Phases and Policies 1872–1913," Yale Economic Growth Center Discussion Paper, no. 294 (August).

Tsuda, Mamoru (1978), *A Preliminary Study of Japanese–Filipino Joint Ventures*, Quezon City: Foundation for Nationalist Studies.

White, Lawrence J. (1974), *Industrial Concentration and Economic Power in Pakistan*, Princeton: Princeton University Press.

World Bank (1982), *World Bank Report 1982*, Washington: World Bank (August).

PART V Foreign Trade and Development

16 Manufactured Exports and Developing Countries: the Thai Textile Industry and the Japanese Experience

IPPEI YAMAZAWA and
SOMSAK TAMBUNLERTCHAI

Frustrated by the stagnation of import substitution (IS), industrialization, and chronic balance of payments deficits, a number of developing countries are promoting industrial exports. But this has usually been difficult compared to IS. Successful exportation of industrial products depends on a number of factors, including demand and competitiveness in terms of price and quality. Only a few export-expansion (EE) industrialization attempts have been successful. A crucial problem for LDCs is thus how an industry can be moved from the IS stage to the EE stage.

The sequential development of IS to EE is observed in Japan's industrialization. Starting later than western countries, Japan imported modern industries, each of which followed the catching-up process. The start of every modern industry was preceded by an increase in imports of the new product, then domestic production developed gradually and became competitive enough to replace imports in the home market. At first, the domestic product tended to be an inferior substitute for the import, and domestic producers expanded their scale by selling at a lower price. This is IS. The product was then exported to less-developed neighbors, and later to other parts of the world. This is EE. The sequence of importation, domestic production, exportation is referred to as the catching-up product cycle (CPC), and is illustrated in figure 16.1.

The CPC originated with Akamatsu before World War II and has been applied to the Japanese experience. The model was originally named the "flying-geese pattern of industrial development," after the shape of the sequential growth curves for imports, domestic output, and exports. The CPC model was developed by Akamatsu in the 1930s (see Akamatsu 1961; Shinohara 1962; Kojima 1973).

The authors wish to express their appreciation to Suppee Teravaninthorn for her assistance in data collection and interviews.

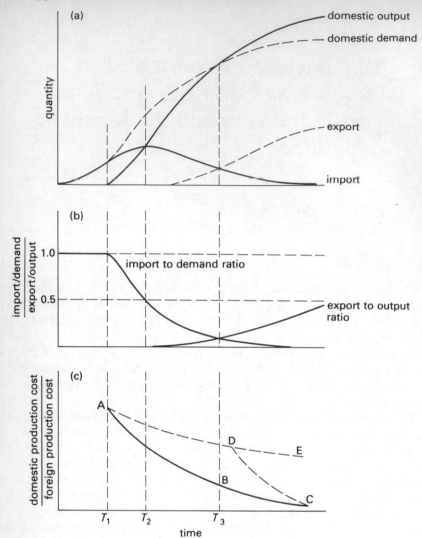

Figure 16.1:   Schematic diagram of the catching-up product cycle model

The development of the Thai textile industry from the IS to the EE stage is the topic of this chapter. After a brief overview of the development of the Thai industry, the Japanese experience and the catching-up cycle model are explained. The Thai textile industry is then examined in greater detail, in the light of the catching-up product cycle model and in comparison to the Japanese experience. The reason why export performance differs among Thai firms, and the export orientation of Thai entrepreneurs are then analyzed.

The Thai Textile Industry

The textile industry in Thailand is typical of development with the active participation of foreign direct investment, and it had the advantage of achieving IS and beginning EE before many other developing countries. In 1978, textiles accounted for 20.5 percent of total manufacturing value added, and 21.7 percent of total manufacturing employment.

Rapid development started around 1960, when the government launched a program providing incentives for private investment in industrial activities. The spinning, weaving, and knitting capacities of textile firms expanded at a spectacular rate. Synthetic fiber production was begun by Toray Nylon Thai, an affiliate of a leading Japanese synthetic fiber maker, in 1963, and a year later Thai Toray started manufacturing synthetic textiles. Teijin Polyester, another Japanese-affiliated firm, opened a synthetic fiber plant in 1967, and others followed. Cotton fabric production increased threefold, from 270 million square yards in 1966, to 835 million square yards in 1978. Synthetic fabrics grew even more rapidly, from 45 to 888 million square yards.

The textile-products export drive started in the late 1960s, when saturation of the domestic market slowed the industry's growth. First, cotton fabric and clothing were exported in small amounts. Synthetic fabric exports began shortly after that. Table 16.1 gives changes in imports as a percentage of demand (M/D), and of exports as a percentage of output (X/S) for woven cotton and synthetic fiber.

Woven fabrics are representative of textile products in Thailand and these ratios measure IS and EE, respectively. A rapid decline of M/D was observed in cotton fabrics, and then, four or five years later, in synthetics. IS appears complete by the early 1970s, and was successfully followed by EE. Both fabrics had export booms (1973 and 1978–79) alternating with stagnation (1974–75 and 1980).

The 1978–79 export boom blessed major Thai textile firms with high profits and quantitative expansion of their business, but at the same time it created a problem. Relying on export demand for 30–40 percent of sales, firms have become concerned with protectionism in Europe and North America, and competition from other Asian exporters in nonquota markets. The Achilles' heel of the Thai textile industry is the high acquisition cost of input materials and the proliferation of substandard weavers.

The Catching-up Product Cycle in Japan

A catching-up product cycle (CPC) in one industry induces that of another mainly through backward linkage. Thus, the CPC of cotton textiles induced the CPC of textile machines and synthetic dyestuffs in Japan during the 1910s and 1920s. When the import need of one CPC is paid for by the EE of an earlier

Table 16.1:   Import substitution and export expansion in the Thai textile industry

	Woven cotton fabric		Woven synthetic fabric	
	M/D	*X/S*	*M/D*	*X/S*
1961	67.2	0.7	–	–
1962	58.8	0.5	–	–
1963	48.6	0.1	100.0	0.0
1964	41.9	0.1	98.2	0.0
1965	31.6	0.0	95.9	1.3
1966	27.9	0.9	65.0	1.7
1967	26.3	0.7	68.4	2.2
1968	17.3	2.1	66.6	8.6
1969	12.6	2.4	63.6	2.8
1970	13.4	0.9	49.0	2.3
1971	10.0	3.5	22.9	2.8
1972	8.9	7.6	17.7	11.3
1973	8.2	12.2	19.0	26.2
1974	7.2	6.1	18.5	13.4
1975	4.6	8.3	12.0	18.3
1976	3.8	19.1	9.0	29.5
1977	3.2	16.8	7.8	29.8
1978	4.6	17.3	10.8	35.7
1979	2.1	16.0	9.5	32.5
1980	1.0	15.2	11.7	28.0

M/D: import/demand ratio; *X/S*: export/output ratio

Source: Custom Department and Thai Textile Manufacturers Association

one, the sequence of the two CPCs will not cause a serious balance of trade problem. Japan's industrialization had adequate time-lags, so it became free of persistent trade deficits in the early 1930s and in the mid-1960s.

In the early 20th century in Japan, fabric production took advantage of earlier developments in weaving silk fabrics, and was viable even on a small scale, so import substitution of fabrics was quickly achieved using imported yarn and indigenous technology. In fact, rayon fabric was immediately export-competitive. Fabric export tended to be preferred to yarn export, because of its greater value added.

Exports of cotton fabrics expanded rapidly after 1900, when large spinning firms started weaving as a vent for their yarn. Rayon fabrics were exported even before IS for yarn was completed. The EE of a fabric may be linked to the IS of the yarn. The decline of the import share of cotton yarn demand was followed by the rise of the export ratio of cotton fabric; and the rapid decline of the import share of rayon yarn was followed by the rise of the export ratio of rayon fabric. The export ratio of both fabrics exceeded 50 percent in the 1930s. Export of synthetic fabric quickly followed the IS of both yarn and fabric in the 1950s, and expanded greatly in the 1960s and 1970s.

In quantity terms (million square meters), the production of cotton fabrics increased from 114 in 1890 to 4,035 in 1937, rayon fabrics from 0.3 in 1918 to 865 in 1973, and synthetic fabrics from 2.9 in 1951 to 2,916 in 1978.

The primary force underlaying CPC development in Japan was improved production efficiency: better utilization of labor, larger scale of operation, advanced technology and equipment, and general improvement in production and management techniques. Both cost reduction and quality improvement occurred, enabling the substitution of domestic for foreign product, first at home (IS) and later abroad (EE); this is the path A-B-C in the bottom panel of figure 16.1.

Fujino's estimates of labor productivity in cotton spinning and weaving show steady increases for both, except during 1905-10, 1918-20, and after 1934 (LTES vol. 11: figure 7). The first two exceptions correspond to severe output reductions after wars. Productivity accelerated during the periods before 1904, when the export–output ratio increased for both yarn and fabric, 1910-15, when both IS and EE were rapid for fabrics, and 1926-31, when fabric exports expanded.

Labor productivity of the two combined increased by 2.65 percent annually in the period 1894-1937, which is about the same as the long-run increase in nominal wages. The capital–labor ratio increased at 2.9 percent, almost parallel to output per worker, which suggests technical progress in the cotton spinning industry was Harrod-neutral or slightly labor-augmenting. The productivity increase was more rapid in weaving, especially after 1910, corresponding to the shift of Japan's comparative advantage from yarn to fabric production. (Data are from LTES vol. 11: 10.)

The IS of cotton textile production had almost no tariff protection, as treaties limited duties to 3 percent until autonomy was gained in 1899. Tariffs were then raised to 8 percent on cotton yarn and 25 percent on cotton fabric. Fabric export to Korea and China benefited from preferential export credits from the Yokohama Specie Bank and expansion of Japan's sphere of influence before World War I. However, both IS and EE in cotton textiles were mainly the result of efficiency improvements.

Japanese rayon production benefited from tariff protection in its IS stage. Most rayon producers obtained technology and equipment from European manufacturers, but they suffered from declining world-market prices for rayon and occasional dumping by Germany and Italy. A 25 percent tariff was levied to offset the difference between domestic cost and the world price.

IS was achieved in rayon by 1930 and exports of both yarn and fabric expanded in the 1930s. A more rapid productivity increase occurred during the IS period (a 23 percent increase in 1926–30) than in the EE period (10 percent increase in 1930–37). This was partly attributable to severe competition with European producers, whose prices declined steadily, by one-third between 1919 and 1926 and by half between 1929 and 1931, and partly to duty-free imports to bonded factories of rayon weavers (see *JCFA* 1974).

Thai Textile Development

In contrast, protection better explains the development of Thailand's textile industry than efficiency improvement. Once domestic production has started, both IS and EE are possible with limited improvement in efficiency, if the importation of competing products is restricted and a heavy subsidy is provided for exports (path A–D–E in the bottom panel of figure 16.1). However, it is costly in the long run to continue EE without efficiency improvements.

Labor productivity has risen in both spinning and weaving since EE began in the mid-1970s. The average compound rate of increase was 15 percent for spinning in 1975–78, and 14 percent for weaving in 1974–78. The increase in spinning was accompanied by a big increase in the capital–output ratio, and a smaller increase in the capital–labor ratio. In weaving, the reverse was true, when adjusted for changes in capacity utilization. Wages rose steadily in the 1970s. The minimum wage set in 1973 has been adjusted upward at an average of around 10 percent a year, and textile wages have kept pace. Raw-material prices also rose. The productivity increase was partly eroded by the rising trend of input prices relative to output prices.

No data are available for labor productivity during the IS period. However, it can be argued that, because capital is a relatively scarce factor of production in developing countries, to maximize output the scarce production factor should be used efficiently. Hence, instead of labor productivity, capital productivity is a better indicator of production efficiency. Capital productivity increased more slowly over the IS period than after 1975, when EE in textiles accelerated. There was little incentive to increase the capital–labor ratio, given the ready availability of labor in the 1960s, which suggests there were only small increases in labor productivity. Improvements in technology and management are discussed in Katano et al. (1976) and Ichimura (1982).

From this, we may conclude that efficiency improvement must have been much less during the IS period, and thus made little contribution to the industry's development. On the other hand, increases in import duties on major textile products suggests a strong role for protection. Tariff rates are given in table 16.3.

The time between increases in effective protection for synthetic fabric and for cotton fabric is consistent with the time-lag in IS between the two types of fabrics. Tariffs on fabrics and garments were further increased in 1978, long after IS appears to have been completed. Although the 80 percent tariff was not

Table 16.2: Productivity increases in spinning and weaving in Thailand, 1966-79

	Spinning			Weaving			Relative wage
	O/K	O/L	K/L	O/K	O/L	K/L	W/P
1966	0.101	–	–	17.1	–	–	–
1967	0.099	–	–	15.9	–	–	–
1968	0.119	–	–	15.0	–	–	–
1969	0.112	–	–	14.3	–	–	–
1970	0.132	–	–	13.5	–	–	–
1971	0.126	–	–	15.4	–	–	405.0
1972	0.137	5.61	38.0	16.7	37.9	1.90	424.8
1973	0.137	5.96	39.0	17.5	42.9	2.05	416.0
1974	0.138	5.59	39.9	17.5	38.5	2.20	394.5
	(0.153)		(36.6)	(26.4)		(1.46)	
1975	0.120	5.03	41.1	20.3	47.7	2.35	534.0
	(0.153)		(33.6)	(26.3)		(1.81)	
1976	0.143	6.12	42.1	26.2	55.7	2.50	554.3
	(0.153)		(40.0)	(22.0)		(2.12)	
1977	0.161	6.85	42.5	22.6	57.6	2.55	571.2
	(0.166)		(41.2)	(26.8)		(2.15)	
1978	0.180	7.80	43.0	25.7	66.7	2.60	580.4
	(0.184)		(42.6)	(27.0)		(2.47)	
1979	0.169	7.45	44.0	25.3	66.1	2.60	567.2
	(0.173)		(43.1)	(26.7)		(2.47)	

O/L   Yarn output (in tons) or fabric output (in 1,000 square meters), divided by the number of employees (on all three shifts)
O/K   Yarn output per spindle or fabric output per loom
K/L   Number of machines (spindles or looms) per employee

Limited employment statistics permit only a rough analysis of efficiency improvement in Thailand. Both O/K and K/L were directly affected by business cycles; because the utilization rate of machines changed over the cycle, the employment level was less varied. Figures in parentheses are adjusted for changes in capacity utilization of the machines

W/P   Average monthly earnings of textile workers (in baht), deflated by the wholesale price index of textile products (1971 = 100)

Source: Computed from data supplied to the authors by the Thai Textile Manufacturers Association

specifically intended to protect domestic fabric production, many people expect a surge in fabric imports from East Asian countries if tariffs are removed.

However, the effective protection rates (EPRs) in table 16.3 overstate the real EPRs, because the estimation is affected by the redundant element of high

Table 16.3: Tariffs on textile imports to Thailand (expressed as percentages), 1960

		1960–62	1962–65	1965–68	1968–71	1971–78	1978–
Cotton yarn	Nominal	–	–	–	25.0	25.0	25.0
	Effective	3.2	3.2	3.2	77.6	77.6	77.6
Polyester/cotton yarn	Nominal	20.0	20.0	20.0	20.0	20.0	20.0
	Effective	25.9	25.9	25.9	25.9	25.9	25.9
Polyester/rayon yarn	Nominal	20.0	20.0	20.0	20.0	20.0	20.0
	Effective	20.0	20.0	20.0	20.0	20.0	20.0
Cotton fabric	Nominal	22.0	35.0	35.0	60.0	60.0	80.0
	Effective	53.7	114.3	114.3	70.7	70.7	390.9
Polyester/cotton fabric	Nominal	37.0	37.0	40.0	60.0	60.0	80.0
	Effective	80.1	80.1	94.8	265.8	265.8	1,051.7
Polyester/rayon fabric	Nominal	37.0	37.0	40.0	60.0	60.0	80.0
	Effective	78.6	78.6	92.9	254.3	254.3	913.4
Outer garments	Nominal	27.5	27.5	30.0	40.0	60.0	100.0
Under garments:							
cotton	Nominal	27.5	27.5	30.0	60.0	60.0	100.0
man-made fibers	Nominal	37.0	37.0	40.0	60.0	60.0	100.0

Source: Nominal rates are from Customs Tariff Decrees (published by the Department of Customs); effective rates have been computed from the same data by Supee Teravaninthorn, using the Corden formula

tariff protection. The degree of real protection can be estimated by the difference in actual prices of homogeneous products between domestic and world markets. Table 16.4 gives prices of Thai products quoted in Bangkok's Sampeng market (PD) and prices posted by Korean and Taiwanese exporters to the world market (PX).

In Sampeng, imports sold for PX plus tariff plus other import charges. The excess of PD over PX for individual products in table 16.4 reflects the degree of tariff protection. Both domestic and world prices fluctuated in response to the business cycle, and the gap decreased for all products in December 1978, when world prices rose in a tight market. The excess was much less than the nominal tariffs of 80 percent, which implies the existence of a redundant element of tariff protection.

Our survey (discussed in a later section) revealed the most important reason for both foreign and Thai investment in the textile industry during the early 1960s was the government's decision to protect industry. Protection was more important than programs under the Investment Promotion Act of 1961, although most of the large firms reported that these did influence their decision to invest. The Act provided foreign and Thai firms with exemption from corporate income taxes for five years, free import of machinery and equipment, and reduced duties on raw-material imports.

Major importers (Japanese trading companies) and Thai wholesalers were encouraged to develop joint-venture production in Thailand with Japanese textile manufacturers. Thai wholesalers monopolized domestic distribution and, during IS, shifted from Japanese to local suppliers. Minor importers, mostly Indian merchants, generally did not venture into local production, and rapidly lost market share in the 1960s.

Thai Exports

EE is more difficult when IS is achieved under protection, rather than through cost reduction, and in such cases, countries tend to resort to various promotional measures for EE. Governmental promotion of textile exports began in Thailand in the early 1970s, using several common incentives.

Import duties on imported materials and business taxes on both imported and domestically produced materials are refunded when production is for export. The textile industry has been the largest beneficiary of such refunds. In 1977, refunds equalled 4.1 percent of the total export value of textile products. Although refunds of taxes and duties on inputs merely enable exporters to buy inputs at world prices, they give some incentive to produce for export rather than for the domestic market.

The Bank of Thailand provides rediscount facilities to commercial banks that, in 1977, for example, enabled them to charge 7 percent (5 percentage points below the ordinary bank-loan rate) in discounting export commercial bills. These are usually three-month credits. The subsidy element equals 1.75 percent

Table 16.4: Domestic and world market prices for selected textile products

Textile	Price category	1978 June 12–16 (June 14)[a]	1978 December 11–15 (December 13)[a]	1979 June 11–15 (June 13)[a]
Cotton yarn 40s (baht/lb)	PD[b]	28.9 (4.5)	35–36 (6.7)	35 (14.7)
	PX1[d]	27.5	34.5	28.0
	PX2[e]	27.8	32.0	33.0
Cotton fabric, broad cloth gray 2210, 50" (baht/yd)	PD[c]	12.5 (43.6)	14.25 (18.7)	14.25 (35.7)
	PX1[f]	9.2	12.4	10.6
	PX2[f]	8.2	11.6	10.4
Polyester/cotton yarn 45s (baht/lb)	PD[b]	38.25 (40.1)	38–39 (14.2)	38–39 (21.4)
	PX1[e]	27.6	35.4	33.4
	PX2[e]	27.0	32.0	30.0
Polyester/cotton fabric 186 threads 47" gray (baht/yd)	PD[c]	11.55 (21.5)	14.2–15.0 (19.1)	14.5 (34.2)
	PX1[f]	9.4	12.3	10.8
	PX2[f]	9.6	12.2	–

PD Domestic price, being a weekly average in the Sampeng market
PX Price in Bangkok of exports from Korea (1) and Taiwan (2), before tariffs and other import charges are added; the original quotes are in US dollars and have been converted to baht at the day's prevailing exchange rate
Figures in parentheses are the premiums of PD over the average of the corresponding PX1 and PX2

a Date of export price quotation
b Cash payment
c 60-days' sight draft
d CIF (cost, insurance, freight)
e FOB
f Sight draft

Sources: PD: compiled by Masahiko Kobayashi, former adviser to the Textile Credit Center, at the Bangkok Bank in Bankkok. PX: original quotes taken from the *Japan Textile News Weekly*

of export value per year. Producers of exports can claim a 3.33 percent reduction in electricity costs. This subsidy is not significant.

Although receiving far less than exporters in Korea and Indonesia, in 1977 Thai textile exporters received a subsidy equal to around 6 percent of the value of exports. The subsidy rate in Korea in 1972 was 27 percent (World Bank 1975), and in Indonesia in 1978, 16–43 percent (IDE 1980). Table 16.4 shows tariff protection raises the domestic price above the export price, and tends to encourage selling at home rather than abroad. The 6 percent subsidy rate compensates only partly for the export-discouragement effect of protection.

Export growth is also affected by restrictive import policies. European and North American countries impose quotas on textile exports from Thailand for individual product categories under bilateral agreements that are part of the Multi-Fiber Arrangement. The Thai government negotiates textile quotas with each country every year and allocates them to individual textile exporters based on past export performance.

Thailand has been able to increase exports under this quota system because the more industrialized countries (including Taiwan, Korea, and Hong Kong) have been severely restricted, while Thai exporters have been given large quotas relative to their supply capacity. However, this slack has decreased recently. In 1978, export quotas on fabrics were 78 percent filled to the United Kingdom, 93 percent to West Germany, 94 percent to Italy, and up to 94 percent to the United States. Knitted shirt quotas were over 95 percent filled.

The exchange rate has also been helpful to export expansion. The baht has long been pegged to the US dollar, which depreciated against most other major currencies during the 1970s. At the same time, only a few minor adjustments were made in the dollar-baht rate, so since late 1971 the baht also depreciated. This helped competitiveness of Thai textile exports, accelerating their expansion.

The recent EE of Thai textile products can be attributed partly to a change in business behavior which, since the mid-1970s, has improved efficiency and quality. The change, obvious in our interviews of Thai textile firm personnel, has been self-reinforcing, as it was caused by an increasing need to sell abroad and by stiff competition in world markets (path A–D–C in the bottom panel of figure 16.1). The change has strengthened the competitiveness of Thai textiles not only abroad, but also against potential imports. As a consequence, real IS ultimately will be achieved, in that there would be no upsurge in imports, if the tariff were abolished.

Why Export Performance Differs

Large firms, which now have 50–80 percent export ratios, in the early 1970s supplied mainly the domestic market. They shifted to foreign markets gradually, initially disposing of excess supplies, and ultimately arranging production to meet specific foreign demands.

During August and September 1979, we interviewed major textile firms in Thailand to learn the relationship between export performance (measured as the percentage of output exported) of individual firms and their production, management, and marketing characteristics. All the sample firms started as import substituters, and none exported before 1971. Although the overall export–output ratio increased to more than 30 percent in 1978, the ratio differs greatly among firms.

The type of product is the crucial factor in the export ratio. But among firms with the same products, the principal determinant, developed from our interviews, is that the shift from domestic sales to exports requires firms to change production and management techniques and to acquire marketing channels abroad, and not every firm can meet these requirements.

The sample, which contains 25 firms, was selected to represent the behavior of major textile firms, and covers all major sectors (spinning, weaving, and clothing) in Bangkok. Inclusion of a few small-scale local weaving firms makes the sample representative of textile firms throughout Thailand. Fiber producers are excluded, with the exception of one that is also engaged in spinning and clothing production. The contents of the questionnaire and a list of the sample firms are reported in Tambunlertchai and Yamazawa (1981). The questionnaire was designed to evalue current government export incentives, quota restrictions of importing countries, future prospects for domestic and foreign demand, and the competitiveness of Thai textile products.

Export ratios of the 25 firms in the sample are classified by major products and by ownership in table 16.5. Many small-scale Thai firms specialize in weaving or making apparel for domestic markets, and thus export less than 10 percent of output. However, both Japanese and Thai firms are among the larger exporters, which contradicts the conventional notion that only multinational firms or joint ventures contribute to export expansion.

Product Category

The major textile product of a firm determines its export performance, a finding consistent with the difference in comparative advantage among product categories. The export ratio is small for polyester/rayon (p/r) and filament (synthetic) fabrics, whereas it is larger for clothing, cotton, and polyester/cotton (p/c) fabrics. Comparative advantage is determined by size and other conditions of domestic and foreign markets (demand), and the difficulty of technological transfer and size of optimum-scale operation (supply). Thus, spinning and weaving costs are significantly affected by the scale of production, scale is determined by the combined size of domestic and foreign demand, and demand in turn depends on price and quality.

Demand and supply conditions differ for individual products. Cotton textiles include those for industrial use, such as canvas and gauze, and textiles for clothing. The industrial category uses coarse yarn and involves easy technological

Table 16.5   Export performance of individual Thai textile firms, classified by products and ownership, in 1979

Major products	Joint venture[a]		Purely Thai-owned
	Japanese management	Thai management	
Cotton fabrics		B (65)	F (95)
			Z (50)
Cotton and polyester/	E (80)	U (50)	D (0) G (0)
cotton fabrics	H (45)	M (0–50)	I (75)
			J (30)
			N (25)
			X (50–60)
			Y (60)
Polyester/cotton fabrics	S (80)		
Polyester/rayon fabrics	T (30)		
	V (20)		
Filament fabrics	K (0–10)	L (25)	
	P (30)		
Clothing	R (100)	A (100)	
		Q (100)	
		W (30)	
Export ratios			
I 0–20%	1	0	2
II 20–40%	3	3 (incl. M)	2
III 40–64%	1	1	3
IV 65–100%	3	3	2

Each entry is an individual firm; the letters A–Z are used to identify firms in both the table and the text; the figures in parentheses are the firm's export ratio

[a] Joint-venture firms are classified by control, rather than by ownership. In one company, the management is controlled by Japanese, even though Thai shareholders together own more than 50 percent because the Thai holdings are fragmented

Source: Interviews conducted by the authors in August and September 1979

transfer. Two Thai firms (B and F) are major industrial suppliers in Southeast Asia.

There is a large domestic market for cotton and p/c for clothing. Simple equipment is used for spinning and weaving, and many firms thus have acquired the technology for producing grey fabrics, which are shipped to Europe, the United States, and Japan. In contrast, only four of the ten companies (H, M, N, and Y) producing cotton and p/c fabrics have dyeing facilities, including affiliated dyeing companies, but these are the largest firms, with between 70,000 and 150,000 spindles. The dyed and finished fabric is shipped to the Middle East, neighboring Asian countries, and domestic markets.

Polyester/rayon suiting (p/r), a cheap substitute for wool, as stable, but limited demand at home for uniforms and other practical garments. It is shipped in piece-dyed form. Technology transfer is more difficult and international competitiveness is limited. Two companies (T and V) specialize in p/r, and two others (M and Y) make it in addition to cotton and p/c fabrics.

Filament fabrics are used for lady's suitings and other outer garments. They are yarn-dyed or piece-dyed, and differentiated by design and weaving technique. This requires significant technical competence, and the joint-venture producers have only a few local competitors (including M). Domestic demand for filament fabrics is limited and a considerable part of domestic sales are believed to be used in border trade. A small amount is exported to Singapore. K, P, and L have only weaving (100–150 looms), dyeing, and finishing facilities, but purchase filament yarn from producers in Thailand.

Garment exports have a relatively short history. Domestic demand has grown and a wholesale market has developed at Bobey Market in Bangkok. Low labor costs contribute much to the competitiveness of Thai garment exports. Competition has been very severe, but export performance has been remarkable in recent years. The BOI (Board of Investment) has limited its aid to firms producing exclusively for export, in order to protect small local producers. Q and R started in 1970–72 as promoted firms with the 100 percent export obligation. Both are supplied fabrics from affiliated spinning–weaving firms (U and H, respectively), but they also use cheap fabrics from Korea and Hong Kong.

W is a joint venture between a Japanese underwear producer and a large Thai textile producer–distributor group, which includes Y. Management and technology at W originally came from the Japanese partner, but both have been successfully transferred to the Thai partner. W did not apply for BOI aid, and has competed with imports for the limited domestic demand. Sales increased as that demand expanded. W has half the domestic market for high-quality goods, sharing it with a Thai-German joint venture.

Production Control and Management

Although inter-firm differences in export–output ratios are largely accounted for by demand and supply conditions for the products of individual firms, divergent export performance among firms producing the same products still needs to be explained.

Quality, packaging, and timely delivery standards are usually higher for exports than for domestic sales. Textile finish is classified into A+, A, B, and C according to the number of frays and streaks. Normally, only A+ and A goods can be exported, B goods are sold locally, and C goods are rejected. Quality inspection is a prerequisite for exports, but the distinction between A and B is less important when production is only for domestic sales. All sample firms which export imposed stricter controls to maintain quality when they started exporting regularly, though they are still less strict than the controls of Japanese firms in Japan.

Closely integrated marketing and production control is indispensable. During the shift to exports, managerial methodology is more crucial than pure production technology. The factory manager is key, and all joint-venture firms, including those with Thai management, have appointed an experienced Japanese manager to this position. He is the last manager to be replaced by a Thai.

Changes in the product mix or production system were introduced by some export-oriented firms, especially those producing cotton and p/c products. For example, production of p/c fabric of 208 threads expanded, whereas 186-thread fabric has been discontinued. Both fabrics are used for shirting. (Threads measure the tightness of the weave; it is the sum of the number of warp and weft threads in an inch.)

Concentrating on one product eliminates frequent adjustment of machinery and thus improves efficiency. Joint-venture companies E, H, and S, and Thai company Y have adopted this strategy. E also adopted a strategic change in product mix, expanding its production of dyed and finished fabrics for shipment to markets in developing countries, thereby fully utilizing existing facilities. On the other hand, few producers of p/r and filament fabrics are enthusiastic about changing their management system and product mix beyond strengthening quality control and technical improvement. This is mainly because they are still oriented toward the domestic market and are eager to export only in the case of a recession at home. They are cautious in expanding and renovating capacity.

Garment producers have had their own export strategy from the beginning, under the 100 percent export obligation. Most major garment exporters have some form of contract with their customers, produce under the customers' brands, and have strict quality requirements. Usually the design, material, and workmanship are specified by the buyers. Once buyers are satisfied with the quality and the ability to meet prompt delivery schedules, they tend to stay with the same manufacturers. T, although without the export obligation, adopted strict quality control at the outset in order to sell under its Japanese parent-company label.

Marketing Channels

The relationship between textile firms and trading companies is complicated and changing. Thus, textile firms in Bangkok have not usually had direct contact with customers abroad; reliable third-party channels have been required. Market channels of individual firms for both domestic and export sale are classified by product and ownership in table 16.6.

Joint-venture firms with Thai management and purely Thai-owned firms sell directly to the Sampeng market. This is because most Thai businessmen in the industry, including Thai partners in joint ventures, started in Sampeng as importer-wholesalers. Even joint ventures with Japanese management sell directly to

Table 16.6: Marketing channels used for textile products, 1979

Ownership	Domestic market		Export market	
	Marketing channel	No. of firms	Marketing channel	No. of firms
Joint venture with Japanese management	JTC (affiliated)	4 (E, S, T, V)	JTC	6 (E, K, P, S, T, V)
	JTC + Direct	2 (H, K)	JTC + Direct	1 (H)
	Direct (partner wholesaler)	1 (P)	FTC	1 (R)
Joint venture with Thai management	JTC + Direct	1 (L)	JTC, FTC	2 (L, U)
	TTC	1 (W)	JTC + Direct	1 (B)
	Direct	4 (A, B, M, U)	Direct	2 (M, W)
Purely Thai owned	Direct	8 (C, D, F, G, I, J, N, X, Y, Z)	JTC + Direct	4 (F, I, J, Z)
			TTC + Direct	1 (N)
			TTC + JTC + Direct	1 (X)
			TTC	1 (Y)
			Direct	1 (C)

Each entry is an individual firm; the letters A–Z are used to identify them in both the table and the text

JTC   Sells through a Japanese trading company
TTC   Sells through a Thai trading company
FTC   Sells through a non-Japanese, non-Thai trading company
Direct Sells through own sales staff, including affiliated wholesalers

Source: Interviews conducted by the authors in August and September 1979

Sampeng through the Thai partners. Japanese trading companies are sometimes used for credit, and risk hedging after sales commitments have been made directly between the textile firm and Sampeng customer.

For export sales, on the other hand, marketing networks of Japanese trading companies are relied on more heavily. Foreign trading companies have not been allowed to participate in the brokerage business since the implementation of the Alien Business Law in 1972, so this is now usually done through proxy trading companies incorporated in Thailand.

Reliance on Japanese trading companies has decreased, and direct sales and the use of Thai traders has increased as Thai management has gained experience. Thus, direct-sales effort has been intensified by both Thai and joint-venture firms. Salesmen are now regularly sent abroad, and trading companies are simply used as export agents after the producer has established sales commitments. Sales of Thai textile goods to other Southeast Asian countries have been handled by small-scale Thai-Chinese merchants.

Japanese joint ventures often rely on non-partner trading companies for exporting. The marketing competence of Japanese general trading companies differs in individual markets. One may dominate in a European country, whereas another may have strong channels to the Middle East. Firms cannot rely only on affiliated traders for orders, but must use companies strong in the target markets. Still, the long-established relationships between Japanese joint ventures and affiliated trading companies are important.

Because a trading company will not sell competing products in the same market, at the outset of export activities Thai firms were handicapped by lack of access to foreign markets. In 1980, BOI began assisting Thai trading companies. By December 1980, 14 companies had applied, only 2 of which had begun operating at the end of 1981 (see chapter 18 below). One of the most active Thai traders is affiliated with a large Thai textile producer-distributor group, with company Y as the nucleus, which creates difficulties in approaching outside textile firms.

Besides the government-assisted trading companies, there are numerous small trading companies. Most are run by Thai-Chinese merchants, and a few by Indians. They engage mostly in importing, but a few also serve as agents for overseas fabric and garment buyers, finding suppliers and inspecting quality and packing. Although almost all fabric exports are handled by Japanese or large Thai trading companies or directly by the manufacturers, smaller trading companies are active in garment exports.

Export Orientation of Thai Entrepreneurs

The degree of export orientation also depends on the attitude of owners and managers. The switch from domestic to export orientation is not easy, requiring substantial effort and a long-term perspective. Thus, the decision not to export after import substitition is achieved may reflect satisfaction with selling in the domestic market, and fear of the risk in expanding production for export.

Among Thai textile firms, those with family management tend to emphasize domestic sales, including border trade. These markets do not require high-quality textiles, and prices are higher than for export sales. Also, because they are small, these firms usually lack the channels and experience needed to deal with exporting. They have thus been interested in exports only during severe recession at home.

Under the Multi-Fiber Arrangement, firms cannot export to Europe or North America more than their individual quotas. A firm's exports can increase only by increasing its share of Thailand's quota, or if there is an increase in the total Thai quota. The former can be done by applying for redistribution of the unfilled quota of others, after a firm has filled its own quota. Under this system, an export-oriented firm must fill its own quota (a given amount to a particular country), even at a loss, every year, and must apply for a gradual increase in its quota. Japanese joint ventures have increased their share in this way. Some Thai firms have not got used to the system and have lost their quota because they have not filled it during peaks in domestic demand.

Educational background and the business experience of managers may be an important element in the differing export emphasis. Thai firms with family management are generally run by first-generation immigrants from China with little formal education. Their firms typically start as traders, or as small-scale manufacturers. Well-established relationships with wholesalers in Sampeng are usual. They aim at high profits over the short run, and emphasize domestic sales. In contrast, a younger group, children of the immigrant businessmen, who have had a formal education (university or commercial college), have gone into exports. Although only a few have been trained in textiles, with their general educational background and foreign-language ability, they are adept at modern management. They have longer-term objectives, including expansion, and are more internationally minded.

Conclusions

Japanese historical experience shows that modern manufacturing industries have developed in what can be called a catching-up product cycle (CPC), a sequence of import growth, domestic production substituting for imports (IS), and expansion into exports (EE). The CPC of cotton, rayon, and synthetic textiles indicate efficiency improvement is the prime moving force in CPC development, partly assisted by government protection.

The CPC is a rational development pattern for a late-starting country with a sufficiently large enough domestic market and potential comparative advantage in the industry concerned. Imports create a domestic market for the new product, local producers gain efficiency through import substitution, and finally competitiveness is tested in world markets. Not every industry can pass through

IS to EE. Many, such as metals, machinery, and chemicals, after achieving IS under protection, have not exported. Constrained by small-scale production, because of small domestic markets and the greater need for technology transfers, these industries can export only with substantial subsidies.

CPC is sometimes challenged by a counter-example – industries introduced into developing countries for the purpose of exporting from the beginning, as has happened in the assembly or processing of electronics and chemicals. This, however, is only possible through foreign firms bringing in capital, technology, parts, materials, and exporting channels – indeed, providing everything apart from the labor force.

Nevertheless, the CPC model provides an analytic framework to assess the performance of industries in contemporary developing countries, and we have applied the framework to the Thai textile industry. Both cotton and synthetic fabric production achieved IS rapidly, and in the early 1970s started EE. Contrary to the Japanese experience, in Thailand the textile industry achieved IS under protection and started EE with government promotion measures. However, EE has become more self-sustaining in the 1980s because of changes in business attitudes toward exporting and cost reduction and quality improvement.

A similar pattern of export development occurred earlier in Korea and Taiwan, and it seems to characterize a historically successful mechanism for developing manufactured exports. Further CPC development of modern industry is, however, hindered in the 1980s by changes in the world-market environment and technology. This includes intensified protection in developed-country markets. Exports of textiles and clothing to Europe and North America are restricted for Korea, Taiwan, and Hong Kong. Thailand initially benefited because the quotas exceeded the supply capacity. But as capacity expands, Thailand will feel more restricted by the quota system.

Policy distortions in developing countries have prevented efficiency improvement. This includes prolonged protection of inefficient local firms from import competition, and negative protection of promising export production with complicated tariff-subsidy systems. Market competition is the most reliable force promoting efficiency improvement during the shift from import substitution to export expansion. At the export-expansion stage, firms meet more severe competition and are thus compelled to improve efficiency. It is therefore important for governments of developing countries to encourage manufacturers to rationalize production and management. Removal of tariffs and other restrictions, and gradual reduction of direct promotional measures can be scheduled, while indirect encouragement is strengthened through business education and subsidized marketing activities.

References

Akamatsu, Kaname (1961), "A Theory of Unbalanced Growth in the World Economy," *Weltwirtschaftliches Archiv*, 86(2).

Ichimura, Shinichi (1982), "Cultural and Institutional Factors and Government Policies in Implementing Appropriate Technologies: The Survey Findings in Indonesia, Thailand and the Philippines," mimeo.

IDE (1980), Ajia Keizai Kenkyujo (Institute for Developing Economies), *Hatsuten-tojo-koku no Seni Sangyo*, Tokyo.

JCFA (1974), Nippon Kagaku Kyokai (Japan Chemical Fiber Association), *Nippon Kagaku Seni Sangyoshi*.

Katano, Hikoji, et al. (1976), "Technology Transfer in Japanese Joint Ventures in Thailand – A Case Study of [the] Textile Industry," ECONCEN Study, no. 19 (June).

Kojima, Kiyoshi (1973), "Reorganization of North–South Trade: Japan's Foreign Economic Policy for the 1970s," *Hitotsubashi Journal of Economics*, 13(2): 1–28 (February).

LTES (*Estimates of Long-term Economic Statistics of Japan*), series edited by Kazushi Ohkawa, Miyohei Shinohara, and Mataji Umemura, Tokyo: Toyo Keizai Shimposha.
   vol. 11, *Textiles* (1979), Shozaburo Fujino, Shiro Fujino, and Akira Ono.

Shinohara, Miyohei (1962), *Growth and Cycles in the Japanese Economy*, Tokyo: Kinokuniya.

Tambunlertchai, Somsak, and Ippei Yamazawa (1981), *Manufactured Exports and Foreign Direct Investment: A case study of the textile industry in Thailand*, Hitotsubashi University, Faculty of Economics, Report Series no. 29.

World Bank (1975), *Industrial Policy and Development in Korea*, Staff Working Paper no. 236, Washington, DC: World Bank.

17 Is the Division of Labor Limited by the Extent of the Market? A Study of Automobile Parts Production in East and Southeast Asia

KONOSUKE ODAKA

Industrializing nations view the automobile industry as symbolic of development, and many have sought to establish domestic production. The development of a domestic machinery industry is one intended result of promoting a local automobile industry. Some time has passed since the initial thrust into auto-mobile manufacturing was made, and it is useful to assess what has happened. Drawing on field studies made in the latter half of the 1970s, this essay reviews the performance of an important segment of the industry, parts suppliers, with special emphasis on the growth of smaller firms in the machinery industry. The overall question is in the title of this chapter: "Is the division of labor limited by the extent of the market?" The answer is "Yes, but ... "

Six Asian nations are studied: five that began to promote the industry in the 1970s (Indonesia, Malaysia, Thailand, the Philippines, and Korea), and Japan, where the industry started in the 1930s, but did not become significant until the 1950s. As part of the analysis, Japan's experience in the 1950s is compared to the experiences in the 1970s of the five other countries (hereafter called the selected countries).

By the 1930s, the technology of auto production had reached a plateau. Although changes have taken place in materials, design, and production engineering, not much innovation has occurred in the basic essentials of auto making. In terms of gaps in technology, one can thus argue that the selected countries were not necessarily worse off in the 1970s than the Japanese industry was in the early 1950s. Yet, in general, the parts industry in the five countries in the 1970s can be considered underdeveloped relative to Japan in the 1950s, in terms of both number and size of suppliers.

As part of the "but ... ," particular attention is paid to job creation and technology transfer. Most of the transfer of technology that has taken place appears to be capital embodied – built into the production equipment. Because most of these machines have been made in countries with relatively higher labor

389

costs, they have tended to be labor-saving. This relates directly to job creation. Analysis of employment in the parts supplier industry in the selected countries in the 1970s, compared to Japan in 1950, suggests the industry has created fewer jobs per vehicle produced than occurred in Japan. Thus achievement of two of the goals of promoting an automobile industry have not been achieved to the extent they were by Japan in the 1950s, and might still have been in the 1970s with different choices of capital equipment.

Focusing on the acquisition of technical skills and the relationship between suppliers and assemblers, the Japanese supplier network and its historical development are examined in the first part of this chapter. This provides a backdrop for looking at the relative underdevelopment of parts suppliers in the selected countries. Besides comparison with the Japanese experience, some observations on Japanese joint ventures in the area are included. Then, drawing on my own research and other data, Philippine metal-working firms are examined in more detail. The international competitiveness of the region's industry is next analyzed, and some of the important differences in the experiences of Japan and the selected countries are then discussed. Emerging from this are reasons for the relative underdevelopment of the selected countries' parts industries.

The automobile industry is characterized by the cooperation of a large number of firms supplying or assembling interchangeable parts or performing certain processing services, and a relatively small number of final assemblers producing the finished product from components supplied by the first group and internally. This structure reflects the fact that the industry is a discrete process industry, with a set of independent, well-defined production processes. Moreover, any machine product may be decomposed into a finite number of machine elements (Odaka 1983). By virtue of these hardware properties, automobile production is amenable to a vertical division of labor among many production units.[1]

An assembler looks for reliable suppliers and subcontractors when it feels the limitation of its own resources: production may be "dissimilar" to its major lines of activities (Richardson 1972), or financial or engineering resources may be constrained. More basically, the degree of vertical nonintegration is determined by the extent of the market for the final product (Stigler 1951).

This division of labor, sometimes termed the American system of manufacturing, has proven highly efficient for producing standard automobiles in large quantities. It was first applied to cars in 1913 by Ford, at its Highland Park Model T plant. The success of Ford's venture symbolized the culmination of technological convergence (a term coined by Rosenberg 1963). The vertical

---

[1] Assemblers are the companies whose names appear on the car. Parts makers are classified as OEMs (original-equipment manufacturers), who sell assemblers parts for newly built cars, or as replacement parts makers. The latter generally supply consumable items such as headlights, oil filters, etc. Companies can, and many do, sell the same item both as original equipment and replacement (repair) parts, but other firms concentrate on one or the other market. Subcontractors provide services such as subassemblies and painting, although the term also is extended to such fabricators as metal stampers.

division of labor in machine making not only enhanced productive efficiency, but also stimulated the creation of new products in the machinery industry, especially during the second half of the 19th century in the United States.[2]

The American system set a precondition which the follower countries in economic development could not but accept. Thus, when countries in postwar Asia decided (for better or worse) to establish their own auto industries, about the only technological choice was to adopt it. Accordingly, initial production began with assembly-line operations based on foreign models. This did not mean, however, that there was no room for minor adjustments. When Toyota built its first plant in Koromo in 1937–38, because the expected maximum ouput was only 500 cars per month, a large-scale plant with limited-purpose equipment did not make sense. The designers thus tried to substitute as much labor as possible for capital equipment, to scale down the size of the plant considerably from western ones, and to adopt a number of general-purpose machine tools in place of specialized ones (Toyota 1958: 605–22). Such attempts nonetheless remained variants of the basic American system. The Japanese industry could not achieve the international price competitiveness until output reached a level that could utilize scale economies, and thus the division of labor.

The Japanese Supplier Network

Japanese car companies feel there are cost savings in relying more on sub-contractors and suppliers than their counterparts in other industrialized countries do. This is illustrated by comparing the gross value added to the finished vehicle by the assemblers: in 1973, it was 18 percent in Japan, 43 percent for the "big three" (General Motors, Ford, Chrysler) in the United States, and 44 percent for Volkswagen and Benz in Germany (MITI 1976: 360–64). Reliance was especially stong in the 1960s (Hayashi 1961: 156–61, 319–29), no doubt reflecting the period's wage differentials by firm size, which meant the typical supplier was paying considerably lower wages than the assemblers.

Saying the car companies rely on parts makers and subcontractors, however, is not the same as saying they are not integrated in their own way. Firms supplying several auto compaines, such as Yazaki Sogyo (wire harnesses and meters) are a minority; most supply just one. There is a vertical division of labor

[2] The parts suppliers and subcontractors discussed in this essay are mostly metal-working shops, broadly defined (firms using machine tools), firms providing electrical items, and those that are subassemblers (rather than fabricators). The SIC classes finished automobiles as transportation equipment, whereas components are spread over fabricated metal parts, machinery, and electrical machinery. (The SIC is a classification structure for the entire national economy. First issued in 1939, it has been revised periodically since, and is published by the US Government, Office of Management and Budget, as the *Standard Industrial Classification Manual*.)

A good description of what machine tools do, written for non-engineers, is found in Engelberger (1980).

between assemblers and suppliers that is generally long-standing and ongoing, and sometimes the assembler is a supplier's sole customer.

There are company-specific associations of suppliers: Kyoho-kai for Toyota parts manufacturers, Takara-kai for Nissan, and so on. As an example of their activities, Kyoho-kai helped spread stricter cost accounting ("value analysis") and quality control (by encouraging quality-control circles). The associations are information clearing houses, and help keep up morale.

A network of parts manufacturers did not develop in prewar Japan. In fact, Hoshino (1966: 92–130) argues that underdevelopment of medium and small-scale machine shops was a major reason why mass-produced machinery production did not develop extensively in prewar Japan. The situation was to a considerable degree a result of the small size of the market.

Only later – beginning perhaps in the war years, definitely by the mid-1950s – did Japanese assemblers decide to cultivate subcontracting networks. For instance, Toyota found few firms acceptable in the 1930s in its search for suitable suppliers, and so decided to produce most parts internally (Odaka 1981: 182–83), a practice that persisted for some years. Accordingly, a substantial share of replacement parts was also produced by the assemblers. In the early 1950s, the proportion (in value) of replacement parts from outside suppliers was only 19 percent in the case of Toyota, 26 percent for Isuzu, and 34 for Nissan. Mitsubishi's rate was higher, 62 percent, but the company's market share was very small. The weighted average of these figures is 32 percent (Kokuritsu Kokkai 1978: 84–85).

Although development of an extensive supplier network began only after World War II, almost from the beginning of the industry the assemblers have taken great care in maintaining cordial relations with suppliers. As Toyota's declaration of purchasing policy puts it, "once affiliated, a parts manufacturer shall be regarded as an organic part of the Corporation; in principle, therefore, standing orders shall be placed with the firm, and as much assistance as possible extended to improve its performance" (Toyota 1939: article 4). This is still in effect.

As suggested by the Toyota declaration, the assemblers have taken a very active interest in increasing the economic and engineering capability of their suppliers, primarily by offering technical assistance. Because the assemblers inevitably have several sources of supply, the parts companies have an incentive to improve quality or reduce price to increase their share of the orders. In other words, the assemblers work closely with their suppliers, but at the same time encourage competition among them in a way that would be more difficult with another division of the same company.[3]

The assemblers had several reasons to promote parts makers. In the period of early rapid growth, the late 1950s and early 1960s, the assemblers faced

---

[3] Toyota's purchasing policy stipulates the number of suppliers for an item (for example, spark plugs) shall be exactly two.

a shortage of financial and other resources; moreover, they were not always self-sufficient in engineering expertise. Consequently, it was beneficial to support the growth of outside suppliers. In other words, assemblers favored subcontracting elements of the production process dissimilar to their own major activities or experience, thus establishing complementarity of activities (Richardson 1972).

Although the suppliers rarely deal with more than one assembler, the degree of dependence varies. Some firms behave very much like wholly owned subsidiaries, whereas others are quite independent in their decision-making. The nature of the relationship to a large extent reflects historical circumstances. Two broad types can be distinguished in the development of Japanese parts suppliers. The first are those previously engaged in other types of metal and machine-goods production. The second type are firms that were either nurtured or spun-off by assemblers.

In both cases, but especially for the former, the initial relationship with the assemblers was established on the basis of the supplier's technological strength. Having gained the confidence of an assembler, the ties were reinforced with friendships and even marriages. Although most of the smaller firms were definitely short on expertise, as well as of managerial capability, they had spent a number of years learning and improving their metal-working techniques. Here again, one finds a framework of engineering, financial, and labor skills to which foreign technology could be added when necessary or available.

All the Japanese automobile assemblers started as producers of metal products of one kind or another. For instance, Toyota is an outgrowth of a leading maker of cotton weaving machines. Nissan's development was based largely on the technological resources accumulated by the two enterprises that joined to form the company; one of the core members, Tobata Casting, had long experience operating an iron foundry. Similarly, Isuzu originated partly from Ishikawajima Shipbuilding, a leading firm in machinery production (see descriptions in Ono and Odaka 1979; Adachi et al. 1981). Consequently, these firms received considerable assistance, both financial and technical, from their parent or sibling firms, which were engaged in non-automobile production.

Long years of trial and error before the war laid the groundwork for the ability to absorb advanced technologies from overseas after the war. Nissan, for instance, managed to learn everything it wanted to know from Austin within just six years (from September 1952 to March 1958). Such an accumulation of manufacturing expertise made it easy, and natural, for the assemblers to extend engineering assistance, if necessary, to others. In any event, when the time was ripe to develop a subcontracting network of parts producers, the assemblers were ready to help the smaller machine shops meet the requirements.

Technological Upgrading

Final-assembly labor productivity rose steadily from the late 1940s to the early 1980s, though in the 1960s the rate of increase slowed significantly, compared to that of the 1950s. For parts, a sustained rise in productivity did not begin until the end of the 1950s, but the pace of the increase had not slowed. This is reflected in the price indexes in figure 17.1.

During the immediate postwar years, economic conditions were not at all favorable to vehicle and machinery production. Demand was suppressed until the start of the Korean War, and capital equipment was generally dilapidated.

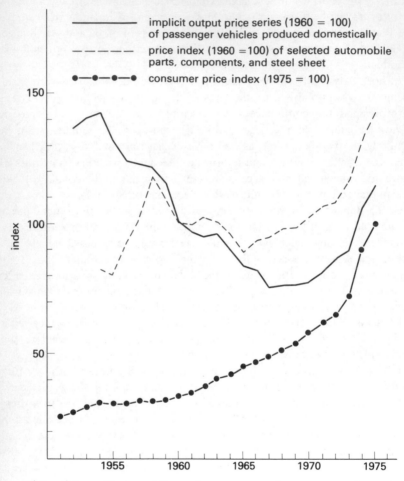

Figure 17.1: Prices of automobiles and auto parts and components, Japan, 1951–75

Sources: Automobile prices were estimated from data in various issues of *Jidosha tokei nempo*. The price index of parts and components was compiled from data given in *Kikai tokei nempo* and by the Bank of Japan's *Bukka shisu nempo*. The consumer price index is from the *Shohisha bukka shisu nempo* (1976 edn)

Production facilities in the Japanese machinery industry in the early 1950s, particularly for machine tools, were poor. With respect to engineering standards, the machine-tool industry was more than twenty years behind the level of the United States in 1950 (Kikai Shinko 1968: 57). According to an American machine-tool mission, which examined 225,000 Japanese machine tools in 1952, only 150 units were "acceptable" (Hayashi 1961: 412-14). As of 1954, machine tools in use for more than a decade comprised over 70 percent of the total, whereas the comparable figure in the United States was 43 percent.

But significant technological upgrading took place in the decade after the war. In 1956, MITI commissioned a group of professional engineers from various parts manufacturers to investigate the characteristics of 25 key automobile components commonly available both in Japan and from abroad (mostly the United States). The detailed reports allow an assessment of the technical level of the industry at the time. Four general conclusions emerge.

(1) The quality of raw materials was superior in some foreign components.
(2) Japanese parts reflected minute and equal attention to both functionally essential and nonessential elements. In contrast, foreign components demonstrated care in processing vitally important areas, while neglecting functionally incidental operations such as exterior polishing.
(3) Engineering performance of the Japanese products was comparable to the foreign components, unless one was exceptionally particular about some details.
(4) Many observers detected overall economic inefficiency in the Japanese production lines.

Table 17.1 summarizes the comparisons. The perceived economic inefficiency implies cheap labor alone could not overcome the effects of other factors, such as small-lot production, resulting in relatively costlier Japanese products. In fact, another 1956 survey found the prices of Japanese auto parts could hardly compete – they were more expensive by from 20 percent (for cast parts) to 100 percent (for some electric parts) (JAPIA 1957, vol. 1: 39).

In many respects, the early 1960s mark a turning point for Japanese auto making, as this is the period when exports began to grow and, in 1965, importation of foreign cars was liberalized. International competitiveness was attained through the assemblers' and parts suppliers' efforts, combined with favorable economic conditions, for which the central government (especially MITI) was partly responsible.

How is this made consistent with the observation that there was little or no sustained upward trend in average labor productivity in real terms prior to 1960? The only answer is that the technological upgrading of the late 1940s and 1950s improved product quality or increased capital efficiency, but did not significantly affect labor efficiency. Thus, after the war, some parts manufacturers had obtained high-quality machine tools from Army and Navy arsenals (Nihon Denso

Table 17.1: A comparison of the Japanese and non-Japanese auto parts and components industries, 1954–55

Parts and components tested	Observations on purely engineering traits			Observations on economic aspects of production engineering	
	Domestic superior	No difference	Foreign superior	Domestic part costly, owing to small production lot	Foreign part showing signs of intensive cost-saving measures
Cast parts					
Pistons[a]	(x)	x			
Piston rings		x			yes
Intake exhaust bulb guides	x			yes	
Wheel hubs and brake drums[a]	(x)	x			yes
Forged parts					
Intake and exhaust bulbs[b]	(x)	x			yes
Tie rod ends[c]	(x)	x		yes	yes
Rear wheel axles			x		yes
Knuckle supports[b]	(x)	x		yes	yes
Universal joints			x		yes
Machine-fabricated parts					
Piston pins[d]		x	(x)		yes
King pins[e]		x	(x)		yes
Miscellaneous components					
Fuel pumps[f]		x	(x)		
Clutch discs			x	yes	yes
Oil seals		x		yes	yes
Brake linings		x		yes	yes

Component					
Water pumps	x				yes
Brake cylinders[d]	x	(x)		yes	
Electrical parts					
Spark plugs			x		
Spark coils	x				yes
Condensers[c]	x	(x)		yes	
Distributors[e]	x	(x)			
Generators and regulators	x	(x)			yes
Body parts					
Back mirrors	x	x			
Electric windshield wipers[d]	x			yes	
Switches		x			
Total					
(1) No functional differences	2	18	5 ⎫	9	15
(2) No functional differences, but superiority in a non-functional aspect	7	6	12 ⎭		

In 12 cases where there is "no (overall functional) difference," the Japanese or non-Japanese component excels in at least one aspect; this is noted in the appropriate "superior" column by (x)

[a] Exterior finish
[b] Precision
[c] Less dispersion
[d] Hardness
[e] Heat treatment
[f] Performance at high speed
[g] Quality of die-casting, pressing, etc.
[h] Quality of materials

Source: Compiled by the author from Jidosha Gijutsu Kai 1955

1974: 23–24), and in the late 1940s the major assemblers sold used equipment at nominal prices to associated firms (Aisan Kogyo 1973: 21–31). In addition, some aeromechanic engineers and other specialists, on returning from military duty, may have joined the industry.

After 1963, importation of foreign technology surged, and in the early 1960s a transformation occurred in the machine-tool industry as one branch after another reached international standards. Parts manufacturers were actively engaged in the installation of more, newer, and increasingly Japanese-made equipment. Gear cutters, gear finishers, and screw grinders were among the last group to be domestically purchased, and some of these are still imported. Around 1965, stamping and forging capability had reached the point where domestic dies were competitive. Die-making is one of the most sophisticated machining operations. (For a general account of postwar technological progress in Japan's machine-tool industry, see Tomiyama (1973: 75–96).)

Not only did the medium and small-scale firms increase the capital intensity of their production facilities; at one level, they pushed it much further than did the larger corporations. Much of their equipment was secondhand – for firms with 10–19 employes, almost two-thirds of the equipment bought in 1960 was secondhand; the proportion declined steadily as firm size (number of employes) increased. New or used, the number of machine tools per employe was higher for the smaller firms, and this tendency held unchanged over time (1960–73). This implies smaller firms sought to renovate themselves through capital deepening.[4]

Changes occurred in the quality and type of basic materials used in automobile production. In particular, lower-grade speciality steels were substituted for higher grades, and then ordinary steel replaced speciality steel. Nonferrous metal, synthetic rubber, and plastic parts were introduced both to cut cost and reduce the automobile's weight, which contributed to greater fuel efficiency. Besides the improvements in production technology, starting in the mid-1960s, the suppliers began to place emphasis on such aspects of organizational efficiency as quality control and cost accounting. The average size of parts-producing firms gradually increased in the 1950s and 1960s. Median employment at firms that were members of JAPIA (the Japan Auto Parts Industry Association) more than doubled between 1956 (82 employes) and 1960 (167), and doubled again in the

---

[4] The comparison is subject to some reservations. For one, the number of employes is inclusive of both production and office workers, but the proportion of office workers is likely to be higher in a larger firm. For another, the ratios are expressed in number of units of machine tools, disregarding their size and economic value, and thus the numbers may overestimate the significance of smaller-sized, cheap machines. Assuming the degree of biases created by these factors remain reasonably constant over time, the intertemporal comparisons remain relevant.

The number of newly installed machine tools per company presents an entirely different picture from the per employe data, for it becomes smaller as the size of the firm decreases. However, it shows a clear increasing trend over time, regardless of firm size. Data are from the 1960 edition of the *Kosaku kikai setsubi to tokei chosa hokoku*.

1960s (252 employes in 1965, 335 in 1970). In 1974, the number was 417. These findings lead to the conjecture that technological innovation in the automobile parts industry was primarily capital-augmenting through the 1950s, after which it became more of a labor-augmenting variety.

Parts Suppliers in the Selected Countries

Almost by definition of being an underdeveloped country, the number of domestic firms that can supply an automobile industry is limited. This means components initially must be imported, and even at later stages the local assemblers have tended to be vertically integrated, manufacturing many parts in their own plants.

In this discussion of parts suppliers in Indonesia, Malaysia, Thailand, the Philippines, and Korea – the selected countries – the Japanese experience in the 1950s has been used as a frame of reference, because the size of the Japanese automobile market then is roughly comparable to that of the selected countries in the 1970s. In 1950–55, the annual production volume in Japan, and the number of vehicles on the road, is more or less the same magnitude as in the selected countries in the late 1970s (table 17.2).

Table 17.2: Number of automobiles (passenger and commercial) in use in East and Southeast Asia, 1978

Country	Automobiles in use ('000)	Size of population ('000)	Population per automobile
Indonesia	890	143,280	161
Singapore	209	2,330	11
Malaysia	702	12,570	18
Thailand	731	45,100	62
Philippines	792	46,350	59
Taiwan	380	17,968	47
Korea	385	3,019	8
Japan (1978)	34,121	114,900	3
Japan (1955)	754	89,276	118
Japan (1950)	257	83,200	324

Sources

1978 values: *Shuyokoku jidosha tokei* 1980 edn: 43
Earlier values: *Jidosha tokei hempo* 1966 edn: 46–47
Population: *Statistical Yearbook of Japan* 1960 edn

Moreover, the degree of international price competitiveness of completed automobiles in the selected countries in the late 1970s is somewhat reminiscent of the Japanese experience in the early 1950s. As an example, the retail price of a typical passenger vehicle made in Japan in 1954 was 1.84 times that of a standard British model (Hayashi 1961: 127).

Despite an apparent similarity in the size of the market, the selected countries have lagged considerably behind 1950s Japan with respect to development of a parts-supplying network. Although it is not easy to determine the exact number of auto parts producers, in 1975 there were at least 95 in Malaysia, and about 195 in the Philippines, compared to 686 in Japan in 1955. The Japanese figure, however, includes general suppliers, which catered to other industries as well as to car production. If one counts only those firms that were members of JAPIA and were direct suppliers of the automobile assemblers, the number is 280 (JAPIA 1957: 9–10; Chee and Fong 1983: table 3–23; Tolentino and Ybañez 1983: 5.22). In any event, the selected countries in the late 1970s were still heavily dependent on imported parts and components. In fact, over 98 percent of the total demand for auto parts and components in Indonesia was imported in 1975 ($30 million worth) (MRI 1979: 12).

The automobile industries in the selected countries have not generated significant numbers of new jobs. To illustrate this, I have computed hypothetical rates of manpower utilization by the auto industry in each of the countries, taking the 1950 Japanese record as the standard of comparison. At that time, the Japanese auto parts industry had yet to introduce the various new production methods that eventually improved labor productivity tremendously; the transformation came after 1960 (Odaka 1978: 127–31). In 1950–51, a completed automobile (passenger or commercial) involved 0.95 man-years of labor (suppliers and assemblers combined), so employment did not quite equal unit output. Applying this ratio to the production figures of the selected countries in 1977, I obtained the potential employment which could have been generated if the subcontracting and parts network had been as fully developed as in Japan in 1950–51. The actual employment figures were then divided by the hypothetical upper bounds to yield the utilization rates. Data are given in tables 17.3 and 17.4.[5]

As expected, the utilization rate is highest in Korea, which has adopted a very aggressive program for the localization of automobile production. Philippine performance reflects the early introduction of domestic content programs, called

[5] The Japanese employment figures do not include motorcycles. The calculated utilization rates are likely to be underestimated, because the average labor productivity of the selected countries was not quite on par with that of 1950 Japan. Moreover, the employment figures in the selected countries may be underestimated because of, among other things, underrepresentation of the informal sector.

The informal sector is "that part of the urban economy of LDCs characterized by small competitive individual or family firms, petty retail trade and services, *labor-intensive* methods of doing things, low *levels of living*, poor working conditions, high *birth rates*, low levels of health and education, etc." (Todaro 1977: 422, italics in original).

Table 17.3: Employment generation by the Japanese automobile industry, 1950–51

Year	Population census	Employment, as reported by Establishment census	Manufacture census[a]	Annual production (passenger and commercial)[b]
1950	76,326	na	67,208	67,095 (35,498)
1951	na	92,316	75,186	82,292 (43,802)

na not available
[a] Establishments with four or more employes
[b] Inclusive of three-wheelers (three-wheeler production is given in parentheses)

Sources

Employment: *Kokusei chosa, Showa 25*; *Jigyosho tokei chosa, Showa 26*; *Kogyo tokei hyo* 1950–51
Vehicle production: *Jidosha tokei nempyo* 1966 edn: 3

Table 17.4: Employment generation in the automobile industries of the selected countries, 1975

Country	Gainful employment in automobile industry	Annual automobile production (passenger and commercial)	Employment generation per unit of automobile produced	Hypothetical rate of utilization of manpower resources (%)
Indonesia	10,700	78,873	0.14	14.1
Malaysia	7,080[a]	60,903[a]	0.12[a]	12.1
Thailand	na	31,029	na	na
Philippines	14,300	48,658	0.29	30.6
Korea	20,900	37,290	0.56	58.4

na not available
[a] 1974 data

Sources

Employment: United Nations *Yearbook of Industrial Statistics* 1978 edn
Production: for Malaysia, from Ajia Keizai Kenkyujo 1980: 185; for the other countries, Odaka 1983: tables 2.4, 4.1, 5.1, and 6.2

the PCMP and PTMP (Progressive Car and Progressive Truck Manufacturing Programs).

The relative underdevelopment in 1980 of domestic manufacturers of auto parts and components in the selected countries is partly reflected in the small size of their operations. Only 3 of 17 factories in the organized sector in Jakarta and Bandung (Indonesia) had more than 50 employes in 1977. Size was even smaller for machine shops in the informal sector; there was single-person ownership of 39 out of the 41 factories surveyed in Bandung in the mid-1970s (Harahap et al. 1978). By the same token, for 50 parts suppliers surveyed in Kuala Lumpur in 1975, the median number of employes was 49 (Chee and Fong 1983: table 3.22).

Compared to these, the Philippine machine shops were somewhat bigger, the average number of employes was 96 (median, 50) for the 27 firms in the Metro Manila area in 1976. Of these, only 11 firms produced metal products, and they were much smaller (average, 49 employes, median, 38) (Albarracin and Tolentino 1978). The average size was comparatively larger in a later Philippine sample, in which another set of 51 metal-working factories were surveyed in Metro Manila. The 49 firms reporting employed an average of 80 workers (median, 53) at the end of 1977 (Albarracin et al. 1979: appendix). By contrast, the average number of employes was 144 in 1955 for 251 Japanese factories which specialized in auto parts. Moreover, 61 general suppliers, firms also catering to other industries, were much bigger in size, employing on average, 1,511 people (JAPIA 1957).

Locally Available Parts

Locally available auto parts are evaluated in terms of both engineering and economic properties. To do this, a table showing certain technological and economic aspects has been prepared for 266 major components. Each of these products is described qualitatively in terms of (1) major production activities, (2) degree of capital intensity and of capital-labor substitution, and (3) the size of the market. The range of parts and components produced in the selected countries is limited. Of the 266 items, 47 have been identified as being domestically manufactured in the late 1970s in one or more of the selected countries. Moreover, the production technologies of the items being manufactured are relatively simple; they either use easily available processes, or face favorable market conditions. The list, however, is not necessarily exhaustive. Table 17.5 provides the characteristics of the 47 items.[6]

Consumable parts (those with significant replacement markets) comprise at least half the list, and three-quarters of the goods characterized by scale economies either have large replacement markets (bumpers) or sizeable non-auto demand (radios). Note that 40 of the items make use of relatively capital-intensive production equipment, the majority of which (27 of the 40) is not easily substitutable by labor.

---

[6] The definition of domestic production lacks rigor. For one thing, products vary greatly in their degree of real domestic content. Only a handful of items are 100 percent local, while in an extreme case an imported item packed in a locally manufactured box was classified as domestically produced.

Of the eight metal-fabricating operations described in the table, joining is the commonest, followed, in order, by pressing, forming, painting, machining, casting, heat treating, and forging. This ordering is largely consistent with the relative frequencies derived from a survey taken in 1973 covering the entire metal-working industry in the Philippines. The Spearmann's rank coefficient between the two is 0.857, which is significantly different from zero at the 10 percent level. This finding is consistent with observations by engineering experts (foreign and native) that forging, heat treating, and casting are the more difficult operations to introduce into the region. In the late 1930s, Japanese skill in forging and large-scale pressing is also said to have been quite primitive (Toyota 1958: 556, 614).

As noted, only part of the locally-manufactured parts and components are used by assemblers as original equipment. An original-equipment manufacturer (OEM), when submitting a part to a joint venture for approval, must pass stringent tests by the assembler's foreign parent. Parts manufacturers in the selected countries have in fact complained that too rigid a standard of quality testing works as a strong (perhaps intentional) deterrent to the progress of domestic content programs.

The adoption of a machine part as original equipment, therefore, is an indication that the quality of the product has reached an internationally acceptable standard. In other words, by choosing original equipment as the object of investigation, one is assured of dealing only with a set of products that are "normalized" for their quality variations.

The last three columns of table 17.5 show 30 of the 47 parts domestically manufactured are used as original equipment in at least one country. For any one of the countries, however, the number is much smaller, and the items are the kind largely unaffected by economies of scale. More specifically, of the 23 original-equipment items made in the Philippines, 20 either have no scale economies or the presence of an extensive non-original-equipment market (as replacement parts or in non-auto uses) provides the scale needed. For Thailand, the proportion is 15 of the 18, and all 5 of the locally-produced original-equipment items in Malaysia also have replacement markets.

In the case of the eight assemblers operating in Thailand in the 1970s, 20 or so items were obtained from local manufacturers of parts and components. Most of the assemblers of passenger vehicles subcontracted the production of radiators, wire harnesses, exhaust systems, seat assemblies, batteries, tires and tubes, carpet, glass, and certain other electrical components (table 17.6).

Indonesia and Malaysia were somewhat behind the other countries in terms of local production of original equipment. We know of only a few items, such as tires, batteries, and paint, that had been adopted in Malaysia (Chee and Fong 1983: table 3.26). Obviously this is due to the small size of the market, but also to the delay in the implementation of an official domestic content program. One subsequently may expect a larger number of locally obtained items in Indonesia, in view of the progress of a domestic content program, although as yet no hard data are available on this point (Harahap et al. 1978: 23).

Table 17.5: Characteristics of production of selected auto parts

(a) Metal parts

Identification no.	Parts and components	Operations								Factor inputs		Market factors				Domestic supplies of OEMs		
		Moulding/casting	Forging	Pressing	Forming	Joining	Machining	Painting/plating	Heat treatment	Capital intensive	Low substitutability	Fast-moving	Non-auto demand	Non-model specific	Scale economies	Malaysia	Thailand	Philippines
3	Intake exhaust valve		O			O			O	O	O	O			O			
7	Timing chain or belt			O		O			O	O	O	O			O			
13	Piston (and liner)	O			O		O			O	O	O			O			
14	Piston ring	O		O			O			O	O	O			O			
16	Cylinder liner	O			O		O		O	O	O	O						
31	Radiator			O	O	O		O		O	X	O					O	O
32	Radiator cap			O	O	O				O	X	O		O				O
35	Water pump	O		O	O		O			O	X	O			O			
47	Fuel pump			O		O				O	O	O	O	O	O			
51	Spark plug	O				O	O			O	O	O	O	O	O			O

59	Alternator or generator
64	Bracket (for electric parts)
71/72	Battery holder and tray
75	Chassis wiring harness
78	Battery cable
81	Muffler
82	Exhaust pipe
88	Fuel tank
92	Wheel disc and rim
110	Door window regulator handle
117	Tool kit
120	Seat frame
139/143	Shock absorber
142	Rear spring (leaf and coil)
150	Brake shoe and lining
151	Brake drum
172	Clutch disc
193	Rear window panel
203/206	Hinge
211/212	Bumper
219	Gear
227	Tie rod
253	Axle shaft
262	Air conditioner
263	Radio

(b) Nonmetal parts

Identification no.	Parts and components	Factor inputs		Market factors				Integrated score			Domestic supplies of OEMs		
		Capital intensity	Low substitutability	Fast-moving	Non-auto demand	Non-model specific	Scale economies	Conditions of factor inputs	Market factors	Total points	Malaysia	Thailand	Philippines
27	Engine gasket	O	O	O			O	2	−2	0			O
33	Radiator hose	OX	X				O	−1	1	0			
38	Fan belt	O	O	O	O	O	O	2	−4	−2			
54	Air filter element	O	O	O	O	O	O	2	−4	−2	O	O	
61	Battery	O	O	O	O	O	O	2	−4	−2	O	O	O
67	Wiper blade	O	X	O		O		0	−1	−1			
93	Tire and tube	O	O	O	O	O	O	2	−4	−2	O	O	
98	Head lining	X			O			−1	0	−1		O	
99	Carpet and floor mat	X			O			−1	−1	−2		O	
100	Door trim	X						−1	0	−1		O	
125/126	Door glass, windshield	O	O				O	2	0	2		O	
130	Head lamp	O	O	O			O	2	−2	0			O

O indicates the presence of the factor designated in the column heading
X indicates the presence of the factor whose effect is opposite that designated in the column heading
Product-specific problems are not taken into account in preparing this table. For instance, domestic production of fuel tanks is likely to occur at an earlier stage because they are too bulky to include in a CKD (completely knocked down) pack and its value added is not substantial

Source: Based on a table of engineering characteristics of automobile components prepared by Siriboon Nawadhinsukh

Table 17.6: Domestic procurement of auto parts by Thai assemblers in the late 1970s

Parts and components	Assemblers								Percentage of locally procured parts and components[a]
	Karna-sutra	Siam	Toyota	United	Sukosol	Thai-Swedish	Isuzu (trucks)	Thai Hino (trucks)	
Metal parts									
Radiator		○	○	○	○	○	○	○	88 (83)
Bracket								○	13 (0)
Wiring harness	○	○	○	○	○	○			75 (100)
Exhaust system	○	○	○	○	○	○	○	○	100 (100)
Fuel tank						○	○		25 (17)
Seat assembly		○		○	○	○			50 (67)
Wheel		○			○				25 (33)
Spring (leaf and coil)		○		○	○			○	50 (50)
Shock absorber		○		○	○			○	50 (50)
Body press parts							○		13 (0)
Radio	○								13 (17)
Electrical equipment		○	○	○	○	○	○		75 (83)
Non-metal parts									
Battery	○	○	○	○		○			63 (83)
Tire and tube	○	○	○	○	○	○	○	○	100 (100)
Head lining		○							13 (17)
Carpet			○	○	○	○			50 (67)
Glass	○			○	○				38 (67)
Rubber parts	○	○		○					38 (50)
Console	○								13 (17)

[a] Figures in parentheses indicate the proportions without taking into account the two truck manufacturers, Isuzu and Thai Hino

Source: Nawadhinsukh 1983

In any event, one may safely infer that domestically manufactured items in Southeast Asian countries in the late 1970s were confined to those with relatively lax engineering constraints, or those which had a wide replacement market. The low volume of production of completed vehicles in these countries did not justify domestic production of a large number of parts – especially parts characterized by the simultaneous presence of scale economies which require heavy outlays for fixed investment, and limited use (only as original equipment). But that is not the whole story of why the region's parts suppliers are relatively underdeveloped.

Japanese Joint Ventures

Through their active involvement in the local production of parts, joint ventures are an important feature of the automobile industry in contemporary Asia. Their participation has been encouraged partly by the governments of the host countries, in conjunction with their industrialization policies, and also by the assemblers, which are mostly either also joint ventures or under licensing agreements with foreign corporations. We now examine Japanese joint ventures in East and Southeast Asia. The major data source for this is a questionnaire survey conducted in 1976 by JAPIA (the Japan Auto Parts Industry Association).

Table 17.7 presents a list of major parts supplied by joint ventures at the same time of the survey. However, these firms were not necessarily OEMs. A good example is spark-plug production in Thailand; so long as engines were imported as part of CKD (completely knocked down) packs, there was no place for a local OEM spark-plug maker.

Once again, one notes that the items are the relatively easy to make products; that is, they are either technologically easy to manufacture, or face large (and expanding) markets. Although some, such as pistons, piston rings, spark plugs, etc., call for relatively high degrees of engineering sophistication, any technological problems can be resolved rather easily by importing capital equipment which embodies the required technology. Purely engineering difficulties are in this sense convertible to a problem of cost accounting – how to finance purchase of equipment.

On the other hand, according to my interviews in 1979–81 in Indonesia, Thailand, and the Philippines, resident Japanese engineers were generally satisfied with the quality of the blue-collar workers, whose operational skills had improved markedly in the 1970s. (The problem of labor-force motivation and skill formation is the topic of a separate study, which is in progress.)

Table 17.8 summarizes selected economic characteristics of the Japanese joint ventures in the region in 1976–77. Although information is scarce, the table nevertheless reflects the relatively more advanced status of Taiwan and Korea, which could supply domestically most of the intermediate goods (including sheet steel). Thailand was the most popular country for Japanese direct investment, if only because it is the biggest outlet for Japanese autos (imported or

Table 17.7: Major products of Japanese joint ventures in auto parts production in East and Southeast Asia, 1976–77

	Country					
Parts and components	*Indo-nesia*	*Malay-sia*	*Thai-land*	*Philip-pines*	*Taiwan*	*Korea*
Metal products						
Intake and exhaust valve					*a	*
Piston (and liner)			**			
Piston ring			*		**	
Connecting rod	*					
Cylinder liner			*		**	
Radiator	*				*	
Spark plug		*	*			
Chassis wiring harness			*	*	*	
Control cable		*				*
Shock absorber	*			**		
Spring (leaf and coil)		*			*	*b
Air conditioner	*		**	*		*
Radio						*
Meter and other electrical parts			*	*	**	*
Bolts and nuts, screws			*			
Heat treatment jobs (subcontracting)						*
Non-metal products						
Engine gasket			*			
Brake lining				*		
Battery	**		**			
Tire and tube			*			
Upholstery		*	*			
Rubber and plastic products					*	

*   One firm present
** Two firms present

a Engine valve
b Spring and fastener

Source: Questionnaire by JAPIA

Table 17.8: Japanese joint ventures in auto parts production in East and Southeast Asia, 1976–77

Country	Number of firms								Average size of employment		
	Total	Manufacturers of metal products	Manufacturers of non-metal products	100% Japanese ownership	Joint ventures with local manufacturers	OEMs	Firms procuring local raw materials, parts and components	Representation by Japanese capital (%)	Total	Manufacturers of metal products	Manufacturers of non-metal products
Indonesia	5	3	2	0	0	5	negligible	47.0	113	78	166
Singapore	1	1	0	0	0	0	not applicable	50.0	7	7	–
Malaysia	3	2	1	0	1[a]	2	1	50.0	114	64	214
Thailand	14	13	1	1	4[b]	9	2	51.0	161[d]	164[d]	120
Philippines	4	3	1	0	1	4	not significant	40.0	85	104	27
Taiwan	8	7	1	1	3[c]	5	6	48.9	250[e]	281[e]	63
Korea	6	6	0	2	4	4	4	56.6	97[d]	97[d]	–
Total	41	35	6	4	13	29	13	49.7	143	152	98

[a] Assemblers
[b] Of which three cases are represented by an assembler, Siam Motors
[c] Of which two are assemblers
[d] Excluding one firm whose employment size was not reported
[e] Excluding two firms whose employment size was not reported

Source: Questionnaire by JAPIA

locally built) in Asia. By contrast, Taiwan and Korea have wished to develop domestic capability in the manufacturing of auto parts, and the Philippines has historically strong ties with the United States.

Average employment at the joint-venture firms was somewhat greater than at the purely domestic parts suppliers (compare tables 17.8 and 17.9). Typically, the local partners originally were commercial companies and thus probably did not have sufficient technological expertise to absorb borrowed technology, let alone the capability of generating appropriate technology of their own design. Consequently, these firms must have been under strong Japanese influence in so far as their engineering activities have been concerned. In any event, most of the imported technology has been capital-embodied, requiring relatively little labor skill for day-to-day operations. There remains some doubt, therefore, as to the extent to which a transfer of technology actually has taken place between the Japanese and local firms.

Philippine Parts Suppliers

To gain a better understanding of the medium and small-sized suppliers in the selected countries, let us look more closely at a sample of 60 Philippine metal-working firms. Surveyed in 1975 and 1977, they are all in Metro Manila. In table 17.9, the firms have been classified into a three-by-three matrix of market scale and engineering characteristics, and data are given with regard to employment, capital assets per employe, and the form of business organization. In this table, one expects:

(1) (keeping the engineering factors constant) the greater the size of the market, the larger the size of the average firm, and
(2) (keeping market factors constant) the higher the level of technology, the higher the capital-labor ratio.

These expectations are by and large met. The proportion of proprietorships is close to 40 percent, and the only firms with assets-per-employe exceeding 100,000 pesos were those having some connection with foreign corporations, either joint ventures or through technology licensing agreements. Only eight firms showed indications of such connections with foreign firms. Of the firms covered, 50 were sampled in 1977, providing additional information on them. Using this data, it is possible to describe some features of Philippine metal-working shops in 1977.[7]

[7] An additional firm, which specialized in production of spare parts and for which information was not sufficiently complete to be included in table 17.9, increases the total size of the 1977 sample to 51. Automobile assembling and parts-producing firms are also described by Watanabe (1979) on the basis of his field study of five assemblers and 114 parts manufacturers in the Philippines in 1976.

Table 17.9:   Basic characteristics of automobile OEMs in the Philippines, 1975–77

| | Market scale requirements | | | | | | |
| | Low | | | | Middle | | |
Engineering require- ments	No. of firms	Average employ- ment	Capital asset per employe (P1,000)	Proportion of proprietorship (%)	No. of firms	Average employ- ment	Capital asset per employe (P1,000)
Low	16	52	17.9[a]	43.8	20	93[b]	30.4[c]
Middle	15	32	49.8[f]	46.7	8	134	30.3[f]
High	0				0		
Total	31	42	28.1[h]	45.2	28	105	30.3[i]

The following rules were used in classifying data in this table. (1) Engineering requirements were ranked low if the activities were commonly available *and* if the degree of capital/labor substitution was high. (2) Market requirements were low if scale economies were absent or if their presence was neutralized by the existence of an extensive market. Relatively higher scores were given for the opposites of (1) and (2)

Only 21 of the firms, fewer than half, were established before 1970; they had started as either repair shops or local machine shops, 6 in the auto industry and 15 in other businesses. A marked increase in the number of parts suppliers occurred after 1973, when the government launched a domestic-content drive called PCMP (the Progressive Car Manufacturing Program). The median age of firms in 1977 was 5.6 years. This compares to 10.8 years in 1955 Japan. Table 17.10 gives the distribution by age of firm.

By eliminating the 30 firms established after 1950 and ignoring the firms which disappeared during the five-year period 1950–55, an estimated median

Table 17.10:   Number of years in operation: selected auto parts manufacturers

No. of years in operation	Philippines (1977)	Japan (1955)
0–4	16	30
5–9	14	61
10–14	9	32
15–19	6	62
20–24	3	16
25–29	1	5
30–	2	25
Total	51	231

Sources: Philippines: Albarracin et al. 1979: appendix
Japan: JAPIA 1957, summary volume: p. 37

| Market scale requirements | | | | | | | | |
| Middle | High | | | | Total | | | |
Proportion of proprietor-ship (%)	No. of firms	Average employ-ment	Cap.asset per em-ploye (P1,000)	Proportion of proprietor-ship (%)	No. of firms	Average employ-ment	Capital asset per employe (P1,000)	Proportion of proprietor-ship (%)
35.0	0				36	74[d]	25.1[e]	38.9
62.5	1	148	140.0	0.0	24	71	46.7[g]	45.8
	0				0			
42.9	1	148	140.0	0.0	60	73[j]	31.6[k]	41.7

[a] Average of 15 observations   [e] Average of 31 observations   [i] Average of 23 observations
[b] Average of 19 observations   [f] Average of 7 observations   [j] Average of 59 observations
[c] Average of 16 observations   [g] Average of 15 observations   [k] Average of 46 observations
[d] Average of 35 observations   [h] Average of 22 observations

Sources: Albarracin, Tolentino, and Ybañez 1979: appendix; Albarracin and Tolentino 1978: appendix

age for Japanese firms in 1950 is 8.1 years. In terms of median age, therefore, Japanese auto parts suppliers in the early 1950s were older by a few years, and thus slightly more experienced, than their Philippine counterparts in the late 1970s.

Although only 2 firms manufactured exclusively for replacement demand, 15 sold primarily to the spare-parts market. The majority of the sample (26 firms) preferred being OEMs, because they felt being a regular supplier to an assembler offered more stability. The replacement market was preferred by 8 firms, because of (1) higher unit prices, (2) considerably less stringent quality standards, and (3) the absence of strict delivery dates; 14 firms indicated no preference.

Major Products

Table 17.11 lists the major products of the sampled firms. Almost all of them require relatively simple metal fabrication or wiring (except for alternators and generators, which are a bit more complex). About 40 of the firms engaged in the production of several categories of parts. This strongly suggests the firms endeavored to maximize the utilization rate of their facilities in the face of a relatively small market, soliciting orders for whatever the shop manager thought he could produce. The surveyed firms were in this respect somewhat reminiscent of the small machine shops in the Shikoku area of Japan around 1934, as described by Waraya (see Odaka 1981).

Only about 20 percent of the firms specialized on one product category; the corresponding figure for Japanese parts producers in 1954 was about 31 percent

Table 17.11:   Principal product of the sampled auto
parts manufacturers in the Philippines, 1977

Product	No. of firms
Metal parts of various kinds[a]	15
Spring	7
Exhaust system	4
Stamped parts	4
Parts for Asian utility vehicles	4
Wiring harness and cable	3
Seat frame	3
Brake and fuel lines	2
Radiator	2
Wheel rim	2
Trim parts	2
Aluminum parts	1
Alternator and generator	1
Total	50[b]

[a] Handle, pin, bracket, etc.
[b] Excluding one firm whose product information is missing

Source: Derived from Albarracin et al. 1979: appendix

(43 of 139 sampled firms). The level was higher still in the case of Japanese
bicycle parts manufacturers at about the same time – 81 percent, or 296 of
366 factories surveyed. Bicycle producers could take advantage of an extensive
market (Hayashi 1961: 285, 289).

Relationship with Assemblers

Contrary to the Japanese experience, the overwhelming majority of the Filipino
parts manufacturers kept multiple ties with the assemblers. Only 5 of the
48 OEMs supplied only one assembler. Although assemblers were the most-
frequently cited source of technological information (38 of 51 firms), only
5 reported receiving substantive technical assistance. The second most-common
source was a firm's own experience (35 firms); 7 firms cited catalogs, trade
journals, and other publications.[8]

[8] The exclusive nature of interfirm relations was by no means common to all branches of the
machinery industry in Japan. In some parts of the industry, where the development of
domestic parts manufacturers preceded that of assemblers, as in bicycles, sewing machines,
and textile machinery, the assemblers and parts manufacturers were not only independent,
but also on relatively equal terms (see Hayashi 1961: 270–78).

Transactions between assemblers and parts suppliers were mostly carried out under standing purchase orders (42 of 48 firms); 5 of these were supplemented by written contracts. Of the 6 OEMs with no purchase orders, 2 had written contracts with assemblers. It is a commonly observed phenomenon in the Philippines that firms experience shortages in working capital because of difficulty in collecting receivables. In our sample, even the 5 firms receiving technical assistance complained of slow payment.

The majority of the OEMs considered that the establishment of a regular subcontracting relationship with their assemblers had contributed to the improvement of their own productive efficiency. The reasons commonly cited were the stability of orders as well as the greater emphasis on quality and delivery timing, which not only improved their utilization rates, but also necessitated additional investment in equipment. In fact, it was a minority view (9 firms) to disclaim favorable impact. This minority was engaged mostly in manufacturing highly marketable products which are either fast-moving or general-purpose. In other words, they enjoyed the benefit of large markets even before PCMP offered them a new market, and thus had less to gain by supplying parts to assemblers.

Other Features

Trade associations did not seem to be much appreciated for their activities, although 35 firms were members. For one thing, the firms realized little tangible gain from membership. Although 20 member companies felt they had received "some benefits," 14 thought they had gained nothing. Benefits included some information, and opportunities to join employe training programs. This is in marked contrast to the Japanese parts makers, which are organized into associations of suppliers to each assembler (see Odaka 1978). In Japan, the trade associations have been instrumental in maintaining cooperative relations among their members not only horizontally (among the parts makers), but also vertically (between suppliers and assemblers).

Very few of the firms used modern business administration practices. Only 16 of the 51 prepared annual budgets; the rest simply set profit or sales targets, and 8 companies did not prepare any financial records at all. Nor did the sample firms normally devote resources to research and development activities, but there were indications that they were not entirely unconscious of the need to do so. There were specialized research staff at 10 respondents, and 2 others said the company owners were engaged in research and development.

Training of the work force was done mostly by informal means – on the job (indicated by 34 firms). Other responses on the multiple-choice questionnaire were workshops, seminars, and lectures (17 firms), and apprentice programs (15); 5 firms engaged in no training activity at all. A few companies sent staff to training courses run by trade associations or even overseas. The prevalence of on-the-job training is not surprising; it has also been the most widely-used method by Japanese medium and small-scale companies (see Koike 1981).

The machine industry is well known for wide fluctuations in the utilization rates of its capital equipment (Kerdpibule 1978: 98-101). Certainly, the machinery industry in prewar Japan was periodically faced with low levels of demand for its products. It is not a purpose of this essay to determine how the Philippine rate relates to international experience, but one suspects the level has been, if anything, rather low. The average utilization rate of the 13 metal-working shops surveyed in 1975 was only 46 percent (range, 11-90 percent); the figure increased slightly, to 54 percent, when 14 manufacturers of non-metal parts were added, but this widened the range to 1-100 percent utilization (Albarracin and Tolentino 1978: appendix).

International Competitiveness

Very often there is an economic cost in the domestication of industrial activities – a relative increase in the unit cost of the completed product, or a decline in quality from international standards. If both the market size and the country's technological capabilities are kept constant, one expects the product price to rise with the domestic content ratio (DCR). The DCR is defined here as the proportion of the product value that is added by domestic production. The greater the number of domestically produced items installed on a completed vehicle, the higher its DCR. The rise in production costs is measured by the cost penalty, the ratio of the marginal costs of automobile production in the country to those costs in industrialized countries.

Drawing on data from Argentina, Brazil, India, Mexico, and New Zealand, Baranson (1969) has empirically determined the relation between the DCR and the cost penalty. In the following discussion, this is referred to as the Baranson curve. A technical problem inherent in the Baranson curve is that the time sequence of when domestic production of parts began is not uniquely determined, because economic, engineering, and natural endowments vary from one country to another. Moreover, the DCR is not necessarily a perfect indicator of the growth of local parts suppliers, as some items – especially functionally important or exportable goods – are manufactured by the assemblers themselves. Examples are engine blocks and transmission gears in the Philippines.

The Baranson curve shifts downward to the right if market size expands, or if the level of technological capabilities is upgraded. There are indications, perhaps as a result of improvement in both of these factors exogenous to the Baranson curve, that the cost penalty in the Philippines began to move downward shortly after 1973 (table 17.12).

Figure 17.2 presents a set of hypothetical Baranson curves. The result is at best highly speculative, as the observations plotted are based on a number of working assumptions. For one, the concept of DCR is not uniform among the countries. While four points for 1977 record cost penalties for a specific model, a four-door Toyota Corolla sedan with a 1.2 or 1.3 liter engine, other points are

Table 17.12: Domestic content ratio and cost penalty in the Filipino automobile industry, 1972–77

Year	Domestic content ratio	Average price of passenger vehicles of all models (Japan = 100)	Annual volume of production of passenger vehicles
1972	0.236	238	12,937
1973	0.320	246	17,360
1974	0.375	236	23,824
1975	0.355	235	28,320
1976	0.716	233	33,817
1977	0.672	201	(35,000)[a]

Data apply to the second half of the year

[a] Estimate

Sources: Domestic content ratio and production: Tolentino and Ybañez 1983: tables 5.7 and 5.1, respectively. Average price ratios were estimated from the average prices of Filipino passenger vehicles, domestically assembled by the five PCMP-participating companies in Ajia Keijai (1980: 148) and price data reported in the *Jidosha tokei nempo* (1980 edn: 12–13)

approximated versions of that model. Thus K_{77} uses the domestic and export prices of the Pony, and P_{72}, P_{73}, and P_{75} are simple estimates of cost penalties in the Philippines for the three years plotted, based on data in table 17.12.

Highly speculative as they may be, the Baranson curves allow several observations.

(1) Both the level and the rate of increase in cost penalty is much higher in the selected countries in the 1970s than those in the original Baranson study, especially when the DCR is kept at low levels.
(2) The curve quickly shifts downward when the production volume increases.
(3) In view of the actual annual level of production of passenger cars, one might expect I_{77} and M_{77} to fall on the curve drawn through P_{72}. That they do not may be explained by two factors. First, the initial target of the Indonesian domestic content program was commercial vehicles. Second, in the mid-1970s Malaysia had not introduced a domestic content program.
(4) The lower level of cost penalty in the Philippines (P_{73}) compared to that of Thailand (T_{77}) may be attributable in part to the introduction of the PCMP in the former, which restricted, among other things, the number of assemblers to five.

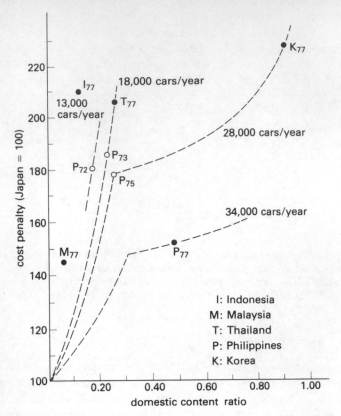

Figure 17.2: Baranson curves for Asian countries for selected output levels

The white points were derived by the author as follows. (1) The officially reported DCRs for 1972, 1973, and 1975 were reduced by a factor of 0.70 to eliminate export earnings and thereby make the DCR comparable to the DCRs in other countries. (The official DCR for the Philippines in 1977 was 0.672.) (2) The average price ratios between Filipino and Japanese passenger cars were adjusted down by a factor of 0.756 to approximate the cost penalties for the specified model (the Corolla 1200 to 1300 cc with four doors); the unadjusted price ratio was 2.01

The Baranson curves have been drawn to have inflection points when the DCR exceeds about 30 percent, as shown by Baranson (1969: 30–31)

Sources
• (black points): MRI (1979: 78) for domestic content ratios (DCRs) and Matsui (1980: 568) for cost penalties
○ (white points): Tolentino and Ybañez (1983: table 5.7) for official DCRs in the Philippines, and Ajia Keiazi (1980: 148) and the *Jidosha tokei nempo* (1980 edn: 12–13) for the average prices of all passenger models domestically produced

(5) In terms of cost penalty, the situation of the automobile industry in Japan in the early 1950s may be likened to that in South Korea in the late 1970s.

A Comparative Perspective

A more fundamental difference between Japan in the 1950s and the selected countries in the 1970s is in the level of technological and entrepreneurial experience, which of course is a function of history. Japan had an obvious advantage compared to the selected countries, because of a longer period of industrial development during which a number of basic industries (iron and steel, shipbuilding, etc.) emerged. This helped Japan accumulate manufacturing know-how as well as a trained industrial labor force.

This is reflected in the fact that the network of parts suppliers was apparently much more developed in Japan in 1950 than in the selected countries in the late 1970s. Furthermore, by the mid-1950s the majority of parts installed on Japanese autos were domestically made. An examination of the engineering characteristics of 25 auto parts revealed at least 13 of them had essentially reached internationally acceptable standards by 1955; difficulties were with their high costs. At the time of the initial domestic CKD production of Austin models in late 1953 by Nissan, for instance, the number of domestically purchased items was 224; by August 1955, the majority of the parts were domestic (Amagai 1982: 124).

The assemblers in the selected countries, with the possible exception of Korea, lacked the kind of strong incentive the Japanese had to develop a domestic network of parts suppliers. First and foremost, almost all the producers of motor vehicles were joint ventures with an assembler from an industrialized country. As such, their role in the diffusion of technology was severely limited, at best secondary, precisely because the resources with which to extend assistance to potential parts suppliers were limited. Second, internationally acceptable parts were readily available at cheaper prices. Third, if it was absolutely necessary, for whatever reasons, to establish domestic parts suppliers, it was more natural for the assemblers to ask the manufacturers of parts in their home countries to set up joint ventures. This was particularly true for Japanese-related assemblers, with their close association with Japanese parts makers.

The production of Jeepneys (four-wheeled commercial vehicles) in the Philippines is, however, an exception to the rule. In the jeepney case, local assemblers used indigenous engineering resources to manufacture motor vehicles of their own design, often in cottage-factory operations. Although functionally essential components (the engine and transmission) are still imported, most of the other parts are domestic. Jeepneys tend to sell for less than other vehicles. In July 1978, the Fiera and Tamarao, two typical Asian utility vehicles (jeepney-style vans) made by Ford and Delta, respectively, cost about 27,000 pesos, whereas a two-door Toyota Corolla was 78 percent more expensive (48,000 pesos) (Ajia Keizai Kenkyujo 1980: 148–49).

The importance of jeeps and jeepneys in the Philippines is illustrated by their share of the stock of automobiles in use. In 1975, they accounted for over 23 percent of the total number of registered cars (161,000 of 687,000) (Tolentino and Ybañez 1983: table 5.3). A similarly indigenous vehicle in the late 1940s and early 1950s in Japan was the three-wheeler, which comprised 32 percent of the total number of automobiles in 1950, and over 50 percent in 1955 (Nihon Jidosha 1966: 46–47).

Table 17.13 summarizes similarities and dissimilarities between the selected countries and Japan with regard to their domestic capacity to engage in automobile production in the specified periods. Conditions were more favorable for Japan on almost all counts, except market size and cost penalty.

Summary and Interpretation

In terms of the size of market and cost penalty, the selected countries in the late 1970s and Japan in the 1950s can be considered roughly comparable. They were similar in that their governments had introduced industrial policies to promote domestic production of automobiles, including parts. Such parallelism notwithstanding, the development of parts manufacturers so far has been rather limited in the selected countries compared to the level achieved in Japan by the early 1950s. In other words, the growth of medium and small-scale machine shops has been sluggish in the selected countries, in as much as parts makers are generally identified with this sector of the economy, although it is true that in the selected countries some parts makers are bigger than the assemblers.

It should be remembered, however, that the subcontracting small-firm sector was also very much underdeveloped in the machinery industry of prewar Japan, and growth probably did not take place until the war years or immediately thereafter. The establishment of a stable auto parts-supplier network has been a relatively recent phenomenon even in Japan.

Examination of the economic and engineering characteristics of the auto parts manufactured in the selected countries shows the items currently produced are those that are relatively easy to make – the technology is simple or is embodied in imported machinery – or are usable in a wider market. Items subject to large-scale economies require, almost by definition, huge investment outlays for capital equipment, and thus are inappropriate for local production, where there is not a large market. These observations suggest the absence of market has been a deterrent to the growth of subcontracting. Adam Smith's law on the division of labor has been applicable to the experiences of these countries, albeit in a negative sense.

Size of market does not explain everything, however. The most striking difference between Japan in the early 1950s and the selected countries in

Table 17.13: Factors promoting and discouraging domestic production of automobiles, the selected countries and Japan compared

Major factors	Items	S vs J[a]	Remarks
Market	Size of market	=	Number of makes and models more numerous in S than in J
	Level of cost penalty	=	Korea (late 1970s) roughly comparable to Japan (early 1950s)
	Development of network of parts suppliers	<	
	Supply of domestically fabricated industrial inputs	<	
Technology	Accumulation of indigenous engineering know-how	<	Predominant role of joint ventures in transfer of technology in S
	Supply of experienced engineers and technicians	<	
Management	Close interfirm relations between assemblers and parts suppliers	<	
	Modernization in managerial practices	⩽	
	Role of trade association	<	Quite nominal in S
Government	Promotion of infant industry policies	=	

[a] Level of the item in the selected countries (S) in the late 1970s relative to the level in Japan (J) in the early 1950s

the late 1970s is the level of technological and entrepreneurial skill. In the case of Japan, both assemblers and many parts suppliers had been involved in manufacturing before becoming part of an automobile industry, and thus had accumulated managerial and engineering resources which were not only instrumental in digesting borrowed technology, but also the source of indigenous growth. Moreover, the development of other basic industries provided the desperately needed outlet for certain machine elements manufactured by the smaller firms.

By contrast, neither of these conditions was fulfilled for machine shops in the selected countries. Hence, they had to rely solely on imported technology, which was generally obtained in the form of joint ventures or licensing arrangements with foreign firms. The foreign partners had little incentive to assist development of local parts suppliers. Why should they, when better and cheaper goods could be imported? In addition, the local assemblers were mostly new, and thus had little expertise to help local parts makers, even if they wished to do so. In the area of parts production, too, it was not always easy to establish local OEMs without help from foreign parts makers. Here again, there remains some doubt as to the extent to which domestic transfer of technology has been accelerated by the presence of joint ventures or technological agreements. On top of these, government policies have had an inherent tendency to favor the importation of relatively capital-intensive equipment. All in all, these circumstances were congenial to the emergence of technological dualism in the machinery industry of certain of the countries under study.

One finds some comfort in the prospering business of homemade designs such as the *becak* and *bejaj* (the three-wheeled passenger carriers in Indonesia) and jeepney in the Philippines. Unique to their particular culture, most of their parts are produced locally. The firms making them are likely to generate interfirm linkages, which may help cultivate indigenous capabilities in machine making. There are many signs such skills exist, for instance, among the agricultural machinery producers of Thailand (Ishikawa 1981: 440–58). Moreover, prospects for the growth of the market for their products is by no means dim. Other things being equal, therefore, the constraints on machinery production in the selected countries imposed by limited markets could be lifted in the 1980s.

To achieve this, more effort is needed to encourage the growth of domestic capabilities in medium and small-scale machinery production. This is especially so in such activities as casting, forging, extruding, squeezing, deep and cold drawing, stamping, machining, and assembling, where elasticities of substitution between capital and labor have been estimated to be significantly greater than zero (Kerdpibule 1978: ch. 5; also see White 1979). Thus, the expectation that an automobile industry would create jobs can be met to a greater extent than it has so far.

This is not to say the smaller firms should be given direct financial assistance by public authorities. Their productive activities will be greatly improved by helping them introduce modern accounting procedures and quality-control measures, by establishing common facilities such as materials testing stations, research and development laboratories, and occupational training centers, as well as arranging group purchases or import of raw material.

From the surveys I and others have conducted, as fragmentary and incomplete as the results are, one feels that perhaps the most crucial factor needed for further development of domestic machinery production is progress in human-embodied technology. This encompasses such factors as entrepreneurship, improved management methods, engineering skills, and organizational and institutional arrangements. Capital-embodied technology can be purchased, and doing so has caused relatively little difficulty, except for the problem of financing it. But for just that reason – the ease with which it is obtained – such an approach has done little to help upgrade the industry or the economy, as distinguished from simply contributing to output growth. Ultimately, for the automobile and machinery industries to succeed in the selected countries, investment must be made in human skills.

References

Adachi, Fumihiko, Keinosuke Ono, and Konosuke Odaka (1981), "Ancillary Firm Development in the Japanese Automobile Industry – Selected Case Studies (II)," Institute of Economic Research Discussion Paper no. 42 (March), Tokyo: Hitotsubashi University.

Aisan Kogyo KK (1973), *Aisan kogyo 35-nen shi.*

Ajia keizai Kenkyujo (Institute of Development Economies) (1980), *Hatten tojo koku no jidosha sangyo*, Tokyo: Ajia Keizai Shuppankai.

Albarracin, Magdaleno, B., Jr, and Arturo L. Tolentino (1978), "Ancillary Firm Development in Asia, Philippine Sub-project, First-year Report," Discussion Paper no. 78-11, Quezon City: Council for Asian Manpower Studies.

Albarracin, Magdaleno B., Jr, Arturo L. Tolentino, and Roy Ybañez (1979), "Ancillary Firm Development in Asia, Philippine Sub-project, Second-year Report," Discussion Paper no. 79-27, Quezon City: Council for Asian Manpower Studies.

Amagai, Shogo (1982), *Nihon jidosha kogyo no shiteki tenkai*, Tokyo: Aki Shobo.

Baranson, Jack (1969), *Automotive Industries in Developing Countries*, World Bank Staff Occasional Paper no. 8, Baltimore, MD: Johns Hopkins Press.

Chee peg Lim, and Fong Chan Onn (1983), "Ancillary Firm Development in the Malaysian Motor Vehicle Industry," in Konosuke Odaka, ed., *The Motor Vehicle Industry in Asia, a Study of Ancillary Firm Development*, Singapore: Singapore University Press.

Engelberger, Joseph F. (1980), *Robotics in Practice*, New York: Amacon.

Harahap, Filino, Wimar Witoelar, Abdul Manan, and Krisihagni Driwindro (1978), "A Report on Ancillary Firms Development in the Automotive Industry: The Indonesian Case," Development Technology Center Report no. 303/ICP-03-76, revised version, Bandung: Institute of Technology.

Hayashi Shintaro (1961), *Nihon kikai yushutsu ron*, Tokyo: Toyo Kezai Shimposha.

Hoshino, Yoshiro (1966), *Nihon no gijutsu kakushin*, Tokyo: Keiso Shobo.

Ishikawa, Shigeru (1981), *Essays on Technology, Employment and Institutions in Economic Development: Comparative Asian Experience*, Tokyo: Kinokuniya.

JAPIA: Jidosha Buhin Kogyokai (Japan Auto Parts Industry Association) and Nihon Kikai Kogyo Rengokai (Federation of Japan Machinery Industries) (1957), *Jidosha buhin kogyo no jittai*, 2 vols, Tokyo.

Jidosha Gijutsu Kai (Society of Automative Engineers of Japan) (1955), "Gaikoku jidosha buhin kenkyu hokoku sho," mimeographed, Tokyo.

Jidosha tokei nempo, published annually by Nihon Jidosha Kogyokai (Japan Automobile Industry Association).

Kerdpibule, Udom (1978), *Planning Development of the Light Engineering Industries, Report on the Philippine Metal-working Study*, Honolulu: Center for Cultural and Technical Interchange between East and West.

Kikai Shinko Kyokai, Keizai Kenkyujo (The Institute of Economic Research, Society for the Promotion of Machinery Industry) (1968), *Gijitsu kakusa no kenryu*, processed, Tokyo (June).

Kim Chuk Kyo and Chul Heui Lee (1983), "Ancillary Firm Development in the Korean Motor Vehicle Industry," in Konosuke Odaka, ed., *The Motor Vehicle Industry in Asia, A Study of Ancillary Firm Development*, Singapore: Singapore University Press.

Koike, Kazuo (1981), *Chusho kigyo no jukuren – jinzai keisei no shikumi*, Tokyo: Dobunkan.

Kokuritsu Kokkai Toshokan, Chosa Rippo Kosa Kyoku (Research and Legislative Department, National Diet Library, Japan) (1978), *Waga kuni jidosha kogyo no shiteki tenkai*, Tokyo.

Matsui, Mikio (1980), "Ajia shokoku ni okeru jidosha seisan taisei no genjo to mondai ten," in Ajia Keizai Kenkyujo (Institute of Developing Economies), *Ajia shokoku no kyusoku na kogyoka to waga kuni no taio*, Tokyo: Sogo Kenkyu Kaihatsu Kiko.

MITI: Tsusho Sangyosho (Ministry of International Trade and Industry, Japan) (1976), *Sekai no kigyo no keiei bunseki* (published annually).

MRI: Mitsubishi Sogo Kenkyujo (Mitsubishi Research Institute) (1979), *Hatten tojokoku ni okeru jidosha kanren seisaku*, 2 vols, Tokyo.

Nihon Denso KK (1974), *Nihon Denso 25-nen shi*.

Nihon Jidosha Kogyokai (Japan Automobile Industry Association) (1966), *Jidosha tokei nempo* (published annually).

Odaka, Konosuke (1978), "The Place of Medium- and Small-Scale Firms in the Development of the Automobile Industry – A Study of Japan's Experience," in *Papers and Proceedings of the Conference on Japan's Historical Development Experience and the Contemporary Developing Countries*, Tokyo: International Development Center of Japan.

Odaka, Konosuke (1981), "Senkan-ki ni okeru shitauke-sei kikai buhin kogyo hattatsu no shoyoin," in Takafusa Nakamura, ed., *Senkan-ki no Nihon keizai bunsei*, Tokyo: Yamakawa Shuppansha.

Odaka, Konosuke (1983), "A Theory of Ancillary Firm Development," in Konosuke Odaka, ed., *The Motor Vehicle Industry in Asia, A Study of Ancillary Firm Development*, Singapore: Singapore University Press.

Ono, Keinosuke, and Konosuke Odaka (1979), "Ancillary Firm Development in the Japanese Automobile Industry – Selected Case Studies (I)," Institute of Economic Research Discussion Paper no. 24, Tokyo: Hitotsubashi University.

Richardson, G. B. (1972), "The Organization of Industry," *Economic Journal*, 82 (327): 883–96 (September).

Rosenberg, Nathan (1963), "Technological Change in the Machine Tool Industry, 1840–1910," *Journal of Economic History*, 22 (4): 414–46 (December).

Shuyokoku jidosha tokei, published annually by Nihon Jidosha Kogyokai (Japan Automobile Industry Association).

Siriboon, Nawadhinsukh (1983), "Ancillary Firm Development in the Automobile Industry of Thailand," in Konosuke Odaka, ed., *The Motor Vehicle Industry in Asia, A Study of Ancillary Firm Development*, Singapore: Singapore University Press.

Stigler, George (1951), "The Division of Labor is Limited by the Extent of the Market," *Journal of Political Economy*, 59 (3): 185–93 (June).

Todaro, Michael P. (1977), *Economics for a Developing World*, London: Longman.

Tolentino, Arturo L., and Roy Ybañez (1983), "Ancillary Firm Development in the Philippine Automobile Industry," in Konosuke Odaka, ed., *The Motor Vehicle Industry in Asia, A Study of Ancillary Firm Development*, Singapore: Singapore University Press.

Tomiyama, Kazuo (1973), *Nihon no jidosha – kuruma wa do kawaru ka*, Tokyo: Toyo Keizai Shimposha.

Toyota Jidosha Kogyo KK (1939), *Kobai kitei*.

Toyota Jidosha Kogyo KK (1958), *Toyota Jidosha 20-nen shi*.

Watanabe, Susumu (1979), "Technical Co-operation between Large and Small Firms in the Filipino Automobile Industry," World Employment Program Research Working Papers, WEP 2-22/WP47 (March), Geneva: International Labour Office.

White, Lawrence (1979), "Appropriate Factor Proportions in Manufacturing in Less Developed Countries, A Survey of the Evidence," in Austin Robinson, ed., *Appropriate Technologies for Third World Development*, London: Macmillan.

18 Trading Companies and the Expansion of Foreign Trade: Japan, Korea, and Thailand

IPPEI YAMAZAWA and HIROHISA KOHAMA

Motivated by the need to increase foreign-exchange earnings, many contemporary developing countries are eager to develop new exports as well as explore new markets for their traditional exports. Being aware of the difficulties involved, they have been interested in Japanese general trading companies (GTCs) because of their successful performance in the process of expanding Japan's foreign trade. Some developing countries, including Korea and Thailand, implemented GTC promotion policies in the 1970s with the expectation this would rapidly expand their exports. Because their GTCs have been set up only recently, it is too early to evaluate their performance fully, or to forecast their future confidently. However, it is possible to assess their early development and, because Japan's GTCs have been the model, to compare development experiences. That is what this chapter does.

The primary function of a trading company is to connect sellers with buyers across national borders and carry out transactions between the two. In this sense, a trading company does commission business. Occasionally it trades on its own account.

A GTC is distinguished from other trading companies primarily by the diversity of products it deals in, and to a lesser extent by the breadth of geographical coverage it offers, and its involvement in both export and import, as well as offshore trade. Japan's GTCs are taken as an efficient model of GTC behavior in the process of expansion and structural change in foreign trade, and used as a basis for comparing the Korean and Thai experiences. We are interested in the applicability of GTC functions over different social, economic, and cultural conditions.

Contrary to the textbook explanation, comparative advantage does not decide actual trade performance; rather, it only affects the potential. Some organizational device is required for realizing the potential. At a minimum, this is undertaken by individual small merchants and direct marketing by manufacturers, but it is done most effectively by GTCs.

Foreign trade transactions require various types of service. (1) The trading company must acquire information on both the demand and supply sides, so it can connect a market which pays the highest price with a producer with the lowest cost. (2) It has to acquire enough skill to conduct complicated customs procedures correctly and promptly, so it is trusted as an intermediary by both sides. (3) In recurrent transactions, it has to organize the supply and demand, so the commodity is produced and distributed to the customers efficiently and regularly. (4) It may provide the seller (or buyer) with credit. (5) It also may arrange such services as transportation and insurance.

To put this in terms of a production function for a trading company, output is the service of conducting a foreign transaction, while inputs are market information, language and trading skills, organizing capability, and the knowledge and capability to perform such services as trade credit, insurance, and shipping. The first three are provided from the employe skill (assets) accumulated inside a trading company. Other services, which may be called trade promoting, are provided by outside firms specializing in them, but the trading company has to procure and combine them at the right time and place. Ability to access these outside sources significantly affects the effectiveness of a trading company.

This analytical framework, although difficult to quantify, is helpful in assessing various characteristics of trading companies and their contribution to the expansion of Japan's foreign trade at different stages of development, as well as to a comparative assessment of contemporary performance by Korean and Thai trading companies. These two countries were chosen because development of GTCs has been encouraged by the government, with Japanese GTCs as a model. However, sociocultural differences from Japan will have significant effects on the success or failure of GTCs in these countries. As a context for the discussion, we outline below the main features of GTCs. We next look at the development of Japanese trading companies before World War II, including the emergence of GTCs, and then examine the postwar evolution of Japanese GTCs. GTC promotion in Korea and Thailand is outlined, and a comparative assessment is made in the concluding section of this chapter.

Main Features of General Trading Companies

The main features of GTCs can be described within the production function framework for trading companies outlined earlier. Diversification of business activity is the most important feature. A successful GTC handles a wide range of goods through a network of overseas branches. Business is not confined to the export and import trade of Japan, but also includes offshore transactions between pairs of foreign countries. However, transactions in goods both supplied and demanded domestically have continued to represent more than half of the trade volume of individual GTCs, reflecting their origins as domestic wholesalers. Diversification contributed to revenue growth and economized handling and information costs. Growth has also enabled GTCs to provide trade financing and other trade-promoting services on more favorable terms.

Diversification enables GTCs to make up for a loss in one commodity or market or in a recession with gains elsewhere, and thus to stabilize revenue over the business cycle. It is more important for GTCs to expand business in the longer run, so as to include goods with growing demand and to enter new markets. The GTCs were quick in finding profit potential in import-substituting production, and committed themselves to importing new technology and equipment.

Superior organizing capability is required for successful diversification. Various organizational devices have to be implemented to explore new commodity or geographic markets. Sole-agent status has often been used with new commodity imports to maintain profits. Suppliers and consumers have been organized to assure a steady flow of goods.

Prewar Japanese Trading Companies

How and why did trading companies evolve so successfully in prewar Japan? In essence, the trading company was an institutional device to economize on scarce resources – people with language and trading skills – by pooling the transactions requiring those skills.

When trade reopened with western merchants in 1859, Japanese were inexperienced in international trade practices, and had little information on overseas markets for their products. Profit-making opportunities existed in foreign trade, but the supply of Japanese with the necessary skills to exploit them was limited. This is typical of backward economies, and the Japanese were further handicapped by their lack of proficiency in other languages, a result of their long national isolation. Although a domestic commercial system was already well established in the mid-19th century, most wholesalers spoke only Japanese, and thus had to rely on trading companies for all foreign transactions. Initially, all exports and imports were handled by foreign merchants. Learning from these merchants, the Japanese started their own trading companies.

Information and skill gradually accumulated through both on-the-job training and a formal commercial education. Despite their initial inexperience and lack of know-how, Japanese firms did have some advantages over their European and American rivals. They charged lower commissions and offered a native's knowledge of how to exploit new demand for foreign products (imports) and to organize new Japanese supply sources for export (see Yamazawa and Kohama 1978: secn 5).

The share of trade held by these new companies expanded steadily, though not rapidly; it was still amost negligible in 1874, when the government announced promotion of direct trade by Japanese. Subsequently, their share increased, aided by the rapid expansion of foreign trade (8-9 percent annually between 1885 and 1900, and 4-6 percent for 1900-20), which was led by commodities with which the Japanese trading companies could capitalize on their advantages. By 1900, the Japanese share had reached about 40 percent of both exports and imports, and by 1920, 70 percent of exports and 90 percent of imports.

As might be expected, the expansion of the Japanese share was closely associated with Japanese industrialization and changes in trade structure, and varied widely among commodities and trading partners. It was most rapid in new export and import commodities, and also rapid in the export of modern industrial goods and the import of investment goods and raw materials closely related to the development of modern industries in Japan. Geographically, expansion was faster in trade with East Asia than with Europe or North America.

The increase in share was supported by the development of trade-promoting services such as financing, insurance, and ocean transportation. At first, these serivces were only available from foreign sources on unfavourable terms. The first Japanese firms in these fields were the Yokohama Specie Bank (1880), Tokio Marine Insurance Company (1879), and Nippon Yusen Kaisha (the NYK line, 1885). All three were financed or heavily subsidized by the government. Because trade-promoting services have been much more competitively offered in the postwar world, trading companies in contemporary developing countries are in a more advantageous position than Japanese trading companies in the 19th century.

Emergence of GTCs

A good deal of experience and knowledge had accumulated by the time World War I provided the Japanese with significant trade opportunities. A number of trading companies had already succeeded in diversifying their transactions both in commodities and trading partners, and by the end of World War I, Mitsui, Mitsubishi, and Suzuki had developed into GTCs, handling a wide variety of commodities with a great number of countries, including non-Japanese trade.

Mitsui led in diversification. Although in the 1910s textiles represented more than 40 percent of Mitsui's trading volume, the share decreased to less than 30 percent in the 1920s. Diversification of trading partners was achieved by the extension of an overseas branch network. Mitsui had 6 overseas branches with 35 Japanese working in them in 1893. The number of branches had increased to 35 (347 Japanese) in 1910, and 57 (1,409 Japanese) in 1919 (Yamaguchi 1974-75). The areas of Mitsui's activities changed: the share of trade with Europe and East Asia (China and Korea) decreased, while that with Southeast Asia, North America, and Australia increased. The other two big trading companies, Mitsubishi and Suzuki, followed Mitsui in diversifying during the 1910s and early 1920s. Smaller trading companies generally specialized in particular commodities such as textiles, steel, or machinery.

It is disputed among business historians whether the GTC served as a core of the *zaibatsu*, financially backed by a group bank and sending personnel to new industrial undertakings, as well as serving as a powerful marketing arm for the group firms. The hypothesis is quite applicable to prewar Mitsui and Mitsubishi, the two major firms. But in the postwar period, control by *zaibatsu* families has been eliminated, and both financial and personal relationships are less exclusive between the GTCs and their affiliated banks and manufacturers. (See Nakagawa 1967; Morikawa 1976.)

Postwar Evolution of Japanese GTCs

Japan experienced rapid economic growth and a drastic change in industrial and trade structure in the postwar period. In the 1960s, this growth centered on heavy industry. The share of such industries as metals, machinery, and chemicals in total manufacturing production was 49 percent in 1950, increased to 61 percent in 1960, and reached 72 percent in 1970 (Ohkawa and Shinohara 1979: table A22). Export structure also changed. The share of heavy industrial goods in total merchandise exports in 1951, 1960, and 1970 was 36, 44, and 78 percent, respectively (LTES vol. 14: table 3). The ten major GTCs also evolved.[1]

Of these ten, Mitsubishi and Mitsui are of *zaibatsu* origin and were already diversified in the prewar period. They were divided into more than a hundred companies by Occupation authorities in 1947, but Mitsubishi reunited in 1954, and Mitsui in 1959. Export substitution of heavy industrial goods was commonly observed for individual GTCs, and was most evident in the case of the Kansai Gomen, five big trading companies in the Kansai (Osaka) area specializing in textiles before the war. They took over some domestic steel distributors to promote steel exports. At the same time, Nissho, Iwai, and Ataka, originally steel and machinery trading companies, extended their businesses to other items.

Although these ten GTCs handle approximately half of Japan's total exports, some large electrical goods and car manufacturers export directly or through their own trading companies. For example, Matsushita Electric Trading was established by Matsushita Electric Industrial to both export Matsushita products and import raw materials and machinery necessary for production. Sony, Toyota

[1] Until a merger reduced the number to nine, the major GTCs have been referred to simply as "the ten GTCs" by the Japanese. They are Mitsubishi, Mitsui, C. Itoh, Marubeni, Sumitomo, Nissho-Iwai (formed by merger in 1968), Toyo Menka, Kenematsu-Gosho (merged in 1967), Nichimen, and Ataka (which was absorbed by C. Itoh in 1977). For more on Japanese trading companies, see Yamamura (1976).

Motor, and Nissan Motor also export directly. While these firms accounted for only a small part of trade in the 1960s, their products became significant exports in the 1970s.

Diversification of Transactions

Diversification of product and geographical markets and transaction type is the most prominent feature of postwar GTCs. This went hand in hand with diversification of the economy. Thus, heavy industrial goods such as metals, machinery, and chemicals were 39 percent of total exports of Japan's GTCs in 1960 and expanded rapidly to 74 percent in 1970. Although this kind of change in export structure was common to every GTC, the change in companies that began as textile trading companies was remarkable. Heavy industrial goods exported by the Kansai Gomen increased from a range of 18-33 percent of their total exports in 1960 to 54-76 percent in 1970; the textile share fell from 50-66 percent to 15-31 percent. Such a sharp decline in the textile share is comparable to what occurred at Mitsui in the prewar period.

Table 18.1 provides the export structure of the ten GTCs in 1960 and 1970. The rate of increase of the total exports of Mitsui, Mitsubishi, Marubeni, Sumitomo, and Nissho-Iwai is above the average of the ten GTCs. This indicates that the greater the scale of the company's initial export level, the greater the rate of increase of exports in the 1960s.

The rate of increase of heavy industrial goods is much higher than that of the total. The rates for chemical products, metal, and machinery are 10.6, 8.2, and 11.5 times, respectively. Although the ten GTCs exported over threequarters of Japan's total metal exports in 1970, their share of machinery is much lower (about two-fifths), because of the prevalence of direct export by manufacturers of electrical machinery and motor vehicles.

The number of overseas branches increased one and a half times between 1961 and 1970, primarily in Europe, Africa, and Australia, as the firms sought to expand in new markets. Mitsui and Sumitomo were the most aggressive in opening new offices (table 18.2).

There was also diversification in the type of transaction, with offshore trade (involving non-Japanese as both buyer and seller) becoming more important, although it comprised only 3-8 percent of the activity of individual GTCs. Exports from Japan provided 14-19 percent of volume, while imports to Japan were 16-26 percent. The fact is, less than half of all the GTCs' volume involved foreign trade. Domestic transactions accounted for 50-62 percent. The GTCs were thus in a good position to hedge between domestic and foreign markets. Although it is difficult to give exact figures, it is widely agreed that domestic transactions have the highest profit margins, followed by importing and exporting. Offshore trading is the least profitable, because of high operating costs, greater risks, and limited experience.

Table 18.1: Export structure of Japanese GTCs, 1960 and 1970[a]

		Foodstuff	Textile	Chemical products	Metal	Machinery	Others	Total
Mitsui	1960	20.2	22.5	13.4[f]	28.6[f]	18.2[g]	14.4	117.4[f]
	1970	30.2	62.9	78.6	246.3	255.2	49.7	722.9
Mitsubishi	1960	24.6	20.2	0.7[g]	20.1[f]	29.9[f]	16.5	111.9[f]
	1970	39.4	51.4	55.8	197.8	259.5	43.2	657.2
Marubeni	1960	8.1	46.6	2.5[g]	11.4[g]	18.5[g]	10.2	97.3[f]
	1970	13.3	75.9	26.1	121.0	249.7	36.1	522.2
C. Itoh	1960	5.0	56.5	1.0[g]	8.3[g]	5.7[g]	7.6	84.1
	1970	14.5	101.6	21.3	94.3	132.9	21.1	385.7
Sumitomo	1960	0.7[f]	0.6[g]	3.2[g]	16.1[f]	4.1[g]	2.6	27.4[g]
	1970	6.0	7.6	34.5	150.8	115.2	11.6	325.6
Nissho-Iwai	1960[b]	1.4[g]	11.9	—	14.5[f]	2.8[g]	4.2[f]	36.7[f]
	1970	8.6	40.6	—	110.7	100.5	31.9	292.3
Toyo Menka	1960	2.5[g]	31.7	0.8[g]	5.1[f]	3.8[g]	7.7	51.6
	1970	25.4	60.6	11.8	32.0	65.3	2.4	197.4
Nichimen	1960	1.6[f]	40.6	1.6[g]	8.0	14.4	6.2	72.3
	1970	10.1	38.7	18.6	39.9	54.5	8.5	170.4

Kanematsu-Gosho	1960[c]	3.4	25.6	—	9.3	11.1	12.1	61.6
	1970	10.7	34.8	—	28.6	28.4	20.4	122.9
Ataka	1960	0.2[g]	4.6	1.2[g]	8.4[f]	3.0[f]	4.7	22.1
	1970	3.9	23.4	12.5	44.3	19.6	8.2	111.8
GTCs total[d]	1960	67.7	260.8	24.4[g]	129.8[f]	111.5[g]	86.2	582.4
		(70.3)	(59.6)	(27.0)	(58.9)	(30.3)	(33.8)	(46.8)
	1970	162.1	497.5	259.2	1,065.7	1,280.8	243.1	3,508.4
		(69.5)	(62.6)	(58.3)	(77.8)	(39.8)	(36.9)	(50.4)
Japan's total[e]	1960	96.3	430.5	90.4[f]	220.3[f]	367.4[f]	254.7	1,459.6
	1970	233.1	794.3	444.2	1,370.0	3,218.9	658.6	6,954.4

All figures in table, except those in parentheses, are in billion yen (i.e. 1,000 million yen)
Fiscal years, except as noted

[a] Export price indexes in 1970 are (1960 = 100): foodstuff, 129; textiles, 103; chemical products, 77; metal, 103; machinery, 94; all commodities, 106
[b] The total of Nissho and Iwai, which were separate companies in 1961
[c] The total of Kanematsu and Gosho, which were separate companies in 1961
[d] Figures in parentheses are GTCs' percentage share of the Japan total
[e] Calendar year
[f] The ratio of 1970 to 1960 exports in this category is above the 5.14 ratio of total 1970 GTC exports to total 1960 GTC exports
[g] The ratio of 1970 to 1960 exports in this category is over 10

Sources: Financial statements of the companies and LTES vol. 14: table 1

Table 18.2: Overseas branches of Japanese GTCs, 1961 and 1970

		Asia	North America	Latin America	Europe	Middle East	Africa	Oceania	Total
Mitsui	1961	23[c]	14	13[c]	6[d]	3[c]	5[c]	3[d]	67[c]
	1970	39	18	26	25	8	14	10	140
Mitsubishi	1961	18	10[c]	10	5	5	4[c]	3[c]	55
	1970	23	17	11	6	7	11	7	82
Marubeni	1961	21	8[c]	9	5[c]	4	5[c]	4	56[c]
	1970	27	15	10	14	6	9	6	87
C. Itoh	1961	15	9	12	5[c]	4	5[c]	3[c]	53
	1970	17	13	12	14	6	8	8	78
Sumitomo	1961	16	7	4[c]	4[c]	1[d]	1[d]	1[d]	34[c]
	1970	20	10	11	11	6	6	6	70
Nissho-Iwai	1961[a]	25	9	9	10	4	5[c]	6	68
	1970	21	12	5	14	6	9	8	75
Toyo Menka	1961	12	7	8	2[d]	3	1[d]	3	36[c]
	1970	17	10	9	8	3	4	4	55
Nichimen	1961	23	12	6	4[c]	3[c]	6	2	56
	1970	20	10	8	9	5	7	3	62
Kanematsu-Gosho	1961[b]	20	9	3	4[c]	3	2	2[d]	43
	1970	15	11	4	7	1	3	6	47
Ataka	1961	12	5[c]	2[c]	4	1[c]	0	3[c]	27[c]
	1970	14	10	5	6	2	2	7	46
Total	1961	185	90	76	49[c]	31[c]	34[c]	30[c]	495
	1970	213	126	101	114	50	73	65	742

[a] The total of Nissho and Iwai, which were separate companies in 1961

[b] The total of Kanematsu and Gosho, which were separate companies in 1961

[c] The ratio of the number of overseas branches in 1970 to the number in 1961 is greater than 1.5, which is the ratio of total GTC branches in 1970 to the total in 1961

[d] The ratio of 1970 branches to 1961 branches is over 3

Source: Company financial statements

Organizing Capability of GTCs

Expansion of heavy industry in the 1960s provided GTCs with ample opportunity for showing their organizing capability. (1) Increasing demand for energy and raw materials led GTCs to explore import sources in such unfamiliar areas as Australia, Latin America, and Africa, where they risked investment in new mines and related infrastructure. (2) The GTCs utilized their information networks to explore American and European suppliers of technology and equipment and joined domestic manufacturers in new import-substituting production. (3) They promoted joint ventures in import-substituting production in Asian and Latin American developing countries and the switching of Japanese exports from final products to intermediate goods and machinery. This contributed significantly to the resumption and further expansion of the share of trade done by Japanese GTCs in Southeast Asia. Equity investments by the GTCs were aimed not so much at the direct return as at a commitment by the new ventures that the GTCs would handle their trade. (4) GTCs also participated as prime contractors or consultants in the exports of plants and equipment, and in aid programs.

Mergers among trading companies specializing in promising products was a common way to expand business activity. Japanese steel firms actively invested in plant and equipment, expanding capacity in the late 1950s at the same time as trading companies took over the export business from domestic steel distributors through a series of mergers. Although equipped with know-how in the steel business and long affiliated with the big mills, the domestic steel distributors were inexperienced in foreign transactions. Thus they searched for partners with overseas experience to expand exports. Their needs were met by the strategy of the big textile trading companies to diversify. Thus Marubeni absorbed Takashimaya-Iida, which specialized in machines and steel, in 1955, and Daiichi Kozai, in February 1960. C. Itoh took over Morioka Co. in October 1961, and Toyo Menka merged with Nankai Co. in October 1963.

It is the organizing capability of GTCs, based on skilled personnel in both top and middle management, that effected the diversification. Human resources are the crucial production factor for GTCs, and they have attracted competent university graduates and trained them on the job to be business experts. GTCs dispatch their staff to affiliated companies as a major source of supply for entrepreneurship in Japan's private company.

Direct Export by Manufacturers

Not all manufacturers in Japan have left overseas marketing to the GTCs; producers of electrical machinery and motor vehicles have exported most of their products directly or via their own trading companies. By the late 1960s, the value of exports by Matsushita, Toyota, and Nissan put them in the same league as the major GTCs.

Why have some manufacturers relied on their own sales efforts, rather than used the established channels of the GTCs? Technical requirements of the products and the timing of export expansion are commonly given as reasons. For automobiles and electrical goods, significant technical know-how and skills are required, and after-sale service has to be provided, so it was not considered profitable for GTCs' branches to undertake the marketing, especially as the volume was small at the start of exporting. Moreover, when exports started in the early 1970s, the big manufacturers were prepared to do their own marketing overseas. However, the technical skill requirement does not completely explain the lack of involvement by GTCs. We hypothesize that in the early 1970s the GTCs simply failed to see the rapid growth of these exports, and let the manufacturers rely on their own sales efforts.

Promotion of GTCs in Korea

Economic reconstruction in Korea began around 1953, and the Park government turned to an outward-looking policy in 1961, when it came to power. Production and export of light industrial goods were promoted by the first five-year development plan, starting in 1962. Although direct export subsidies (1961-63) and an export–import link system (1963-65) were short-lived, both export financing on concessional terms and tax exemption for export income have been available for all designated foreign trading companies since 1962. The overvalued currency (50 won to the US dollar in the 1950s) was devalued to 130 won in 1960-61, then to 250 won in 1963-64. Chemicals and heavy industry began to be promoted in 1972 with the third five-year plan. The export share of heavy industrial goods in Korea's total exports passed 40 percent in 1979. Major imports shifted from consumption goods to intermediate goods in the mid-1960s, and the import share of raw materials and fuels began to increase in the 1970s.

In Korea, an exporting firm is eligible for preferential financing and tax exemption. The Korean Productivity Center in 1980 listed 405 firms earning more than half of their income from handling foreign transactions. The companies were divided into four groups: import agencies (62 firms), firms engaged in both exports and imports (102), companies involved in export, import, and domestic wholesaling (66), and firms combining foreign and domestic trading with manufacturing (175).

The first group, import agencies, generally were subsidiaries of manufacturing companies. The next two groups were small and medium-size trading companies, generally specializing in a limited number of commodities. It is the manufacturer–trader group that predominantly characterizes the Korean handling of export expansion. A few of these originated as export agents and integrated back into manufacturing, but many others started as manufacturers who extended their business to handling exports of their products. Added to the last group are many other manufacturer–traders who earn less than half of their revenue from exporting, but are still eligible for financing and tax exemption.

Non-Korean trading companies are not officially allowed to handle foreign transactions on their own account, but in practice they engage in Korean exports and imports through branches in Korea or occasional visits by their employes. In 1980, the Seoul branch of a Japanese GTC had a staff of 10 Japanese and 40 Koreans, another had 24 Japanese and 100 Koreans. Foreign firms concentrate primarily on imports, and are not inclined to handle small-lot exports of small and medium-scale manufacturers. The role of non-Korean trading companies has decreased over time, but Japanese trading companies still handled over 10 percent of total exports from Korea in 1977–79.

Korean exports were at a turning point in the early 1970s. The largest exports, textiles and clothing, had been decelerating since 1974, because of European and North American quota restrictions under the MFA (Multi-Fiber Arrangement). Some sections of heavy industry had the capacity to supply exports by then, and the Korean government planned to change its export structure by developing new export commodities and new quota-free markets. Non-Korean trading companies were not interested in the new exports, and Korean manufacturer–traders lacked the skills required to develop new markets. Big, competent, domestically owned trading companies were needed, and this led the Korean government to implement promotion of GTCs in 1975.

The eligibility requirements and preferential treatment accorded GTCs in Korea are listed in table 18.3; promoted GTCs are also eligible for general export

Table 18.3: Eligibility requirements and preferential treatment for Korean GTCs

---

Qualification

1.	Capital	2 billion won
2.	Annual export performance	2 percent of total export in previous year
3.	Number of export items	5 (1 million US$ or more)
4.	Number of overseas branches	20

Preferential treatment

1. Preferential treatment in international tender
2. GTCs can import major raw materials when they are not final demander
3. GTCs can use more than two banks for the letter of credit for importing major raw materials
4. Overseas branches of GTCs can hold more foreign exchange than other trading companies
5. GTCs can hold more than two branches in one country
6. Tax reduction and exemption for the GTC's commission of export and import

---

Source: Ministry of Trade and Industry, Korea

promotional measures. The requirements reveal the Korean government's intention of promoting trading companies that export many types of products and have global information networks. Thirteen companies were designated as eligible for preferential treatment. They have to renew their status every year, and in 1981 there were eleven, ten backed by major manufacturing groups and one run by the government.

Sam Sung started as an importer in 1952, subsequently began cotton spinning, sugar refining, and wool textile production, and then expanded into the export of textiles in the 1960s. In the 1970s, Sam Sung started production and export of electronics, steel, and chemical fertilizers. Dae Woo was established in 1967 as a trading company for exporting tricot (a fabric used primarily in women's clothing), then moved into manufacturing textiles, and later into making and exporting steel, rolling stock, chemical fertilizer, and other heavy industrial goods. In 1980, Dae Woo had 54 overseas branches with 260 Korean expatriates.

Sang Yong, Han-Il Synthetic Fiber, and Sun Kyong are large textile makers. Kukje, Hyo Sung, and Sam Hwa are manufacturers of rubber products, including tires and footwear. Ban Do is an electronics maker, and Hyun Dai is backed by the Hyun Dai group, which produces cement, machinery, and ships. Koryo Trading was established by the Korean government for promoting the exports of small and medium-scale firms.

For the ten private GTCs, 60 percent of exports are from within their own groups. Only Hyun Dai specializes in trading as a separate marketing arm for its group; the others are more closely tied to their manufacturing sections. The expansion of designated Korean GTCs has been remarkable. Although it is partly due to their efforts in exploring new exports and new markets, it is also due to inclusion of existing exports by large manufacturers from within their own groups in order to meet GTC eligibility requirements.

Table 18.4 presents the export structure of Korean GTCs and total Korean exports in 1977 and 1979. GTCs' export volume grew at an annual rate of almost 36 percent for 1977–79, and their share of total exports increased from 26 to 34 percent over this period. Although the share of manufactured exports shows only a slight increase in both the Korean and GTC total, exports by GTCs of heavy industrial goods increased remarkably, and represented 47 percent of GTCs' exports in 1979. This is compared to 21 percent of exports by Japanese trading companies in Korea (up from 18 percent in 1977) (Sai 1980: 73). Korean GTCs have been active in exploring new markets, particularly in Latin America and Africa. The performance of Korean GTCs has so far justified their promotion by the Korean government.

Table 18.5 compares the scale of operation of Korean and Japanese GTCs. By 1979, Korean GTCs had reached a scale of operation more or less comparable to Japanese GTCs in 1960, when they had started to diversify. For this and other reasons, our comparison is with Japanese GTCs as of 1960, rather than with contemporary Japanese GTCs. The 1960 Japanese figures are

Table 18.4: Export structure of Korean GTCs

	Total			GTCs				
	1977[a] (1)	1979[a] (2)	1979/ 1977 (3)	1977[a] (4)	1979[a] (5)	1979/ 1977 (6)	(4)/(1)[b]	(5)/(2)[b]
Agricultural product	326.4 (3.2)	518.9 (3.5)	1.59	48.9 (1.8)	89.8 (1.8)	1.84	15.0	17.3
Marine product	621.0 (5.9)	855.5 (5.7)	1.38	100.8 (3.6)	111.4 (2.2)	1.11	16.2	13.0
Mineral product	116.4 (1.1)	110.6 (0.7)	0.95	43.8 (11.6)	11.3 (0.2)	0.26	37.6	10.2
Manufactured goods	9,410.4 (89.8)	13,570.5 (90.1)	1.44	2,576.1 (93.0)	4,889.5 (95.8)	1.90	27.4	36.0
Heavy and chemical industries	3,778.0 (36.1)	6,061.5 (40.3)	1.60	879.8 (31.8)	2,414.9 (47.3)	2.74	23.3	39.8
Light industries	5,632.4 (53.8)	7,509.0 (49.9)	1.33	1,696.3 (61.2)	2,474.6 (48.5)	1.46	30.1	33.0
Textile	3,246.2 (31.0)	4,502.9 (29.9)	1.39	933.8 (33.7)	1,343.2 (26.3)	1.44	28.8	29.8
Total	10,472.4 (100.0)	15,055.5 (100.0)	1.44	2,769.6 (100.0)	5,102.0 (100.0)	1.84	26.4	33.9

Figures in parentheses are percentage shares of total exports

[a] In million US dollars
[b] Percentage

Source: Korean Traders Association

Table 18.5: A comparison of Korean and Japanese GTCs

	Korea (1979)		Japan (FY1960)		Japan (FY1978)	
	Average (9 GTCs)	Dae Woo[a]	Average (12 GTCs)	Mitsubishi[a]	Average (9 GTCs)	Mitsubishi
Overseas branches (number)	29	56	41	55	103	138
Overseas staff[b]	51	116	189	308	647	873
Total proceeds[c]	561	1,120	411	871	11,969	21,314
Proceeds per branch[c]	19.3	20.4	10.0	15.8	116.1	154.4
Proceeds per employe[c,d]	5.2	4.3	2.2	2.8	18.5	2.2
GTCs' share of total exports (percentage)	33.9		47.6		48.1	
GTCs' share of total imports (percentage)	4.7		63.9		51.2	

[a] Dae Woo Industrial and Mitsubishi Corporation are the largest GTCs in their respective countries
[b] Number of expatriate employees only; Korean data are for 1977
[c] In million US dollars. Korean figures include only export and import; Japanese data also include offshore trade and domestic (within Japan) transactions
[d] Total proceeds divided by the worldwide total number of employes

Source: Financial statements of the companies

converted at 360 yen per US dollar, whereas in 1979 the rate was 219 yen and the export price index had risen 38 percent. This means the Japanese numbers for 1960 should be multiplied by 2.27 to be comparable with the 1979 data.

A big difference between Korean and Japanese GTCs is in the small share of imports handled in the Korean case. The predominance of exports in part reflects the shifting of existing exports to the GTCs, while leaving imports in existing channels. Exports were 85 percent of Dae Woo's trading volume of 528 billion won in 1979. In contrast, exports were 17 percent of Mitsubishi's volume, just over half the level for imports and a third of domestic sales. The major Japanese GTCs have relied on domestic transactions as their most stable and profitable activity, with imports second.

The Korean government has expected designated GTCs to contribute to the modernization and export expansion of small and medium-scale firms, through close affiliation with the latter. Korean GTCs had advanced 70 billion won to 839 related small and medium-scale firms by 1976, and this had increased to over 128 billion won to 1,333 related firms by the end of 1977. The share of products of small and medium-scale firms in GTCs exports reached 28 percent in 1976 and almost 28 percent in 1977. But many problems of linkages between small and medium-size firms and GTCs remain (see Hwang 1978).

GTC Promotion in Thailand

Thailand experienced rapid industrialization during the 1960s and 1970s. Manufacturing production expanded at over 10 percent annually between 1960 and 1972, and although it has slowed somewhat, the rate was still as high as 9 percent in the late 1970s. Industrialization was initially oriented towards production of modern consumption goods by firms encouraged by import restrictions and an investment promotion policy. The BOI (Board of Investment) gave privileges to both Thai firms and Thai–foreign joint ventures for domestic production of textiles, automobiles, household electrical appliances, etc., including exemption from the corporate income tax and duties on imports of materials and machinery.

Major import items shifted from consumption goods to machinery and industrial materials. The share of consumption goods declined from 35 to 12 percent between 1960 and 1975. Crude oil was 22 percent of imports in 1979. Exports of textiles and processed food started in the early 1970s. At the same time, the BOI began shifting its policy emphasis toward export promotion. Since 1972, exporting firms under official BOI promotion have been granted such special incentives as exemption from tariff and business taxes on capital equipment and raw materials used for production of exports, as well as exemption from export duties and taxes on a certain amount of export income. Newly built spinning and weaving facilities are promoted only if they export a certain percentage of their output (see chapter 16 above).

Although primary commodities still accounted for threequarters of the exports in the late 1970s, the composition had undergone a radical change; the combined share of the four traditional exports (rice, rubber, tin, and teak) was almost halved, from 66 percent of total exports in 1960 to 35 percent in 1979, while such new commodities as tapioca, maize, and sugar increased share. Traditional primary exports have long been handled by scores of medium-size specialized trading companies of Chinese and European origin. Rice export is conducted by more than a hundred firms, but is dominated by some 18 groups, 5 of whom, the Five Tigers, control over 20 percent of rice exports by private firms. However, rice exports to several countries, including Indonesia, Japan, Sri Lanka, and India, are now government-to-government sales.

In the export of rubber, tin, and teak, European trading companies have acquired close contact with domestic supply sources, including primary processing factories, in part by advancing money. Some European trading companies operating in Thailand have been active in primary product trade since the early 20th century, including the East Asiatic Company (incorporated in 1897) and Louis T. Leonowens Ltd (1905) in the timber business. European trading companies have also long engaged in importing, for example B. Grimm & Co. (1878) and Diethelm & Co. (1906) in cosmetics, pharmaceuticals, and scientific instruments. Since the 1970s, these companies have entered manufacturing and begun exporting canned foods and textiles. Some have become Thai firms, with the majority of shares owned by Thais.

Small and medium-size trading companies run by Chinese Thai and Indians have long been engaged in the import of consumption goods from China, India, and other parts of the world. However, small and medium-size exporters are handicapped by a lack of marketing channels and unreliable supplies from their manufacturers. In addition, import-substitution production in Thailand has compelled them to explore new areas in order to stay in business. Exports of garments and accessories is one promising direction, and an increasing amount is being exported to the Middle East and Europe. Such products of small and medium-size manufacturers have not been handled by the bigger trading companies.

Japanese trading companies returned to Southeast Asia in the mid-1950s, when Japanese exports resumed in this historic market. The ten major Japanese GTCs and dozens of medium-size trading companies had opened offices in Thailand by the mid-1960s. They quickly adjusted to the industrialization promotion policies initiated by the Thai government and shifted their emphasis from exporting from Japan to domestic production by organizing joint ventures between Japanese manufacturers and Thai wholesalers in Sampeng, the textile wholesale market. Their handling of finished products from Japan decreased, while the handling of imports of materials and machinery from Japan increased. Today one of the affiliates of a Japanese GTC has 29 joint ventures in Thailand, and exports agricultural products, processed foods, and textiles. Katano and Smutrakalin (1976) estimate that between a third and a half of Thailand's foreign trade was handled directly and indirectly by Japanese trading companies in the mid-1970s.

The Thai government has had a liberal policy toward foreign trading companies. Unlike other Southeast Asian countries, they were permitted to do the same business as Thai firms. However, the Alien Business Law in 1972 excluded foreign trading companies from indent business (importing goods as an agent against a domestic buyer's specific purchase orders, often at an unspecified best-efforts price). This meant Japanese GTCs would have to participate in transactions as prime contractors and pay business taxes. Nonetheless, the Japanese continued to do indent business through controlled Thai corporations.

Under the liberal policy, the Japanese GTCs have been able to exploit their access to industry and agriculture in Thailand. However, the long-run scope of their activities is limited by various factors. Increasingly, management, if not control, of joint ventures is being taken over by Thais. The number of Japanese employes in manufacturing and trading firms fell from 561 to 416 between 1975 and 1979, because of a work-permit regulation. Even without such factors, the high cost and great difficulty of recruiting in Japan have led to reductions in overseas Japanese staff.

In October 1978, the BOI started promotion of Thai GTCs. As shown in table 18.6, both the qualifications and privileges are basically similar to those of Korea. Through qualification, the BOI intends to encourage new export goods through the new trading companies. Unlike Korea, Thailand has not begun to export heavy industrial goods; instead, efforts have been made to find new exports related to existing manufacturing and agro-industrial activities. Both the first and fifth privileges in table 18.6 are given to exporting firms under the pre-existing promotion scheme, while the second encourages small manufacturers to use GTC services, and the third, fourth, and sixth are aimed at reducing the initial cost of international marketing.

Fourteen companies had applied, and five, each affiliated with a large manufacturing group, had started operations, by the end of 1980. Texport International was formed from the export division of the Saha Union group and benefited from taking over existing exports of textiles and accessories from member firms, thus easily attaining its export target for 1980. On the other hand, SCT (Siam Cement Trading), another leading promoted trading company, has had to exploit export supply sources outside its group, because of increased domestic demand for the group's major products, primarily cement and construction materials. (See *Business Review* September 1980, and the *Bangkok Post* of 1980 December 31.)

Three other firms (S.M. International Trading Corp., International Trading Development Corp., and Bangkok International Trading Corp.) have experienced great difficulty fulfilling the BOI requirements on the amount and composition of exports. They have had particular difficulty in finding new export items. Supported by groups specializing in certain products, they have not been successful in securing products from outside their group. The five promoted

Table 18.6:   Eligibility requirements and preferential treatment for Thai trading companies

Qualification

1.	Capital	30 million baht (50 million baht within 3 years)
2.	Ownership	Thai-owned company which can be listed at the Stock Exchange of Thailand within 5 years
3.	Export performance	1st year: 300 million baht 2nd year: 400 million baht 3rd year: 500 million baht
4.	Export composition	traditional primary commodities: less than 20 percent existing manufactured goods: less than 50 percent new export goods: more than 30 percent
5.	Information network	must organize a marketing network and operate in the overseas markets

Preferential treatment

1. Exemption of import duties and business taxes on imported raw materials for the production of export goods
2. Exemption of business taxes to the companies who supply export commodities to the promoted international trading companies
3. Permission to deduct the paid-up income tax of overseas branches
4. Special allowance to deduct essential expenses for international marketing
5. Export financing by the Bank of Thailand with concessionary terms are available
6. Promoted international trading companies can maintain a foreign-currency deposit account

Source: Board of Investment, Thailand

trading companies together handled only about 5 percent of Thailand's exports in 1980, and to do that, relied on the overseas networks of their parent companies.

Evaluation of GTC Promotion in Korea and Thailand

The following features emerge from our discussion of the development of trading companies in Korea and Thailand. First, the focus of government promotion has been on subsidizing trading activity under market competition, rather than the establishment of state trading companies or the granting of monopolistic handling of certain products.

Second, government promotion made a significant contribution to the establishment of domestic GTCs in Korea and Thailand, and to their rapid expansion in Korea in the late 1970s. Greater emphasis on exports, the growth of overseas branch networks, and the diversification of traded commodities have all been promoted under government guidelines. Rapid expansion of the GTCs' share of Korean exports in the 1970s was made possible by the GTCs taking over the existing export activities of affiliated large manufacturing companies and other small and medium-size firms. The Thai GTCs started later, also with support of large parent manufacturers. In the prewar period, Japanese GTCs likewise benefited from the back-up of affiliated companies, but in the postwar period their business has extended to non-affiliates.

Third, the dominance of exports in total transactions unfavorably affects the profitability of Korean GTCs, in view of the Japanese experience that domestic and import transactions have provided greater profits than exports. The small share of imports relates directly to the emphasis placed on export expansion by the government; the low level of domestic transactions reflects the fact wholesaling has not developed as much in Korea as in Japan.

Finally, drastic changes have taken place in the world trading environment during the past half-century. Large manufacturers in developing countries in the 1980s are more experienced in international trade and are less handicapped by lack of access to shipping, insurance, and foreign-exchange banking than Japanese firms in the 19th century. Foreign trading companies (which now include the Japanese) are no less active today in exploiting new export supply sources in developing countries than western merchants were in Japan in the late 19th century.

The last three features lead us to expect the continued dominance of the manufacturer–trade type of GTC, rather than the Japanese type GTC. Affiliation with a manufacturing group has helped the early expansion of GTCs, but further growth and diversification may be limited by the size and production capabilities of the group.

Indigenous trading companies have an advantage over outsiders, because of easier, closer contacts with domestic producers and consumers. This is supported by the existence of competent indigenous trading companies specializing in the trade of certain primary products. Moreover, foreign trading companies generally are less active in promoting new exports than are domestically owned trading companies.

Compared to specialized traders, GTCs benefit from their diversity, which makes it easier for them to adjust to both short-run business cycles and long-run changes in comparative advantage. While specialized traders often provide their customers with as good service as the GTCs, the GTCs have an advantage as companies.

Thus, in answer to the question "Is it worthwhile to promote indigenous GTCs, in the face of the huge cost incurred in developing overseas branch networks?" our answer is "Yes." Indigenous GTCs are needed, if contemporary developing countries are to take full advantage of international trade opportunities.

References

Hwang Myong-soo (1978), "The Linkages and the Division of Labor in GTCs in Relation with Expediting Export of the Medium and Small Scale Enterprises," *Journal of Dangkook University*, vol. 12.

Katano, Hikoji, and Phitaya Smutrakalin (1976), *The Role of Japanese Trading Companies in the External Trade of Thailand*, ECOCEN Study no. 14 (March).

LTES (*Estimates of the Long-Term Economic Statistics of Japan*), series edited by Kazushi Ohkawa, Miyohei Shinohara, and Mataji Umemura, Tokyo: Tokyo Keizai Shimposha.

vol. 14, *Foreign Trade* (1979), Ippei Yamazawa and Yuzo Yamamoto.

Morikawa, Hidemasa (1976), "Sogo shosha no seriritsu to ronri," in Mataji Miyamoto et al., eds, *Sogo shosha no keiei-shi*, Tokyo: Toyo Keizai Shimposha.

Nakagawa, Keiichiro (1967), "Nihon no kogyoka katei ni okeru 'soshiki sareta kigyosha karsudo'," *Keiei shigaku*, 2(3).

Ohkawa, Kazushi, and Miyohei Shinohara, with Larry Meissner, eds (1979) *Patterns of Japanese Economic Development*, New Haven, CT: Yale University Press.

Sai Jun Mei (1980), "Japanese Trading Companies in Korea," *Chosun*, August: 70–88.

Yamaguchi, Kazuo, et al. (1974–75), "Mitsui bussan kabushiki kaisha hyakunen-shi," mimeographed, Tokyo.

Yamamura, Kozo (1976), "General Trading Companies in Japan — Their Origins and Growth," in Hugh Patrick with Larry Meissner, eds, *Japanese Industrialization and its Social Consequences*, Berkeley, CA: University of California Press.

Yamazawa, Ippei, and Hirohisa Kohama (1978), "Trading Companies and the Expansion of Japan's Foreign Trade," in *Papers and Proceedings of the Conference on Japan's Historical Development Experience and the Contemporary Developing Countries*, Tokyo: International Development Center of Japan.

The Contributors

Likhit Dhiravegin is a member of the Faculty of Political Science, at Thammasat University, Bangkok.

John C. H. Fei is Professor of Economics and a member of the Economic Growth Center at Yale University.

Yujiro Hayami is a professor in the Faculty of Economics at Tokyo Metropolitan University.

Susumu Hondai is an associate professor in the Department of Economics at Daito Bunka Gakuen University, Tokyo.

Masao Kikuchi is an economist at the National Research Institute of Agricultural Economics, Tokyo, and at the time of writing he was a Visiting Fellow at the International Rice Research Institute in the Philippines.

Yukihiko Kiyokawa is a professor at the Institute of Economic Research, Hitotsubashi University, Tokyo.

Hirohisa Kohama is an economist at the International Development Center of Japan, Tokyo.

John K. Lynam is an economist at Centro Internacional de Agricultura Tropical in Cali, Colombia.

Ashoka Mody is on the faculty of the Centre for Development Studies in Trivandrum, Kerala, India.

Honorata A. Moreno is Assistant Professor of Economics at the University of the Philippines.

Sudipto Mundle is on the faculty of the Centre for Development Studies in Trivandrum, Kerala, India.

Le Thanh Nghiep is an economist at the International Development Center of Japan, Tokyo.

Konosuke Odaka is a professor at the Institute of Economic Research, Hitotsubashi University, Tokyo.

Kazushi Ohkawa is Emeritus Professor of Economics at Hitotsubashi University, Tokyo, and Director of Research and Training at the International Development Center of Japan, Tokyo.

Akira Ono is a professor in the Department of Economics at Hitotsubashi University, Tokyo.

Hugh Patrick is R. D. Calkins Professor of International Business at Columbia University. At the time of writing, he was Professor of Economics and a member of the Economic Growth Center at Yale University.

K. N. Raj is on the faculty of the Center for Development Studies in Trivandrum, Kerala, India.

Gustav Ranis is the Altschul Professor of International Economics at Yale University and a member of the Economic Growth Center.

Gary Saxonhouse is Professor of Economics at the University of Michigan, Ann Arbor.

Somsak Tambunlertchai is Associate Professor of Economics at Thammasat University, Bangkok.

Juro Teranishi is a professor at the Institute of Economic Research, Hitotsubashi University, Tokyo.

Ippei Yamazawa is a professor in the Department of Economics at Hitotsubashi University, Tokyo.

Yasukichi Yasuba is a professor in the Department of Economics at Osaka University.

Index